Wilderness Journey

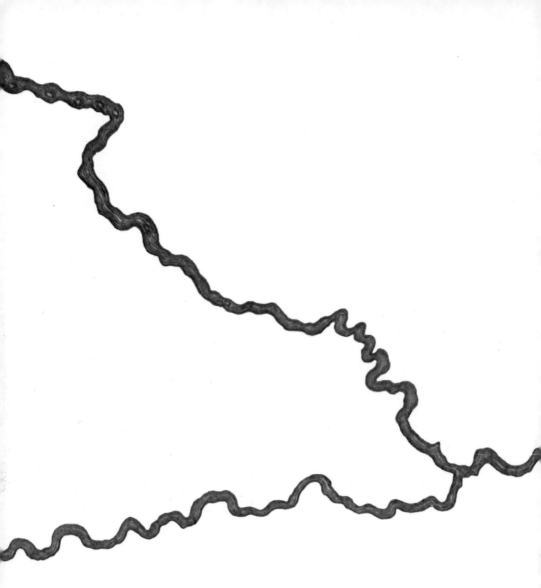

Missouri Biography Series
William E. Foley, Editor

Wilderness Journey

The Life of William Clark

William E. Foley

University of Missouri Press   Columbia and London

William Clark, portrait by
Charles Willson Peale.
Courtesy of the Independence
National Historical Park.

Copyright © 2004 by
The Curators of the University of Missouri
University of Missouri Press, Columbia, Missouri 65201
Printed and bound in the United States of America
All rights reserved
First paperback printing, 2006
5 4 3 2 1   10 09 08 07 06

Library of Congress Cataloging-in-Publication Data

Foley, William E., 1938–
    Wilderness journey : a life of William Clark / William E. Foley.
        p. cm. — (Missouri biography series)
    Includes bibliographical references and index.
    ISBN 978-0-8262-1663-2 (alk. paper)
  1. Clark, William, 1770–1838. 2. Explorers—West (U.S.)—Biography. 3. Lewis and Clark
Expedition (1804–1806). 4. West (U.S.)—Discovery and exploration. 5. West (U.S.)—
Biography. 6. Governors—Missouri—Biography. 7. Businessmen—Missouri—Saint Louis—
Biography. 8. Missouri—Biography. I. Title. II. Series.
F592.7.C565F65 2004
917.804'2'092—dc22

                                                                                      2003027195

♾ This paper meets the requirements of the American National Standard
for Permanence of Paper for Printed Library Materials, Z39.48, 1984.

Designer: Kristie Lee
Typesetter: Crane Composition, Inc.
Printer and binder: Thomson-Shore, Inc.
Typefaces: Minion, Timbrel

*The University of Missouri Press gratefully acknowledges the support of the
William T. Kemper Foundation in the publication of this book.*

For Martha, my journey partner

Contents

Preface

I N THE GRAND NARRATIVE of American progress and achievement William Clark stands proud and tall at the side of his friend and partner Meriwether Lewis, almost as if joined at the hip. The phrase "LewisandClark" rolls off the tongue as if it were a single word. Their daring and remarkable journey to the Pacific has become a source of national pride, and William Clark's contributions to that great odyssey have been well documented. No mere sidekick, he was the expedition's principal cartographer, waterman, and Indian diplomat. The stalwart redhead provided a welcome and steadying presence as he and Lewis guided their tiny band through wilderness territory in search of a practicable passage to the western sea, but in spite of the notoriety surrounding his renowned exploratory venture, William Clark's story is little known.

His tragic and flawed partner Meriwether Lewis and his equally tarnished brother George Rogers Clark have commanded far greater attention than the man on whom they both came to depend. In a drawing titled "Clark's mother," Far Side cartoonist Gary Larson captured that irony. His cartoon shows Clark's mother with a newspaper in hand, admonishing her son: "Here it is again, William! Front page! 'Lewis and Clark Expedition Declared a Success!' . . . See what I mean? His name is *always* first! . . . I tell you, son, if you don't do somethin' about this now, you'll be playin' second fiddle in the hist'ry books!"

In truth, William Clark is not an easy person to fathom, and any effort to take his full measure must draw from the totality of experiences in a life that spanned nearly threescore and ten years. His was a long and complicated journey that began in the gentrified world of Revolutionary Virginia and ended in the booming western entrepot of St. Louis nearly seven decades later. William Clark devoted the greater part of his life to public service as a soldier and as a government bureaucrat. The peripatetic official's assignments frequently placed him at center stage in the national quest to possess and occupy North America's vast westward expanses and prefigured many of the U.S. government's future efforts to shape the region's development.

Important as it was, the Voyage of Discovery represents only a single episode in what was for Clark a lengthy wilderness journey. The celebratory tone of so many of the bicentennial observances intended to honor Clark seems to belie the reality of a lifetime in which disappointment, pain, and adversity all too often crowded out public adulation and private contentment. That should not be taken to mean that his was a life bereft of satisfaction, success, and happiness, for such was not the case. But it does suggest that the totality of William Clark's experiences makes him far more interesting and human than some heroic figure on a pedestal.

A complex individual, William Clark lived a life replete with contradictions. He was a lifelong government official who was never elected to a single office. His only attempt to win popular approval at the polls ended with a humiliating loss. Clark lived most of his life in the rustic and unfinished American backcountry, but he always bore the mark of his aristocratic upbringing. He was neither snobbish nor arrogant, but his gentlemanly bearing proved to be a serious handicap in an age when politicians had to affect a common touch if they wanted to be successful. Clark was a leader who knew how to take charge and whose actions commanded the respect and loyalty of those who served under him, but unlike many of his cohorts in business, government, and the military, he was reluctant to give offense to those willing to give him his due. This ninth-born child in a family of high achievers always seemed eager to please. Whether in personal conversation or in official negotiations, Clark usually sought to occupy the middle ground.

William Clark did not wed until he was thirty-seven, but he relished the joys of marital bliss and was a doting husband and father. Twice married, he found comfort in his companions and the seven children they bore him. But along with the familial happiness that had always eluded his friend Lewis, Clark had to endure more than his fair share of sadness and sorrow in a life filled with personal tragedy. Despite the difficulties and losses he had to bear and the demands of an active and involved life, William Clark steadfastly attended to his responsibilities as a son, brother, husband, and father.

For someone who savored the comforts of home, Clark was seldom there. He seems to have been a man constantly on the go. Until the very end of his days he routinely journeyed to Kentucky, eastward to the Atlantic seaboard, and into Indian Country for both business and pleasure. We know about his travels because he kept detailed journals logging his frequent trips. As a novice militiaman, Clark initiated his lifelong practice of keeping a journal, and it was no happenstance that his systematic writings provide the most complete coverage of the Pacific expedition.

His methodical and meticulous record keeping and attention to detail helped make him an efficient public servant and a careful businessman. Clark had a remarkable talent for keeping abreast of his voluminous public and private accounts. While he was scrupulous in his oversight of public business, Clark had no qualms about using his position to secure government appointments and contracts for family and friends.

Clark knew how to enjoy himself and have a good time. He delighted in sharing a dram and perhaps a ribald tale with traders in a frontier outpost, but he seems to have been equally adept in carrying on a polite conversation in a Washington, D.C., drawing room. Yet despite his congenial nature and gregarious ways, he seems to have formed few close attachments beyond the confines of family. He seldom chose to reveal his true thoughts on personal matters to anyone outside the family circle.

Indian diplomacy occupied much of Clark's time. The dutiful soldier and bureaucrat never wavered in his commitment to an expansionist national agenda that expected Indians to surrender their lands, abandon their traditional ways, and acquiesce to the dictates of the U.S. government, but the consequences of the very policies that Clark so vigorously championed frequently moved him to demonstrate genuine concern for the plight of destitute native people increasingly threatened with extinction. His attempts to intercede on their behalf prompted Indian-hating frontier settlers to brand him an Indian lover. Paradoxically, many of the very people whose dispossession and forced relocation Clark helped engineer chose to view the red-headed chief as their friend. They turned to him when faced with a problem and trusted him as much as they did any outsider.

Like so many of his contemporaries, William Clark succumbed to the evils of slavery. An indulgent parent who found it difficult to deny the whims of his prodigal sons, Clark could be cruel and indifferent to his slaves. His treatment of York following the expedition was particularly reprehensible, but his longtime servant and companion was not alone in receiving his master's wrath. Clark did show solicitous concern for his old and infirm slaves, but his insistence on viewing his African American servants as possessions made it possible for a man who modeled decency and integrity in most facets of his life to treat them shamefully.

For a man with the good fortune to be born into a family with some means, Clark had to struggle to make ends meet on his government salary. Financial reverses caused by the demise of the Missouri Fur Company and the collapse of the Bank of Missouri compounded his problems. Clark possessed extensive landholdings, but until late in life many of their titles were still in dispute. At the time of his death William Clark was able to bequeath princely sums to his heirs, but most of those gains had been long deferred.

Difficult as the challenges he faced might have been, William Clark refused to allow his misfortunes to overwhelm him, and only rarely did he permit himself to dwell on his disappointments and failures. Throughout his life he exhibited a dogged perseverance and determination that made him among other things a successful explorer, soldier, territorial governor, Indian diplomat, and family man, and above all else a steadying presence and a comfort to those who knew him best.

Acknowledgments

Forty years ago while researching a doctoral dissertation on Missouri territorial politics, I first became interested in William Clark and realized that his was a story worth telling. Assuming that someone else would soon tackle that assignment, I moved on to other projects, including several in which Clark was a crucial supporting player. The approach of the Lewis and Clark bicentennial caused me to once again cast my thoughts in Clark's direction, and an early retirement option afforded me an opportunity to undertake the task I had contemplated at the beginning of my academic career.

Along the way I have benefited from the generous support and assistance of numerous individuals and organizations. Jim Goodrich, the executive director of the State Historical Society of Missouri, was among the first to urge me to consider a Clark biography, and I am grateful for his encouragement and for two research grants from the society's Richard S. Brownlee Fund that helped underwrite my research. I also appreciate the ongoing support that I have received from the Missouri Historical Society and its president, Robert Archibald. My 2001 MHS Research Fellowship at the Missouri Historical Society allowed me to plumb their marvelous archival holdings, which include the largest single collection of Clark family papers. The Filson Historical Society, another important repository of Clark materials, also awarded me a research stipend to support my work in their collections. Numerous other individuals have facilitated my work on this book, and I wish to single out the following for special mention: Lynn Gentzler, Laurel Boeckman, and Christine Montgomery at the State Historical Society in Columbia; William Stolz and John Konzal at the Western Historical Manuscript Collection in Columbia; Carolyn Gilman, Emily Troxell-Jaycox, Duane Sneddeker, and Dennis Northcott at the

Missouri Historical Society; Eric Sandweiss, formerly at MHS and now at Indiana University; Mark Wetherington, Jim Holmberg, and Rebecca Rice at the Filson Historical Society; Ken Winn and Lynn Morrow at the Missouri State Archives; Michael Everman at the St. Louis Circuit Court Records Project; Beverly Jarrett, Clair Willcox, and John Brenner at the University of Missouri Press; Perry McCandless, Mary Ellen Rowe, David Rice, John Sheets, Ruth Hirner, Mollie Dinwiddie, Barbara Wales, and Marian Craig at Central Missouri State University; Robert Cox at the American Philosophical Society; Glenn McMullen at the Indiana Historical Society; Gordon Julich at the Jackson County Parks Department; Sharon Silengo at the North Dakota Historical Society; Amy Mossett, Three Affiliated Tribes at the Fort Berthold Reservation; and Loy Morrow and Jennifer Bottomly-O'Looney at the Montana Historical Society. Walter Schroeder and James Harlan at the University of Missouri–Columbia provided the map showing the route of the Lewis and Clark expedition. April Foley adapted my computer software to accomodate my research needs. Jim Ronda provided encouragement along the way, read the manuscript, and offered many helpful suggestions, as did Bob Moore. Finally, my wife, Martha, to whom this book is dedicated, has been with me in this and all of my other endeavors, and only she knows how much I value her companionship and loving support.

Wilderness Journey

One

The West Beckons

T HE CLEARING SKIES that had supplanted the previous day's rain clouds must have seemed a good omen to John and Ann Rogers Clark and their four youngest children, Lucy, Elizabeth, William, and Frances. Many forces nudged them westward as they set out from their Caroline County, Virginia, farmstead on October 29, 1784, on their way to make a new home for themselves on Beargrass Creek a short distance southeast of Louisville, Kentucky.[1] The settled parts of the Old Dominion appeared to be economically stagnant, if not in decline. Years of tobacco cultivation had taken a toll on eastern Virginia's once fertile soils, and the lure of the abundant new lands in the greater Ohio Valley was irresistible.[2] In eighteenth-century Virginia, land holdings and slave ownership were the yardsticks by which status and success were measured. The modest estates and few slaves that John Clark had inherited were sufficient to bestow social respectability and more than a nodding acquaintance with some of Virginia's better families, but like so many other members of the lesser gentry, he continued to hope for more. Already in his late fifties, John Clark must have sensed that time was fleeting when he finally yielded to Kentucky Fever and joined the growing exodus of Virginians bound for "Cantuck" in search of a new and better life.

William Clark, then a lanky fourteen-year-old with red locks that matched his father's, left no account of his thoughts about leaving the only home that he had known. One can only surmise that the youngest of the Clark sons looked forward to the opportunities that a move to Kentucky might afford him. Too

1

young to take up arms during the Revolutionary War, Billy, as he was known to family members, had been relegated to following the conflict vicariously through the military feats of older brothers Jonathan, George Rogers, John Jr., Richard, and Edmund, all of whom had served as officers in Virginia fighting units. Perhaps he sensed that at long last he would have a chance to test his own mettle and prove himself on Kentucky's dark and bloody ground. What neither Billy Clark, nor anyone else for that matter, could possibly have imagined was that this trip was merely the first step in a longer journey, one that for the next half century would take him all the way to the Pacific, lead to a lifelong career in public service, and make him an active participant in a national quest to possess and occupy North America's vast westward expanses.

The intertwined roots of William Clark's family tree were deeply embedded in the Virginia soil that he and his parents were about to abandon. The earliest of his paternal forebears to arrive in America was John Clark, an Englishman from County Kent who settled on the James River in the late seventeenth century. Family lore credits the bonny Scottish lass he married with introducing the familiar red hair into the Clark family's gene pool, but the destruction of the pertinent Virginia records by fire makes it impossible to identify her name or to verify those assertions.[3] Documented Clark family genealogy begins with the first John Clark's son Jonathan, who was born circa 1695 and died in Virginia in 1734. At the time of his death, Jonathan left a widow, Elizabeth, and four surviving children including William Clark's father, John, who had been born on October 9, 1725, in King and Queen County, Virginia. In 1749 the younger John Clark married his cousin Ann Rogers, scion of another pioneering Virginia family. The Rogers clan traced its ancestry to Giles Rogers, who had come to America from England sometime in the latter part of the seventeenth century. In the small world of early Virginia, marriages sometimes forged complicated connections among the early arriving families. The intricacies of the marital links between the Clark and Rogers clans were such that John Clark's mother, Elizabeth, and his wife, Ann, were both granddaughters of Giles Rogers.[4]

Ann Rogers, who had been born in King and Queen County on October 20, 1734, was barely sixteen at the time she married twenty-five-year-old John Clark. Over the course of the next quarter century the couple had ten children. William Clark was their ninth. Shortly after their marriage John and Ann Clark left the place of their birth to take up residence on a 410-acre wilderness tract on the Rivanna River in Albemarle County, Virginia, not far from Shadwell, the estate where Thomas Jefferson had been born six years earlier. By the time the Clarks arrived in the remote and undeveloped Virginia Piedmont, Thomas's father, Peter Jefferson, a well-known wilderness surveyor, had retreated eastward with his family to occupy a larger and better house on the James River.

Meanwhile, the newlywed Clarks set up housekeeping in an unimposing log house located on lands that John had inherited from his father in the shadow of the little mountaintop where Thomas Jefferson later built Monticello. The first two of the Clark's ten children were born there: Jonathan in August of 1750 and George Rogers two years later in November. Like Thomas Jefferson's mother, Jane Randolph Jefferson, John and Ann Clark were not especially enamored of the remote, sparsely populated wooded hills on the eastern edge of the Blue Ridge Mountains, for when John's bachelor uncle, also named John, willed him property in Caroline County, the young couple wasted little time in returning eastward to the more settled confines of that location. Ironically, not long before the Clarks abandoned their isolated wilderness home in Albemarle, Peter Jefferson had returned to neighboring Shadwell with his family.[5]

By 1754 the Clarks and their two young children were settled in the domicile in Caroline County's southwest corner that they would call home for the next thirty years. It was a busy neighborhood. The road from Fredericksburg to Richmond passed nearby, and the County Line Baptist Meeting House was less than a mile away. William Clark was born there on August 1, 1770. It was likewise the birthplace of seven of his siblings: Ann (born in 1755), John (1757), Richard (1760), Edmund (1762), Lucy (1765), Elizabeth (1768), and Frances (1773).[6]

Ann and John Clark were caring and loving parents who maintained lifelong connections with their numerous progeny. When the Clark children grew to maturity and scattered to distant places, they continued their cherished family conversations by exchanging letters. Those communications, filled with news, gossip, and business matters, attest to the closeness of their bond and their shared concern for one another's welfare. John Clark's letters written shortly after his first two sons set out on their own expressed the timeless concerns of anxious parents: "This leaves us all well I thank God, but we are under some onease apprehensions at your not coming down [to see the family] & at your brother [George] setting out for the back country." But along with parental worries there were joys to be shared. The elder Clarks passed along to Jonathan the happy news that his sister Ann planned to marry Owen Gwathmey, and the proud parents signaled that they expected their eldest son to return home to share the day with his family.[7]

Whenever anyone in the expanding family circle failed to keep the others adequately apprized of his or her comings and goings, the delinquent correspondent was apt to receive a friendly reprimand. The absence of a letter was always cause for concern. The close-knit Clarks never hesitated to turn to each other for advice and counsel. At the time seventeen-year-old Edmund was preparing to join Jonathan in military service, John and Ann Clark reminded their older son about his obligations to his younger brother: "we religh on your advice & direction to him who I make no doubt will redily follow such directions as you proscribe. He is young and unexperienced. We fear he may keep bad company."[8] William Clark's letters to his siblings and later to his own children continued the chain unbroken.

In his later years William Clark often emulated his parents' example in guiding his own children. When they failed to heed his advice, he stood ready to forgive their shortcomings. During his frequent absences from home, he always kept in touch by letter. William's parenting differed from his father's only in the degree of indulgence he granted his children. William Clark seems to have been even more lenient than his attentive father had been.

John and Ann Clark's household was seldom a dull place. Their Caroline County residence was a popular gathering spot for members of their extended family as well as for friends and neighbors. A nearby relative who sometimes called at the Clark home remembered William's father as "a man of amiable excellent character, of sedate thoughtful appearance and not apt to say much in company."[9] The elder Clark's seeming reserve appears not to have diminished the hospitality that visitors to the Clark home came to expect. In his attempts to keep son Jonathan posted on the latest neighborhood news, he reported in August of 1772 that "most of the young people about here are engagd in Keys Dance which will be at our house on Monday 24th . . ."[10] Although Billy was barely two at the time, the experience of growing up in a house where dances, parties, and family gatherings were an integral part of life was destined to leave a lasting imprint. Participation in those events along with attendance at weddings, funerals, public proceedings, barbecues, horse races, and cockfights introduced the Clark sons to the rituals of planter society and prepared them for their roles as proper gentlemen. One can credit Caroline County's social milieu for nurturing the sociability, gregarious nature, and gentlemanly bearing that forever marked William Clark's public demeanor.

Valuing books and learning was another product of Clark's gentrified Virginia upbringing. John and Ann Clark prized literacy and saw to it that all of their children were able to read and write. As members of the landholding class, they made sure that their sons received proper instruction in what they deemed to be the fields of knowledge essential for a rising young man, notably mathematics, history, geography, and natural history. Their efforts to provide their boys with well-rounded educations also included hands-on lessons in the practical arts of farming, surveying, and horsemanship—equally vital skills for all would-be gentlemen farmers.

The older Clark sons, Jonathan and George, attended Donald Robertson's School about six miles away in King and Queen County. Jonathan, a typical high-achieving firstborn, was more attentive to his studies and a better student than the more high-spirited second son, George, whose primary interests lay outside the classroom. The Clark boys were in good company at Robertson's school, where James Madison and John Taylor of Caroline were also students. Known for his high standards and rigorous expectations, the Scottish schoolmaster was a graduate of the University of Edinburgh, a disciple of the Enlightenment, and the husband of Ann Clark's younger sister Rachel. Billy was too young to attend his Uncle Donald's school, but under the tutelage of his older brothers he later came to embrace the Scotsman's rationalist principles.[11]

The emphasis Enlightenment thinkers placed on mathematical laws as determinants of the natural order of the universe no doubt caused the Clarks to stress the mastery of mathematical skills in the education of their children. The family's handwritten and well-worn copybook attests to that. Books were costly, and Dicky Clark, among others, spent hours carefully copying for future reference detailed instructions for making calculations using decimals, compounding interest, figuring square and cube roots, and a host of other similar mathematical procedures. Assorted tables of weights and measures could also be found among the little volume's meticulously hand-scripted contents. Through the years all of the Clark boys, including William, filled the book's unused blank pages with their calculations and solutions to problems.[12]

A belief in a rational and orderly universe failed to shake John and Ann Clark's faith in a higher power. As communicants of the Anglican Church, they labored to convey their religious convictions to their numerous progeny. To be sure, they did not wear religion on their sleeves, nor did they embrace the enthusiasm espoused by the eighteenth-century Awakeners, but they held fast to the tenets of their faith. In April of 1777 the couple counseled their eldest son, who was then recovering from smallpox, that "should you go to war before you come down, I expect it will be a long long time before we see you again, perhaps never in this life . . . our blessings attend you—and we shall pray by the help of God to that same great God almighty to guide, govern and protect you in all your undertakings."[13]

Of his numerous siblings, William Clark's two eldest brothers exerted the greatest influence on him, even though he was only two years old in 1772 when both left the family home to venture out on their own. Unlike in many ways, Jonathan and George both retained lifelong ties with their youngest brother, and he in turn revered them equally. The diligent and scholarly Jonathan secured a position as deputy clerk in what was then Dunmore County and quickly earned high marks for his job performance.[14]

A clerk's life had little appeal for the more impetuous and risk-prone George, who headed west hoping to make use of his surveying skills. After crossing the Blue Ridge and the Alleghenies, the Clarks' nineteen-year-old second son reached the forks of the Ohio for the first time in June 1772. He and his traveling companions boarded canoes at Fort Pitt and headed downriver as far as the mouth of the Kanawha, camping out along the way, sleeping, as one of them put it, on gravel stones rather than feathers. After leaving the river at Kanawha they headed back to Virginia overland. Notwithstanding the rigors of frontier living, the western country had captivated young George Rogers Clark. Later that same year, in the company of his father, he returned to Grave Creek on the Ohio, about 130 miles below Fort Pitt near present-day Wheeling, after passing through what one member of their party described as "the Hilleyest Country I ever saw." With winter approaching, John Clark left George "keeping house" on the banks of the Ohio and returned home equally smitten by the West's possibilities.[15]

The onslaught of white settlers staking out claims along the Ohio River provoked violent clashes with a resident Indian population fearful that the land-hungry hordes would soon drive away the wild game they relied on for sustenance. Raids, retaliations, and occasional massacres, initiated by whites as often as by Indians, exacted a bloody toll on both sides. In 1774, Virginia's Royal Governor Lord Dunmore summoned the militia to suppress the Indian resistance and uphold Virginia's claims to the region. With nary a twinge of conscience concerning the legitimate demands of native people who for generations had hunted, farmed, and made their homes in the contested zone, the Clarks lined up in support of the governor's offensive. From their vantage point the Indians stood as obstacles to their ambitious plans for transforming the region into cultivated fields and prosperous farmsteads. Lord Dunmore's War gave the bold and audacious George Rogers Clark a proper initiation in the ways of war and left him firmly convinced that force was the best response to Indian recalcitrance. When William Clark came of age in Kentucky fifteen years later, he followed his older brother's example and enlisted for military service against the still powerful and defiant Indians.

Lord Dunmore's War ended in a momentary defeat for the Shawnee, whose leaders signed a peace accord requiring them to surrender all claims to Kentucky and to cease interfering with traffic on the Ohio River. The next year (1775), with an appointment as deputy surveyor for the Virginia-based Ohio Company in hand, George Rogers Clark headed to Kentucky for his first visit that far west. Along with laying out lands for the company, Clark set about acquiring tracts for himself and for his family in what he called "this Beautifull Cuntry."[16] John Clark's plans to take a look at Kentucky for himself that summer never materialized, but the expectations born of his son's prediction that once he had seen the country he would never rest until he got to live in it lingered on.[17]

George Rogers Clark and his gentrified associates set about to convert the Kentucky hunting ground into a commercial landscape. True to the interests of their class, they wasted little time in elbowing aside the long hunters who had preceded them to Cantuck. The resulting destruction of the middle ground occupied by Daniel Boone and his compatriots doomed the informal arrangements that had allowed Indian and white hunters to maintain a tenuous, albeit volatile, coexistence in the backcountry wilds. In the spring of 1776 an extralegal assembly in Harrodsburg elected Clark and attorney John Gabriel Jones to represent the western settlements in the Virginia Assembly and to lobby for making Kentucky a separate county. Late that year Virginia's legislative body responded affirmatively by formally staking its claim to the newly created county on its far western reaches.[18] The decision was a victory for the Virginia land speculators that George Rogers Clark represented and a fatal blow to the rival Transylvania Company, headed by the wealthy and powerful North Carolinian Richard Henderson, who had his own plans for the region.

While George maneuvered to establish Virginia's elite as the arbiters of property rights in the Kentucky backcountry, war clouds of a different sort loomed along the distant Atlantic horizon. Discontented colonists resisted efforts by their British rulers to extract new taxes and tighten control over the thirteen seaboard colonies. Boston, home of the famed "Tea Party," had become a hotbed of opposition to the unpopular Parliamentary measures, but as the tensions escalated in 1774–1775, the Clarks, like many of their Virginia neighbors, appeared ready to embrace the cause championed by the northern colonists. Members of the Clark family lined up early with other Virginia Patriots, and when the citizens of Dunmore County met in February 1775 to elect two delegates to a Virginia Convention summoned to consider the issuance of a call for independence, they chose Jonathan Clark as one of their representatives. He was present at Old Saint John's Church in Richmond when Patrick Henry spoke the words destined to make him forever famous: "Give me liberty or give me death."[19] Billy was not old enough to comprehend the import of these dramatic happenings, but in the troubled times that followed, he must have sensed the anxiety that filled the Clark home as his parents tracked the ebb and flow of America's struggle for independence through the lives of their soldier sons.

The Revolutionary War was never far from the Clark household. All of William Clark's five brothers distinguished themselves and honored their family through military service. Jonathan, the eldest, was the first to answer the call to duty. He served briefly as a first lieutenant in Dunmore County's American Independent Company of Riflemen prior to his acceptance of a captain's commission in the Eighth Virginia Infantry Regiment of the Continental Line in early 1776. His first assignment took him to southern Virginia, and southward from there to Charleston, South Carolina, and Savannah, Georgia, before he returned to his home state for a brief furlough. Following his advancement to the rank of major, he proceeded to the mid-Atlantic region, where he fought with his regiment in several key engagements including Brandywine, Germantown, and Monmouth. His role in the successful assault against the British fort at Paulus Hook, New Jersey, in 1779 helped earn him a promotion to lieutenant colonel the next year. As the primary arena of combat moved southward, Colonel Clark advanced with his unit to Charleston, where he was taken prisoner when British forces occupied that city on May 12, 1780. Following his parole a year later, he returned to Virginia and sat out the few remaining months of the conflict. Several years later, the Virginia Assembly commissioned him a major general in the militia, making him the second of the Clark sons to attain a general's rank. His brother George Rogers Clark had previously earned that distinction.[20]

John Clark, Jr. was a captain in the same Virginia regiment as Jonathan, but he did not make it to Charleston. During the Battle of Germantown, John Jr. was taken prisoner and confined by the British for the next five years, forced to spend a part of that time on the prison ship HMS *Jersey* in New York's Wallabout Bay. The squalid conditions and deprivation to which the American prisoners were subjected took a heavy toll. The fatalities on the New York prison hulks numbered in the thousands. John Clark's plaintive letters pleading for money and clothes and detailing his sorrowful plight had to have been a source of great distress to his family. Despite the poor state of his health at the time of his exchange, John Clark, Jr. remained undaunted and even rallied sufficiently to join the Marquis de Lafayette's forces in Virginia for a brief period during the war's final campaign. He never fully recovered from the consumption he had contracted during his confinement and died at his parents' home on October 29, 1783. The Clark family blamed the conditions of John's British captivity for causing his untimely passing at age twenty-six, and that conviction added anger to their sorrow and planted the seeds of William Clark's dislike for the British.[21]

The subsequent shocking disappearance of fourth son Richard Clark, better known to family members as Dicky, only compounded the family's grief. Richard, a lieutenant in the same Illinois Regiment commanded by George Rogers Clark, had come through the war unscathed. But after leaving Louisville unaccompanied, en route to Vincennes, he was never seen again. Family members opined that he either was killed by the Indians or drowned while attempting to cross the White River. William Clark always assumed that Dicky had died at the hands of hostile Indians even though some accounts suggest that his riderless horse had later been found. Even for seasoned travelers, the western country could be a dangerous place.[22]

Edmund Clark was a few months shy of his eighteenth birthday when he joined the Eighth Virginia Regiment as a lieutenant in 1780. Barely two months later he fell into British hands at Charleston with his brother Jonathan. Edmund was exchanged shortly before the war's end and mustered out of military service a few months later.[23]

Among Billy Clark's older brothers, the confident and courageous George Rogers Clark attained the most fame and notoriety. His daring attempts to secure U.S. claims to the much-contested trans-Appalachian region and to open the way for full-scale settlement there made him a rising star in the early days of the young Republic. When he reached Harrodsburg in December of 1776 carrying a small store of ammunition that he had procured from Virginia officials, central Kentucky was under siege. With the encouragement and support of British officials at Fort Detroit, Shawnee war parties had launched an offensive against the exposed and vulnerable Bluegrass settlements. A Christmas Day attack took the lives of John Gabriel Jones, George Rogers Clark's fellow delegate to the Virginia Assembly, and three other members of his traveling party. Clark realized that the outbreak of the American Revolution had brought dramatic changes for the backcountry settlers, and he concluded that a new strategy would be required to safeguard the region from its British and Indian foes. He hurried back to Williamsburg, where he won Governor Patrick Henry's support for a secret military offensive against British posts north of the Ohio.[24]

Following his return to Kentucky with the Virginia and Pennsylvania volunteers he had recruited for his western campaign, George Rogers Clark established a base camp on Corn Island at the Falls of the Ohio. His plan was more popular in Virginia than in Kentucky. Many rank-and-file Kentuckians resented his decision to exchange his major's commission in the Kentucky County militia for a colonel's commission in the Virginia Line, the new state's regular army. That action confirmed their assessment that the rough-edged but imperious Virginia gentleman was an interloper with an agenda far different from their own. Neither his charm nor his passion could persuade them of the necessity for venturing so far from home. They were much more concerned with defending their own doorsteps against enemy marauders than in joining the larger Revolutionary struggle.[25]

Those setbacks did not deter Clark from his mission. With characteristic boldness and bravado he launched a successful assault against British-controlled Kaskaskia. Using the element of surprise, Clark and a ragtag force of fewer than two hundred recruits, mostly easterners, occupied the Mississippi River outpost on the second anniversary of the Declaration of Independence. Following his victory at Kaskaskia, Clark persuaded many of the Illinois Country's French-speaking residents to join the American cause, and their tacit support

George Rogers Clark, portrait by Mathew H. Jouett, ca. 1825. Jouet based this depiction of William Clark's older brother in middle age upon a posthumous portrait by John Wesley Jarvis. Courtesy of the Filson Historical Society, Louisville.

along with an approving nod from Spanish officials in St. Louis enabled the forces under Clark's command to extend nominal American control to Cahokia and Vincennes with relative ease.

News of Clark's campaign soon reached the British post at Detroit. Canada's Lieutenant Governor Henry Hamilton, known to the Americans as the "Hair Buyer" because of his alleged practice of purchasing enemy scalps from the Indians, hastily organized an expedition to reimpose British authority in the region. His forces, augmented with the Indian allies he had recruited, encountered only slight resistance and easily ousted the handful of Americans occupying Vincennes. Hamilton chose not to advance to Clark's headquarters at Kaskaskia immediately, deciding instead to wait for better weather.[26]

Counting upon the British to assume that he would not be foolish enough to attempt a march across the muddy swamplands that separated Kaskaskia from Vincennes in the dead of winter, George Rogers Clark once again took advantage of the element of surprise. After slogging through the wilderness for eighteen days, Clark's dwindling Illinois Regiment, with assistance from an equal number of French Creole volunteers, caught Hamilton unawares—he was playing cards when the assault against Fort Sackville began. With fewer than 150 troops and the aid of a local populace with no particular allegiance to either side, Clark retook Vincennes. The French were not all that fond of Clark's Virginians, but they cared even less for the British. Given a choice, most of them probably would have opted to sit out the conflict.

When a party of pro-British Indians came upon the scene oblivious to what had just happened, Clark's Indian-hating forces killed, scalped, and mutilated the hapless warriors with relentless fury. Those bloody actions were intended to send other Indians a message they would understand: their British allies were as weak as old women and unable to protect them. Clark accepted Hamilton's surrender at Fort Sackville on February 23, 1779, and packed the British official off to a Williamsburg prison, where he was kept in chains until his parole the next year. The gains of Clark's victory at Vincennes, though much celebrated, proved fleeting. In truth Clark occupied rather than conquered the region. The ultimate object of his northwest campaign, the ouster of the British from Detroit, remained unrealized. Plans for an assault on the northern post had to be abandoned when Clark's pleas for assistance with the project fell on deaf ears.[27]

Conditions were as unsettled as ever in Kentucky, where Indian raids continued to wreak havoc among the scattered settlements. Fearing that all that he had accomplished might be lost, George Rogers Clark led a raiding party across the Ohio in the summer of 1780. The expedition sacked Shawnee towns on the Scioto and Great Miami and destroyed hundreds of acres of unharvested corn in a by then all too familiar scenario. But Clark's heavy-handed recruiting tactics and his confiscation of corn and whiskey from local settlers also had aroused considerable ire that was only partially placated by the positive results and the distribution of proceeds from the sale of the Indian loot.[28]

The failure of eastern authorities to provide adequate provisions for his troops placed Clark in a difficult position and forced him to borrow money and pledge his own assets to secure the notes he signed to cover his expenses. At war's end when officials of both the Confederation and the state of Virginia declined to reimburse his outlays, he faced financial ruin. The cash-strapped Virginia Assembly had lobbied to have Congress assume the costs of Clark's campaigns in the Northwest, but when he was unable to produce vouchers to account for his precise expenditures, U.S. officials declined to reimburse him. At that point, Virginia's legislators seemed content to reward the services of their state's youngest general with no more than an elegant sword, which he allegedly broke and discarded in anger and disgust.[29] This sudden reversal of fortunes took a toll on the man that Virginian John Randolph had earlier proclaimed the "Hannibal of the West." George's attempts to find solace in the bottle only accelerated his personal and financial decline. Eventually he would be forced to turn to his younger brother William for assistance in sorting out his troubled finances and salvaging his remaining assets.

While George Rogers Clark waged war against the British in distant western lands, the Revolutionary conflict inched ever closer to the Caroline County farm where Billy Clark still resided with his parents and sisters. The situation seemed especially dire in early 1781. Lord Cornwallis, the British commander, had captured Williamsburg and launched an assault against Charlottesville before his fortunes suddenly changed. In a dramatic turn of events General George Washington, with assistance from the French naval fleet, forced Cornwallis's Redcoats to lay down their arms at Yorktown. Even though the British general's 1781 surrender for all intents and purposes marked the end of the war, both sides kept their troops in the field for another two years, pending the drafting of a formal peace accord.

By 1783 America's changing circumstances suggested to John Clark that the time for him to pull up stakes and head west might finally be drawing near. For nearly a decade he had contemplated a move to Kentucky, but as long as British Redcoats and their Hessian hirelings occupied America's coastal seaports and Indian raiding parties stalked the backcountry, all such plans had been kept on hold. As those threats diminished, a sense of optimism had replaced the gloom of the war's darkest days. The belief that a new era had dawned was much in evidence when the Clarks joined their neighbors at the Caroline County courthouse in April of 1783 for a barbecue celebrating an end to the war with England.[30]

Even as exuberant Americans gathered in various places across the land that spring to mark their victory, diplomats representing the Continental Congress were still in Paris hammering out a final settlement. The provisions of the Treaty of Paris, concluded later that year, were exceedingly favorable to the fledgling American Republic. Not only did George III's negotiators agree to recognize American independence, but they also cast aside the assurances they had given their Native American allies and ceded to the United States jurisdiction over all territories east of the Mississippi, save for Florida.

As the returning Clark sons assembled at the home of their parents in 1783, they seemed eager to claim the spoils of the victory that they had helped make possible. George Rogers Clark had come eastward to press his claims for compensation, but when he traveled to Richmond, Virginia's financially pressed leaders took advantage of the war's end to relieve the young general of his duties with no more than a hearty thanks for his services.[31] George was still smarting from this latest setback when he received a letter from Thomas Jefferson, Virginia's former governor and a family acquaintance, inquiring if he might be willing to lead an exploratory party to the West. This was the first time that Jefferson had seen fit to put in writing his thoughts about a transcontinental western expedition.[32]

His timing was not propitious. Clark waited a few weeks before responding: "Your proposition respecting a tour to the west and North west of the Continent would be Extreamly agreeable to me could I afford it but I have late discovered that I knew nothing of the lucrative policy of the world supposing my duty required every attention and sacrifice to the Publick Interest but must now look forward for future Support."[33] It obviously was a sore subject, and Jefferson opted not to pursue the matter. He had no inkling that in a curious twist of fate twenty years later he would turn to George's younger brother William for assistance in bringing his long-deferred plan for exploring the West to fruition. One can only wonder if George bothered to mention Jefferson's proposal to brother Billy in 1783.

George's disappointments were not the family's only concerns in 1783. Their homecoming had turned somber when John Clark, Jr. succumbed to the ravages of consumption in late October. But the Clarks understood that loss and disappointment were a part of life, and they pressed ahead even in the midst of sorrow and grief. The day following his brother's burial, Jonathan set out for Kentucky to initiate arrangements for his father's pending move westward. Rain and snow impeded Jonathan's progress, but by mid-December he was surveying lands at Beargrass Creek, the location not far from the Falls of the Ohio that George Rogers Clark had selected for their parent's new home. John Jr.'s recent death seems to have been very much in Jonathan's thoughts, because in a diary noted for the brevity of its entries he took time to record a folk remedy someone had recommended for the treatment of the dreaded consumption—a tea made from green oats. By the end of May in 1784 Jonathan was back in Virginia reporting to his family.[34]

With the preliminary arrangements in Kentucky now completed, John and Ann Clark began final preparations for vacating their Virginia farm. In sorting through the accumulated possessions of a lifetime, choices had to be made. Transporting everything they owned was out of the question. Some things were undoubtedly given to family and friends planning to remain in Virginia, while the other items that had to be left behind were auctioned off at a mid-September sale at the farm.[35] As their scheduled departure date drew near, the tempo must have accelerated as the elder Clarks directed family members and their dozen or so African American slaves in packing goods of every description into trunks, barrels, and boxes and in rounding up the livestock that had been carefully culled from the family herds and flocks for transport to Kentucky.

Optimism undoubtedly ran high. A new home under construction outside Louisville was being readied for their occupancy. Even so, the prospect of imminent departure from the familiar Virginia countryside must have occasioned some second thoughts and more than a few tears as the departing members of the Clark family said their good-byes and bade farewell to kinfolk and friends. The prospect of leaving homey comforts and severing ties from the well-established support groups was especially difficult for women like Ann Clark who long had drawn solace and encouragement from those neighborhood networks.[36]

This uprooting was a matter of choice for members of the Clark family, but for the African American slaves they compelled to accompany them, there was no option.[37] Slaveholding was an essential strand in the fabric of eighteenth-century Virginia society, and like most other slave owners the Clarks expected their human chattel to do their bidding without question or complaint. They comforted themselves with the belief that they were good slave masters because they adhered to a code of conduct that required owners to do right by their slaves as long as their slaves did right by them. And to the Clarks' way of thinking slaves did right by obeying their masters and following orders. From their vantage point, slavery was a part of the natural order of things, and they, like so many others, simply turned a blind eye to the system's inhumanity and cruelty.

The Clarks' African American slaves so unceremoniously removed to Kentucky probably had little time to dwell on their misfortunes, for they would have been assigned primary responsibility for loading the wagons and pack animals that had been secured to transport the Clark family and its belongings. And more likely than not, the able-bodied among them were expected to walk most of the way herding livestock and pushing wagons when they became mired in mud. The late October departure date the Clarks chose was not optimal. Travelers destined for Kentucky usually set off in September, hoping to take advantage of dry roads before the onset of the October downpours. Those rains were needed to raise the Ohio's lower late-summer water levels sufficiently to permit flatboats to float safely downstream before wintertime ice floes again closed the river. As the Clarks discovered, timing was everything.

After leaving their Virginia farm, the Clarks joined a caravan heading northward through Maryland and Pennsylvania. Their initial destination was Redstone Landing, a busy river port on the Monongahela River in western Pennsylvania, not far from Pittsburgh. To get there they had to cross the Blue Ridge and the Allegheny Mountains. On a good day a sturdy wagon could advance as much as twenty miles, but the rains and perhaps even early snows that the Clarks encountered in the mountains impeded their progress as they struggled to maneuver wagons and animals through the hilly terrain along bad roads. Inns and other establishments scattered along the route offered the weary travelers a nighttime resting place and refuge from the inclement weather. But in all likelihood to avoid the costly "tavern prices" the Clarks and their retinue spent more than a few nights camping out under shelter of the canvasses that covered their wagons, perhaps scratching the flea and insect bites that bedeviled wilderness travelers until the winter frosts temporarily eliminated the source of their discomfort.[38]

When they belatedly reached Redstone Landing (now Brownsville, Pennsylvania) there was insufficient time to arrange for the necessary flatboats before winter's onset closed the Ohio to traffic for the season. Having missed that deadline, John Clark, who had first visited Redstone a decade earlier with his son George, scurried to secure winter lodgings where his party could await the arrival of spring thaws. By mid-February all was in readiness for them to continue their journey to the Falls of the Ohio. The local builders had finished construction of the bulky flatboat that John Clark had purchased to transport his family to its final destination. Once their goods and supplies had been stowed away, their livestock had been tethered in rows across the deck, and all of the passengers were safely on board, the Clarks were ready to begin their descent downriver.

There was plenty to capture Billy Clark's attention. No doubt he spent more than a little time observing the boatmen guiding the cumbersome river craft downstream, and perhaps he even tried his hand at the rudder without realizing that one day he would earn a reputation as an expert waterman. There were other sights to behold as he surveyed the unending succession of unfamiliar scenes passing before his eyes, including the lush Kentucky canebrakes that livestock found so appealing. As their boats neared the mouth of the Kentucky River, someone spotted a canoe filled with Indians, but the sighting occasioned no alarm.[39] The Clarks had taken precautions to fortify their vessel, but more important, they erroneously assumed that George Rogers Clark's daring actions along with recent post-Revolutionary accords had restored peace to the Indian Country.

There was greater excitement a short time later when their boats approached a clearing where an old Virginia acquaintance, Captain Robert Elliott, had built a cabin and begun making other improvements. John Clark, accompanied by one of his slaves, went ashore to confer with Captain Elliott, but he learned that his former neighbor was away on a hunting trip. Elliott's wife, Mary, somewhat embarrassed by the family's humble abode and unaccustomed to entertaining guests in her primitive surroundings, opted not to invite a family of the Clarks' social status to come ashore and share a meal while they awaited her husband's return. Thus rebuffed, the Clarks continued on their journey. Only later did they learn that on that same evening a party of hostile Indians fell upon the tiny settlement, burned the cabin to the ground, and killed four persons. Mary Elliott managed to escape with her baby daughter, but news of the Indian assault dramatized for the Clarks the ever-present dangers that still lurked in the Kentucky wilderness.[40]

That stark reminder did not diminish the elation they experienced when the Falls of the Ohio came into view. On March 3, 1785, more than four months after they had left their Virginia home, the Clarks went ashore at Louisville eager to begin a new life on the frontier. The town was already a thriving place with its own fort, one or more stores, a new courthouse, and well over one hundred clapboard houses and log cabins. Louisville was a city with considerable promise. Its future prospects seemed endangered only by the unhealthy pools of stagnant water that stood in low-lying places behind the town.[41]

The Clarks hurried off to occupy the home awaiting them on the nearby South Fork of Beargrass Creek. When they arrived there, efforts to transform what one contemporary observer called a "rich and beautiful country" into a proper plantation were already well under way.[42] Their new residence was built of logs with stone chimneys framing each end. The structure measured forty feet by twenty feet with two large rooms on each side of the central hallway. At the time of their arrival it may have been a single-story dwelling, but sometime before 1799 a second story of identical proportions would be added. The property that John Clark initially dubbed Ampthill, and later renamed Mulberry Hill, faced northwestward in the direction of Louisville and Fort Nelson, General George Rogers Clark's military headquarters.[43] Billy Clark was now a westerner, and Mulberry Hill was his new home.

Billy, no doubt, was pleased to see his brother George, who he discovered had been ailing. There were problems aplenty with the Indians. John Clark wrote to Jonathan, who had remained in Virginia, that the Indians "have lately kild & taken a family within 3 or 4 miles from me and are repeatedly doing mischief on the external parts of the countrey." The elder Clark complained about the shortage of commanding officers capable of taking charge of the local militia, hinting broadly that Jonathan might join the family in Kentucky where he could put his experience as a military officer to good use. By the next spring George's health had improved, but the Indian troubles persisted. Two more of the Clarks' neighbors had been lost while out scouting, but their deaths had been avenged when the militia killed three Indians in retaliation.[44]

Kentucky's anxious residents demanded action, and a council of field officers in Harrodsburg authorized an expedition against the Wabash Indian towns even though their authority to mount an expedition outside Kentucky was

Mulberry Hill, the Clark family home near Louisville, was William Clark's principal residence between 1785 and 1803. Courtesy of the Filson Historical Society, Louisville.

questionable. They named George Rogers Clark, who held the rank of brigadier general in the Virginia militia, to take command. Everything that could went wrong, and the star-crossed venture proved to be a complete fiasco from beginning to end. By the time the expedition reached Vincennes, grumbling in the ranks prompted Clark to arrest and reprimand a militia colonel from Lincoln County. Clark's actions combined with a chronic scarcity of provisions caused the Lincoln County unit to desert his command and head for home. Following their hasty departure, the campaign had to be abandoned and the remaining militiamen soon followed the deserters back to Kentucky.[45]

In an effort to procure badly needed rations, the disgruntled militiamen forcibly appropriated for public use a supply of goods and merchandise belonging to Laurent Bazadone, a Spanish merchant in Vincennes whom they conveniently accused of illegal trade with the Indians. General Clark clearly sanctioned their actions, but when the aggrieved Bazadone subsequently attempted to hold him responsible, Clark placed all blame for the incident on one of his subordinates. Clark did agree, however, that the Spaniard deserved what he got. Bazadone took the matter to the courts, where he secured a judgment against the general. That award threatened George Rogers Clark's Indiana lands, and on the eve of his departure for the Pacific in 1803, William Clark was still attempting to settle the case for his by then generally discredited older brother.[46]

The Clark family's first two years in Kentucky (1785–1786) were not easy. John Clark was obliged to borrow money to purchase a few cattle and other necessaries, but despite these initial hardships he expected that things would soon improve.[47] Meanwhile, Billy appears to have taken to his new surroundings with nary a glance backward in the direction of Old Virginny. Not long after his arrival in Kentucky, he helped survey the Beargrass lands his father had recently purchased from the estate of George Meriwether (a relative of Meriwether Lewis). No doubt Billy's older brother George, who had returned to his parents' home to recuperate, offered him some practical tips prior to his first assignment as a surveyor's apprentice. The youngest of the Clark boys also devoted himself to the mastery of the survival skills that were so essential to successful wilderness living. There was much to learn, but he had an excellent teacher at hand.

A seasoned and experienced frontiersman, George Rogers Clark was well qualified to instruct his younger sibling in the arts of hunting, shooting, and navigating in the woods. With the benefit of George's expert guidance, it was not long before the rapidly maturing William felt comfortable in venturing forth into the countryside on his own. A faint pencil entry recorded in the Clark family Mathematics Copy Book stated "William Clark Junr. found a mans fresh bone Sunday the 23rd of March 1787 as I was coming from the falls Ohio."[48]

While neither as polished nor as scholarly as the absentee Jonathan, George was mindful of the importance of the more traditional components of a proper gentleman's education. There were fewer schools and tutors on the Kentucky frontier than there had been in Virginia, so William was mostly home schooled. The deficiencies of William Clark's education have been well documented. Anyone familiar with his writings can attest to his creative and inconsistent spelling and capitalization and his occasionally tortured syntax. In his journals of the expedition one can find innumerable variations in spelling as in the oft-cited case of the word Sioux, which he spelled twenty-seven different ways. Likewise Clark rendered flour as flower, and transformed botanist and naturalist into botents and natirless. Because he spelled phonetically it is not difficult to determine his intent as in the case of "looner" for lunar or "wrighting" for writing.[49]

William Clark was acutely aware of his shortcomings in these areas, for when Meriwether Lewis dispatched a part of his partner's private journal to Thomas Jefferson from Fort Mandan in 1805, he cautioned the president that "Capt. Clark dose not wish this journal exposed in it's present state, but has no objection, that one or more copies of it be made by some confidential person under your direction, correcting it's grammatical errors &c."[50] For the same reason, following Lewis's death, Clark asked Nicholas Biddle to take charge of preparing the expedition's journals for publication. Sensitive though he may have been about his inadequate language skills, Clark had higher academic priorities, as he made clear in one of his early journals: "Learning does not consist in the knowledge of Languages, but in the knowledge of things to which language gives names (Science and philosophy)."[51] Indeed it is easy to make too much of Clark's linguistic shortcomings. Spelling variations were commonplace even in the writings of the best-educated Americans, and over the course of time Clark's spelling improved. The first edition of Noah Webster's *Blue Back Speller* did not appear in print until 1783. William Clark's "wrighting," while not always florid, was generally clear and concise. His vocabulary bespoke someone who was well read, and while he might spell velocity "verlocity," he knew the word's meaning. Clark seldom used more words than necessary to deliver his message, and his simple and to-the-point style offers an unadorned eloquence that modern readers still find captivating.

While he did not have the advantages of a classical education, Billy Clark was an eager learner whose natural inquisitiveness prompted him to pursue knowledge throughout his lengthy life. He shared his brother George's fondness for history, geography, and natural history and occasionally found time to enjoy an entertaining novel. He was already developing skills as a draftsman and cartographer. At a young age he extolled the importance of trigonometry, astronomy, navigation, geometry, architecture, and land surveying. The Clarks obviously saw to it that Billy kept to his books. His math skills were improving. He took time to calculate the distance from Charles Town to London using only the givens that Boston in New England bears west from London a distance of 3,227 miles and Charles Town in South Carolina bears south from Boston a distance of 797 miles.[52]

By the time that William Clark reached his eighteenth birthday in 1788, the amiable, physically fit six-footer stood ready to strike out on his own whenever the first promising opportunity came his way. A product of gentrified Virginia and backcountry Kentucky, he mirrored his upbringing in both worlds. From his close-knit and high-achieving family he acquired his steady habits, his ambition and desire to succeed, and his personal qualities of honesty and integrity. The unhappy consequences of George's sometimes-volatile temperament and his growing intemperance alerted William at a young age to the dangers of inconstancy and excess. As he matured, William became a steadying presence in his much-admired older brother's troubled life. It was a role that he would master and frequently put to good use—notably in his friendship with Meriwether Lewis and his dealings with Indians.

Throughout his life, the amiable William Clark was eager to please and reluctant to offend. In a telling encounter with a pair of British traders at Fort

Mandan during the winter of 1805, one of them reported that Meriwether Lewis "could not make himself agreeable to us," but he hastened to add that Captain Clark's "conversation was always polite, for he seemed to dislike giving offense unnecessarily." Sociability and good manners were the hallmark of a Virginia gentleman, and of William Clark as well. He would later put many of these same qualities to good use in his roles as a diplomat and negotiator. Clark was neither snobbish nor arrogant, but his gentrified upbringing left an indelible imprint of class consciousness. Proper deportment and association with the right people were important to Clark. During his early days as a young officer in the U.S. Army, Lieutenant Clark confided to his sister that a fellow officer's wife "was of low burth & less breading [breeding.] She is not noticed at all."[53]

Family ties and kinship were obviously important. There were other lessons imparted by members of his immediate family. The example of his brothers had taught him about honor, duty, and public service. His Anglican parents had also transmitted to him their belief in a higher power and his conviction "that religious duties consist in doing justice, loveing mercy, and endeavouring to make our fellow creatures happy."[54]

But such altruistic notions did not dampen his appetite for financial gain. From his father's aspirations born of the larger world of eighteenth-century Virginia, William Clark learned to value land as a measure of status and success and to believe that its ownership helped ensure personal freedom and independence. He also absorbed the spirit of Enlightenment thought and a commitment to the republican principles that Virginia's Revolutionary generation embraced so ardently. To his discredit, he failed to see any inconsistency between those political beliefs and his attitudes about slavery and race. He was by no means alone in that failing, but his blind adherence to such notions allowed him to treat his fellow human beings in a manner that contradicted his normally decent impulses.

William Clark's Kentucky years did not fundamentally alter the basic precepts that he had carried with him from Virginia. The distinctive conditions of the American frontier simply opened new avenues for realizing his well-established ambitions. In Kentucky he was able to master the skills that were essential to wilderness living, and for the first time he encountered native people in the flesh. His introduction to rampaging Indians killing his friends and neighbors and attempting to foil his family's pursuit of a better life brought home the realities of the conflicts that he had heard his brothers discuss around the Virginia hearth. The drive for self-preservation was strong, and he willingly looked forward to going on the offensive against these pesky nuisances who stalked his new homeland. But he already must also have had a glimpse of the larger dilemma that he would spend much of his life attempting to resolve. What was to be the fate of the hostile and beleaguered Indian people struggling to protect themselves against an onslaught of white settlers who threatened to take away their tribal lands and to destroy their traditional modes of living? But there would be time to ponder such questions in the future, and for now, as he stood on the threshold of adulthood, William Clark seemed ready to tackle any challenges that might come his way.

Two

Kentucky Apprenticeship

WITHIN A FEW SHORT YEARS Billy Clark and his family were comfortably settled at Mulberry Hill just outside Louisville. The Clark farmstead with its numerous improvements was beginning to take on the appearance of a proper plantation. Its cultivated fields, commodious two-story log residence, detached kitchen, slave quarters, and other assorted outbuildings and gristmill gave it an established look that the Clark's Beargrass neighbors must have envied. George Rogers Clark pronounced his father's family "by far the best settled of any persons in this part of the Cuntrey."[1]

The well-ordered Clark homestead belied the turmoil and uncertainty swirling around the Kentucky countryside. Cantuck in the 1780s was a cauldron of contesting factions and warring parties at odds over how to protect their exposed settlements against Indian attacks, defend their interests against outside speculators and land grabbers, and gain commercial access to the vital Mississippi River from a foreign power. Some Kentuckians saw statehood as the best way to address their problems, while a handful of others openly flirted with the possibility of separating the western province from the struggling American nation and joining forces with imperial Spain.[2]

The Clarks stood aloof from the factional squabbling, preferring instead to focus their attention on the task of claiming and improving their lands. John Clark, the family patriarch, was growing older, and he showed little interest in entering the public arena at this stage in his life. George, whose glory days were already behind him, foreswore any interest in politics after likening Kentucky politicos to "a swarm of hungrey persons grasping for bread," and Billy was neither old enough nor sufficiently established on his own to join the debate.[3]

At Beargrass as elsewhere, Indian raids remained a serious problem. The ever-present threat of attack kept the watchful settlers perpetually on edge. Like many of his neighbors, George Rogers Clark placed the blame at the doorstep of national leaders whom he accused of prolonging the conflict with their ill-advised policy of showering the Indians with kisses and presents.[4] Under the circumstances, Kentuckians relied upon local militia as their first line of defense.

When Kentucky volunteers launched a series of impromptu retaliatory militia strikes across the Ohio River into the heart of Indian country, U.S. government officials complained that they had overstepped their bounds and were only making matters worse. Indian people were as divided as their Euro-American neighbors over proper strategies for defending their interests in the contested region. On both sides of the Indian-white divide proponents of the sword battled it out with those who favored negotiation.

The ratification of the U.S. Constitution and the election of George Washington as the new Republic's first president in 1788 brought renewed hope to those Kentuckians who believed that the stronger national government led by the Revolutionary hero would be able to rein in the errant tribesmen stalking the western countryside. But they were sorely disappointed when hostile Wea and Miami raiders returned to the warpath early the next year following their usual winter hiatus.[5]

Unwilling to wait for federal authorities to respond to this latest outrage, Major John Hardin raised a force of two or three hundred militiamen at Louisville intent on chastising the offending Weas. William Clark, who had just observed his nineteenth birthday, was among the volunteers enlisting in Hardin's company that summer. Given his family's commitment to duty, its well-established military traditions, and the ongoing threats to Kentucky's frontier settlements, his decision to answer the call came as no surprise. Hardin's 1789 expedition to the Wea towns on the Wabash marked Billy Clark's entry into the public arena and gave him his first taste of military life. It also afforded him an opportunity to hone skills that would prove exceedingly useful for his future advancement.[6]

During Hardin's campaign the novice soldier kept a journal documenting his travels, a practice that he quickly transformed into a lifelong habit. Perhaps he had gotten the idea from observing his brother Jonathan faithfully record his daily whereabouts in a diary, but any similarities in their journal-keeping practices ended there. In contrast with Jonathan's terse entries of no more than a few words, William favored an expansive daily log with room for personal observations. Billy Clark's journal of the Hardin expedition conveys the wide-eyed wonder of a youthful traveler venturing into unfamiliar territory for the first time. The scenes he witnessed frequently moved him to employ superlatives. The middle fork of the White River was "the Delitefullest River" he had ever seen, and not long thereafter when he came upon an open expanse covered with tall grasses and "Butyfull" purple flowers, he labeled it the most delightful plain he had ever laid his eyes upon. "Delitefull" and "butyfull" were his favorite adjectives, and there seemed no insufficiency of places to which they might be applied.[7]

William Clark kept meticulous records throughout his lengthy career. His precision and attention to detail made him a better civil servant and businessman, and to this day Clark's journals and voluminous correspondence are a treasure trove of information about the early-nineteenth-century American frontier. By the time he and Meriwether Lewis began their journey to the Pacific in 1804, William Clark was a practiced journal keeper. It was no mere happenstance that his systematic writings provided a more complete record of the Pacific expedition than his better-educated but mercurial partner's more episodic chronicle. Clark also used his 1789 trek with Hardin across the Indiana wilderness to practice his map-making skills. The maps that the novice draftsman sketched already gave hints of an accomplished cartographer in the making.[8]

Hardin's actual campaign did not amount to much. On August 5, 1789, the company set out from Clarksville at the foot of the Falls of the Ohio across from Louisville—coincidentally the same location that Lewis and Clark would use as a staging area for the Corps of Discovery fourteen years later. Hardin's army marched overland without encountering a single Indian until the fifth day, when it came upon a recently abandoned campsite. Following that discovery, Major Hardin dispatched two small mounted units to search out the enemy. Billy Clark was among those deployed. As they traveled down a well-worn road leading to the Wea towns, the sound of an Indian bell alerted the advance guard to their nearby presence. Thus forewarned, the eager troops rushed forward. Clark and his companions crossed to within fifty yards of the Indian encampment and opened fire. Members of the advance guard joined in the fight. When the battle was over the Kentuckians had killed eight Indians (four men and four women), taken two children prisoners, seized sixteen horses, and confiscated plunder worth more than £150. Three of their number had been wounded in the skirmish, but Clark was not one of them.[9]

Having momentarily satiated their thirst for revenge, the men of Hardin's poorly disciplined company elected not to press their campaign against the main enemy force ensconced in the nearby Wea strongholds. They headed instead for the relative security of Vincennes. While en route, a disagreement broke out within the ranks over their proposed route of travel, and fifty of the volunteers announced that they intended to go no farther. At that point the feuding troops auctioned off the Indian loot they had seized and divided the proceeds among themselves. With their share of the spoils in hand, members of the disaffected faction struck out on their own. Clark dutifully remained with the main force as it proceeded according to plan to the French settlement of Vincennes. Clark was not very impressed with the "old starved place" on the banks of the Wabash and its low French-style buildings that were, according to him, base but clean. The French preference for village living over the commonplace scattered farmsteads on the Anglo-American frontier surprised him. In time Clark would become well acquainted with French ways and customs, but for the moment they seemed strange and different. After a brief respite at Vincennes, the remnant of Hardin's company returned to Clarksville, arriving on August 18.[10]

Clark's initial military venture had lasted barely two weeks and accomplished little of strategic importance, but it had been a learning experience for the youthful recruit. Clark appears to have acquitted himself honorably. The conduct of some of his comrades in arms must have given this inexperienced warrior much to ponder. He undoubtedly had plenty of questions for the seasoned veteran George, who was more knowledgeable about these matters. Whatever he may have thought about the ill-disciplined militia, the excitement of his initial campaign left him ready for more.

After a six-week pause, Billy Clark set out with sister Elizabeth's husband, Colonel Richard Anderson, a cousin whose name was also William Clark, and several others intent on joining a new army forming for yet another Indian campaign. When that expedition failed to materialize, Billy took time out for a hunting trip with friends. Billy Clark's family connections and his eagerness to participate in military service persuaded General Arthur St. Clair, governor of the Northwest Territory, to offer the lad a captain's commission in the militia company at Clarksville the very next year.[11] No doubt his family approved.

On February 7, 1790, one month after he received his commission, the novice militia officer embarked on a six-week reconnaissance through central Kentucky. His journal fails to disclose the object of his trip, but it does suggest that he used the opportunity to introduce himself to local militia leaders. He also found time for socializing. As with most nineteen-year-old males, Billy exhibited a decided interest in the fairer sex and seems to have been particularly drawn to the Slaughter residence and the young ladies who resided there. On those blustery winter days when he chose not to venture out for business or pleasure, Clark contented himself in his quarters with a good book. His choice was Tobias Smollett's *Roderick Random,* a picaresque novel about a shameless Scottish rogue with a penchant for farce, horseplay, and violence.[12]

Clark's precise whereabouts in the ensuing months are unclear, though a notation that his son Meriwether Lewis Clark penciled many years later on his father's 1798 journal of a trip to New Orleans and the East Coast states that William Clark made his first trip to the gulf port in 1790.[13] That may account for his failure to join Hardin's company for General Josiah Harmar's disastrous 1790 expedition against Miamitown. Whatever his reason for absenting himself from the campaign, he had little cause to lament his decision once he heard that the savvy Miami leader Little Turtle, with assistance from his Shawnee and Delaware allies, had bested the overconfident Americans and left them bleeding and in tatters. News of Harmar's debacle only stiffened President Washington's resolve to assert U.S. authority in the troubled Northwest, but anxious Euro-American residents in the Ohio Valley worried that Little Turtle's victories might embolden neighboring tribes to renew their assaults against unprotected American settlements. Washington had appointed General Arthur St. Clair as Harmar's replacement. Biding their time to allow St. Clair to regroup his forces in preparation for a renewed assault against Miamitown planned for the latter part of 1791, federal officials arranged for Kentucky's recently appointed militia commandant Brigadier General Charles Scott to launch a diversionary spring offensive against the Wabash towns.[14]

William Clark and more than eight hundred other Kentuckians volunteered to serve with Scott's command, which set out for the Wea town of Ouiatanon on the banks of the Wabash River on May 23, 1791. On the eve of Billy Clark's departure with the Scott expedition, James O'Fallon, an as yet unmasked scapegrace who recently had married the beauteous Fanny Clark, pronounced his new brother-in-law a brave youth of solid and promising parts.[15] O'Fallon's assessment of the youngest of the Clark boys appears to have been on the mark. Billy proved himself more than able to handle the tough going that Scott's men encountered as they made their way through dense patches of briers and brush and across the wooded and hilly countryside. Lightning strikes, torrential downpours, and swollen streams added to the miseries of their 155-mile march. There were other distractions as well. A court martial delayed their progress, and stealthy Indian raiders stole two horses from the advance guard. When the expedition reached the Wabash River, General Scott divided his force, sending a party under Colonel Hardin to a nearby Kickapoo village, while he and the remainder of his company proceeded to Ouiatanon. Scott's little army overtook and burned both towns and destroyed their outlying cornfields and gardens. The Indians lost an estimated thirty warriors, most of them shot from the riverbanks as they attempted to flee in their canoes. Scott seized fifty-eight Indian women and children prisoners as a cautionary notice to other would-be miscreants, though he released seventeen of the most debilitated and sent them away bearing warnings for their tribal leaders.[16]

Following the demolition of their principal targets, Scott ordered a detachment under the command of Colonel James Wilkinson to Kithtippecanuck, an Indian town eighteen miles up the Wabash River at Eel Creek, not far from the junction of the Tippecanoe and Wabash. Clark was a member of Wilkinson's force, which exchanged fire across the river with the Indians for about ten minutes before the tribesmen retreated, as Clark supposed "with considerable loss." The Kentuckians then sacked the abandoned town, a stockaded village with sturdy shingle-roof dwellings, a tavern, and other substantial improvements emblematic of the Indian-European culture that had flourished along the Wabash during much of the eighteenth century. The scene was far different from what Billy Clark had expected. After observing, "those Indians appeared to be Welthy," he made it a point to enumerate the thousand bushels of corn, kettles of bear oil, plows, carts, supplies of salt and sugar, and the cattle and hogs that the Weas and their trading partners had accumulated. Following orders, the militiamen wiped out these fruits of Indian labor and destroyed all of their goods and improvements.[17]

Traveling conditions were no better for Scott's army during its homeward trip. Heavy rains continued to impede its progress. Several horses, worn down with fatigue and stuck in the mud, had to be left behind, and to make matters worse provisions were in short supply. When the expedition attempted to cross the White River, ten horses drowned amidst what Clark termed "Much Confusion." After delivering their Indian prisoners to the regular army at Fort Steuben, the tired and hungry militiamen hastily proceeded to Louisville for a final muster prior to their discharge. Billy Clark had many tales to tell to members of his family, who were always a willing audience. Never one to pass up a party, he may have detoured briefly with his comrades to Colonel John Campbell's home to take advantage of his generous offer to provide the returning fighting men with beef, mutton, and as much grog as they could drink.[18]

Jubilant Kentuckians joined Colonel Campbell in saluting the destruction of the Wabash towns, but any lingering elation was dashed at year's end when the shocking and grisly details of the subsequent annihilation of General Arthur St. Clair's army at Miamitown became known. The campaign launched to avenge Harmar's defeat had turned into yet another rout when forces led by Little Turtle and Blue Jacket ambushed the U.S. expedition. Fleeing in panic, the surviving troops left behind a battleground strewn with the corpses of their fallen comrades. The heavy casualties in what came to be known as St. Clair's Defeat made it one of the worst U.S. military setbacks at the hands of Indians in American history.[19]

Congress, equally unprepared for the stunning news of yet another humiliating loss at the hands of the Miami and their allies, responded by authorizing an increase in the size of the U.S. Army, now to be known as the Legion of the United States. Efforts began immediately to raise the additional troops required to meet the legion's newly authorized strength. William Clark's commission as a lieutenant in the regular infantry, dated March 7, 1792, was among the first to be issued in the wake of congressional attempts to bolster the military.[20]

Within a month of his appointment William Clark was back in Virginia visiting family and friends. Their happy reunion allowed Billy to bring everyone up to date on the latest Kentucky happenings. He discussed land transactions and other business matters with Jonathan and Edmund. There also must have been a great deal of talk about his pending entry into the regular army, accompanied no doubt by some brotherly advice. In nearby Fredericksburg Billy shopped for the articles that every properly attired young officer needed. His purchases there and later in Pittsburgh included such standard fare as stockings, breeches, a jacket, hat and hat cover, knee buckles, a pair of shoes for himself and a set for his horse, gloves, and buttons. He also acquired a whip and spurs, a blanket, a pocket dictionary (which he sorely needed), tooth brush, watch chain, razors, fishhooks and line, gun lock, memo book, tin kettle and cup, powder, five pounds of coffee, and also had his watch repaired. Thus suitably outfitted, the good-looking twenty-one-year-old scion of the Clark family cut a fine figure. By mid-April it was time for him to head west and take up his duties as a soldier in the regular army.[21]

Spring came later than usual in 1792, for on his route to Pittsburgh Clark encountered frost and snow on more than one occasion, and at one point found himself forced to spend the night in a dirty, disagreeable house tavern. The brand new officer reported for duty at Fort Washington in Cincinnati on May 15. Shortly after his arrival, General James Wilkinson, the post commander, sent him on to Kentucky to deliver some dispatches and to initiate a recruiting campaign.[22] His posting at Fort Steuben, located just across the river from Louisville, must have seemed a plum assignment. It was undoubtedly the work of the transplanted Kentuckian Wilkinson, eager to court this well-connected young officer. Wilkinson's ambition matched his audacity. William advised brother Jonathan in September that he had been ordered to recruit his part of the company in Kentucky. He already had enlisted ten men, and he confidently predicted that he would attain his quota in Lexington within a few days. Despite his own success, the pace of the overall recruiting campaign was going too slowly to suit the eager novice, who fretted that it might take another year before the army could marshal sufficient manpower to chastise the Indians properly.[23]

From his Kentucky post Clark reported that the Miami, emboldened by their triumph over St. Clair the previous year, were trying to unify the northern tribes

James Wilkinson, portrait by Charles Willson Peale. As an aspiring junior officer in the U.S. Army, William Clark lent a sympathetic ear to Wilkinson's criticism of Anthony Wayne. Courtesy of the Independence National Historical Park.

for action against the United States, and to the south the Creeks were busy harassing settlements along the Cumberland. Representatives of the northern tribes shunned U.S. orders to assemble at Vincennes, because given their recent successes they felt little pressure to negotiate.[24] Under the circumstances, the best the Americans could do was stall for time to complete a military buildup prior to launching a new offensive under the command of General Anthony Wayne. With great reluctance President Washington had named the rambunctious, headstrong, and hard-drinking general, best known by his nickname "Mad Anthony," to superintend the new Legion of the United States. A compromise choice, Wayne had won the position primarily because the president and his advisers considered him the least of all evils. Persistent rumors that the other principal contender, Brigadier General James Wilkinson, had intrigued with the Spaniards to promote Kentucky's secession made him even less acceptable than the obstreperous Wayne, whose appointment Washington acknowledged to his old friend, Virginia Governor Henry Lee, as an embarrassment. The self-serving Wilkinson lobbied vigorously for the post, and when he did not get it, he promptly launched a campaign to discredit Wayne and force his removal. Wilkinson's rancorous vendetta against Wayne divided the officer corps into contending factions.[25]

Cognizant of the fate of his predecessors in the Northwest Territories, the ordinarily rash General Wayne opted to pursue a more cautious course as he set about to recruit, train, and supply an army of sufficient size before he engaged the enemy. Critical of Wayne's seeming inaction and drawn to Wilkinson's bluster, Lieutenant Clark and many of his fellow officers cast their lot with the wily Kentuckian. Eventually Clark developed serious misgivings about his choice, but for the moment, like so many others young Clark succumbed to Wilkinson's guile and flattery.[26]

While tending to the mundane matters of military life at Fort Steuben, the congenial Clark took advantage of his prerogatives as an officer—albeit a junior one—to enjoy occasional diversionary moments: a game of billiards, a round of drinks with fellow officers, or a social visit with nearby friends and acquaintances. Something so simple as a letter from a faraway relative brought pleasure and helped relieve the monotony. Brother Jonathan wrote from Virginia to enquire how things were going and to invite Billy to serve as a godparent for his newborn niece. He happily accepted.[27]

But duty soon called, and Lieutenant Clark, then assigned to the greenplumed Fourth Sub Legion, was ordered to take charge of convoying a supply of clothing to Fort Knox at Vincennes. The midwinter journey up the Wabash put the young lieutenant to the test as his command struggled to move the bulky cargoes upstream. When the boats became stuck on the rocks, sandbars, and snags that low wintertime water levels left more exposed, his men had to plunge into the frigid waters to dislodge them. Snow and freezing temperatures did not make their tasks any easier. Perhaps Clark learned some valuable navigational techniques from the seasoned voyageurs in charge of a boat belonging to French merchants from Vincennes that had joined the military convoy for protection. Every lesson learned contributed to his developing talents as a waterman. The same held true for his hunting skills. Clark's matter-of-fact reports of going ashore and killing several turkeys, a deer, and a bear suggest he was well on his way to becoming the crack marksman who would soon be given command of an elite rifle company. Once the convoy arrived safely at Fort Knox, the junior officer spent the day meticulously inventorying the goods consigned to his care before concluding that four pairs of shoes were missing. By year's end Lieutenant Clark was ensconced back at Fort Steuben and able to usher in the new year of 1793 at his parents' nearby home with family and friends.[28]

Clark soon was on the move again. The year was barely a week old when he was dispatched to Fort Washington with a supply of provisions. From there he continued northward to Forts Jefferson and Hamilton (both in western Ohio), and appropriately at Fort Hamilton he joined in raising his glass in celebration of General Washington's birthday. His next assignment was to oversee construction at the mouth of the Kentucky River of a blockhouse and garrison for use as a fortified corn storage facility for the army. Despite the swampy conditions, the axmen and artificers under his command immediately began felling trees and constructing the new fortification, and within three weeks Lieutenant Clark reported that the timbered structures were nearly finished and ready to receive and dispense corn shipments. The Ohio River outpost provided a convenient stopping point for passing travelers. Military expeditions routinely paid a call, often bearing the latest news and intelligence. A report of recent army promotions received Clark's full attention, even though he was suffering from a stomach disorder that was to become a recurring problem for him. He was by no means alone in his predicament. Illness was a common occurrence in a frontier soldier's life, and diarrhea was a chronic complaint. Colds, fevers, and more serious maladies also took their toll, and absent a physician, Lieutenant Clark attempted to doctor his ailing troops as best he could. Bleeding and sweating were among the remedies in his medical bag, but caring concern was probably his best medicine.[29]

Clark was solicitous of the welfare of his men, but he also took care to maintain discipline within the ranks. The young officer conducted regular inspections and dispensed punishments—presumably the prescribed number of lashes well laid on—for infractions ranging from filth and neglect of duty to sleeping while on watch. The latter was a particularly serious offense given the recent reports of renewed Indian assaults. Lieutenant Clark worried about the army's poor condition when two companies of "horrid looking invuleads [invalids]" about to be deployed at Forts Steuben and Knox stopped briefly at his post. The arrival of five gallons of whiskey and orders for his reassignment in early June may have lifted his spirits momentarily. Clark was soon to be on the road again.[30]

He headed down the Ohio with a consignment of corn and merchandise destined for the Chickasaws as part of an effort by the United States to lessen Spanish influence among the southern tribes. After reaching the Mississippi he found an expectant Chickasaw party awaiting his arrival, and they escorted his expedition overland to their villages, where the goods were distributed. It was then back northward to Louisville and from there to the Ohio posts where the army had begun constructing winter quarters after it became evident that General Wayne's planned offensive would have to be postponed until the following year. At Fort Washington Clark found smallpox raging through the camp in late November. No doubt he was relieved when he received orders to return to Fort Steuben with a shipment of clothing for the troops stationed there. When spring arrived, he saw to it that he was inoculated against smallpox.[31]

Following a brief respite in Louisville and its environs, Lieutenant Clark once again had to forgo the relative comfort of his officer's quarters at Fort Steuben. In early December he departed for Vincennes to begin a tedious and laborious five-month command. The journey was even more difficult than the one he had made the previous winter. After escorting a party of Chickasaws as far as the mouth of the Wabash, he dispatched them homeward with a twenty-day supply of provisions. Having depleted their stores to accommodate the departing Indians, Clark's men found themselves largely dependent on their rifles for subsistence. Such disagreeable circumstances were worse for privates than for their officers, who received larger rations and better accommodations even in the wilderness. Desertion was a common problem, and when two of his men fled, Clark made an unsuccessful effort to locate them before proceeding on. In relating the story of this unhappy journey to his brother Jonathan, William later complained, "I like to have starved." He arrived in Vincennes tired, cold, and hungry. The residents welcomed the familiar face of the bedraggled young officer and saw to it that he was included on the guest list for a ball hosted by the townspeople on the following day. The congenial French Creoles knew how to enjoy themselves, but even their succession of balls and entertainments proved insufficient to alleviate Clark's mounting boredom and fatigue.[32]

When representatives of the Potawatomi and Kickapoo nations, summoned to Vincennes for discussions with U.S. officials, began arriving in mid-February of 1794, they were not in a particularly receptive mood. At their initial meeting the disgruntled tribal leaders produced a red wampum belt that had accompanied a Spanish invitation to form an alliance against the Americans. Since they had declined the offer, the Indians expected the U.S. government to compensate them handsomely. The presents were not immediately forthcoming, but the Americans had laid in an ample supply of liquor to grease the wheels of diplomacy. The generous libations left the Indian delegates too inebriated to continue the talks the following day. When the discussions did resume, even the free-flowing alcohol failed to produce results satisfactory to either side. Neither did the much-anticipated distribution of gifts do the trick. Lieutenant Clark reported that the drunken tribesmen had threatened him, but he ignored their disrespectful conduct and went off to join local townspeople for a game of cards. The discontented tribesmen finally departed, and shortly thereafter Clark happily bid adieu to Vincennes and headed back to Louisville for a visit with his parents.[33]

The weary young officer was pleased to find them in good health. A prime topic of conversation undoubtedly was brother George's recent involvement in a French scheme to outfit a filibustering expedition against the Spanish posts along the Mississippi. The unhappy combination of George's failing finances, the U.S.

government's refusal to compensate him for the debts he had incurred from his participation in the Revolutionary War, and his fondness for the bottle made the once renowned hero of the West susceptible to the overtures of a foreign power. The Revolutionary French Republic's declaration of war on both Great Britain and Spain in 1793 had given rise to expectations in America's western territories that a decisive French victory might end Spanish and British meddling there.

To the dismay of President Washington and his Federalist supporters, France's minister to the United States, Edmond Genet, had embarked upon a campaign to increase U.S. support for his revolutionary government and to launch expeditions from U.S. soil against Spanish outposts along the Gulf Coast and the Mississippi River. George Rogers Clark had accepted a commission from Genet designating him major general in the French army and commander-in-chief of the French Revolutionary Legions on the Mississippi. Defying the provisions of the president's 1793 Neutrality Proclamation, Clark placed an advertisement in the *Kentucky Gazette* seeking recruits, to whom he promised land grants and a share of any lawful plunder they seized. Spain's refusal to open the Mississippi to American traders and its attempts to woo western tribes had angered many Kentuckians, some of whom expressed interest in his proposition. The scheme collapsed when the French failed to deliver their promised financial assistance and the federal government threatened action against U.S. citizens who lent their support. George Rogers Clark hastily disassociated himself from the quixotic venture. After conferring with the family, William simply reported that "the expedition that was going against Louisiana I believe is given out," but in his brother's defense he observed that the Spanish threat to the United States had not diminished given the recent reinforcement of their Mississippi River garrison at New Madrid.[34]

Following his brief detour to Mulberry Hill in late March of 1794, Lieutenant William Clark returned to duty at the Ohio bases, where preparations for General Wayne's forthcoming campaign were well under way. Clark's recurring intestinal complaint seems to have struck him again, but he reported that he took "some medison it work me verry well."[35] At Fort Washington the commanding officer placed Clark in command of sixty infantrymen and twenty dragoons assigned to escort a supply train carrying clothing and provisions to General Wayne's headquarters at Fort Greenville. Having already endured unpleasant details at the mouth of the Kentucky River and at Vincennes in little more than the space of a year, these latest orders prompted the somewhat disgruntled junior officer to complain to his brother that it appeared that "all action & laborious commands fall to me."[36]

The sizable convoy, which included no fewer than seven hundred packhorses, was a tempting target for Indians unsettled by the growing military buildup in the region. It had scarcely advanced eighteen miles from Fort Washington when a war party of about sixty Indians began firing upon the advance guard that Lieutenant Clark had deployed. The dragoons charged to support the advance unit and the engagement continued for about fifteen minutes, until Clark and the remainder of the infantry at the rear of the convoy came to their rescue. By Clark's telling, their arrival sent the Indians into hasty retreat, causing them to leave behind one dead warrior, seven rifles, forty blankets, and a quantity of provisions. Lieutenant Clark suspected that the Indians had suffered far greater casualties because in his words "they bled plentifully in several places." His losses numbered eight men killed, two wounded, and a few horses destroyed by the fleeing Indians. Having turned back the enemy raiders and buried its dead, the convoy proceeded on to Fort Greenville under Clark's command.

To his chagrin, Lieutenant Clark received little credit for his "officer like conduct" in successfully dispatching the attacking Indians and seeing the supply train through to its destination. The accolades for valor and bravery went instead to a subordinate officer attached to the caravan, who in Clark's judgment foolishly led an impulsive initial charge only to be forced to retreat. Thoroughly disgusted by his treatment and feeling slighted by General Wayne, Clark declined an offer to become adjutant and quartermaster for the Fourth Sub Legion and announced his intent to resign unless his application to command a corps of riflemen was honored.[37]

The continuing discord within the officer corps, fueled by Wilkinson's ongoing efforts to undermine General Wayne's authority, undoubtedly added to Clark's growing disaffection with army life. Wilkinson frequently shared with Clark disparaging remarks about their obstinate commander's conduct, and the young lieutenant proved to be a sympathetic listener. General Wayne ignored the carping and second-guessing about his strategies and pressed ahead with his methodical offensive. By midsummer all was in readiness, and in late July he finally ordered the force of thirty-five hundred regulars and militia at his disposal to advance northward to engage the enemy. The stage was set for the Battle of Fallen Timbers, the first important engagement in William Clark's military career.[38]

Along the line of march to the Miami villages on the Maumee River in northwest Ohio, the going was tough, as the troops marched through thick woods, brush, and waist-high patches of nettles, built a bridge to cross the river, and erected a fortified encampment that Clark called a "trifling garrison." All of this caused considerable grumbling among the ranks, including more than a little from the junior officer from Kentucky who faulted his commander for failing to adopt "Some grand stroke of Enterprise" that offered a means for ending the war and compelling the Indians to make peace. General Wayne remained steadfast in his plan and rejected all such proposals—most of which emanated from Clark's friend Wilkinson. When a falling tree came within inches of crushing to death "His Excellency" (Clark's favorite term for his commander), the lieutenant wrote in his journal that the incident "had nearly deprived Certain individuals of theire A.W. & Particular persons of their concequence."[39]

The Indians had taken cover in an area of broken and uprooted trees recently felled by tornadic winds, thus accounting for the battle's name. As General Wayne's army approached, the warriors began their customary practice of fasting to prepare themselves for the combat that they assumed was imminent. After two days of waiting for the expected assault, many of the Indian fighters left their ambush to go in search of food. General Wayne chose that moment to attack, and his troops overwhelmed the dispersed and hungry band of about nine hundred Indians and their Canadian allies.[40] During the heated engagement, which lasted little more than an hour, Lieutenant Clark led a column of sharpshooting riflemen against the retreating Indians and Canadians. True to form, Wayne's victorious soldiers fell upon and burned numerous Indians towns in that region, and cut down and destroyed hundreds of acres of corn and more than a few haystacks. They also erected an impressive new fortress, aptly named Fort Defiance, as a direct challenge to Britain's continuing presence in the Northwest Territory. The thrill of victory even caused William Clark to have second thoughts about his future plans. After advising his brother about the army's recent triumph, he confided to him, "I want much to quit service but cant whilst an army crowned with succkess."[41]

Wayne's triumph at Fallen Timbers momentarily silenced his critics (Clark among them), and it proved a major blow to Indian efforts to retain control over the territories north of the Ohio. The northern tribes' British friends had turned their backs on them. The commander at Fort Miami had declined to come to their aid and even refused to allow their besieged warriors to take refuge within the walls of his garrison. News that British negotiators in London had agreed to withdraw their troops from their forts south of the Great Lakes under the terms of the recently concluded Jay Treaty further undercut the Indians' bargaining position. Abandoned by their British allies and facing the prospect of starvation, the once defiant Shawnee, Delaware, Miami, Wea, and Piankashaw nations had few remaining options.

In 1795 more than a thousand Indians representing more than a dozen tribes assembled in the shadow of Fort Greenville, where General Wayne in full dress uniform opened the proceedings with appropriate pomp and ceremony before laying down his terms. In the negotiations that followed the Indian leaders

Anthony Wayne. William Clark served under Wayne's command and participated in the general's celebrated victory at the Battle of Fallen Timbers. Courtesy of the Library of Congress.

eventually acceded to the new realities and affixed their marks to the Treaty of Greenville, which opened present-day Ohio to American settlement and for all practical purposes ended hostilities in the Northwest. William Clark witnessed the signing ceremonies for the historic agreement that concluded the campaign his brother George had launched more than a decade earlier. He also filed away for future reference mental notes on the protocols of Indian diplomacy.[42]

With the gradual cessation of fighting in the Indian Country, the rush of victory gave way to the monotony of regular military routines for William Clark and his army companions. Reenlistments were declining and desertions were on the rise because "the service has become so sevear in escorting provisions from the Ohio to the out garrisons that the men cant undergo the fatigue & live on the present allowances of provisions." Clark, who had long since begun to tire of the military regimen, once again contemplated resigning from the service in favor of "some more honourable imployment for my youthful days." He understood that his prospects for advancement were bleak in an army declining in size and dominated by an aging officer corps whose members seldom resigned. He asked his brother Jonathan for assistance in locating a new position, and confided to brother Edmund that he believed the possibilities for opening an extensive and successful trade on the Mississippi River were especially promising at this particular moment.[43] Notwithstanding his determination to seek his fortunes in some civil capacity, true to his nature William elected not to act precipitously.

As he continued to weigh his options, there was sad news from home. His sister Elizabeth had died at the age of twenty-six following complications from childbirth. The entire family took the news very hard. Billy's parents, who were showing the signs of their age, reported that they were attempting to "bear our loss with fortitude [with the] hope that it will be not long before we get recinciled." George and younger sister Fanny were now living at Mulberry Hill. Both had their share of problems. George's health and his fortunes continued to decline. Fanny, a raven-haired beauty, had suffered a nervous breakdown following a 1793 confrontation that prompted the family to banish her feckless husband, James O'Fallon, who obligingly died not long thereafter. She had returned to her parents' home with her two infant sons John and Benjamin, where the comforts of home and loving family support soon restored her to health and allowed her to marry once more.[44]

The steadfast and protective Billy secured a leave in the spring of 1795 to return home and check on his family. His homecoming seems to have given all a lift in spirits, but no one was more rejuvenated than Billy himself. In his case, the magic tonic turned out to be the attentions of an unnamed young lady. The infatuated suitor found himself torn between the wiles of love and the call of duty. In fact, his clumsy attempts at courting had made the usually punctual young officer late in returning to his post. Fortunately for him, General Wayne proved understanding. The lovesick young Clark reported to Fanny, his confidant when it came to matters of the heart, Wayne "is a reasonable as well as a Galant man, and had Some *Idea* of my *Persute*, he treated my inatention as all other good fathers would on the Same acasion."[45]

In subsequent letters to his dear sister, he continued to press for details about the latest social gatherings in Louisville and news about the young ladies of his neighborhood and, no doubt, one young woman in particular. Nothing came of that brief courtship, and the young lieutenant was left to follow the counsel that he had urged upon a fellow officer equally unlucky in love. Clark had admonished him to "meet his fate like a valuent Soldur, who after a long and Serious *Siege* is repulsed and falls a Victim to his *Foe.*"[46]

The episode had left Lieutenant Clark with a more positive view of General Wayne and even made camp life seem more bearable. Momentarily rejuvenated, he reveled in the sights of soldiers arrayed in splendid dress marching on parade to the accompaniment of drums, fifes, bugles, and trumpets. He found amusement in the roaring of the cannon and the yells of the guards on their maneuvers. The antics of inebriated Indians likewise contributed to the mirth.[47] Geopolitical realities soon intruded on these momentary diversions. Renewed reports of Spanish military activity along the Mississippi River and possible incursions at Chickasaw Bluffs (present-day Memphis) alarmed officials in the Washington administration. These alleged actions by the Spanish government threatened to further destabilize the region and undermine U.S. efforts to open the Mississippi to American commerce.

On September 10, 1795, General Wayne dispatched Lieutenant William Clark along with a sergeant, corporal, and fifteen privates under a flag of truce to deliver to Manuel Gayoso de Lemos, the governor of Natchez, a strongly worded message demanding an end to Spanish intrusions on American soil. Clark's reconnaissance expedition was also intended to provide U.S. authorities with an up-to-date assessment of current conditions along the Mississippi. The decision to assign William Clark to undertake this vital mission was a shrewd one that demonstrated General Wayne's confidence in the young soldier's abilities. Not only was he familiar with the route of travel, but also his selection as the American messenger must have been unsettling to Louisiana's Spanish officials, who were well aware that his brother George had long been a proponent of military action against their exposed Mississippi River installations.[48]

Clark traveled as far as New Madrid, where he conferred with Gayoso aboard *La Vigilante*, the flagship of the tiny fleet the Spaniards had deployed to patrol the Mississippi. Prior to his meeting with Gayoso, river travelers had confirmed the Spanish presence on U.S. soil and had provided detailed descriptions of their recently completed military installation at the Chickasaw Bluffs, known as Fort San Fernando. Clark delivered General Wayne's message and also pressed the Spanish official for an explanation of their recent incursions into U.S. territory. When his justifications failed to persuade the young American, Gayoso simply shrugged and declared that it was a ministerial decision. Notwithstanding their obvious differences of opinion, Clark made it a point to note that the governor and his officers had treated him with every politeness during his stay at New Madrid. Having completed his business there, Lieutenant Clark headed back to Fort Greenville to deliver his report.[49]

On November 4 he presented his findings to General Wayne and no doubt showed him the pen-and-ink sketches he had drawn of Fort San Fernando and *La Vigilante*. While the Spanish forces may not have constituted an imminent threat, their intrusions across the Mississippi were clear violations of U.S. territorial rights. Wayne forwarded Clark's report along with his own to the War Department. When it reached Philadelphia in December, Clark's report elicited favorable comment from federal officials, but any concerns about his findings quickly evaporated following receipt of word from Madrid that Thomas Pinckney had reached an accord with the Spaniards. The Treaty of San Lorenzo, commonly referred to as Pinckney's Treaty, was quite favorable to the United States. It guaranteed U.S. citizens access to the Mississippi and the right of deposit at New Orleans. Spanish officials had concluded that the plan for transforming Louisiana's vast expanses into a protective barrier was not feasible and would be too costly. Manuel de Godoy, Spain's savvy foreign minister, had warned, "You cannot lock up an open field." He might well have added, especially with the Americans breathing down your necks. Within little more than a year the Spaniards abandoned Fort San Fernando and burned it to the ground.[50]

Shortly before Lieutenant Clark set out on his inspection tour along the Mississippi, Ensign Meriwether Lewis had reported for duty at General Wayne's headquarters. Lewis, who was four years younger than Clark, had been born in Albemarle County, Virginia, not far from where Clark's parents had once resided. The Clarks knew the Meriwethers, Lewis's maternal relatives whose name he bore. Prior to receiving a commission in the regular army, Lewis had served briefly with the Virginia militia during the Whiskey Rebellion. Two weeks after Clark's departure from Fort Greenville, Ensign Lewis became inebriated—hardly a novel occurrence in the military—but his provocative and insulting words and gestures aimed at a fellow officer, Lieutenant Elliott, followed by the issuance of a challenge to fight a duel, prompted Elliott to prefer charges against him. Lewis stood accused of violating the first and second articles of the seventh section of the Rules and Articles of War and also of conduct unbecoming an officer and a gentleman. Charges against privates were one matter, but against an officer were quite another. When Clark returned to Fort Greenville in early November, Ensign Lewis's imminent court martial must have been the talk of the officers' quarters. On November 6, Major Shaylor convened the court-martial against the young officer. The court waited six days before issuing its findings, but to the relief of Clark and many others, its verdict exonerated Lewis of all charges. General Wayne upheld the court's findings and pronounced that he fondly hoped this would be the last instance of a trial of this nature in the legion.[51]

Lewis's total vindication allowed him to continue his military career. Immediately following the verdict General Wayne reassigned Lewis to the elite rifle company commanded by his fellow Virginian Clark. The duration of their initial service together was brief, for as Clark later informed Nicholas Biddle, "Capt. Lewis was appointed an Ensign and arranged to the Company which I commanded a fiew months before I resigned." In a move that he had long contemplated, William Clark resigned his commission on July 1, 1796, following his return from the extended leave he had been granted the previous November to attend to some business in Kentucky and to visit his brothers in Virginia.[52]

Many factors influenced his decision to leave the service: poor health, a desire to improve his financial prospects, a yearning to try his hand in the world of commerce, and a sense of obligation to his aging parents and his brother George, who increasingly stood in need of his assistance. Most of all, Clark's prospects for advancement in the army seemed unpromising. Though to his way of thinking he had performed his duties ably and always acquitted himself honorably, his superiors had failed to accord him the recognition he coveted and expected. Such disappointments rankled, even though the always circumspect Clark confided his thoughts only to close family members.

Even before Billy resigned, George had offered him twelve thousand acres of his Tennessee lands in return for help with his tangled financial affairs. George gently nudged his younger brother when he wrote, ". . . if you intend to leave the Army the sooner you can do it with propriety the better as you have served long enough to qualify yourself for any further military Imploy which is all you could wish for or at least all the advantage you could expect in the present state of affairs." Even as he exited the army, the feud between Generals Wayne and Wilkinson raged white-hot; it would not be resolved until Wayne's sudden and unexpected death the next year left Wilkinson standing alone. But that was no longer Billy Clark's concern as he turned his attention to family matters. His first assignment was to get a still for his father, and after that he faced the daunting prospect of putting George's finances in order. Perhaps he expected that a few shots of his father's very own version of Kentucky whiskey flowing from the new family still would fortify him for the challenges he faced at home.[53]

When Billy arrived at Mulberry Hill he found his parents well, but the same could not be said for poor George, who had badly sprained his ankle and was left to hobble around with the assistance of a stick. Sometime previously the ailing older brother and his younger sibling had come to an understanding authorizing William to dispose of any or all of George's property, settle his debts to the extent that he could, and otherwise attend to his business affairs. Jonathan had attempted to assist George from afar, but aside from lobbying politicians in Richmond and Philadelphia to grant his brother relief, there was little that he could do for him in Virginia. William's first task was to deal with the creditors who relentlessly hounded George on the streets and in court. He first headed to Lexington, Kentucky, where he unsuccessfully attempted to settle suits that the Federalist curmudgeon Humphrey Marshall and the heirs of William Shannon had filed against George.[54]

Rebuffed in his initial efforts to sort out the complex problems that threatened George with financial ruin, William Clark returned to Mulberry Hill to recuperate from what he referred to as his lengthy indisposition. He surveyed some of the lands claimed by George and set about "doing what parts of his business I could which I found in a very unfinished situation." Among other things George transferred ownership of his landholdings to William and to his father John in an effort to shield them from the claims of his creditors.[55] In rushing to the aid of his brother, William assumed obligations for legal fees, taxes, and other related expenses that jeopardized his own financial standing, subjected him to endless suits and litigation, and threatened to leave him impoverished. In the long run, George's properties, along with some he inherited from other family members, helped make William Clark a wealthy man. By the time of his death William Clark was able to bequeath princely sums to his heirs, but those gains were long deferred. Throughout most of his career he had to rely on his soldier's pay and/or civil servant's salary to sustain the standard of living to which his family had become accustomed. That was no easy task.

In 1797 William Clark's immediate prospects seemed bleak, but he refused to shirk his duty to his family, and most particularly to his poor dear brother George. In August he set off for Vincennes to respond to a suit filed by Laurent Bazadone that threatened George's Indiana landholdings. After conferring there with local authorities about the case, William Clark traveled on to the

Illinois Country in search of documents that might help buttress his brother's defense. He took advantage of his trip to Kaskaskia to reconnoiter the nearby settlements in Spanish Illinois. On September 6 he visited the village of Ste. Genevieve, the oldest settlement in present-day Missouri, as a guest of the local commandant François Vallé II, one of the wealthiest men in Spanish Louisiana. Given Clark's interest in entering the world of Mississippi River commerce, the powerful Creole entrepreneur was a most promising acquaintance.[56]

From Ste. Genevieve Clark proceeded upriver to St. Louis, where for the first time he glimpsed the city that he would call home during the final thirty years of his life. Upper Louisiana's thriving capital, with its commanding view of the Mississippi, had in the three decades since its founding become an important fur trading entrepôt. Moses Austin, another American who visited the city in 1797, described it as "better built than any Town on the Missisipi . . . [with] a Number of wealthey Merchts. and an Extensive Trade."[57] The most cosmopolitan and prosperous of Upper Louisiana's settlements, St. Louis boasted a racially and ethnically diverse population of one thousand inhabitants and more than two hundred houses, which as Clark noted were all built in the French style. The grandest dwelling in town, Auguste Chouteau's two-story stone mansion with its surrounding galleries and its well-appointed interior, might even have reminded Clark a little of the great houses of Virginia that he had known in his youth. Like his fellow American Austin, Clark's initial impression of the city was quite favorable. He toured the town and "found it to be in a thrieving state." The former soldier took note of its fortifications, including a small fort and five stone guard towers, and also reported seeing some Indian mounds located about half a mile above the town.[58]

The city's most distinguished citizens, including Lieutenant Governor Zenon Trudeau, a New Orleans–born French Creole in Spanish service, Auguste and Pierre Chouteau, prominent fur merchants and members of St. Louis's founding family, and their bilingual brother-in-law trader Charles Gratiot, a friend to Americans and to George Rogers Clark, welcomed the young Kentuckian with the same gracious hospitality that by then he had come to consider a mark of French character. After supping with the lieutenant governor, Clark attended a ball at the residence of Pierre Chouteau where he saw "all the fine girls and buckish Gentlemen," and once again experienced the French joie de vivre, with the amiable Gratiot serving as his interpreter and host. One must surmise that the conversation that evening was animated, the company enjoyable, and the libations plentiful, for Clark did not retire to the Gratiot home until the wee hours of the morning.[59]

After his sojourn in St. Louis, Clark returned to the American side of the river, only to discover that sickness and fever were rampant there. At Kaskaskia he secured the papers that he had gone in search of, but unfortunately he too succumbed to the illness that gripped the countryside. In his case, it left him stricken with several large boils on his legs and thighs. Clark's rundown physical condition made him susceptible to this infectious malady. On September 18 he recorded in his journal, "No sleap last night for me. I have a violent hed ake [headache] to day." Confined to his quarters, he found time to write a letter to Kentucky. Once he had healed sufficiently to permit him to mount a horse, he returned to Vincennes, where, in spite of his weakened condition, he succeeded in having Bazadone's twenty-four-thousand-dollar suit against George dismissed. William Clark attributed the successful outcome to proper attention, hard pleading, and some expense on his part. He had, he informed his brother Edmund, ridden two thousand miles in behalf of George's interests during the course of 1797. William returned to Mulberry Hill on October 9 bearing the good news that he had secured George's property on the other side of the Ohio, but once home he found his mother and brother suffering from the fever that was making its rounds that fall. For his part William continued to experience its lingering effects until mid-December.[60]

During his convalescence William turned his thoughts to a commercial enterprise that he hoped might improve his own lagging fortunes and enable him to launch a new career as a merchant. On March 9, 1798, he set out from the rapids of the Ohio with a shipment of tobacco destined for New Orleans, accompanied in all likelihood by his trusted servant York.[61] When he reached the Mississippi, Clark joined four other boats headed downriver. During the often tempestuous voyage, strong winds and storms repeatedly battered their boats and forced them to hug the shore. One particularly violent blow impaled Clark's vessel on a snag and terrified the crew. The sinking of another boat in the convoy left its owner with only the few bales and kegs the crewmen had dragged from the river. Things slowly improved. At Yazoo Clark was pleased to find U.S. forces occupying a post that the Spaniards had recently abandoned, and along the lower Mississippi the "butifule" sugar plantations caught his eye.[62]

Following his arrival in New Orleans, Clark supervised the unloading of his boat and rented a warehouse to store his tobacco. The city's streets were abuzz with talk about the likelihood of war between the United States and France. Reports of angry Americans chanting "millions for defense but not one cent for tribute," in response to France's recent attempt to exact a bribe from the United States in what had come to be known as the XYZ Affair, had fueled speculation in the port city that the Adams administration might soon go to war against France and its ally Spain. The rumors of war did not prevent Clark from going about his business. He sold his tobacco and made a brief trip back

Auguste Chouteau Mansion, by J. C. Wild. William Clark frequently attended business and social gatherings at this elegant St. Louis residence. Courtesy of the State Historical Society of Missouri.

upriver to Natchez, where he delivered some horses to the U.S. Army post there. He returned to New Orleans and set sail immediately for Philadelphia on board the *Star,* a ship fortified with six guns, to check on mercantile opportunities in the eastern markets.[63]

The ocean voyage was far from routine. An encounter with a French privateer that previously had seized two U.S. ships as prizes and a subsequent run-in with Spanish authorities over their attempts to shield the French vessel kept the Americans at bay until Governor General Manuel Gayoso de Lemos finally cleared them to proceed. Stormy seas, illness on board, and a diet of little more than fish added to the trip's unpleasantness. An outbreak of yellow fever in Philadelphia forced the *Star* to alter its course yet again and dock at New Castle, Delaware. Clark proceeded from there to Jonathan's home in Virginia by way of Baltimore. After the long and arduous voyage, Clark welcomed the diversions of Baltimore, where he took care of some business, attended church, witnessed a raucous congressional election, took in a play, and visited with his Kentucky friend Father Benoit Joseph Flaget. The friendship between the Catholic priest and the Episcopalian Clark endured, and sixteen years later in St. Louis he called upon the then Bishop Flaget to baptize his three oldest children.[64]

On his way to Virginia Clark passed through the new Federal City of Washington that was soon to replace Philadelphia as the national capital. Clark reported that the city, then under construction, was much scattered. The stonework on one wing of the Capitol building was nearly finished, as was the President's House. Shortly afterward he settled in at Jonathan's Spotsylvania County home for nearly a month in the company of family and friends. He returned to Kentucky via the Ohio River, arriving back home on December 24 in time to mourn the passing of his mother, who died that very day.[65] Ann Clark was sixty-four years old. Her death was especially hard on her husband of nearly fifty years, who was in poor health and sensed that his days also were numbered. He said so when he wrote to advise his son Edmund that "your dear mother has left us, I my self expect will shortly follow her I trust to a place of happiness where care and trouble will be no more."[66]

John Clark's final words to Edmund proved prophetic, for he died at Mulberry Hill on July 29, 1799, of complications from a violent pleurisy that had settled on his lungs. He was interred beside his beloved wife in the nearby family burial plot in the presence of all of the Clark children who lived in Kentucky.[67] The house at Mulberry Hill must have seemed a very lonely place to William once both of his parents were gone. He remained there with only the company of George and the slaves he had inherited. Tragically, George continued to sink deeper into the throes of alcoholism. Only a short time before his father's death William had confided cryptically to Jonathan that "Brother George has given up more so [to] that vice which has been so infamous to him."[68]

John Clark left his entire estate to William, save for a modest bequest of slaves and property that went to his grandsons John and Benjamin O'Fallon, whose ne'er-do-well father had left them penniless. Any property that might have gone to George would immediately have been claimed by his creditors; Jonathan and Edmund were well settled in Virginia, and daughters Ann, Lucy, and Fanny were all married and comfortably fixed. Under the provisions of John Clark's will, William inherited the house and lands at Mulberry Hill; the horses, cattle, sheep, and hogs; the still, plantation utensils, and household and kitchen furniture; any collectible debts, except for what son-in-law Charles Thruston owed him; eight slaves, including York, who later accompanied his master on his western expedition; and the Illinois lands that George had deeded to his father. In his will John Clark appointed his son William, sons-in-law Richard Anderson, William Croghan, and Charles Thruston, and friend Benjamin Sebastian to be the executors for his estate.[69]

William oversaw the estate's final settlement and continued to look after other business matters for family members, such as tending to the removal of a squatter on lands claimed by brother Jonathan or responding to the suit that Laurent Bazadone had managed to resurrect against George. With his father's passing he now had to take a more active role in the management of the daily activities at Mulberry Hill, but he relied heavily on the family's trusty slaves to look after the crops, tend the livestock, operate the mill, and take care of maintenance needs and routine chores. A farmer's life never seemed William Clark's preferred calling. During his solitary moments in the quiet old house he occasionally picked up a book. One title on his shelf was *A History of India*, which neighbor John Thruston recently had returned with his thanks for its loan. By year's end the family was faced with more sadness. Charles Thruston, younger sister Fanny's second husband, was killed by one of his slaves two weeks before Christmas. As Jonathan Clark's friend Abraham Hite aptly observed, "Poor Fanny is an unfortunate girl."[70] Following Thruston's death, Uncle William also took an increased role in looking after his beloved younger sister's sons by her first marriage, John and Benjamin O'Fallon. Their bachelor uncles George and William treated them as if they were their own children.

By May of 1801 the boredom of his quiet life prompted the peripatetic Clark to set out once again in search of new and different opportunities that just might yield the elusive fortune which always seemed just beyond his grasp. He traveled a total of 1,820 miles before returning to Kentucky in mid-August. Between two visits with Jonathan in Virginia, he sandwiched in a trip that included stops in Philadelphia, New Castle, Baltimore, and Washington, D.C. While in the Federal City in June, he called on his army friend Meriwether Lewis, who was then occupying rather Spartan quarters in the as yet unfinished East Room in the President's House, where not long before Abigail Adams had hung out her laundry to dry. Lewis had accepted Thomas Jefferson's invitation to serve as his private secretary and general aide and had taken up residence with the widowed president in the executive mansion shortly after he had been sworn into office.

Lewis and Clark probably reminisced about their time together at Fort Greenville, and maybe the two bachelors discussed their failed efforts to woo the ladies. Lewis did ask his friend Clark to attend to some land business in the backcountry for him.[71] The visit also afforded Clark an opportunity to meet America's recently inaugurated third president. Jefferson undoubtedly inquired about Clark's brother George as well as other family members he knew. The president would not forget their visit and neither would Clark, who headed back to Jonathan's Virginia plantation where the eldest Clark son's decision to join his siblings and their families in Kentucky must have been a prime topic of conversation. William undoubtedly echoed George's reassurances to well-fixed Jonathan that he need not fear serious repercussions from Kentucky's 1799 protests against the Alien and Sedition Acts.[72] Kentucky was republican but no hotbed of radicalism. Before his departure for home, William also volunteered to assist his brother in any way he could.

While en route back to Louisville, William stopped briefly in Cincinnati to confer with Judge John Cleves Symmes, who was hearing Bazadone's on-going case against George. Once he reached Mulberry Hill the news that awaited him was not good. His mill had gone up in flames that also destroyed his tools, mill saws, and millstones along with several hundred bushels of grain and a quantity of leather. He was at a loss to explain the fire's cause. It was a severe blow for the financially hard-pressed Clark, eased only slightly by news that the current year's wheat and corn crops were doing reasonably well. The prospects for the fruit harvest seemed less promising. Despondent over his recent losses, he lamented to his brother, "I am fearfull nature has intended me for the Sport of fortune, and appeerencus appear to justify aprehentions—I never went from home any time, but before I returned was informed of Some loss or misfortune."[73] Even so, William Clark was not one to allow adversity to get the better of him. Family members and friends looked to him for assistance and for support in times of need. His willing hand and steady presence were a source of strength and comfort to all who knew him, but dependable as he was, he was not impervious to moments of self-pity.

In the New Year, William's time for feeling sorry for himself had ended, and the reliable youngest brother returned eastward to take charge of escorting Jonathan's slaves and household goods from Virginia to Kentucky in prepara-tion for his brother's much anticipated move. Traveling in winter was not easy, and it cost more. William advised his brother that he had been forced "to feed high & give Whiskey frequently" to sustain his party against unseasonably cold temperatures. It was slight compensation for the hapless African Amer-ican slaves who bore the brunt of transporting Jonathan's possessions across the muddy and snow-covered roads. They completed their journey without serious incident, save for a minor domestic dispute involving three of the slaves. But after reaching their destination there was little time for rest and recuperation. In late February they began work on the construction of a new house for Jonathan and his family. The new residence was only one of a num-ber of improvements in the neighborhood, where plans were well under way for the establishment of a new school. Louisville was thriving, but William suggested to his brother that any additional furniture he might need for his new residence would be less expensive in Pittsburgh. The work at Jonathan's new plantation went well, for only a month later William was sufficiently con-fident to predict that by the time Jonathan arrived in June, "I flateer my Self I

Shall have a house for you a garden &c."⁷⁴ Billy Clark had repaid his older brother's efforts in facilitating their parents' move to Kentucky nearly two decades earlier.

Jonathan Clark and his family reached the Falls of the Ohio on July 6 and eight days later settled into their new quarters at Trough Spring just east of Mulberry Hill. Brother Edmund joined the family the same year, and with his arrival in Kentucky all of the surviving Clark siblings were in residence in the vicinity of Louisville. While William celebrated having all of his brothers and sisters nearby, yet another judgment against George, whose finances had become inextricably linked with his own, threatened them both with financial ruin. This latest crisis forced William to take drastic measures to stave off bankruptcy. He sold the farm he had inherited from his parents along with a lot that he owned in Louisville, and he and George moved across the river to the Point of Rocks on the opposite side of the Ohio, where they occupied a simple cabin that was a considerable step down from their residence at Mulberry Hill. According to William's calculations, between 1796 and 1803 his expenditures in George's behalf totaled $6,205.95. In 1803 alone, his cash outlays for his debt-ridden brother had amounted to $3,656.25, not a paltry sum for someone who was for the moment unemployed. Little wonder that he had been forced to put his farm up for sale.⁷⁵ William Clark's prospects had never seemed gloomier. The success he so coveted had thus far somehow eluded him. His efforts at soldiering, farming, and business had produced only modest gains, but unknown to him, destiny was about to call. Past disappointments would soon become only a distant memory as Clark heeded Meriwether Lewis's call to assist with a project of epic proportions—a task for which his Kentucky apprenticeship had prepared him better perhaps than even his friend Lewis and the president had dared to imagine.

Three

A Most Welcome Invitation

THE LETTER BEGAN LIKE so many other communications that had come to William Clark: "Herewith inclosed you will receive the papers belonging to your brother Genl. Clark, which sometime since you requested me to procure and forward to you; pray excuse the delay which has taken place . . ." But when his eyes moved ahead to the second paragraph, the younger Clark soon sensed that his old friend Meriwether Lewis had more on his mind than brother George's business affairs. "From the long and uninterrupted friendship and confidence which has subsisted between us," Lewis continued, "I feel no hesitation in making to you the following communication under the fulest impression that it will be held by you inviolably secret until I see you, or you shall hear again from me." As Clark read on, the true purpose of this confidential message became clearer. Thomas Jefferson had selected Lewis to lead a small military expedition to the Pacific, and he was inviting Clark to join the enterprise and participate with him in "it's fatiegues, it's dangers and it's honors" because, as he put it, "there is no man on earth with whom I should feel equal pleasure in sharing them as with yourself."[1]

The expedition's primary objective was to ascend the Missouri River to its source and if practicable to proceed from there to the Western Ocean via the Columbia or Oregon rivers. Jefferson anticipated that their discoveries would at long last reveal the much-vaunted Northwest Passage. Along the way the voyagers would be expected to gather information about the geography of the country through which they passed, identify the names and locations of the various Indian nations they encountered, describe their manners and customs, languages, occupations, and articles of trade, and record useful information about plants, animals, and minerals. "In short," as Lewis put it, Jefferson intended for them "to collect the best possible information relative to whatever the country may afford as a tribute to general science."[2]

As for Clark's role, the president had authorized Lewis to offer him a captain's commission with appropriate pay and emoluments along with such portion of land as was granted to officers of similar rank for their Revolutionary services. The commission would, if Clark wished, be permanent, and Lewis assured him that for this mission, his situation would "in all respects be precisely such as my own." Should Clark not choose to attach himself to the exploring party in an official capacity, Lewis gave him the option of accompanying the expedition as far upriver as he wished. He had been solely responsible for Clark's selection and was prepared to offer terms that would be difficult for him to refuse.[3] The joint command was likewise his idea. He obviously liked and trusted Clark. Lewis's brief stint of service under his command had alerted him to the Kentucky soldier's congenial ways, his leadership qualities, and his steady and reliable habits. Along with the wealth of experience in frontier soldiering and wilderness living that Clark would bring to the enterprise, Lewis somehow sensed that his dependable friend also would provide a steadying influence to counterbalance his own emotional ups and downs. From Meriwether Lewis's perspective, William Clark was the best man for the job.

Clark was every bit as eager to cast his lot with Lewis, whom he admired and respected, and the proposed terms of engagement were all that he could have asked for. His availability was no secret. On more than one occasion he had signaled his interest in a governmental appointment. When Secretary of War Henry Dearborn asked him to recommend possible sites for a military post at the mouth of the Ohio, Clark sensed an opening. He provided the secretary with a complete description of the locality where in 1780 his brother George Rogers Clark had established a garrison known as Fort Jefferson. But more important, the younger Clark showed Dearborn's letter and his response to George, who followed them up with a personal note to the president endorsing his brother's observations about the place's strategic importance. George's letter seems to have been calculated to give him a pretext for confiding to his longtime friend Jefferson that brother Billy was in need of a job. The old soldier advised the chief executive that he had long since abandoned any interest in the pursuits of his youthful days, but suggested that his youngest brother might be of service to the administration: "he is well quallified almost for any business. If it should be in your power to confur on him any post of Honor and profit, in this Countrey in which we live, it will exceedingly gratify me."[4] Better

Meriwether Lewis, portrait by
Charles Willson Peale. The artist
painted this portrait the year after
Lewis returned from the Pacific.
Courtesy of the Independence
National Historical Park.

that such a special pleading come from an old friend than directly from the applicant.

William Clark had first met Jefferson in 1801 when he visited Lewis at the President's House. Jefferson could not have failed to notice the striking resemblance he bore to his older brother George Rogers Clark. A conversation about George's financial problems and his western military campaigns might even have caused the chief executive to hearken back to his earlier attempts to encourage western exploration. Indeed William Clark's carefully worded response to Lewis's invitation to join the Corps of Discovery suggests that the idea of a Pacific expedition was not an entirely novel one for him: "The enterprise &c. is Such as I have long anticipated and am much pleased with—and as my situation in life will admit of my absence the length of time necessary to accomplish such an undertaking I will chearfully join you in an 'official Charrector' as mentioned in your letter . . ." Clark echoed Lewis's estimate that the proposed endeavor would likely be fraught with danger and peril, but he hastened to add that "no man lives whith whome I would perfur to undertake Such a Trip &c as your self, and I shall arrange my matters as well as I can against your arrival here." A few days later Clark reconfirmed his eagerness to join the expedition in letters he sent to Lewis and the president.[5]

Their agreement to conduct the U.S. government's pioneering scientific expedition launched a formidable partnership that cemented a lasting friendship and caused the names Lewis and Clark to be linked together in perpetuity. It also profoundly changed both men's lives. The offer could not have come at a more opportune moment for Clark, whose fortunes were at low ebb. Lewis's letter reached him at Clarksville, where he and George Rogers Clark were still sharing quarters in a small log house on Clark's Point. It was a scenic spot with a commanding view of the Falls of the Ohio, but aside from its natural beauty there was not much to recommend it. In contrast with Louisville, Clarksville was a forlorn and desolate place. When Josiah Espy visited the town in 1805, he called it a deserted village and described George Rogers Clark's abode as a lonely cottage that the celebrated warrior had done little to improve. Little wonder that William Clark jumped at the chance to join the president's proposed western tour with its proffer of "honors and rewards."[6]

Thomas Jefferson's grand design for western exploration was no quixotic scheme. His vision of an Empire of Liberty was born of years of study and reflection about America and its future prospects. The author of the Declaration of Independence had high expectations for the young American Republic he had helped create. As president, he was intent on staking out a U.S. claim to North America's vast and contested western expanses. The expedition was also a product of Jefferson's intellectual grounding in Enlightenment thought and his lifelong fascination with scientific inquiry. Exploration science was all the rage, and as British diplomat Edward Thornton observed at the time the American leader approached him with his plan for a western expedition, Jefferson was "ambitious in his character of a man of letters and of science, of distinguishing his Presidency by a discovery. . ."[7] Jefferson very much hoped that his venture would occupy a place among the acclaimed voyages he had studied, but he also had a grander ambition for his country, whose future he had come to believe would be linked to the American West.

The sage of Monticello had cast his thoughts westward long before Robert Livingston and James Monroe inked the deal in Paris transferring the Louisiana Territory to the United States. Collecting books was a lifelong habit for the bibliophile Jefferson, whose library was one of America's largest. He once told a friend that during the years he spent traveling abroad as a representative of the U.S. government, "I purchased everything I could lay my hands on which related to any part of America." His vast collection of works on American geography and travel supplied the raw material for his imaginings about the American West and helped whet his appetite to become a patron of exploration.[8]

On more than one occasion Monticello's armchair explorer had contemplated the benefits that might be derived from a transcontinental expedition.

Thomas Jefferson, portrait by
George Caleb Bingham. Clark
rightly called Jefferson "the main-
spring" of the Pacific expedition.
Courtesy of the State Historical
Society of Missouri.

As previously noted, he first mentioned the idea to George Rogers Clark in
1783, but when the general declined to participate, Jefferson quietly shelved the
matter.[9] During his stint as minister to France, Jefferson had encouraged John
Ledyard to pursue his plan for crossing the North American continent from
west to east. In the 1790s, Secretary of State Jefferson supported the American
Philosophical Society's efforts to sponsor an overland expedition to the Pacific
via the more traditional westward route. French botanist Andre Michaux, then
in the United States, had asked the society to back the project, and Jefferson set
about to raise the necessary funds. Before the scheme could come to fruition,
Michaux was diverted by his countryman Edmond Genet's attempts to promote filibustering expeditions against Spain's North American territories—the
very same intrigues that also managed to ensnare George Rogers Clark. When
Michaux jumped ship, the American Philosophical Society abandoned its plans.[10]

Jefferson was acutely aware that Spain, France, Great Britain, and Russia all
had designs on the American West, but it was a new acquisition for his library
that stirred him to action. Less than a year after he had assumed the office of
the American presidency, the scholarly Virginian picked up a copy of Sir Alexander Mackenzie's *Voyages from Montreal,* a publication that chronicled his successful trek to the Pacific through Canada. The chief executive was familiar

with the British explorer's pioneering voyage across the North American continent, but it was Mackenzie's call for expanded British commerce and settlement in the American Northwest that caught his attention and reawakened his old fears about Great Britain's designs on the far West. The Scot's words jolted the president and hastened his decision to launch, under the sponsorship of the U.S. government, an exploratory expedition not unlike some of those initiated by America's rival imperial powers. William Clark understood and appreciated Thomas Jefferson's pivotal role in the unfolding of the grand venture on which he was about to embark. In a letter to Lewis he referred to the president as "that great Chaructor the Main Spring of its action."[11]

Jefferson had first broached the subject of his proposed western enterprise with members of Congress on January 18, 1803, when he sent them a confidential message seeking legislative authorization for a special appropriation of twenty-five hundred dollars for that purpose, far less than the expedition's eventual price tag of thirty-nine thousand dollars. The president had considered including that request in his annual message to Congress, but at Secretary of the Treasury Albert Gallatin's urging he decided to keep his plan under wraps because it contemplated an expedition outside of the United States.[12] Notwithstanding his efforts to shield the mission from public view, Jefferson briefed British, French, and Spanish diplomats about his project in a move calculated to forestall possible efforts to impede the expedition's progress through North America's contested zones. By casting the venture solely as a scientific enterprise, he attempted to disguise his larger purposes. The British and French seemed satisfied with his explanations, but the wary Spanish officials remained more skeptical and attempted to throw cold water on the scheme.[13]

Because all of these preparations predated France's agreement to sell the Louisiana Territory to the United States, Jefferson concocted a similar subterfuge to camouflage the mission's true objectives in order to stave off criticism from his political foes at home. As he explained to Lewis, "the idea that you are going to explore the Missisipi has been generally given out: it satisfied public curiosity, and masks sufficiently the real destination." Taking his cue from the president, Lewis asked Clark to advise any potential recruits he might enlist "that the direction of this expedition is up the Mississippi to its source," with the assurance that those chosen would be fully apprized of the real design before they were formally engaged.[14]

Clark's acceptance letter did not reach Lewis until July 29. Concerned because he had not yet heard from the man he hoped would accompany him, Lewis had advised Jefferson from Pittsburgh that in the event Clark declined his offer, he had settled upon Lieutenant Moses Hook as a replacement. But that contingency was quickly set aside, and the relieved Lewis reiterated yet again, "I could neither hope, wish, or expect from a union with any man on earth, more perfect support or further aid in the discharge of the several duties of my mission, than that, which I am confident I shall derive from being associated with yourself."[15]

News of Clark's decision to join the expedition won applause all around. When Jefferson notified Secretary of War Dearborn that "William Clarke accepts with great glee the office of going with Capt. Lewis up the Missouri," the secretary responded, "Mr. W. Clark's having consented to accompany Capt. Lewis, is highly interesting, it adds very much to the balance of chances in favour of ultimate success." Given Lewis's mood swings, both the president and Dearborn seemed reassured knowing that Clark would be there to take charge if needed.[16]

By the time that Clark came aboard, preparations for the Voyage of Discovery were already well advanced. The president had sent Lewis to Philadelphia, where some of the nation's leading scientific lights gave him crash courses in natural history and the sciences and also tutored him in the latest techniques of scientific measurement and observation. Jefferson enlisted the assistance of his friend, the noted physician Dr. Benjamin Rush, in acquainting Lewis with "those objects on which it is most desirable he should bring us information."[17] Rush, a member of the American Philosophical Society, willingly complied with the president's wishes. In addition to compiling a list of questions to guide Lewis's inquiries relative to the natural history of the Indians, Dr. Rush also gave him directions for preserving the health of expedition members and saw to it that his medicine chest was well stocked with the famous purging pills he had patented.

At Jefferson's urging, several of Rush's scientific colleagues at the University of Pennsylvania also agreed to lend a hand. Botanist Dr. Benjamin Smith Barton, anatomist Dr. Caspar Wistar, and mathematician Robert Patterson all assisted with Lewis's scientific instruction, as did astronomer and surveyor Andrew Ellicott, who advised him on making celestial observations.[18] Lewis proved himself to be an apt pupil, but a host of competing demands limited the hours that he could devote to his studies. Of necessity, the task of assembling the supplies and equipment required for the two-year expedition occupied much of his time. In a letter he wrote Clark from Pittsburgh on August 3, Lewis informed his new partner "the articles of every discription forming my outfit for this expedition have arrived in good order."[19]

At Harper's Ferry he had procured an experimental iron canoe frame and fifteen stockpiled old 1792 contract rifles fitted with new lockplates. Lewis's lengthy packing list included mathematical instruments of various kinds, rifles, powder horns, bullet molds, flints, knives, and other accoutrements, gunpowder and lead, blankets, coats, woolen overalls, socks, hunting shirts, and assorted clothing, kettles, axes, chisels, files, nails, fishing line, tin trumpets, iron spoons, tin cups, steels for striking fire, oil cloth for wrapping and securing items, assorted medicines, and a vast array of merchandise for Indian presents including white wampum, glass beads of various colors, cloth, scissors, looking glasses, needles, thread, vermillion, knives, tomahawks, wire, colored ribbons, tobacco, combs, and blankets. It was a store that could not have failed to impress his waiting partner. According to Lewis, everything was in readiness for his journey down the Ohio, with the exception of a boat he had ordered to transport the supplies that was still under construction.[20]

He had other important information to relay. The Louisiana Purchase was now official. On July 14 the president had received the French treaty ceding the immense western territory to the United States. Good news travels fast. Rumors of the pending transfer had been circulating in the western country for weeks, and by July 24 Clark reported from Louisville that newspaper accounts seemed to confirm them.[21]

While Clark awaited Lewis's arrival at Louisville, he was anything but idle. The prospect of being virtually incommunicado for at least two years made it incumbent that he put his own business affairs in good order prior to his departure. Clark was particularly eager to forestall any legal actions during his absence that might jeopardize the extensive tracts of undeveloped land he and other members of his family claimed. On July 28 George Rogers Clark formally conveyed to William two disputed parcels containing 73,962 acres in Livingston County, Kentucky, including the future site of the town of Paducah. To no one's surprise their old nemesis Humphrey Marshall sniffed out the transfer, which he then challenged on grounds that he had a prior agreement with George Rogers Clark to assign him parts of those tracts. William promised Worden Pope a thousand acres "if he would see to the recording of the deed from G R Clark to myself and otherwise attend to my interest in those lands." On the eve of his departure, William also was still attempting to settle his brother's long-running dispute with Laurent Bazedon. He had turned to Henry Hurst, clerk of the General Court of the Indiana Territory, for assistance. Hurst, an old friend and a staunch ally of William Henry Harrison, advised him as late as August 23 to expect considerable trouble in the matter. With that in mind, Hurst volunteered to notify anyone of Clark's choosing in the event that Bazedon initiated further legal steps while he was away.[22]

Brother George, who had come to depend heavily on his younger sibling, would sorely miss him for reasons both personal and financial, but so too would many friends and acquaintances who looked to him as a font of information regarding land claims in Kentucky and the Illinois Country. Shortly after Clark headed down the Ohio in the fall of 1803, Robert Breckinridge advised Major William Preston in Virginia that he was unable to provide answers for his questions concerning the Illinois Grant because Captain William Clark had set out westward and Breckinridge could not obtain reliable information from any other source.[23]

Even as he attempted to wrap up any loose ends involving his personal business, William Clark clearly had set his thoughts on his "western tour" as he called it. Like his partner, Clark also did his homework. He did not have members of Philadelphia's scholarly community at his disposal, but he did have access to books and other sources of information. In his spare moments Clark compiled random notes on diverse subjects ranging from hygiene and diet to medical treatments and scientific notation. His observations included practical assessments of the relative merits of various foods and the best ways to prepare them. Clark's jottings suggested that a diet combining vegetables, fruit, and meat was best, but as he already knew, the desired varieties were seldom available to wilderness travelers.[24]

His notes also contained some practical tips that he filed away for future reference. Parsnips, carrots, and beets were deemed more nourishing than potatoes, but potatoes were to be preferred over turnips. Most vegetables, he wrote, are more easily digested when boiled. Potatoes mixed with other vegetables make a good soup that is rendered more nourishing with salt and toasted bread. He also touted the merits of fruit, which he claimed dulled the acrimony of bile and lessened body heat. With regard to meat, he reported that wild animals were more easily digested than tame ones and also more nourishing. In preserving meat, it was best to bleed the animals thoroughly and in the case of poultry to remove the intestines. When it came to drinks, tepid water quenched the thirst best, and ice was dangerous, he warned, when taken on an empty stomach. Persons with gout and rheumatism should avoid cider, and three or four glasses of wine at dinner were sufficient. According to his sources, rest facilitated digestion, but sleep retarded it. It was best, he concluded, to avoid sleep on a full stomach. And finally he recommended more and smaller meals as preferable to large ones.[25]

Clark also attempted to better inform himself in matters of academic science. From his readings he prepared a series of scientific notes and questions on biology, medicine, and other matters. One of his questions was: "How many ways do we acquire a knowledge of plants?" His notes included references to the physiological arrangements of the famed Swedish naturalist Carolus Linnaeus. Clark probably compiled these notes sometime after Lewis joined him at Louisville, since his partner carried with him copies of botanical works on the Linnaean system of classification. While Lewis deservedly is credited as the principal source of the expedition's important contributions to zoological and botanical knowledge, his partner had also learned a thing or two about scientific observation and description.[26]

Clark's firsthand knowledge of the frontier and its native peoples was even more valuable, as evidenced by the practical advice he offered Lewis in the matter of employing an Indian interpreter. Lewis had been very much determined to secure the services of John Conner, an Indian trader who had long resided among the Shawnee and Delaware Indians on the White River in present-day Indiana. Conner had expressed an interest in taking part in the proposed venture, and Lewis and Jefferson both considered him qualified for the task of interpreting. When Conner failed to respond to a formal invitation to join the expedition, Lewis turned to his partner in Kentucky for assistance, instructing him to spare no pains in his efforts to locate him. Clark, who was unacquainted with the elusive trader, complied with Lewis's wishes. A messenger carrying a letter from Clark managed to track him down only to be told that he was unwilling to accept the offer on the terms that Lewis had proposed. Clark assured his partner that Conner was no great loss, pointing out something that apparently neither Lewis nor Jefferson had picked up on—Conner did not speak any of the languages of the tribes residing west of the Mississippi. Clark knew that there would be plenty of suitable applicants for the interpreter's position in St. Louis, and Lewis quickly embraced that assessment as his own. Clark the westerner was already demonstrating his usefulness.[27]

He took to heart Lewis's injunction that he be on the lookout in his neighborhood for "some good hunters, stout, healthy, unmarried men, accustomed to the woods, and capable of bearing bodily fatigue in a pretty considerable degree." In his letter of acceptance, Clark promised to direct his efforts to the temporary engagement of a few suitable men. Less than a week later he reported some success, but lest his soon-to-be partner consider his actions too hasty, he was quick to add that he had declined to encourage several gentlemen's sons because "they are not accustomed to labour and as that is a verry assential part of the services required of the party." No one was better qualified to screen the applicants. Clark's frontier military experience, his familiarity with life in the woods, his standing in the Louisville community and extensive connections there, and his practiced eye in taking the measure of a man equipped him perfectly to make wise choices. By late August Clark had identified several likely prospects whom he described as "the best woodsmen & Hunters" among the local crop of stout young men.[28]

The failure of Lewis's drunken boat-builder to complete his vessel as promised detained him in Pittsburgh until the end of August, and following his departure low waters on the Ohio slowed his journey downriver. A few days of respite in Cincinnati coupled with a visit to the nearby fossil beds at Big Bone Lick, Kentucky, further delayed the expedition's progress.[29] Lewis finally arrived at Louisville on October 14, where his reunion with Clark brought the two partners together for what must have been a joyful occasion. It was the first time they had seen one another since they had agreed by correspondence to lead Jefferson's grand western journey. During the course of the next several days the men must have reminisced about old times and looked forward to exciting new future adventures. They brought each other up to date on the preparations they had made for the journey and selected a handful of men who would form a nucleus for the Corps of Discovery, many from the cadre that Clark had assembled for consideration. Recruits Charles Floyd, Nathaniel Pryor, William Bratton, John Colter, Reuben Field, Joseph Field, George Gibson, George Shannon, and John Shields were later known as the "nine young men from Kentucky." With the exception of Shannon and Colter, who had joined the expedition prior to Lewis's arrival at Louisville, the other seven all enlisted at the Falls of the Ohio. The Field brothers, whose father, Abraham, was a resident of Jefferson County and well known to the Clark family, seem to have been two of Clark's earliest choices, since their official enlistment date was August 1, 1803.[30]

Also joining the expedition there was York, William Clark's African American slave, though no one considered his enlistment important enough to mention at the time. William Clark and York were approximately the same age and had grown up together. York had long served as William's personal servant, and when John Clark died in 1799 he had bequeathed to his son his enslaved companion since childhood, who would then have been in his late twenties. York had frequently accompanied his master during his previous travels, so Clark's decision to take him to the Pacific must have come as no surprise. How York felt about joining the expedition and leaving his wife in Louisville is not known, but as someone who was regarded as a piece of property it is a safe bet that the decision had not been left to him. Sadly, that was not destined to change. In the journals Clark routinely referred to his African American traveling companion as "my servant," perhaps as a way to avoid the harsher implications of his slave status. Whatever York's sentiments may have been on the occasion of his departure from Louisville, the Kentucky slave could never in his wildest imaginings have dreamed that his participation in this great excursion would one day bring him fame beyond measure. Clark would have been equally astonished to learn of his servant's acclaim.[31]

The newly assembled corps maneuvered the expedition's boats through the Ohio's rapids to Clarksville, where the men encamped until October 26. They then continued downriver on their way to the Mississippi. The early going was anything but pleasant for Captain Clark, who within a few days of their departure

was taken violently ill with an old complaint that he referred to as "a contrac-
tion of the muskelur system." Lewis looked after his ailing partner, and his
treatment, in all likelihood a dose of Dr. Rush's powerful purgatives, brought
Clark temporary relief. When the party arrived at Fort Massac, a venerable
military outpost downstream from the mouth of the Tennessee River, the detachment of troops Captain Lewis had arranged for had not yet arrived. All
was not lost, however, because during their stopover Lewis and Clark secured a
preliminary agreement from George Drouillard to act as an Indian interpreter.
The son of a French Canadian trader and a Shawnee mother, whose name the
Americans commonly rendered with the anglicized spelling of "Drewyer," Drouillard served as an interpreter and proved to be one of the expedition's best hunters
and most valuable members.[32]

By the time the party reached the Ohio's junction with the Mississippi on
November 14, Clark had recovered sufficiently from his illness to make a complete survey of the site and to measure the width of the two rivers at that location. The site was already well mapped, but this practice run allowed the
expedition's leaders to test their skills at determining longitude and latitude.
Clark also was well enough to join Lewis and a small party for what must have
been for him a nostalgic visit to the nearby location where in 1780 George
Rogers Clark had constructed the installation that he had called Fort Jefferson
in honor of Virginia's wartime governor. The fort had been abandoned after
only a year, and William Clark reported to his brother Jonathan that the site
was now overgrown with trees. While Lewis and Clark were reconnoitering the
old fortification, several crew members left to guard the boats defied orders
and stole away to some trader's huts on the Spanish side of the Mississippi,
where they went on a drunken binge. This would not be the last such incident,
and the captains clearly had their work cut out for them if they were going to
impose order within the ranks of this motley and as yet undisciplined band of
recruits.[33]

Indian peddlers regularly approached river travelers offering them food and
game, and a contingent of Shawnee Indians now living on the Mississippi's
western bank sold Lewis and Clark assorted wild meats from their sizable
store. Clark was unable to join in a repast prepared from their restocked larder
because his former complaint had returned with a vengeance. This time Lewis's
ministrations failed to have the desired effect, leaving the hapless commander
to cope with the discomforts of violent pain in the stomach and bowels. Lewis
made his ailing partner some soup from a grouse that one of his men had
killed. But relief would have to await their arrival in Kaskaskia, where some
new and more potent medicines finally did the trick. In the interim Clark did
not stray far from the boats, confining himself to tasks that were not unduly

strenuous. The stoic soldier carried on as best he could, and only revealed the full extent of his infirmities in letters to family members.[34]

Clark was too unwell to accompany Lewis when he paid a call on Louis Lorimier, the commandant at Cape Girardeau. The mixed-blood Canadian trader, who cast his lot with the British during the Revolutionary War, had fled to Spanish Louisiana not long after that conflict ended. George Rogers Clark had destroyed Lorimier's trading post in the Ohio country, but all had been forgotten, and the colorful commandant and his Shawnee wife treated the visiting American officer to a comfortable and decent supper.[35] Prior to his departure for the Pacific Lewis arranged for Lorimier's son to attend the U.S. Military Academy at West Point, despite his initial misgivings that the youth might encounter racial discrimination.

The captains resumed their ascent upstream, and when the expedition passed the Grand Tower, a prominent Mississippi River landmark now known as Tower Rock, William Clark drew a map showing its location with a sketch of their keelboat anchored nearby. Rivermen regarded the unique geological feature that French explorer Jacques Marquette had observed in 1673 as equivalent to the equinox on western waters, and crew members appear to have honored the local custom requiring first-time passersby to treat their fellow travelers to drinks or be ducked in the river.[36]

The expedition's slow progress up the Mississippi (frequently little more than a mile a day) made it clear that the boats were seriously undermanned. At Kaskaskia Lewis and Clark augmented the nascent Corps of Discovery with the addition of twelve men chosen from among the local garrison. They also arranged to procure a store of winter provisions for their expanded force. Unexpectedly, Clark found himself thrust into the role as the expedition's principal record keeper when Lewis curiously abdicated his responsibilities as a diarist. For reasons that still puzzle modern scholars, Lewis abandoned his practice of keeping a daily journal in November 1803. Aside from a few fragmentary jottings, he did not again put pen to paper to resume work on his field notes until April 1805. During that unexplained hiatus, Clark honored Jefferson's instructions that they carefully document the expedition and accurately record their scientific observations. Already a practiced journal keeper, the methodical Clark attended to this important business. Were it not for his faithful efforts, much of the journey would have gone undocumented. The expedition's journals remain a testimony to his commitment and perseverance.

Undoubtedly, Clark's slowly improving health made it easier for him to accomplish the task. A dose of aloin, a derivative of the aloe plant procured in Kaskaskia, finally ended his discomfort and put him on the road to recovery. Clark's visit in the old river town must have seemed eerily reminiscent of his 1797 stay there, when he likewise had paused to recuperate from a lingering illness. But this time the opportunity to renew old acquaintances and the comfortable quarters provided him by Captain Amos Stoddard, a fellow army officer, and William Morrison, a prominent local merchant and future business partner, undoubtedly made his brief sojourn considerably more agreeable.[37]

The conversations that he and Lewis shared with their Kaskaskia hosts yielded important and disturbing information—rumor had it that Charles Dehault Delassus, the Spanish lieutenant governor in St. Louis, intended to bar them from ascending the Missouri River. This startling news prompted Captain Lewis to set out on horseback for Upper Louisiana's capital city carrying official documents confirming the Louisiana Purchase. Lewis assumed, incorrectly as it turned out, that his papers would end Spanish attempts to obstruct the expedition's progress.[38]

Clark's familiarity with St. Louis, his nodding acquaintance with some of the city's leading citizens, his previous experience in dealing with Spanish officials, and his amiable ways all suggest that he would have been a better choice to initiate those conversations with Delassus, but the assignment fell to his partner because as he noted in a letter to his brother Jonathan, he was still too weak to undertake the trip. Lewis was very much put off when Delassus confirmed his intent to prevent the American expedition from entering Spanish territory while he awaited instructions from officials in New Orleans. That decision was born of the lieutenant governor's certain knowledge that his superiors were still reeling from the shocking news that Napoleon, contrary to his assurances, had agreed to sell the Louisiana Territory to the United States and their belief that the Lewis and Clark expedition posed an added threat from the expanding republic on New Spain's eastern border. Lewis advised Jefferson that the Spanish official was a tyrannical despot whom local inhabitants feared more than they feared God.[39]

He overstated the case. The impoverished former French aristocrat could be overbearing, but as a Spanish bureaucrat his powers were in decline by the time Lewis met him. The pending transfer lessened his influence in the province and hampered his attempts to uphold Spanish authority during the regime's waning days. The desertion of longtime allies already positioning themselves to accommodate the incoming Yankees compounded his frustrations. Once his superiors gave him the word to facilitate the transfer to American authorities at St. Louis, Delassus managed the proceedings with dignity and grace, though in frustration, he did scribble "the devil take all" as a parting comment in his Indian ledger.[40]

While Lewis was making his way overland to St. Louis to confer with Spanish officials, Clark guided the river craft up the Mississippi to Cahokia, where he arrived on December 7, the same day Captain Lewis finally sat down with Lieutenant Governor Delassus in St. Louis. Following his session with Upper Louisiana's ranking official, Lewis did not tarry long in the capital city. On December 8 he crossed the river to Cahokia, where he informed the waiting Clark that Delassus would not permit them to spend the winter along the lower reaches of the Missouri as they had planned. Lewis and Clark chose not to press the issue and elected to locate their temporary quarters on the American side of the Mississippi, somewhere in the vicinity of the mouth of the Missouri. The lateness of the season had made their decision not to contest the Spanish commandant's decision much easier.[41]

Two days later the Americans resumed their journey upriver in search of a proper site for their winter camp. When their little fleet approached St. Louis with the American colors flying, Clark reported that "the admiration of the people were So great, that hundreds Came to the bank to view us." After anchoring along the riverfront, Lewis and Clark made their way up the steep path to the bluff that protected the settlement from the Mississippi's rampaging waters. As they made their rounds, Clark must have noticed that the river town he had first visited six years before was as vibrant as ever and, as Captain Stoddard noted, quite comparable to America's eastern seaport cities.[42]

During his brief stopover Clark encountered several old friends from Vincennes and Kaskaskia during a gathering at the lieutenant governor's residence. In his conversations with the American travelers, Delassus sought to make amends by invoking the hardships and dangers of winter travel as a reason for his decision to deny them permission to ascend the Missouri.[43] If the Spanish lieutenant governor was not very accommodating, the same could not be said for most other St. Louisans. In private conversations, out of the governor's hearing, Antoine Soulard and Auguste Chouteau proved useful contacts for initiating the flow of what would soon become a steady stream of valuable information. Soulard, Upper Louisiana's surveyor general, allowed Lewis to peruse his copy of the province's 1800 census, and Auguste Chouteau loaned him a manuscript map depicting the Missouri as far as the mouth of the Osage.[44]

The following day Clark headed upstream in a steady rain in pursuit of a suitable location for a winter camp. Lewis did not accompany him, choosing instead to return to Cahokia to continue his quest for information to supplement what he had managed to collect in St. Louis.[45] Before month's end, Lewis was able to notify the president that he had obtained three maps: one of the Osage River, a general map of Upper Louisiana, and a map of the Missouri River from its mouth to the Mandan nation. He also acquired a manuscript copy of the journal of James MacKay and John Evans's travels on the Upper Missouri that he was having translated into English.[46]

Upriver, Clark had settled upon a site for his camp immediately opposite the mouth of the Missouri at the River Dubois, or Wood River. That particular spot afforded a good harbor for boats, was sufficiently elevated to protect the structures against flooding, was surrounded by a game-rich hunting ground, and was located within the bounds of the United States. Work crews, under Clark's supervision, immediately began building a road and hewing logs, and within a few days they had started raising the first cabins.[47] Since it was intended only as a temporary encampment, the structures or "huts" as Clark called them did not have to be as sturdily built as those required for a more permanent installation.

The flurry of activity did not go unnoticed. Curious river travelers and nosy neighbors could not resist the temptation to check out the scene. Shortly after the expedition's arrival, Clark reported that three inebriated Potawatomi Indians braved high winds and violent waves while crossing the Mississippi for a firsthand look. A local farmer who also came calling returned a few days later bearing a load of turnips. The mail from Cahokia brought a letter from Charles Gratiot in St. Louis offering to provide his friend Clark with a horse and any other assistance he might need. When a passing party of Delaware Indians paid a visit to Camp River Dubois, Clark recognized one of the chiefs who had been present at the signing of the Treaty of Greenville. Perhaps in honor of old times or good conduct, Clark gave him a bottle of whiskey.[48] Such were the comings and goings at the temporary outpost.

The buildings under construction suggested a military camp in the making, but the expected discipline was not yet in evidence. The arrival four days before Christmas of reinforcements dispatched from Captain John Campbell's company of the Second Infantry Regiment stationed in Tennessee had not helped matters. Clark, sensing that Campbell had used the opportunity to rid himself of some of his problem soldiers, cryptically noted "those men are not such I was told was in readiness at Tennessee for this Comd. & &."[49] On Christmas morning soldiers discharging their weapons in a holiday salute awakened Clark, who soon discovered that some of the celebrants were already drunk and at least two of them had been in a fight. Since it was Christmas, Clark indulged the men, who frolicked and hunted all day before feasting on the turkeys they had killed and the butter and cheese that had been purchased especially for the occasion. In the spirit of the day, three Indians who joined in the festivities received a bottle of whiskey. Notwithstanding a few likely hangovers, the soldiers were back at work the following day completing a storeroom and working on the chimney for Clark's cabin. Before year's end the simple structures at Wood River were ready for occupancy.[50]

As the camp neared completion, Clark turned his attention to shaping up his troops and imposing a sense of order in the encampment. In consultation with Lewis he organized a plan for the guards, issued revised orders, and banned a local resident from selling liquor to the men in his party. On New Year's Day, in an attempt to improve his men's marksmanship, Clark staged a shooting match with several local sharpshooters who had joined them for the day's goings on. He offered a dollar prize to be shared by the contest's two best shots. In that initial encounter the country boys won the top prizes, but with practice Clark's soldiers managed to best the locals in subsequent matches.[51]

All the while Captain Lewis remained in Cahokia, occupying the more comfortable quarters that were available there and tending to what Clark described as "business important to the enterprise." The coleaders kept in touch, and Clark never seems to have questioned the arrangement, nor did he see cause to complain. In a mid-January letter written at Camp River Dubois, Clark reported to his brother-in-law William Croghan in Kentucky, "I have not been from my Camp to any house since my arrival here," but as he later added, "my situation is as comfortable as could be expected in the woods, & on the frontiers . . ." There was plenty to keep him occupied at the camp. He compiled lists of names identifying the most suitable candidates for membership in the permanent corps. He also sought to impose stricter military discipline. On January 6 Clark addressed the company and ordered two men guilty of fighting, drunkenness, and neglecting their duties to build a hut for a local woman employed to do laundry and sewing for the detachment.[52]

Clark was soon sufficiently confident about the situation in camp to venture out into the adjacent countryside to inspect an ancient Indian fortification consisting of nine mounds arranged in a circle, once a part of the Cahokia complex, where he found great quantities of earthenware and flints. During that foray Clark again experienced the hazards of winter travel. While attempting to cross a frozen pond, he broke through the ice and plunged into the frigid water. Upon his return to Camp River Dubois he discovered that his wet feet had frozen to his shoes, prompting him to take the necessary precautions against frostbite. While Clark was recovering from the effects of his dousing, James MacKay came calling. The Scottish fur trader had conducted an expedition up the Missouri River in the 1790s with John Evans in search of a route to the Pacific Ocean. It had also been their intent to establish a chain of forts to halt the penetrations by British traders into Spain's North American domains.[53]

Neither man made it to the western sea, but after returning from his travels, MacKay drafted a large-scale map delineating the Missouri River's sixteen-hundred-mile course to the Mandan villages with the aid of surveys supplied by his assistant Evans. The poor copy of the MacKay-Evans map Lewis had acquired in Cahokia persuaded the American captains that a more exact copy

would be an invaluable tool. From sources in Cahokia and St. Louis they
learned that the map's draftsman resided at a small Missouri River settlement
only a short distance above St. Charles, and in contravention of the Spanish
commandant's orders they dispatched Private Joseph Field on a secret mission
to seek him out. Under the cover of a hunting trip, Field slipped into the Spanish territory undetected and persuaded the knowledgeable Scot to return with
him to Camp River Dubois. Like most Upper Louisianans he was eager to make
a favorable impression on the Americans and obliged Clark with the latest version of his chart of the Missouri. MacKay's map, commonly referred to as the
Indian Office map, served as Lewis and Clark's route map during the first leg of
their Missouri River journey.[54]

With the valuable new information supplied by MacKay, Clark was soon cal-
culating the distances from Camp River Dubois to the Mandan nation and
preparing projections of the time that would be required for them to complete
their journey to the Pacific. His estimate that they could return home by sometime in late 1805 missed the mark by nearly a year, but his more accurate projections of the number of men who would be required to maneuver the loaded
boats upriver sent Lewis back to St. Louis in search of additional French boatmen who could be hired for the first year of travel. Clark took charge of retro-
fitting the fifteen-ton, fifty-five-foot keelboat to accommodate the additional
oarsmen needed to propel it against the swift Missouri currents. He also supervised the construction of storage lockers along both sides of the boat, with lids
that could be raised to form a shield in the event of an attack, and directed the
mounting of a small swivel cannon in the bow and two blunderbusses on
swivels attached to the cabin in the stern. Clark's sketches of the fortified vessel
suggest that it bore a greater resemblance to a 1790s Spanish river galley than to
a traditional western keelboat.[55]

Captain Lewis finally arrived at Camp River Dubois on January 30, where he
found his partner once again ailing. Clark had told his brother that he had
considered himself fully recovered until he suffered this latest relapse. Lewis,
his doctor, sent Private Shields out in search of walnut bark that he used to prepare a folk remedy. Within a few days Clark's condition had improved sufficiently to allow him to accept invitations to two balls in St. Louis. The lure of
the city and its entertainments was too powerful for the campbound Clark to
resist, and he headed off to the provincial capital to once again sample the delights of French hospitality. Lewis joined him there later in the month.[56]

In St. Louis Clark was a guest of Pierre Chouteau, better known locally as
Cadet. As gentlemen renowned for their conviviality and as businessmen with
an eye on the future, Pierre and his brother Auguste wasted no time in ex-
tending a hand of friendship to the visiting American officers. When Clark

mentioned the American president's desire to meet with western tribal leaders during a conversation with Cadet Chouteau, the savvy merchant volunteered on the spot to lead a delegation of Osage chiefs to the Federal City. Well aware of Chouteau's long experience with the Osages and his influence in their camps, Captain Lewis encouraged Clark to proceed with the arrangements. They recognized that no other nonnative could serve them so well in persuading the headmen from the powerful tribe to visit the president or to observe American authority.[57]

Once again Clark took advantage of the gracious Creole hospitality. Besides providing a welcome diversion from camp life, his visits in the comfortable Creole homes also gave him an opportunity to learn more about the immense trans-Mississippi territory he and Lewis were preparing to traverse. The Chouteau brothers' vast experience in trade and Indian relations and their local renown as community leaders made them excellent advisers. For their part, the French merchants capitalized on these get-togethers to acquaint the Americans with their personal views on matters ranging from appropriate forms of government—they preferred a military one—to Indian policy. They also took advantage of their growing friendships to strike bargains for the sale of merchandise to outfit the corps and its retinue, which now numbered nearly forty-five.[58]

A conference with a Kickapoo chief and discussions with an army contractor kept Lewis at Camp River Dubois and prevented him from attending a dance in St. Louis, but he clearly longed to rejoin his partner and their friends in the capital. Since this marked the first time that both senior officers were to be absent from the winter camp at the same time, Captain Lewis issued detachment orders placing the trusted and experienced Sergeant John Ordway in charge while they were away. The general orders directed the men to continue with their assigned duties and not to leave camp without Ordway's permission. Lewis also limited the daily whiskey distributions to the legal ration. After mid-February, when Delassus received orders from New Orleans to proceed with the region's transfer to U.S. authorities, both Lewis and Clark began spending more of their time in St. Louis.[59]

U.S. and French officials designated Captain Amos Stoddard to act for their respective governments during the transfer ceremonies in St. Louis. Clark was in the city when a contingent of twenty citizens welcomed the American commandant. Lieutenant Governor Delassus presided over a great dinner and parade during which he announced his readiness to deliver the province to the U.S. officer. Not all of Upper Louisiana's ancient inhabitants were as sanguine as the Chouteaus seemed to be about their prospects under the new regime. For many rank-and-file Louisianans, the thought of being governed by the rambunctious Americans was understandably unsettling.[60]

Clark was an eyewitness to those historic events. Captain Stoddard and Lieutenant Governor Delassus invited him to accompany them on a reconnaissance of the local fortifications, which he pronounced to be in a "retched state." Immediately afterward he and Lewis sat down to yet another sumptuous and well-attended dinner hosted by Delassus, carried off in Clark's words with a "great deel of formality and parade." The Spanish regime was going out in style. Stoddard shared his proposed plans for governing the territory with Clark, who gave them his ringing endorsement. Clark did manage to steal enough time away from his comings and goings in St. Louis to write to his brother Edmund asking him to purchase him several additional riverfront lots in Clarksville.[61]

Stoddard's reception in St. Louis had been cordial, but the official ceremonies of transfer had to be postponed until March 9 and 10 after ice on the river delayed the arrival of the U.S. garrison and the Spanish lieutenant governor became ill, perhaps from too much partying. During the interim Clark briefly returned to Camp River Dubois to check things out. To his chagrin, he discovered that Sergeant Ordway had experienced difficulties in his attempts to manage the bored and restless detachment. In defiance of orders, some of the men had slipped off to visit a neighboring whiskey shop under the pretense of going hunting. Fighting and drinking remained the principal sources of release from the tedium and monotony of camp life.[62]

Clark almost certainly was back in St. Louis in time to witness the raising of the Stars and Stripes and the firing of a salute at the formal ceremonies marking Upper Louisiana's transfer to the United States on March 9 and 10. Stoddard reported seeing tears in the eyes of the French inhabitants as he addressed them, but he denied that they were tears of regret—a conclusion probably more patriotic than accurate.[63] Not long after that momentous occasion, Lewis and Clark lent Stoddard a hand with local Indian policy. The American captains joined Pierre Chouteau and Charles Gratiot on a mission to turn back 110 Kickapoo Indians bent on making war on the Osages. The assignment, which anticipated Clark's post-expedition responsibilities as U.S. Indian agent, momentarily diverted them from final preparations for their western journey.[64]

Back at Camp River Dubois, Clark superintended last-minute modifications to the keelboat and oversaw the parching of additional stores of corn and meal rations. Eager to find out if their efforts to persuade the Kickapoo band to return home had been successful, Clark dispatched a courier in search of information concerning their whereabouts. To his relief, the messenger returned bearing a letter from François Saucier, the commandant at the nearby settlement of Portage des Sioux, announcing that Indians had crossed the Mississippi and headed homeward. Lewis and Clark's foray into Indian diplomacy had been successful, and Clark so advised his partner, who had stayed in St.

Louis.[65] Before returning to camp, Lewis arranged to send Jefferson slips from wild plum and Osage orange trees growing in Pierre Chouteau's garden, along with written descriptions of both plants. Additionally, in an attempt to reciprocate for the many courtesies he received from influential members of Upper Louisiana's Creole establishment and to cement their attachment to the incoming American regime, he recommended Auguste Pierre Chouteau, Charles Gratiot fils, and Louis Lorimier, Jr., for appointments to the newly established U.S. Military Academy at West Point.[66]

Lewis made it a point to be present at Wood River for the March 28 courts-martial of John Shields, John Colter, and Robert Frazer on charges of misconduct. The proceeding lasted for the better part of a day, and when Clark read the verdict during parade the following evening, Shields and Colter "asked the forgivness & & promised to doe better in the future." The captains apparently accepted their assurances and pardoned them for their offenses, for there is no record to show that any punishment was meted out. With that matter resolved, the captains turned their attention to the final selection of members for the permanent detachment. After they had made their choices, they divided them into three squads and appointed Charles Floyd, John Ordway, and Nathaniel Pryor as sergeants. A few days later Sergeant Ordway proudly informed his parents in New Hampshire about his good fortune and the great rewards he expected his service would bring.[67]

Once the detachment was in place, Clark resumed his final packing. On April 7 he and Lewis returned to St. Louis to attend the gala dinner and ball hosted by the new American commandant. Captain Stoddard spared no expense, spending $622.75 for the grand affair that began on Saturday evening and did not conclude until nine o'clock the following morning.[68] Clark, who had helped underwrite the costly event with a $200 loan to his fellow officer, tarried in St. Louis for a few more days "attending to Sunderey Stores &c.," before resuming his duties at Camp River Dubois, where he compiled a memorandum of items that were still needed. Unable to locate the hair pipes they recently had purchased from Chouteau, he advised his partner that the tubular beads so popular with the Indians were a necessity.[69]

Lewis acknowledged Clark's memo and dispatched instructions for paying the troops. He sent along some small flags and a supply of mosquito nets— items they could surely use—and also informed Clark that Chouteau had procured seven French boatmen or engagés to man the canoes as far as the Mandan villages.[70] Prior to Pierre Chouteau's departure for Washington, Lewis also drafted an effusive letter of introduction extolling the French merchant's hospitality and the assistance he had provided. Clark used it as a model for similar letters he sent his Kentucky relatives. Clark may have borrowed his partner's flowery phrases, but the sentiments expressing his warm regard for Pierre Chouteau and his wife, Brigitte, were genuine.[71]

Those letters were hardly in the mail when Clark received a devastating blow. On May 7 Private Colter returned to the camp carrying a packet from Captain Lewis forwarding the commission Clark had anxiously been awaiting. But he was in for an unexpected surprise. When he opened the document, Lewis's co-commander discovered that he had been given a second lieutenant's rank rather than the captain's commission the president had promised him. To add insult to injury, this was a grade below the one he had held when he resigned from the army in 1796. An accompanying letter from Secretary Dearborn explained that "the peculiar situation, circumstances and organization of the Corps of Engineers is such as would render the appointment of Mr. Clark a Captain in that Corps improper."[72] In fairness to Dearborn, he had to operate under the constraints of an 1802 statute designed to shrink the military establishment during peacetime, and there were no vacant captain's slots at the time. This shocking revelation came like a bolt out of the blue, and Lewis attempted to break the news as gently as possible. "It is not such as I wished, or had reason to expect," Lewis wrote his fellow officer, "but so it is—a further explaneation when I join you. I think it will be best to let none of our party or any other persons know any thing about the grade, you will observe that the grade has no effect upon your compensation, which by G-d, shall be equal to my own."[73] And so it was to be.

Neither man ever mentioned it again in public, though as Clark later confided to Nicholas Biddle, at the time he was preparing the expedition's journals for publication, "my feelings on this Occasion was as might be expected." Throughout the journey Lewis held true to his promise and treated his partner as an equal in every respect. In the journals and ever after it would be Captains Lewis and Clark. Nonetheless, it had been a mortifying development for Clark, who true to form chose not to make an issue of it. Clark's most expansive remarks on the subject were included in his letter in response to a query from Biddle: "You express a desire to know the exact relation which I stood in Point of Rank, and Command with Captain Lewis—equal in every point of view—I did not think myself very well treated as I did not get the appointment which was promised me. As I was not disposed to make any noise about the business have never mentioned the particulars to any one, and must request you not to mention my disappointment & the Cause to any one." The closest Clark ever came to making a statement about the incident occurred shortly after his triumphant return from the Pacific in the fall of 1806 when he returned his commission to Secretary Dearborn with the cryptic observation that "having answered the purpose for which it was intended, I take the liberty of returning it to you."[74] For Clark, who was usually a man of few words, that was enough

Henry Dearborn, portrait by
Charles Willson Peale. Dearborn
served as secretary of war during
Thomas Jefferson's administration.
Courtesy of the Independence
National Historical Park.

said, and Dearborn surely got the message. Nearly two centuries later in a special White House ceremony on January 17, 2001, President William Jefferson
Clinton by special act of Congress posthumously conferred on William Clark a
military commission promoting him from lieutenant of the Corps of Artil-
lerists and Engineers to captain in the Regular Army with an effective date of
March 26, 1804. Captain Clark would be pleased.

At the time the disappointed officer chose to persevere. He had invested too
much in this expedition and its success to turn back at the last minute. Taking
this latest disappointment in stride, he was hard at work the following morning to ensure that everything would be in order for their pending departure. It
was an unseasonably hot day, but he opted to take his men on a trial run, perhaps in part to take his mind off of the previous day's unpleasantness. They
loaded the boats and traveled a few miles up the Mississippi while Clark took
practice readings with his compass. The next day Clark moved the detachment
into their tents at the Wood River camp and waited for instructions from Lewis
in St. Louis. When Lewis's letter arrived on May 13, Clark dashed off a hurried
response advising his partner that their three boats were loaded and set to depart. His final memorandum enumerating the articles in readiness for the voyage illustrates the scale of the proposed undertaking: 3,400 pounds of flour,

3,700 pounds of pork, several thousand pounds of parched corn and meal, 700 pounds of lard and grease, 560 pounds of biscuits, 112 pounds of sugar, 120 pounds of candles, 50 pounds of soap, 50 pounds of beans and peas, 750 pounds of salt, 21 bales of Indian goods, and tools of every description. Last-minute jitters caused Clark to worry if they had procured enough presents to accommodate the Indian multitudes they were likely to encounter during their voyage. Such concerns were soon put aside, and the following day the Corps of Discovery set out from Camp River Dubois westward bound.[75] Thanks to his friend Meriwether Lewis's invitation, William Clark was embarking on a journey that had rescued him from a humdrum existence at Clarksville and was about to launch him down an exciting and life-altering path.

Four

Westward Ho!

WILLIAM CLARK'S DEPARTURE from Camp River Dubois in the Spring of 1804 was a defining moment in his event-filled life. Not only did it mark the beginning of his grand voyage to the Pacific, but it also thrust him into the pages of history in the company of Meriwether Lewis. Forever after Clark would be remembered as Lewis's partner in America's pioneering scientific expedition. While circumstances may have relegated Clark to second billing, the two men functioned as a team. Clark was no second fiddle. Because each allowed the other to play to his particular strengths, theirs was a formidable partnership. Clark's substantial contributions to the pioneering venture earned him momentary public acclaim and, more important, what amounted to a federal sinecure for life.

His journal entry describing the launching of the Corps of Discovery was predictably terse and to the point: "I Set out at 4 oClock P.M. in the presence of many of the Neighbouring inhabitants, and [we] proceeded on under a jentle brease up the Missourie . . ." The phrase "we proceeded on" quickly became a familiar part of the Lewis and Clark lexicon and came to symbolize the tenacity and perseverance that characterized the efforts of Clark and all corps members during their lengthy and arduous trek across the North American continent.[1]

On the morning of May 14, 1804, all was in readiness for the corps to begin its journey, save for the weather. Lewis, still in St. Louis finalizing arrangements for the Osage chiefs to accompany Pierre Chouteau to Washington, had left his coleader in command. None of Clark's subordinates had the slightest inkling of the army's recent refusal to grant him a captain's commission, and true to form, the dependable officer gave no hint of the lingering disappointment and resentment that he harbored as a result of that decision. As always, Clark remained a professional soldier prepared to do his duty.[2]

For most of the day gusty winds and a torrential spring downpour kept the expedition's boats moored along the Mississippi riverbank, while members of the corps eagerly waited for the storm to subside so they could bid adieu to the out-of-the-way campsite they had called home for the past five months. When Captain Clark, as he was still called, finally gave the order to cast off, a member of the departing party fired a single salute, and the little fleet consisting of a fifty-five-foot keelboat with twenty-two oars and two flat-bottom pirogues, one with six oars and the other with seven, headed in the direction of the nearby Missouri, while a small gathering of onlookers waved a final good-bye.[3] So began the great western expedition Thomas Jefferson had sent in search of a commercial passage between the Missouri River and the Pacific Ocean. He had no way of knowing that no such connecting link existed, but the mission was destined to forever change William Clark's life.

Choppy waters and the lateness of the hour forced the tiny flotilla to put ashore on the first island it came to in the Missouri. Members of the corps spent a miserable night there in a driving rain that extinguished their camp-fires, and when they resumed their journey the following morning, conditions on the rain-swollen stream continued to hinder their progress. Several times during the two-day trip to St. Charles, crew members had to disengage the expedition's merchandise-laden flagship from snags and river debris. Clark, already an experienced waterman, quickly discerned that the keelboat's overloaded stern was exacerbating the problem.[4]

At midday on the sixteenth, the corps finally reached St. Charles, a settlement of a hundred or so French-style buildings strung out along a narrow strip of land adjacent to the river and standing in the shadows of the little hills that gave the town its nickname, *Les Petite Cotes*. The rustic village's mostly French and mixed-blood residents seldom impressed anyone. In 1796 Victor Collot opined that "it would be difficult to find a collection of individuals more ignorant, stupid, ugly, and miserable," and his French compatriot Nicolas de Finiels suggested that the inhabitants of St. Charles exhibited the "Indians' habits without possessing any of their cruelty." William Clark, better attuned to the realities of backcountry living, was more charitable in his assessment, describing the town's residents as "pore [poor], polite & harmonious." He might well have added hospitable, for on his very first night in town Charles Tayon, the former Spanish commandant, and François Duquette, a prominent local merchant lately down on his luck, invited him to sup with them at Duquette's hill-top residence overlooking the river.[5]

The sociable Clark clearly delighted in the local diversions, but they also gave him cause for concern. He worried that some of his as yet undisciplined soldiers chafing from several months of relative confinement and restless in anticipation of a protracted tour of duty might bring discredit on the army they served. Clark's orders read to the troops following their arrival admonished them to be on their best behavior and warned that if they failed to deport themselves properly, he would deploy the entire outfit to "a more retired place" outside of St. Charles.[6]

His fears were not unfounded. On their very first day at St. Charles, three soldiers sneaked into town without permission to sample the local delights. Upon their return to camp the officer in charge placed the delinquents under guard, and Clark summoned a court-martial to consider the allegations against them. William Werner, Hugh Hall, and John Collins stood accused of having been absent without leave. In addition, Collins also faced the more serious charges of behaving in an unbecoming manner at a local ball and being disrespectful to his superiors. The tribunal found all three guilty as charged and sentenced Werner and Hall to each receive twenty-five lashes on their bare backs, with double that number to be inflicted on Collins. The military panel suggested that Werner and Hall's prior good conduct entitled them to consideration for leniency, but it declined to urge clemency for Collins, who previously had faced charges of drunkenness and pig stealing. As the officer in charge, Captain Clark reviewed the court's findings and after setting aside the punishments for Werner and Hall, he ordered Collins flogged that evening in the presence of the entire party. Clark clearly did not intend to tolerate defiance of military discipline within the corps' ranks, but he was equally determined to maintain the support and respect of the troops under his command.[7]

Bloody back notwithstanding, Collins presumably returned to duty the following day and well may have been among those whom Clark assigned to a detail charged with rebalancing the keelboat's cargo by moving some of it from the stern to the bow. The commander had other things on his mind as he fretted over a report that one of his brothers was ill. Perhaps it was George, whose decline has already been noted. Whichever the sibling and whatever the malady, it was not fatal. Clark returned home more than two years later to find his three remaining brothers still alive and well.[8]

Meriwether Lewis finally arrived in St. Charles on May 20, escorted by a company of influential civic leaders who had traveled from St. Louis to see the Corps of Discovery depart. The following day Captains Lewis and Clark said their final good-byes, and at half past three on the afternoon of May 21, 1804, the voyagers began their trek upriver to the sounds of huzzahs from well-wishers gathered at water's edge.[9]

The first few weeks amounted to a shakedown cruise as the crews struggled to familiarize themselves with the vagaries of the unpredictable Missouri. Experimenting with their poles, oars, sails, and tow ropes to determine the best way for moving vessels against the Missouri's stronger currents kept them occupied. Under optimum conditions, with the benefit of a favorable breeze, the boats could advance as many as twenty miles in a single day. The smaller red and white pirogues were easier to handle than the larger keelboat, whose curved bottom and shallow draft made it susceptible to overturning. Its design facilitated cordelling or towing in the shallower waters closer to the riverbank, but the watermen quickly discovered that the fully loaded vessel weighed down with cargo could also easily become lodged on a sandbar.

As the expedition made its way upriver, friendly onlookers occasionally hailed its passing from scattered shoreline clearings. On their second day out, a small Kickapoo party presented the corps with several freshly killed deer, true to an earlier promise they had made to Clark. The commanders returned the favor with two quarts of whiskey.[10] French and American settlers residing along the river also greeted the travelers with outstretched hands and offers of fresh provisions. They supplied butter, eggs, and milk to complement the wild game provided by their native neighbors. The exploring party stopped briefly at Boone's settlement nine miles above Femme Osage Creek in St. Charles County, but the family patriarch Daniel Boone was notably absent. Clark made no mention of the well-known Kentucky hunter whose wanderlust had brought him to the western fringes of white settlement, and he assuredly would have done so had their paths crossed. In all likelihood the venerable pioneer was away on a hunting trip when the expedition passed by.[11]

The Corps of Discovery did not have the river to itself. At this season the traffic was heavy as trappers and traders from the Upper Missouri headed for St. Louis in canoes piled high with furs collected during the previous winter. Some of the river travelers passed along useful information. The French-Canadian trader Regis Loisel offered advice about Indian tribes farther upstream and also supplied them with letters of introduction to his associates in the Indian country. A short time later they encountered Pierre Dorion, one of Loisel's interpreters, also on his way to St. Louis. Clark described Dorion, who had lived among the Sioux for twenty years, as "a verry confidential friend of those people." Because Jefferson had stressed the Sioux nation's military and economic importance, the Americans were desirous of finding an interpreter who could speak the Sioux tongue, so it came as no surprise when they struck a deal with Dorion to accompany them back upriver as far as the Sioux coun-

Lewis and Clark at St. Charles, May 21, 1804, by Charles Morgenthaler. Courtesy of First Bank in St. Charles, Missouri.

try. His fluency in the French, English, and Siouan languages made him an ideal candidate.[12]

Indian diplomacy was only one of their many concerns. There were dangers aplenty facing even the most experienced members of the corps. Lewis miraculously escaped serious injury when he lost his footing while scaling the three-hundred-foot Tavern Bluff to take in the commanding view.[13] He somehow managed to halt his plunge, but his near miss must have provided a sobering cautionary note even for Clark. During the early going Lewis frequently went ashore to scout the countryside for "curious plants and shrubs," while Clark typically remained at the helm of the keelboat, directing the crews as they maneuvered the vessels through the perpetual perils of underwater logs and caving banks.[14]

An incident on May 24 put Clark's rivermen to the test when swift currents hurled the keelboat against a sandbar, causing its towrope to sever. Several alarmed crew members struggling to prevent the vessel from capsizing plunged into the water and held onto its upper side. After reattaching the rope they managed to pull the stranded boat into the deeper channel near the bank. It was a harrowing experience, especially for the non-swimmers, but when it was over Clark reported that all were in good spirits.[15]

Captain Clark in all likelihood used that incident at the Devil's Race Grounds to give his men additional instruction in the arts of navigation, and shortly thereafter Captain Lewis issued new orders reorganizing the detachment and regularizing procedures to ensure that each of the boats would be properly manned at all times. The measures proved very salutary. Little more than two weeks later, when one of the boats struck a snag near present-day Arrow Rock, Missouri, Clark proudly heralded his crew's deft handling of the dangerous situation and proclaimed, "I can Say with Confidence that our party is not inferior to any that was ever on the waters of the Missoppie."[16] Such conduct may even have allowed Clark to dare to hope that the unruly corps might yet coalesce into a cohesive and disciplined unit.

The men's strenuous labors produced hearty appetites. To supplement the daily rations dispensed from the company's stores of dried corn, Indian meal, flour, salt pork, and grease or lard, hunters from the party routinely scoured the countryside in search of fresh meat. During this initial leg of their journey, wild game was abundant. On June 30 Clark observed "Deer to be Seen in every direction and their tracks ar[e] as plenty as Hogs about a farm, our [hunters] Killed 9 Deer today."[17] They did not want for food, but the lack of vegetables and fruit in their diet undoubtedly contributed to such chronic complaints as dysentery and boils, painful disorders that Clark knew about firsthand.

As corps members settled into their routines, Clark was freer to leave the boats and reconnoiter the countryside. On a June morning when fierce headwinds momentarily had stalled the expedition's progress, he disembarked and began walking along the shoreline across the river from the high bluff in western Missouri where he later erected Fort Osage. Making use of the skills he had first learned as a young lad in Kentucky, he killed a deer, established a camp, and built a fire while waiting for the stranded boats to catch up with him. When the gusty winds persisted, Clark anticipated a lengthy stay and elected to go hunting on a nearby willow-covered island. Unfortunately, when he attempted to cross to the isle, he became mired in mud and had to crawl back to the shore. Even Clark was able to see the humor in his predicament as he dragged his mud-covered body back to his camp.

Once there, he scraped off the mud, washed his clothes, and fired his gun to signal his location. George Drouillard, who had been dispatched to find him, quickly answered with a second salute. By the time the expedition's premier hunter reached Clark's encampment at dusk, he had bagged a fat bear and a deer. They cooked some of the meat on a fire that Clark had stoked in an effort to drive away the swarming mosquitoes and gnats, and following their hearty repast, the two weary men quickly fell asleep on beds made from bark that Clark had peeled from nearby trees. The following morning the duo rejoined the boats with the remnants of their game in tow.[18] William Clark's wilderness skills were still very much intact.

Clark, who clearly enjoyed such diversionary jaunts, often strolled along the riverbank. Three weeks later while on one of those outings he followed some fresh animal tracks across a small wooded strip that unexpectedly opened onto a boundless grass-covered prairie stretching as far as the eye could see. He commented in his journal, "This prospect was So Sudden & entertaining that I forgot the object of my prosute [pursuit] and turned my attention to the Variety which presented themselves to my view."[19] It was easy for a curious explorer to become distracted by the natural beauty that surrounded him at every turn.

As the expedition neared present-day Kansas City, John Collins was up to his old tricks. While on duty, the notorious miscreant tapped the company's whiskey barrel and became inebriated. The errant soldier compounded his offense by inviting his pal Hugh Hall to join in his mischief. Stealing from the corps' scarce liquor supply was serious business, and not surprisingly a court-martial pronounced both men guilty. Collins, by then familiar with the routine, received one hundred lashes and Hall fifty.[20] Such was the nature of frontier army life.

On July 4, 1804, members of the corps marked the twenty-eighth anniversary of American independence by firing the swivel gun mounted on the bow of the keelboat at daybreak and again at twilight. Immediately following the evening volley each man enjoyed an extra gill of whiskey dispensed in honor of a day that had special meaning for William Clark, whose family members had been ardent patriots in 1776. But on that particular anniversary day Clark did not confine his thoughts to America's past. As he surveyed what to his eyes were lush virgin prairies beyond the pale of civilization, the son of Virginia planters also looked forward and contemplated his countrymen one day transforming these verdant spaces into hay fields and cultivated gardens. Using imagery more characteristic of the romantic style favored by Lewis to describe a scene where "nature appears to have exerted herself to butify the senery by a variety of flours [flowers] <raiseing> Delicately and highly flavered raised above the Grass, which Strikes & profuse the Sensation, and amuses the mind," Clark wondered about the placement of "So magnificent a Senery in a Country thus Situated far removed from the Sivilised world to be enjoyed by nothing but the Buffalo Elk Deer & Bear in which it abounds & [page torn] Savage Indians."[21]

Later that month the Corps of Discovery observed a milestone of its own when it reached the mouth of the Platte River, an important reference point for travelers on the Missouri, above which the mighty river's currents slowed down appreciably. Since its departure from Camp River Dubois, the expedition had followed the meandering but fast-flowing river for 642 miles, and in recognition of their steady progress the captains pitched camp at a place they dubbed Camp White Catfish for a few days of rest and recuperation. Cognizant that they were approaching the heart of Indian Country, Lewis and Clark took advantage of their layover to dispatch George Drouillard and Pierre Cruzatte to summon leaders from nearby Oto and Pawnee villages for a meeting with their new "American fathers." To this point on the journey, they had encountered relatively few native people since their departure from St. Louis.[22]

While they waited for the arrival of emissaries from the neighboring tribes, the men used their respite at Camp White Catfish to dry out goods that had become soaked during the trip upriver. For his part, Clark seized the opportunity to work on his sketch map of the lower Missouri and its tributaries. Unable to maintain a steady hand on the wind-tossed barge, he moved his writing desk to a tent in the nearby woods where he had to battle mosquitoes the size of houseflies.

Clark continued drawing in his solitary refuge until the scouts returned with a report that the Oto and Pawnee tribes were still out on the prairies hunting. Disappointed, but with no more time to spare, the corps broke camp and moved on. A short time later when Drouillard unexpectedly encountered a small Oto hunting party, he hastily invited the band to parley with the Americans at a nearby prominence Lewis and Clark would dub "Council Bluff." The captains welcomed the opportunity and began preparing to initiate their much-anticipated meetings with western tribes.

As he waited for the Oto delegation to arrive, William Clark celebrated his thirty-fourth birthday on August 1, 1804. Then at the midpoint of his life, Clark remained unmarried and childless, his labors had earned him few monetary rewards, and he had yet to settle firmly upon his life's work. But for the moment he was embarked upon a great adventure with his friend Lewis, and that was good enough. Less inclined than his partner to introspection on such occasions, Clark contented himself with a hearty meal before matter-of-factly recording the day's events in his journal:

> a fair morning. Sent out two men after the horses & one back to examine if the Indians have been there, [blank] Beever Cought last night, the air is Cool and pleasing Prepared the Pipe of Peace verry flashey. wind rose at 10 oClock and blowed from the W.S.W. . . . those Prairies produce the Blue Current Common in the U.S. the Goose Berry Common in the U.s, two Kind of Honeysuckle which I have Seen in Kentucky, with a paile Pink flower, also one which grow in Clusters about 4 or 5 feet high bearing a Short flour in clusters of the like Colour. the leaves Single. 3 Deer & an Elk Killed to day. This being my birth day I order'd a Saddle of fat Vennison, an Elk fleece & a Bevertail to be cooked and a Desert of Cheries, Plumbs, Respberries Currents and grapes of a Supr. Quality. The Indians not yet arrived. A Cool fine eveninge Mus-

quetors verry troublesome, the Praries Contain Cheres, Apple, Grapes, Currents, Rasp burry, Gooseberris Hastlenuts and a great Variety of Plants & flours not Common to the U S. What a field for a Botents [botanist] and a natirless [naturalist]

Mosquitoes aside, it had been a pretty good day.[23]

At sunset on the following day six chiefs and headmen representing the Oto and Missouri nations arrived at Council Bluff, where they exchanged warm greetings with the Americans, who offered them food and tobacco. The Indians reciprocated with a gift of several watermelons. Despite the cordial atmosphere, each side remained wary of the other's intent. Clark recorded in his journal "[every?] man on his Guard & ready for any thing."[24] The cautious Clark had been raised to believe that native people were bloodthirsty "savages," and his experiences in the Indian wars on the Kentucky and Ohio frontiers had reinforced those popular images.

As he and his partner prepared for their first formal meeting with an Indian delegation since leaving St. Louis, they were eager to get things right. Drawing inspiration from an idealistic scheme for persuading western tribes to abandon their savage and nomadic habits in favor of the sedentary and more productive ways of their Euro-American neighbors and to encourage trade with them, Jefferson had instructed Lewis and Clark to

> treat [the natives] in the most friendly & conciliatory manner which their own conduct will admit; ally all jealousies as the object of your journey, satisfy them of it's innocence, make them acquainted with the position, extent, character, peaceable & commercial dispositions of the U.S.[,] of our wish to be neighborly, friendly & useful to them, & of our dispositions to a commercial intercourse with them . . .[25]

Given their predisposition to view the Indians with fear and distrust, it was a tall order. How in a brief exchange did one convey Jefferson's complicated message to peoples who knew little about the Americans or their ways? In arranging the session, Lewis and Clark resorted to the practices and protocols that had evolved during long years of negotiations with eastern woodland tribes.

Not surprisingly, the proceedings at Council Bluff, albeit on a smaller scale, bore a striking resemblance to those Clark had witnessed as a young soldier at Vincennes and Fort Greenville. The American troops paraded in dress uniform before their Indian guests who had assembled under the shade of an awning hastily fashioned from the barge's mainsail. In accordance with the president's directives, Captain Lewis delivered a lengthy speech in which he attempted to acquaint the tribal leaders with the U.S. government's peaceful intent and its

Captains Lewis and Clark Holding Council with Indians. The expedition's coleaders held frequent councils with the native people they encountered during their western tour. In this woodcut published in the 1810 edition of Patrick Gass's account of Lewis and Clark's journey, the military uniforms are historically accurate, but the Indian costumes are not. Courtesy of the Library of Congress.

interest in promoting trade. The American colors symbolically flapped in the breeze on a nearby standard as one of the chiefs responded to Lewis's message with an obliging nod and a special plea for a dram of whiskey and a little powder. Clark's closing remarks quickly became ancient history once he spread out an assortment of medals and presents he had selected from the expedition's stores for distribution among the tribal leaders. Captain Lewis concluded the event by demonstrating the air gun specially made for him in Philadelphia by gunsmith Isaiah Lukens. That remarkable weapon, capable of firing multiple shots without reloading or producing any sign of smoke, seldom failed to evoke a response of puzzlement and awe. Everyone at the Council Bluff gathering seemed pleased with what had transpired, most of all the American captains, who viewed the proceedings as a trial run for future conferences with the more numerous tribes awaiting them upriver.[26]

Challenges of a different sort soon demanded the attention of the expedition's commanders. The day after they broke camp at Council Bluff, Private Moses Reed announced that he had left his knife behind. The captains gave him leave to retrieve it, but when he failed to return within a reasonable time, they correctly surmised that he and the French boatman known as La Liberté had fled into the wilderness. Desertion was a capital offense, and the commanders wasted little time before dispatching four men with orders to track down the missing men and bring them back "dead or alive."[27] They successfully apprehended both deserters, but while en route back to camp, the French engagé slipped away from his captors and took refuge among the Otoes. Reed was less fortunate. Once in custody he confessed to having "Deserted & Stold a public Rifle Shot-pouch Powder & Bals." Lewis and Clark ordered him dishonorably discharged, required him to run the gauntlet four times and assigned him to perform hard labor until he could be returned to St. Louis. Clark estimated that Reed probably received fifteen hundred lashes.[28]

After having missed the conference with the Americans, the influential Oto and Missouri tribal leaders Little Thief and Big Horse belatedly arrived at the camp to plead for U.S. assistance in arranging a truce with rival Omaha leaders, who were still out in the prairies on their summer hunt. Eager to proceed, Lewis and Clark declined to wait for the Omaha to return. Their refusal irked Little Thief and Big Horse, who went away disgruntled and unmoved by the presents the Americans had given them. By then Clark's thoughts were elsewhere as he turned his attention to caring for the seriously ill Sergeant Charles Floyd.[29]

Clark first mentioned the soldier's sickness on July 30, and in the ensuing days the young Kentuckian, whose father had served with George Rogers Clark, took a turn for the worse. All attempts to treat what Clark called bilious colic had failed to halt his decline, and by August 19 his condition had so deteriorated that Clark elected to sit with him through most of that night. Sensing that the end was near, Floyd told Clark that "he was going away" and asked him to write a letter, presumably to his parents. A short time later with Clark at his side, the young soldier expired "with a great deel of composure." Charles Floyd was only twenty-two.[30]

The saddened members of the corps buried their comrade with full military honors on a high bluff overlooking the Missouri at present-day Sioux City, Iowa, where they erected a cedar post bearing his name, rank, and date of death. Lewis read the funeral service for a man who according to Clark "at all times gave us proofs of his firmness and Deturmined resolution to doe Service to his Countrey and honor to himself." Sergeant Floyd, the expedition's only fatality, in all likelihood died from the complications of a ruptured appendix, though some medical authorities have hypothesized that he may have suffered from tularemia, a disease spread by ticks and flies or by eating infected wild game. Whatever the cause, it was a very somber moment for all of the corps, but especially for William Clark, who had recruited him and also knew his family.[31]

Two days later Captains Lewis and Clark polled members of the corps to

Floyd's Grave Where Lewis and Clark Bury Sergeant Floyd, by George Catlin. The grave site of the expedition's only casualty is situated on a bluff overlooking the Missouri River near present-day Council Bluffs, Iowa. Courtesy of the Smithsonian American Art Museum.

ascertain their preferences for Floyd's replacement as a sergeant. When the votes were tallied, Patrick Gass was the clear winner. In announcing his appointment to fill the vacant post, the commanding officers declared that this expression of confidence by a large majority of his comrades "further confirmed . . . the high opinion they had previously formed of the capacity deligence and integrety of Sergt. Gass."[32]

As the Pennsylvania-born soldier with a knack for carpentry took up his new sergeant's duties, the corps entered the arid, windswept High Plains. In his journal Clark reported marked changes in the landscape as well as in the flora and fauna. When he and Lewis set out to visit a place known to the Indians as the mountain of evil spirits, they had no difficulty locating the conical shaped South Dakota landmark because, Clark noted, "the Surrounding Plains is open void of Timber and leavel to a great extent." Local native people considered the site haunted and stayed away, but Lewis and Clark, dismissive of what they viewed as Indian superstition, scaled the sacred mound for a better view of the seemingly endless stretches of treeless, grassy prairies dotted with grazing elk and buffalo. In an effort to refute Indian claims that the flocks of birds peren-nially swarming about Spirit Mound indicated a spiritual presence, the ratio-nalist Clark concluded that in truth they were attracted by insects propelled there by the force of the local winds.[33]

At the mouth of the James River three young Indian lads advised the cap-tains that a large Sioux party was encamped nearby. Sergeant Pryor and the in-terpreter Dorion immediately sought them out for the purpose of arranging a council. At the time, Clark was feeling unwell as a consequence of an upset he attributed to some spoiled hominy, but by the following day he had recovered sufficiently to work on a speech for the upcoming meeting with the Sioux.[34]

Presently, Dorion showed up accompanied by seventy Yankton Sioux, the first bona fide nomadic Plains Indians Lewis and Clark had encountered. The numerous Sioux, who were relative newcomers to the High Plains, had moved west, acquired horses, and adopted a nomadic lifestyle that enabled them to occupy a crucial role as suppliers and middlemen in a trade involving the ex-change of buffalo from the western hunting grounds, agricultural products from the river villages, and merchandise from Canadian-based British traders. The Americans sent the Yanktons a few token gifts to facilitate Dorion's prepa-rations for the upcoming assemblage. At high noon the following day the well-decorated Sioux delegation, decked out with paint, porcupine quills, feathers, bear claws, leggings, moccasins, and different-colored buffalo robes, gathered under the shade of an oak tree. A few carried fusils but most bore only bows and arrows. The finely attired females who accompanied them were dressed in petticoats and white buffalo robes.[35]

Not to be outshone by their native counterparts, the American soldiers donned their blue and red dress uniforms for the occasion. Lewis initiated the proceed-ings by delivering the remarks that Clark had composed for the occasion framed in the stilted parlance used for Indian diplomacy. The message adhered to the prescribed script by extolling the benefits of trade with the Americans and urging the Sioux to make peace with their neighbors. Because of Jeffer-son's special interest in the Sioux nation, Lewis invited their leaders to send a delegation to confer with their new Great Father at his home on the distant eastern shore of this great island they inhabited.[36]

The captains presented the principal chief, Shake Hand, with a red officer's coat, a cocked hat with a red plume, an American flag, a commission, and a large medal bearing Jefferson's image, all symbols designed to convey U.S au-thority. Four lesser chiefs received gifts appropriate to their status. After pass-ing around the ceremonial pipe, the Indians retired to divide up their presents, smoke, and eat. When the Sioux began their ceremonial dances that night, the Americans courteously stayed late to witness the performances.[37]

The following day the Yankton chiefs and headmen had their chance to speak. They welcomed the promises of friendship and trade while reminding the Americans that they had received similar assurances in the past from the Spaniards and the British. The Yanktons emphasized their needs and made it clear that they expected the Americans to hold fast to their promises to send traders to their villages. They also availed themselves of the opportunity to ask Lewis and Clark for ammunition and whiskey. After listening to Dorion's interpretation of the Indian speeches, Clark gave a brief reply from the notes that he had scribbled hastily. With so much at stake, diplomats on both sides had to choose their words carefully. From Clark's point of view all had gone according to plan and there was reason to be pleased, but he might have done well to ponder the ominously prophetic, cautionary utterances of one chief who had warned: "I fear those nations above will not open their ears, and you cannot I fear open them."[38]

Before saying his good-byes to Dorion, now reassigned to escort a party of Sioux leaders eastward to confer with U.S. officials, Clark asked for some last-minute assistance with the Sioux vocabulary he was compiling. It was tedious and exacting work, for as Clark later observed, "In taking vocabularies [the] great object was to make every letter sound." More useful for Clark's purposes was the information he gained from Dorion during those parting moments concerning tribal customs and internal Sioux divisions.[39]

By early September there was already a chill in the morning air, a sure signal that winter came sooner on the High Plains. Almost daily Lewis and Clark discovered new and unfamiliar animals that needed to be catalogued and described for science—mule deer, pronghorns, jackrabbits, magpies, and coyotes, to name a few. The cute but elusive prairie dogs particularly captivated the American explorers. When they came upon a prairie dog town that according to Clark's reckoning covered four acres, the men scrambled to capture some of the distinctive little creatures, first by digging into their holes and when that failed by pouring several barrels of water into their underground tunnels. For all of their exertions, they managed to capture only two of the furry critters, one dead and the other alive. This surely was an animal worthy of President Jefferson's attention.[40]

Joy reigned supreme in the camp on September 11 when the missing George Shannon, gaunt and bedraggled, rejoined the company after spending "12 days without any thing to eate but Grapes & one Rabit, which he Killed by shooting a piece of hard Stick in place of a ball."[41] Shannon, a notoriously poor hunter, had become separated from the others while pursuing some of the expedition's lost horses. After Sergeant Floyd's death, Clark must have been much relieved not to lose another of the Kentucky recruits.

A two-day hiatus in mid-September ordered for the purpose of drying out

rain-soaked baggage and equipment afforded Lewis and Clark an opportunity
to take stock of their situation. They reconsidered their original plan for sending Corporal Richard Warfington's contingent back to St. Louis with dispatches,
journals, reports, and assorted plant and animal specimens intended for Jefferson and other government officials prior to the onset of winter. Since both men
needed additional time before submitting those items for the president's inspection, they agreed to delay Warfington's departure until spring.[42]

Not long after passing Loisel's trading post on Cedar Island, Clark began observing renewed signs of recent Indian activity as he trudged over the rough
ground overgrown with the ubiquitous prickly pear, which, he complained,
"nearly ruined [my] feet."[43] Three boys who swam out to meet the American
boats confirmed that they were nearing the Teton Sioux villages. The captains
dispatched the Indian lads to the Teton camp with twists of tobacco and an invitation for tribal leaders to meet the Americans at the mouth of the Bad River
the following day.

Lewis and Clark had long anticipated meeting the fractious and formidable
Tetons, who called themselves Lakota. Having learned from St. Louis–based
traders of the tribe's penchant for harassing river travelers, the American captains braced themselves for what proved to be a dramatic encounter with the
Brulé, one of seven bands of the Lakota tribe, at Bad River at the site of present-
day Pierre, South Dakota. Both sides had much at stake as they contested for
control of the river and trade in the region. The well-armed Americans with
their seemingly ample stores of weapons and merchandise posed a threat to
the tribe's dominance in the area, and the Brulé leaders were determined to
exact a price before allowing the expedition to proceed. For their part, Lewis
and Clark sought an alliance with the powerful Lakota bands that would acknowledge U.S. sovereignty and allow American traders to operate in the region with the intent of driving out the well-entrenched British operatives then
doing business with the Brulé.[44]

Over the course of the next four days, a tense confrontation unfolded as the
wary parties faced off against one another. During their first meeting Lewis
and Clark offered the Brulé tribal leaders Black Buffalo, the Partisan, and Buffalo Medicine gifts of food. Not to be outdone, the Lakota chiefs reciprocated
by providing the Americans with meat. Those ritualistic gestures failed to reduce the underlying tensions. The absence of a qualified interpreter hindered
efforts to communicate, and the resulting confusion prompted Lewis to cut
short his prepared remarks and move ahead to the parading of the troops and
the distribution of gifts, activities designed to produce a positive response. The
complexities of intratribal politics also intruded. A decision to award Black
Buffalo a military coat and hat angered his rival the Partisan, who felt slighted.[45]

Lewis and Clark's attempts to awe and entertain the Brulé delegation with a demonstration featuring the scientific instruments and assorted curiosities they carried with them proved less enticing than a jug of whiskey. The visiting chiefs, who had come aboard the keelboat, quickly emptied the bottle, and when the captains declined to offer them more, they registered loud complaints. The Partisan feigned drunkenness, according to Clark, "as a Cloake for his rascally intentions." In his dealings with native people, Clark was predisposed to classify Indians as either good or bad, and he had no difficulty in placing the Brulé Sioux in the latter category. Sensing trouble, Clark removed the rowdy chiefs from the boat. With the assistance of a small military detachment he escorted them to the shore, where he still hoped to effect reconciliation. They went reluctantly, and when their pirogue reached land, three of the young Sioux seized the cable while another hugged the mast. The Partisan declared that since the Americans had not provided sufficient presents they would not be allowed to proceed. Obviously irritated, Clark vowed not to accede to such bullying and drew his sword while his partner, who had remained on board the keelboat, ordered the troops to prepare to defend themselves. Clark's dramatic gesture underscored the seriousness of the situation, but his composure under duress ultimately contributed to defusing the tension. According to corpsman Robert Frazer's recollection sixteen years later, at Captain Lewis's direction he had been set to discharge the swivel gun until Captain Clark signaled for him to hold his fire. Fearful that innocent bystanders might be harmed, Black Buffalo responded by seizing the rope and commanding the youthful warriors to withdraw.[46]

Still surrounded, Clark ordered his military escort back to the keelboat and chose to stand his ground with only the interpreters at his side. A war of words ensued between the chiefs and Clark, who made it clear that his party intended to proceed upriver. Declaring that "we [are] not squaws but warriors," Clark warned them that their great father the president of the United States possessed vast power. The Brulé countered with their own threats, but when a larger well-armed military contingent again came ashore to assist Clark, the chiefs retreated to confer with one another. After waiting a few minutes for a reply, Clark offered his hand in friendship to Black Buffalo and the Partisan, but they refused to shake. Thus rebuffed, Clark and his troops climbed into the pirogue and rowed back to the barge. In an effort to prevent them from leaving without distributing additional gifts, Black Buffalo and three other tribesmen waded in after the Americans, asking to join them on the keelboat. Clark relented and allowed them on board before raising anchor and proceeding about a mile to a willow-covered island where they posted guards and retired for the night.[47]

They awakened the next morning to discover that a sizable Sioux party had followed them upriver and was waiting for them onshore. At the request of Black Buffalo, who was still on the boat, Lewis and Clark agreed to permit the women and children to inspect the vessel. Gradually the Brulé leaders softened their tone and expressed a desire to entertain the American travelers properly, perhaps believing that their example might inspire the parsimonious Americans to greater generosity. Still desirous of coming to an understanding with the Brulé, Lewis accepted their invitation and went ashore. When he failed to return after three hours, an uneasy Clark sent one of the sergeants to check on his partner. He came back a short time later to report that all was well and that Lewis had consented to remain there for the night.[48]

When Clark joined Lewis on land, the waiting Indians picked him up and carried him on an elegantly painted buffalo robe to the council lodge, where as a mark of respect they placed him next to Black Buffalo. Shortly thereafter Lewis was brought in, in a similar fashion. The U.S. flag that Lewis and Clark had given the chief was on display, and so were the Spanish colors, but the Americans chose not to make it an issue. Following the ritualistic smoking of the ceremonial pipe and routine speechmaking, Black Buffalo spread before his guests a feast of Teton dishes. Clark partook only sparingly of the dog meat, a Teton delicacy, opting for the pemmican and potatoes instead.[49]

At dusk the food was cleared away and the Indians began dancing and singing to the accompaniment of tambourines and instruments made from deer and goat hooves. According to Clark, several highly decorated women came forward carrying poles to which they had attached scalps, guns, spears, and war implements taken by their male relatives as trophies of war. This war dance was no doubt intended to impress the visiting Americans in the same way that their military parades had been designed to overawe the Indians. It was a game that two could play. At midnight the captains excused themselves, declined the offer of Indian women for the night, and retired to their boats. The custom of providing obliging female companions was intended as a gesture of hospitality and an instrument of diplomacy, and their refusal was interpreted as a rebuke.[50]

Clark did not sleep well that night, and apparently neither did the Indians. Early the next morning the four chiefs who had spent the night on the boat continued importuning the captains not to depart. The Americans agreed to stay after being told that another large Sioux contingent was expected that evening. When Clark was returning to the keelboat following the nightly festivities, a crewman steering the pirogue lost control and snapped the anchor cable attached to the larger vessel. Clark ordered all of the men to their stations to steady the keelboat that had been set adrift. Hearing all of the commotion, the Indians onshore rushed to the scene in response to rumors that the Omaha were attacking. In short order two hundred Sioux warriors showed up ready for action. When it became clear what had happened, some of them withdrew but others remained at the ready. Their presence alarmed Lewis and Clark, who feared that they intended to rob the anchorless boat. It was to be another sleepless night for Clark.[51]

The situation did not improve on the following day. Having failed to find the anchor now buried somewhere in the sand, the captains improvised and ordered it replaced with rocks so they could resume their journey upriver. Once again the Indians attempted to block their departure. Wearied by their lengthy and sometimes unpleasant dealings with this band, the American commanders were determined to brook no further delays. Yet again they resorted to a threat of force as Clark stood next to the swivel cannon with a lighted fuse in his hand. As a final parting gesture, Clark threw a few twists of tobacco to one of the chiefs, telling him that if he was the great man he claimed to be he should take the tobacco and show his influence by allowing them to proceed without further interference. This final showdown ended peacefully when the Sioux leader jerked the rope from the hands of one of his young guards and handed it to the bowsman. The tense days and nights had taken a toll on Clark, who reported that he was feeling unwell, but as they began to distance themselves from the contentious band he finally enjoyed a good night's rest.[52]

The confrontations at Bad River had been a contest of wills, and while the Americans refused to allow the Tetons to intimidate them, the powerful Sioux remained similarly unbowed within the confines of their Upper Missouri strongholds. The tortuous diplomatic maneuvering made it possible to avoid bloodshed, but otherwise the situation remained as muddled as ever. Throughout the ordeal William Clark held his own. His calm and deliberate conduct prompted Sergeant John Ordway to observe, "Capt. Clark used moderation with them." Such restraint surely tested the patience of Clark, who branded the Tetons "great rascals [that] may be justly termed the pirates of the Missouri," but the incident must have been equally trying for Sioux leaders determined to maintain their dominant position in that country.[53]

With the encounter at the Bad River barely behind them, members of the exploring party began noticing abandoned Arikara earth lodge villages emptied a few years earlier by a smallpox epidemic. On October 8 the Americans made their first contact with the diminished but still formidable tribe that cultivated corn, beans, squash, and tobacco, hunted, and traded their surpluses for British trade goods acquired from the Sioux and other neighboring western tribes. Clark described the sedentary Arikaras as "Dirty, Kind, pore, & extravegent, possessing natural pride." As was so often the case, Clark's disparagements spoke as much to his generalized beliefs about the retarded state of Indian development and the superiority of Euro-American ways as it did to the realities of Arikara life.[54]

Given their recent experiences with the Tetons, Lewis and Clark were understandably wary as they approached the river dwellers. While Captain Lewis set out to confer with Arikara leaders, Captain Clark remained at the ready, posting a military guard on shore and a sentinel on the boat. In his journal he wrote, "all things arranged both for Peace or War."[55] Such measures proved unnecessary as the Arikaras extended a welcoming hand to the Americans. Rain and strong winds that by Clark's reckoning produced waves "as high as [he] ever Saw them in the Missouri" forced a one-day delay in their talks. Their abbreviated sessions followed the now predictable routine of speechmaking and gift exchanges, but it was York who stole the show. According to Clark, "Those Indians wer much astonished at my Servent, They never Saw a black man before, all flocked around him & examind. him from top to toe, he Carried on the joke and made himself more turibal than we wished him to doe." He added that York built upon his celebrity by displaying his strength and regaling his audience with tall tales. It was a novel and welcome experience for the African American slave to be the center of so much attention and admiration, and clearly he made the most of it.[56]

Clark reported receiving "every civility" from their hosts, who eagerly sought U.S. assistance for ending conflict with the neighboring Mandans in the hope that they could woo them away from their associations with the Sioux. Once again Captains Lewis and Clark claimed to have declined the companionship of women offered by tribal elders as a token of friendship, but other members of the corps proved more susceptible to the attentions of the Arikara women, who according to Clark were "verry fond of caressing our men &c."[57] If Salish and Nez Perce oral traditions are to be believed, Clark was not always so chaste.

On October 13 the commanders ordered Private John Newman confined on charges of mutinous expressions. Although the records do not indicate the precise nature of the infraction, it was serious enough to merit a sentence of seventy-five lashes and his removal from the corps. The switching greatly distressed the Arikara chief Eagle Feather, who explained to Clark that his people considered such demeaning treatment a worse fate than execution. The Arikara, he noted, did not even whip children. No doubt he would have been equally astonished to learn that such punishments were regularly meted out to African American slaves such as Clark's servant York, who had made such an impression on his people.[58]

Bridging cultural gaps was seldom easy. A few short days after the Newman

York, watercolor by Charles M. Russell, 1908, photo by John Smart, 1986. This twen-
tieth artistic representation of York at the Mandan/Hidatsa villages made heavy use
of Karl Bodmer's paintings of the Mandans. Courtesy of the Montana Historical
Society.

incident, Eagle Feather, known to his tribesmen as Piahito, joined Clark and
interpreter Joseph Gravelines for a hunting expedition. As they strolled through
the countryside, Clark's companions regaled him with "many extraordinary
stories." After listening to Eagle Feather's explanations of Arikara traditions
about turtles, snakes, and the spiritual powers of a special rock or cave on a
nearby river, Clark shrugged them off as mere superstition and declared them
not worth mentioning. The explorer's bent toward scientific investigation
made him more receptive to Gravelines's explanation of the migratory patterns of the pronghorn herds they observed moving downriver.[59]

    There were new discoveries of other kinds. On October 20 Pierre Cruzatte
became the first corpsman to meet up with a live grizzly, an animal that expedition members erroneously referred to as the white bear. The one-eyed fiddle
player wounded the beast while hunting, and its ferocious appearance so alarmed
him that he fled the scene, leaving behind both his tomahawk and his gun.
When Cruzatte returned to retrieve his weapons, the fierce creature had de-

parted, but the tale of his encounter did nothing to diminish the animal's notorious reputation among his traveling companions.[60] Two days later a violent attack of "rheumatism in the neck" laid Clark low. The severe pain virtually immobilized him until Lewis's application of a heated stone wrapped in flannel brought temporary relief, and none too soon. For on that very day they came upon a Teton Sioux party suspected of stealing horses from the Mandans. When Lewis and Clark declined to respond to their calls for assistance, the Sioux withdrew to the satisfaction of the American party. Their departure eliminated the most immediate source of concern, but Clark's stiff neck continued to trouble him for several more days.[61]

As the expedition moved in the direction of the Mandan and Hidatsa towns in central North Dakota, a light dusting of snow provided a sure sign that winter was fast approaching. Despite the close proximity of their villages and their similar agrarian lifeways, the Mandan and Hidatsas were distinct tribes with different languages. On October 24 members of the corps met a Mandan chief out on a hunting trip and were reassured by his warm welcome and his willingness to smoke with their Arikara traveling companion Eagle Feather. They mistakenly interpreted his actions as an endorsement for their plan to arrange a peace between those two tribes and unite them in an alliance against the troublesome Sioux.[62]

For the Mandans, these American newcomers were simply the latest in a long line of strangers who had come to their villages seeking friendship and trade. The Mandan and Hidatsa towns were crucial hubs in a vast northern plains network that annually brought large numbers of Indian and white traders to their doorsteps. Despite their earlier losses to the ravages of smallpox, the Mandan and Hidatsa villages along the Missouri and Knife rivers retained a combined population of perhaps as many as six thousand, perhaps six times the number of people who then called St. Louis home. The Upper Missouri villagers turned out to observe the little American fleet as it approached. On October 26, Captain Lewis hastily made his way to Mitatunka, the first of the Mandan towns and the home of Shehekshote or White Coyote. The village with its dome-shaped earth lodges was soon to become a familiar haunt for the visiting Americans, especially after they erected their winter headquarters just across the river from it. Clark, still complaining of a sore neck, remained on board the keelboat, where he hosted a deputation that stopped by for a smoke.[63]

The following day he felt good enough to visit Mitatunka, and while there he met René Jusseaume, a resident trader who had once spied for George Rogers Clark in the Illinois Country. Past services notwithstanding, William Clark judged Jusseaume to be cunning, artful, and insincere. No doubt recalling the difficulties they had encountered in making themselves understood to the Brulé

Bird's Eye View of Mandan Village, by George Catlin. During the expedition's winter sojourn at Fort Mandan in 1804–1805, Clark occasionally visited the nearby Mandan villages. Courtesy of the Smithsonian American Art Museum.

Sioux, the American captains set aside their initial misgivings about the Frenchman and employed him as an interpreter anyway.[64] At a second Mandan village located on a nearby elevated plain overlooking the river, Lewis next conferred with Black Cat or Posecopsahe, whom the Americans subsequently determined to be the principal Mandan chief. As with neighboring Mitatunka, the sizable earthen lodges at Black Cat's village were surrounded with a picket stockade.[65]

Captain Lewis invited representatives from the two Mandan towns and the three nearby Knife River Hidatsa villages to attend a general council on October 28. Many of the Minataris or "Big Bellies," as Lewis and Clark called the Hidatsas, showed up for the gathering, but gale-force winds prevented representatives from Mitatunka from crossing the river and forced a postponement of the meeting. While they awaited the arrival of the delegation from White Coyote's town, Lewis and Clark quizzed Jusseaume and Black Cat about some of the participants who would be attending the conference. The council assembled the following day in a makeshift shelter fashioned out of boat sails and designed to shield the gathering from the gusty winds that already had delayed the proceedings. Lewis's lengthy oration advised the Missouri River tribes that they were now under the rule of the Americans, who henceforth would supply them with trade goods from St. Louis. He also urged the Mandans and Hidatsas to come to terms with the neighboring Arikaras, and to the delight of the American captains, leaders from both tribes smoked a ceremonial pipe held out by Eagle Feather. It was only later that they learned that an exchange out of their hearing had been far less cordial.[66]

Each of the principal chiefs received a medal, a dress uniform, and a few other small presents. Lewis also gave the Mandans a corn grinder, and while they oohed and aahed as was expected, Alexander Henry the younger, a partner in the North West Company and a target of the American scheme to supplant the British traders, later reported, no doubt with glee, that the Mandans had broken up their prized gift and used the metal to make arrow barbs and other similar instruments. Such information would have come as a great surprise to the Americans, but it was one more indicator of the depth of the cultural chasm that Lewis and Clark were expected to bridge.[67]

That evening a prairie fire racing across the distant grass-covered plains momentarily distracted the American officers and their men, but by the next morning the conflagration had burned out, and their thoughts returned to the previous day's negotiations as they anxiously awaited formal replies to their proposals.[68] It was a hopeful sign when representatives from the nearest Mandan village came bearing gifts of corn. The corn was especially welcome, since members of the corps had consumed most of the provisions Clark and his men had packed at Camp River Dubois. The responses from the Hidatsas were slower to come and more ambiguous. Boasts about America's great military power had alarmed and annoyed the wary tribe that maintained close ties with British traders from the Hudson's Bay and North West companies.

With cold weather fast approaching, Lewis and Clark understood that they needed to decide upon a location for their winter headquarters before the Missouri iced over. A short reconnaissance convinced Clark that the scarcity of both wood and game farther upriver dictated a site somewhere below their current encampment. Clark found a suitable place well supplied with wood a few miles below the Knife River on the Missouri's north bank, just across from Mitutanka. Lewis concurred with Clark's choice, and by early November work was under way there on a fortified structure that the Americans called Fort Mandan in honor of their neighbors. That came as good news to Shehekshote, who was understandably eager to have the American commissary near his village and less accessible to the rival Hidatsas.[69]

For the third time in his military career, Clark found himself charged with building a frontier military installation from the ground up. The sudden flurry of activity attracted many visitors to the construction site, including Toussaint Charbonneau, a French-Canadian trader who resided at one of the Hidatsa towns. Clark gave this accounting of their initial meeting: "a french man by Name Chabonah, who Speaks the Big Belly language visit us, he wished to hire & informed us his 2 Squars were Snake Indians, we engau him to go on with us and take one of his wives to interpet the Snake language." The decision to employ Charbonneau and his young wife, Sacagawea, as interpreters unexpectedly added a woman to the ranks of the all-male party.[70]

A Shoshone by birth, she had been taken captive in a war with the Hidatsas, who had given her the name Sacagawea or Bird Woman. Charbonneau's second Shoshone wife was known as Otter Woman. As Clark's journal makes clear, Charbonneau had used the Shoshone women's linguistic skills to help him wrangle an interpreter's job from the Americans. After the expedition ended, Lewis awarded the Frenchman barely passing marks for his performance. Clark, in contrast, had warmed to Charbonneau and Sacagawea and their young son Jean Baptiste, dubbed by Clark as "Pomp." Clark's fondness for the Charbonneau family is unquestioned, but even though he and Lewis later shared the Indian tipi they used for their quarters onshore with Bird Woman and Pomp, contrary to later mythology there is not a scintilla of evidence to suggest that Clark and Sacagawea were ever romantically involved.

Fort Mandan began to take shape as the work crews felled the towering cottonwood trees and hauled the heavy timbers to the construction site. Patrick Gass, the expedition's most skilled carpenter, and British trader François Antoine Larocque left the only descriptions of the log fort that served as a winter quarters for the corps. The A-shaped fortress's two sides each contained four huts below with a second story above for storage, and in the angle between the two rows of cabins they built two storage rooms. The fort's third side was enclosed with a large picket stockade fence. With winter fast approaching, the triangular configuration shortened the construction time by eliminating one exterior wall from the traditional square military fortress. By mid-November the cabins were far enough along to permit a transfer of goods and supplies from the boats and to allow the men to occupy their still unfinished spaces. When a hunting party returned on November 19 with a large supply of freshly killed game, an adjacent smokehouse was ready to receive it. Indians from the neighborhood regularly dropped by to inspect the fort's log buildings and stone chimneys as they began to take shape.[71]

In their continuing conversations with the villagers, Lewis and Clark soon detected that at least some of the tribal leaders had developed second thoughts about the wisdom of embracing the American schemes for reorienting the

Sacagawea *(Sakakawea).* Courtesy of the State Historical Society of North Dakota C1109. This statue portraying the expedition's only female member stands on the grounds of the North Dakota State Capitol.

Upper Missouri trading patterns. Fears that former trading partners might retaliate alarmed the Mandans, and their neighbors the Hidatsas had really never signed on to the U.S. proposition in the first place. Despite his close proximity, Hidatsa chief Le Borgne or One Eye visited Fort Mandan only once after their initial conference.

The large number of British traders from the North West and Hudson's Bay companies at work among the Upper Missouri tribes clearly posed a potential obstacle to U.S. designs for the region. In an attempt to ward off possible interference from their agents, Lewis sent Charles Chaboillez, head of North West Company operations on the Assiniboine River, a copy of a British passport instructing His Britannic Majesty's subjects to permit the expedition to pass without hindrance or impediment and to further in any way possible its scientific objects. Jefferson had secured the document from British officials as a precautionary measure after providing assurances that the expedition's purposes were scientific and not commercial. In his letter to the British firm's agent, Lewis requested a "mutual change of good offices."[72]

In late November Nor'Wester François-Antoine Larocque, who was then wintering among the neighboring Hidatsas, accepted Lewis's invitation to come to Fort Mandan. During what was to be the first of many such visits, Lewis and Clark warned him not to distribute British flags and medals among the village tribes. After assuring them that he had no such intention, the trader listened politely as his hosts outlined the new U.S. regime's trading policies, after which he confided privately in his diary that during his stay "a very Grand Plan was schemed, but its taking place is more than I can tell although the Captains say they are well assured it will."[73]

While Lewis continued to work his way through the maze of British and Indian politics, Clark spent much of his time during the final months of 1804 superintending construction at Fort Mandan. In late November a Sioux and Arikara attack on a Mandan hunting party produced a call to action in the American camp. Clark assembled a squad of twenty-three well-armed men and headed for the Mandan town across the river, but the sudden show of force so alarmed the startled villagers that Clark had to scramble to explain he had come to volunteer his services for a joint campaign against the enemy raiders. The incredulous tribal leaders declined his impetuous proposal with assurances that there would be ample opportunities to avenge their losses after the weather improved. Clark came away thinking that his offer had gratified them, but in truth they must have been shaking their heads in disbelief.[74]

Not long thereafter Clark may have figured out why the tribal leaders had been so quick to dismiss his proposal for military action in the dead of winter. He and fifteen of his men had joined a Mandan hunting party, and while they were out, the temperatures fell to twenty-one degrees below zero Fahrenheit, leaving more than a few of their number suffering from frostbite. Clark apparently was not one of them, but he did note that hunting in the ten-inch snow had left him "much fatigued."[75]

Upon his return Clark lined his gloves and had a cap made from the skin of a lynx with three-inch fur. Those efforts came none too soon, for the temperature dropped to forty-three degrees below zero on December 17. It was a good time to stay indoors, and Clark spent much of that cold day conversing with Hugh Heney, a North West Company agent wintering among the Hidatsas. Heney had arrived at Fort Mandan on the sixteenth carrying a letter from his superior Charles Chaboillez promising to assist the Americans in any way he could. Eager to capitalize on the offer, Clark worked his charm on the knowledgeable Nor' Wester, whom he quizzed at length about the Sioux. According to Larocque, Clark took extensive notes and pored over Heney's sketch map of the region between the Mississippi and the Missouri, along with some Indian drawings the British trader had obtained from tribes living farther west. Heney was barely out the door when Clark set about to add this new geographic and ethnographic intelligence to his own maps and charts.[76]

The native resistance to U.S. plans for its newly acquired western territories and the presence of so many British traders in the vicinity of the Upper Missouri convinced Clark that a military presence would be required to secure American control over the region. With that in mind, during his spare time that winter at Fort Mandan, he drew up a plan for a series of frontier forts/trading posts to protect U.S. trading interests, to maintain peaceful relations with the Indians, and to implement the scheme he and Lewis had outlined for Larocque. Historian Ernest S. Osgood called Clark's 1805 document "the first plan for the defense of the Far West." Significantly, over the course of the next several decades the U.S. government established posts in the vicinity of two-thirds of the sites identified by Clark.[77]

The British traders were not the only regular callers at the American winter quarters. Well before the finishing touches had been applied, the installation, which Larocque described "as almost Cannon Ball proof," had become another stop on the Upper Missouri social circuit. Members of the region's culturally diverse trading communities often went calling on their neighbors to escape the boredom that accompanied their lengthy winter confinements, and Clark reported that the Mandan chiefs were fond of staying over at the fort. Christmas Day in 1804 was an exception. On their "great medicine day," the Americans closed the doors to outsiders.[78]

Once the gate swung shut, the celebration began. Two discharges from the swivel gun followed by a round of small arms from the whole corps ushered in this most special of holidays that serendipitously coincided with the fort's completion. Captain Clark gave each man a glass of rum prior to the first official flag-raising ceremony at Fort Mandan. Lewis ordered a second round of Christmas cheer in honor of the day, and the festivities got under way in earnest. Sergeant Ordway reported, "we had the best to eat that could be had & continued firing, dancing & frolicking the whole day." Each mess had been supplied with special rations of flour, dried apples, and pepper to ensure a proper Christmas feast. A few of the men took advantage of the day's warmer temperatures to go hunting, but most remained inside the fort, where they joined in the music and dancing that continued until 9 p.m. In a post-Christmas celebration on the twenty-sixth, Lewis and Clark took time out for a game of backgammon, perhaps the continuation of a match begun the day before.[79]

At the conclusion of their Yuletide festivities, the Americans again rolled out the welcome mat to the steady stream of visitors that traveled up the path to Fort Mandan. In the New Year the blacksmith's forge became the fort's most popular attraction and a profitable enterprise that helped keep members of the corps well supplied with corn. Indians eager to have their metal axes and hoes repaired brought them to the obliging smith, who became a favorite among the visiting Indians. When every last such implement had been put in working order, he began manufacturing war axes to sell for corn. It was a thriving business. One Hidatsa leader, not particularly fond of the Americans, told British trader Charles Mackenzie that the only two sensible men at Fort Mandan were the worker of iron and the maker of guns.[80]

Curious outsiders regularly came to examine the weapons, scientific instruments, and other technological marvels the explorers carried with them, and others arrived simply to while away a few hours swapping stories, exchanging information, and enjoying the company of corps members. Clark particularly welcomed conversations with anyone possessing information about the territory west of Fort Mandan. When White Coyote dined there on January 7 he gave Clark a sketch of the western country as far as the high mountains. Clark continued to produce cartographic sketches that he eventually put together to create what he referred to as a connected plate showing the Missouri all the way to the Great Falls, based upon the information he obtained from Indians and traders along with his own observations and ideas.[81]

Larocque and Mackenzie continued to be regular visitors. In mid-January Larocque was there again, this time to return a book that he had borrowed from the Americans. In view of their warming friendship, he inquired if he might be allowed to accompany them on their journey to the Pacific. When he returned two weeks later to have Lewis repair his compass, he once again pressed for permission to join the expedition. Lewis and Clark firmly rejected the young Canadian's persistent requests. They were not about to allow a foreign national to accompany their military expedition or for that matter to share their geographic discoveries with an agent of the North West Company.[82] Conversely, the British traders did not think much of the American's quixotic schemes for introducing U.S. trading factories into the region.

Larocque's traveling companion Mackenzie acknowledged that the Americans had treated them with "civility and kindness," but he developed a dislike for Captain Lewis, whom he reported "could not make himself agreeable to us—he could speak fluently and learnedly on all subjects, but his inveterate disposition against the British stained, at least in our eyes, all his eloquence."[83]

While clearly no Anglophile, the congenial Clark elicited a more sympathetic reaction because in Mackenzie's words, "his conversation was always pleasant, for he seemed to dislike giving offence unnecessarily." The British trader's characterization was not far from the mark.[84]

The well-worn road leading to the fort was a two-way street that also allowed the Americans to make their way to the nearby Mandan villages. On January 1, 1805, the captains granted permission for sixteen of their men to go to Mitatunka to usher in the New Year. They had been invited to entertain the villagers with the music and dancing that so amused visitors at the fort. The American revelers fired a single volley to announce their arrival at the gates of the neighboring Mandan town. Having captured the attention of their hosts, the musicians in the group launched into a tune using a fiddle, tambourine, and sounding horn and followed it with another salute. For much of the day the jovial celebrants' music and dancing played to rapt audiences. York's agile performance and François Rivet's attempts to dance on his head were especially well received.

At midday Clark made his way to the village to see how things were going and to make amends with tribal members allegedly offended by previous American actions. After making the rounds of most lodges, Clark claimed success and declared that all but a few malcontents were much pleased with the day's proceedings. To show their appreciation, the Mandans offered their guests a diverse sampling of Mandan cuisine and afterward gave members of the traveling troupe three buffalo robes and thirteen strings of corn. Clark returned to the fort early in the evening, and the others straggled in later that night or the following morning, many after accepting more intimate expressions of gratitude from native women. Pleased with their reception, the entertainers next took their show to Black Cat's village, but it was Lewis's turn to monitor those proceedings.[85]

The visits continued throughout the winter. On January 5, 1805, several members of the corps witnessed a performance of the Buffalo dance during which young Mandan males offered their naked wives to tribal elders for sexual purposes in the belief that such ceremonies would draw the buffalo near and that hunting prowess could be transferred from one man to another through sexual relations with the same woman. On that evening several of the expedition's hunters who were in attendance happily embraced an opportunity to participate in the Mandan ritual. All of this was quite baffling to Clark, who described the scene to Nicholas Biddle in 1810 for inclusion in the history of the expedition that he was then preparing for publication. As James P. Ronda has pointed out, Clark was no modern ethnologist, but he did record observations about the things he witnessed. He may have failed to grasp the Indian rationale for peculiar customs, but in the case of the buffalo dance he shunned the prudish moralizing adopted by many of his contemporaries. Biddle considered such practices so scandalous that he chose to render his account in Latin, and Clark's seeming failure to exhibit sufficient moral outrage in this instance later drew a reprimand from England's Poet Laureate Robert Southey.[86]

The interlude at Fort Mandan did allow Lewis and Clark to devote greater attention to the ethnographic assignment Jefferson had given them. Their observations were replete with cultural bias, but the absence of impartial detachment did not negate the value of the information they recorded about indigenous cultures. They accorded some of the items in Jefferson's list of questions greater attention than others, and the Mandans fared better in Clark's descriptions than many of their indigenous counterparts. Their settled and peaceable ways and their prosperity seem to have impressed Clark, who called them "the most friendly, well disposed Indians inhabiting the Missouri. They are brave, humane and hospitable." In his observations Clark was particularly attentive to matters involving tribal polity and decision-making. Indeed his preoccupation with the rituals of Indian diplomacy gave him a superior understanding of tribal deliberative processes that undeniably facilitated his work as a negotiator and diplomat.[87]

As the winter progressed, the pursuit of the scarce game became ever more difficult. In early February, with the fort's larders nearly empty, Clark embarked on a nine-day hunting expedition with sixteen of the corps' best hunters. Despite the slim pickings, they managed to kill forty deer, three buffalo, and nineteen elk, but some admittedly were "so meager that they were unfit for use."[88]

During Clark's absence, Sacagawea gave birth to a son, Jean Baptiste Charbonneau. This was the young Shoshone woman's first child, and she had to endure a long and painful labor. In an effort to hasten the delivery, Lewis resorted to an Indian folk remedy suggested by René Jusseaume and gave her a small portion of a rattlesnake's rattle in water. Lewis's scientific instincts made him skeptical about the efficacy of the treatment, but he acknowledged the child had been born only a few short minutes after he administered the potion. Clark returned just in time to greet the fine young boy he usually referred to as Pomp.[89]

Lewis and Clark continued working on the journals, maps, and natural history specimens they were readying for shipment downriver under the care of Corporal Warfington. Sometime in February or March of 1805 Clark completed an impressive large map of the western part of North America. He also prepared two other important geographic documents: the first summarized the rivers, creeks, and most remarkable places along the Missouri River from River Dubois to the Mandan villages, and the second provided estimated distances for the Missouri and its subsidiary streams beyond the Mandan villages. In making his maps of their journey, Clark seldom relied on the complicated techniques of celestial navigation that his partner had labored so hard to master. He employed instead the less sophisticated system of dead reckoning, using a compass, a watch, and a log line and reel to calculate speed, distance, and direction. He carefully recorded those figures in a daily logbook before transferring them to a gridwork map. In his attempts to extrapolate distances from Indian sources at Fort Mandan, Clark's preconceived notions about western geography led him to conclude erroneously that only a half day's travel separated the Missouri from the great river of the West. That proved, as they would soon discover, a serious miscalculation.[90]

Along with his map, Clark devoted a great deal of time at Fort Mandan to the compilation of a great chart classifying fifty-three Missouri River tribes, most of which resided east of the Rocky Mountains, in nineteen separate categories. That systematic schema provided Jefferson and his policy makers with useful information about major western tribes, but Clark's matrix also imposed a fixity that grossly oversimplified the complex character of Indian cultures.[91]

In preparation for a spring departure, the men began the difficult task of dislodging the two pirogues and the barge from the still frozen river. Once those vessels had been freed from the ice, work crews set about repairing them and also building canoes as a replacement for the keelboat that would soon be heading back downriver. The new vessels hewed from cottonwood logs were corked, pitched, tarred, and put in readiness to help transport the corps and its supplies as it proceeded along the upper reaches of the Missouri.[92]

By late March the ice in the river was breaking up, and the pesky insects that had so bedeviled them before the onset of winter had returned. As the members of the permanent corps anticipated the resumption of their journey to the Pacific, Clark reported "all the party in high Spirits. They pass but fiew nights without amuseing themselves danceing possessing perfect harmony and good understanding toward each other." During their winter confinement, members of the corps seem to have bonded, and the once poorly disciplined and unpredictable soldiers came together to form the cohesive and disciplined kind of company that the tasks ahead would require. This must have pleased both of the captains.[93]

On April 1 Clark directed that the boats be put into the river in anticipation of the pending departure. As previously noted, the keelboat, too large to navigate the waters upstream without great difficulty, would be returning to St. Louis under the command of Corporal Warfington and the members of the temporary detachment and three of the French engagés. The remaining twenty-six members of the permanent corps, the interpreter Charbonneau, his wife,

Sacagawea, their infant son Jean Baptiste, and Clark's slave York planned to continue their voyage to the Pacific in the original red and white pirogues and the six new dugout canoes.[94]

As the time for their leaving neared, Clark kept busy writing dispatches and letters. With Lewis's assistance, he drafted a letter to President Jefferson to accompany the journal that he had prepared for Jefferson's perusal. Concerned that the erudite chief executive might find his writings lacking, Clark was at pains to fend off any such criticism. He explained to Jefferson, "you will readily perceive in reading over those notes, that many parts are incorrect, owing to the variety of information received at different times. I most sincerely wish that leasure had permitted me to offer them in a more correct form. Receive I pray you my unfained acknowledgments for your friendly recollection of me in your letters to my friend and companion Captn. Lewis. And be assured of the sincere regard with which I have the honor to be Your most obedient and Humble Servent." The letters that he sent to other friends and relatives were less difficult for him to compose. To his friend William Henry Harrison he sent an abbreviated account of his travels with a summary view of the Missouri and its tributaries as far north as Fort Mandan. That letter and Lewis's longer communication to Jefferson would soon be widely circulated in the United States and abroad and give a waiting world its first information about the expedition and its progress.[95]

Clark's letters to brother Jonathan and brother-in-law William Croghan were necessarily brief. He apologized to Jonathan that his official duties had kept him so busy that he had been unable to include a "full detail of occurrences." Clark hoped that the rough notes he was sending Jonathan would provide an adequate accounting of his activities. The three trunks filled with gifts of Indian clothing, animal skins, assorted plants and seeds, and other miscellaneous curiosities intended for family members and friends were apt to draw even more interest. Packed away in one of the chests were the buffalo robes that York had secured for his wife and his friend Ben, another Clark family slave. York's status had not afforded him the opportunity of learning to read and write, so these gifts would have to suffice for the time being. Clark sent the customary salutations to family members and concluded by advising them not to expect his return before July 1806, because the country he was about to enter was extensive and unexplored. And on that cautious but determined note, William Clark was prepared to proceed on.[96]

Five

On to the Pacific

THE CORPS OF DISCOVERY resumed its westward trek to the Pacific on April 7, 1805. On the eve of their departure from Fort Mandan, Lewis rightly declared that the little band of explorers was "in excellent health and spirits, zealously attached to the enterprise and anxious to proceed [without] a whisper of murmur or discontent, [acting] in unison with the most perfect harmony." The company was a far cry from the motley, ill-disciplined crew that had left Camp River Dubois nearly a year earlier. During their five-month winter sojourn at Fort Mandan, members of the corps had become an extended family bound together by a collective purpose, a determination to succeed, and a spirit of camaraderie. The change in mood was palpable. Clark's often-melancholy partner pronounced it one of the happiest times in his life. In a momentary rush of exuberance, Lewis even dared to liken their travels to the legendary explorations of Christopher Columbus and Captain James Cook.[1] That renewed sense of optimism may also account for Lewis's decision to resume regular journal writing after a lengthy and unexplained hiatus.

All of this must have been very comforting to William Clark, who spent much of his final day at Fort Mandan holding discussions with Kakawita, an Arikara chief who had come there to confer with the Americans before they left. He assured the tribal leader that his new Great Father Jefferson would always protect his dutiful children, then presented him with a certificate of good conduct, a small medal, a carrot of tobacco, and a string of wampum as tokens of the U.S. government's friendship. With that out of the way, he turned his attention to the final packing and preparations for departure. After dispatching the expedition's former flagship to St. Louis under the command of Corporal Richard Warfington, Clark and the members of the permanent party headed upriver.[2]

The keelboat, carrying official government dispatches, documents, and specimens prepared especially for the president, along with assorted private letters and gifts for family and friends of corps members, reached St. Louis six weeks later with its precious cargoes intact. An interested onlooker who boarded the boat in St. Charles reported seeing a great many curiosities, including moccasins, buffalo robes, goat skins, live animals, and the heavyset Eagle Feather much pitted with the smallpox, then on his way to Washington to confer with U.S. officials. After a false start the Arikara leader headed eastward, where he met with Jefferson and Secretary of War Dearborn among others before he succumbed to an unspecified illness in the federal capital in April 1806.[3]

In what seems to have been a minor miracle, the caged prairie dog and one of the magpies somehow survived their lengthy journeys and arrived at the President's House in mid-August. When Jefferson returned from his annual summer retreat at Monticello, he examined those living creatures from the distant prairies before he began poring over the documents that Lewis and Clark had forwarded for his inspection. In Louisville, Clark's family must have been equally delighted with the cache of papers and curiosities that he had sent for their amusement and edification.[4]

With the keelboat safely on its way downstream, the little fleet of two pirogues and six canoes carrying the expedition's permanent party headed westward into a country known only to its indigenous inhabitants. Captain Clark, who was at the helm, carried with him the map that he had carefully drafted using new information collected from various Indian sources during the long hours of his Mandan winter. He hoped that his efforts to fill in some of the blank spaces on existing maps would make it easier for them to chart their course during this next phase of their journey.

Captain Lewis walked ahead to the lower Mandan village where members of the corps rendezvoused with him that evening. In one final gesture of friendship a Mandan chief presented Clark with a fine pair of moccasins as a parting gift, perhaps to replace the ones he had sent downriver to his family. As the convoy passed by the river towns, crowds of villagers turned out to see off the little band of wilderness travelers. They knew that the Corps of Discovery planned to cross the mountains, and the Hidatsas who had raised Sacagawea and named her Bird Woman probably assumed (erroneously as it turned out) that if she and her baby reached Shoshone country they were not likely to return.

The tiny flotilla was barely under way when one of its newly fashioned canoes took on sufficient water to ruin a bag of biscuit and two-thirds of a barrel of powder—an ominous sign of things to come. To ensure that one of them would always be available to take charge in such emergencies, Lewis and Clark agreed to take turns walking onshore, which both often did to stretch their legs or to collect scientific data. On the days that Clark drew the overland assignment, Charbonneau, Sacagawea, little Jean Baptiste, and York frequently accompanied him. The young native woman was a fount of useful information concerning the region's plant and animal life, and her sojourns with Clark helped forge a friendship that persisted after the expedition had ended. During one of their initial strolls, Janey, as Clark would later call her, harvested some wild artichokes for Lewis to examine and describe.[5]

The signs of spring were everywhere—budding trees, greening hillsides, prairies ablaze with blooms, and, not to be overlooked, the return of the troublesome mosquitoes. Corps members also began noticing more beaver, an animal whose liver and tail provided the hungry palates of expedition members with tasty new delights. Onshore, Clark saw numerous traces of recent Indian activity in the area, presumably left by the Assiniboines, whom he considered potentially dangerous, but as the expedition passed through what is now western North Dakota and eastern Montana there were no direct contacts with members of that band or any other for that matter. The native people in that region had elected to monitor the exploring party's actions from a discrete distance. If the Indians were not a problem for the travelers, high winds and strong currents were. Crews regularly had to resort to towropes to propel even the smaller river craft. Blowing sand added to the general misery and made sore eyes a universal problem, prompting Clark to complain that they had to "eat, drink, and breathe sand."[6]

Given the tough going that the corps was experiencing, the expedition's arrival at the mouth of the Yellowstone was cause for a small celebration. Members of the little community pulled out the fiddle for an evening of singing and dancing in their tattered and torn clothing while one and all enjoyed a dram of liquor. The accompanying hilarity momentarily allowed them to put aside thoughts about past and future toils.[7]

During her periodic walks with Captain Clark, Sacagawea continued to call his attention to distinctive and unfamiliar plants such as wild liquorice and breadroot. Lewis pronounced breadroot tasteless, but he opined that epicures might find the popular food source known to the engagés as white apple useful as a substitute for wild mushrooms in ragouts and gravies. Those same bon vivants might also have savored the wilderness cuisine of Sacagawea's husband, Charbonneau, who won plaudits for his culinary skills, most particularly for his ability to prepare boudin blanc, a sausage made by stuffing buffalo intestines with well-kneaded prime cuts of meat, liver, kidney suet, salt, pepper, and flour.[8]

The French interpreter may have been a good cook, but he was a poor sailor. Turbulent waters terrified Charbonneau, who could not swim. Unfortunately, he was at the helm of the white pirogue on May 14 when a sudden squall threatened to capsize the vessel. Frozen with panic, the hapless navigator abandoned the rudder and in desperation cried out to his maker for help. Contrary to their normal practice, both Lewis and Clark were onshore when the crisis occurred. They watched helplessly from afar as the out-of-control boat appeared to be on the verge of sinking. Their hearts dropped as they contemplated the loss of the vessel and its precious contents, which by their reckoning included virtually everything indispensable to the success of their enterprise. Attempts to shout orders from the shore proved fruitless, and it was only Pierre Cruzatte's resolute action in tandem with some heroic rowing by crew members that kept the pirogue afloat. Sacagawea did her part. With babe in arms, she miraculously managed to retrieve any number of valuable articles before they were washed overboard and lost to the churning waters. It had been a harrowing experience for all concerned, and the final outcome was better than anyone could have expected. The medical supplies sustained considerable damage, as did some gunpowder and garden seeds, but amazingly all else was soaked but otherwise unharmed. Rainy weather subsequently hampered efforts to dry out the salvaged articles.[9]

The travelers were now in grizzly country, and their encounters with the awesome beasts never failed to engender fear and dread. Not all of the wild's dangerous creatures were so sizable, as William Clark discovered when he narrowly averted stepping on a small but ferocious rattlesnake while hiking across the countryside. As the expedition proceeded into the high country in late May, morning temperatures still hovered near freezing, and the water sometimes turned to ice on the oars. Captain Clark caught a glimpse of a high mountain to the west, and by May 26 he was prepared to proclaim with certainty that the distant snowcapped peaks he had seen were in fact the Rockies, but Lewis had been the first to confront the possibility that the snowy barrier might stand astride the good comfortable road that they had expected to conduct them through the fabled passage to India.[10]

A short distance above the entrance of the scenic Montana stream that Clark named the Judith River in honor of his beloved Judith (Julia) Hancock, he came upon a recently abandoned Indian encampment. After examining some moccasins that had been left behind, Sacagawea pronounced that they belonged to a tribe that resided east of the Rockies and north of the Missouri, probably the Atsina or the Blackfeet, either of which the Americans believed might well cause them trouble. Shortly thereafter a pile of decaying buffalo carcasses, the remains of a herd stampeded over a nearby cliff, filled corps

Captain Clark and His Men Shooting Bears. Like several expedition members, Clark was a skilled marksman. Courtesy of the Library of Congress.

members' nostrils with a powerful stench that they interpreted as added evidence of the recent presence of Indian hunters in the area.[11]

The steep perpendicular bluffs from which the buffalo had plunged were interspersed with romantic-looking sandstone formations that from a distance gave an appearance of ancient ruins, but those wondrous geological formations lining the Missouri also produced shoals and rapids in the river below that made their travel even more treacherous than usual. Once again the men had to resort to the towropes, but the muddy and slippery banks frequently forced them to wade in icy waters up to their armpits. When their moccasins became mired in the mud, they were reduced to trudging barefooted across jagged rocks. But as Clark approvingly observed, the faithful fellows bore their painful exertions with scarcely a murmur. It was little wonder that he and Lewis chose on more than one occasion to dispense a ration of grog from their rapidly dwindling supply.[12]

When they reached the confluence of the Marias and Missouri rivers on June 2, Lewis and Clark faced an unexpected challenge that produced a rare difference of opinion among members of the corps. None of the Indian sources had mentioned the river's division at this point, and the leaders were left to decide which fork to follow. A wrong choice could waste precious time and leave the corps stranded in the mountains during the dead of winter. A preliminary assessment inclined both of the captains to believe that the southern fork was the true

Missouri, but because the muddy waters of the northern branch, or the Marias River as Lewis named it, more closely resembled those they had been traveling, most others in the party considered it the more promising route. Eager not to make a hasty judgment they would later come to regret, the commanders elected to gather more information. Lewis led a small party to inspect the north fork, while Clark headed south with another crew to investigate that branch.[13]

After satisfying himself that the stream he was assigned to survey continued in a southwesterly direction with sufficient depth, width, and rapidity, Clark returned to camp convinced that it was the Missouri. The fast-paced march up and down the steep river hills and gullies and across the dry hard plain had left Clark and his men much fatigued. Lewis joined his partner back in camp two days later, equally weary from his travels. After putting their heads together, they reaffirmed their determination to pursue the southern course even though most of their subordinates still believed that the northern branch was a better option. As it turned out, Lewis and Clark's analytical skills had not failed them, and as geographer John Logan Allen has pointed out, they once again demonstrated their competence and intelligence by correctly deducing the right answer from a contradictory set of facts.[14]

During their deliberations the captains made some other important decisions. Recognizing that they would soon be crossing through the mountains, they concluded that the time had come for them to lighten their loads and leave the larger red pirogue behind. After tying the boat to some trees on an island at the entrance of the Marias River and covering it with brush, they also prepared a large underground cache similar to the ones used by Indians for storing agricultural products. Among other items, Lewis and Clark stowed away the blacksmith's bellows, hammers, and tongs, two muskets, beaver traps, furs, foodstuffs, and "superfluous baggage of every description" far too heavy to lug through the rugged terrain ahead. Nearby they also buried an axe with canisters of powder and lead as backups they might return to retrieve in an extreme emergency.[15]

Because most members of the party still questioned the wisdom of following the southern fork, Lewis decided to travel ahead by land in search of positive proof to affirm the correctness of the southwestern course that they planned to pursue. The Indians had advised the Americans that they would pass a series of falls on the Missouri River before they reached the by then not far distant mountains. Lewis set out to find those falls, after leaving the superior waterman Clark in charge of the boats.[16] Prior to the river convoy's leave-taking, Clark supervised some last-minute repairs to their canoes and firearms.[17]

Sacagawea was very ill at the time. Medical authorities have long assumed that she suffered from a pelvic inflammation, but Carolyn Gilman's recent surmise that the Indian woman's problems may have resulted from a miscarriage seems equally plausible and would explain Clark's comment, "if She dies it will be the fault of her husband as I am now convinced." Alarmed by her steadily worsening condition, Clark resorted to the then common medical procedure of bleeding, a tactic strongly endorsed by Lewis's mentor and the expedition's medical authority, Dr. Benjamin Rush. Clark initially concluded that the treatment had been helpful. Undoubtedly more beneficial was his decision to move the feverish young woman out of the sun's direct rays to the covered part of the pirogue. When her condition remained grave, he administered some medicine from the medical chest. Acting in Lewis's stead, Clark also tended to the less serious aches and pains of corps members battered by their attempts to maneuver the boats through the rushing waters and rocky shoals.[18]

Lewis, who was also unwell, pressed forward on his quest to find the Missouri rapids. The sound of falling water came as music to his ears and removed any lingering doubts about the stream's identity. Even though the distant murmurs had revived his spirits, the Indian reports had not prepared him for the grandeur of the scene that greeted him when he reached the lower falls on June 13. In fact, as he soon discovered, there were no fewer than five separate falls on the river. Lewis, attuned to the literary conventions of the day, openly pondered how he could do justice to these wonderful marvels with only a pen at his command. His appetite had returned as he happily settled down beside the churning waters to enjoy a plate piled high with prime cuts of buffalo meat, bone marrow, trout, and parched meal, all seasoned to his liking with pepper and salt. The following morning he dispatched a messenger bearing a letter advising Clark of the good news, and he continued searching for words adequate to describe these "pleasingly beautiful and sublimely grand" vistas.[19]

When Clark first beheld the great cataracts several days later, he echoed his partner's thoughts, declaring, "this is one of the grandest views in nature and by far exceeds anything I ever saw." But in contrast with the romantic impulses that captivated Meriwether Lewis, Clark's scientific turn of mind took charge as he methodically calculated the various dimensions of the many distinctive features of the succession of cataracts that comprised the Great Falls of the Missouri. At the second falls Clark marked his name, the date, and the height of the rapids on a nearby willow tree before recording in his journals the exact measurements taken from his surveys. Clark's matter-of-fact descriptions of this great spectacle contrasted markedly with his partner's eloquent rhapsodies composed in the popular romantic style.[20]

Clark established a base camp a short distance from the first of the great falls, while he and Lewis settled their plans for portaging around these great obstacles. Lewis's preliminary reconnaissance had led him to conclude that the

Great Falls of the Missouri, by A. E. Mathews. Clark responded to this spectacular scenic wonder by attempting to measure and calculate its dimensions, while his partner Lewis searched for romantic phraseology that would properly capture its natural beauty. Courtesy of the Montana Historical Society.

terrain south of the river offered the most promising route. It fell to Clark to determine the most feasible and direct path around the falls, and he soon realized that the portage would be far more formidable than imagined. He methodically surveyed and marked the entire eighteen-mile route, placing stakes sometimes at intervals as short as a quarter of a mile. He concurred with Lewis's assessment that the white pirogue, the last of their original boats, was far too heavy to haul across the lengthy portage he had laid out, and far too large to navigate the Missouri's increasingly shallow streambed. Lewis planned to replace the weighty vessel with a lighter leather boat made from animal skins stretched over the iron frame specially made for him at Harper's Ferry, Virginia. But even if the portable experimental boat proved successful, they still faced the daunting task of transporting overland the smaller dugout canoes that were too heavy to be carried across the portage on the shoulders of crew members. The commanders directed the men to begin constructing some crude wagons mounted on wooden wheels fashioned from cottonwood logs. Even with the carts, the task of portaging all of the canoes and equipment took a full month, far longer than the few days the captains had anticipated.[21]

While Clark oversaw the transport of the goods, Lewis focused his energies on assembling the iron boat, a project whose efficacy his partner already had begun to doubt. Sacagawea was still ailing, and Charbonneau had pressed Clark to allow the couple to return home. Lewis's assorted remedies, including mineral waters from nearby sulfur springs, poultices made from Peruvian bark, and a dose of laudanum, may not have been the reason for her recovery, but whether because of or in spite of those treatments, she steadily improved, to the relief of all of her male traveling companions, who no doubt had given more than a fleeting thought to who would care for the baby if something happened to her.[22]

As the portage crews traveled along the path Clark had marked out for them, the double soles they applied to their moccasins afforded scant protection from the rough ground and prickly pears they had to navigate while bearing their heavy loads. Clark marveled at the stamina of his troops, and simply reported, "to state the fatigues of this party would take up more of the journal than the other notes which I find scarcely time to set down." The strenuous demands of the portage took a toll on Clark, whose old intestinal problems returned to plague him. As if those challenges were not sufficient, he narrowly escaped being swept away by a summer flash flood while inspecting the countryside with his regular traveling companions Charbonneau, Sacagawea, and little Jean Baptiste.[23]

When gathering storm clouds ominously signaled a need for their little party to seek shelter, they sought refuge under a rock ledge near the bottom of a large ravine. Shortly after they were ensconced in their newfound haven, the heavens unleashed a driving downpour that sent torrents of water, mud, and rocks rushing into their safe spot. They scrambled up the hill barely in time to avoid being carried away by the rampaging currents. York, who had parted company with the others to go hunting, returned to the scene fearing that they all had been lost. Clark's large compass, his umbrella, Sacagawea's cradleboard, and the baby's clothing and bedding were the only casualties of the sudden deluge, and a salvage party later managed to retrieve the valuable compass from the muddy debris.[24]

That same summer storm also sent hailstones as large as seven inches in circumference raining down on members of a nearby transport party making its way along the route that Clark had marked out for them. The men returned to camp naked, bruised, and bleeding from the pounding they had received. The delays occasioned by the difficult portage gave rise to a growing concern over their failure to have reached the mountains this late in the season. While the crews continued their struggles to haul the expedition's goods around the falls, Clark prepared a backup copy of his map for burial at the site of the portage with the thought that he would be able to reclaim it later if his original drawings were accidentally destroyed.

"Draught of the Falls of the Missouri and Portage." Entry of ca. July 2, 1805. Voorhis Journal #1. Courtesy of the Missouri Historical Society. Clark's cartographic drawing showing the Great Falls of the Missouri and the portage he staked out around them includes his meticulous measurements and survey data.

Such preoccupations caused the Fourth of July in 1805 to pass with scant notice and only some brief dancing in the evening. Lewis continued to labor on his
iron boat, but the unexpected absence of pine trees required for making the tar
needed to seal the boat ultimately doomed the project and forced the troops to
resort to building more dugouts to take the place of the white pirogue that they
had been forced to ditch. Clark took charge of that final task, while Lewis occupied himself collecting and preserving specimens of unfamiliar plants.[25]

On July 15, a full month after they first reached the Great Falls, the portage
had been completed and the expedition was ready to forge ahead. Though relieved that they had avoided contact with potentially hostile tribes during their
trek across what is now Montana, Lewis and Clark now worried that a failure to
secure horses from friendly Shoshones for the mountain portage between the
Missouri and Columbia rivers might eventually doom their enterprise. In the
face of such uncertainty, the captains abandoned their plan for sending a small
contingent to St. Louis with a progress report as they had promised to do in the
letters they had forwarded from Fort Mandan. They now feared the departure
of even two or three men might discourage those left behind and jeopardize
the expedition's upcoming trek through the mountains. The members of their
little band understood that they were about to enter the most perilous and difficult part of their journey, but like all good soldiers they remained resolute
and were prepared to succeed or perish together.[26]

While the expedition still had not made contact with the Shoshone, the signs
of their presence were everywhere. Fearing that the sounds of their hunters'
guns might cause the Shoshones to leave the river and retreat into the mountains, Clark set out with an advance party to seek them out before they had a
chance to flee. Having recognized familiar scenes along the river, Sacagawea assured Lewis and Clark that they were in Shoshone country. On July 25, Captain
Clark arrived at the confluence of the Three Forks of the Missouri, rivers that
he and Lewis later christened the Jefferson, the Madison, and the Gallatin in
honor of the president and his secretaries of state and treasury. Clark was feeling unwell at the time, suffering from a fever and sore feet caused by the punc-
tures of the ubiquitous prickly pear spines. A dose of Dr. Rush's purgative pills
and a hot water bath applied to his cut and blistered extremities failed to alleviate his symptoms.[27]

When they camped at the place where the Hidatsas had taken Sacagawea
prisoner five years earlier, Lewis ordered the erection of a small bower to shield
his feverish partner from the excessively warm temperatures inside their leather
tipi. Lewis continued to administer medicines to his ailing friend. Clark's fever
and achiness gradually subsided, only to be replaced by a boil on his ankle that
made it exceedingly painful for him to walk and forced him to stay close to the

boats. This was hardly the way that he would have chosen to spend his thirty-fifth birthday, which understandably he allowed to pass unnoticed.[28] Big game was becoming scarcer in the rugged and barren countryside through which they were now traveling, but the scientific-minded explorers continued to discover new and different animals to catalog, including Lewis's woodpecker, the blue grouse, pinon jay, western meadowlark, bushy-tailed woodrat, and kit fox.

Sacagawea, now fully recovered, advised Lewis and Clark that they were nearing the location where the Shoshone went in early fall to hunt buffalo, and that news prompted Lewis to initiate yet another search to locate the elusive tribe. Left behind, Clark chafed under his confinement and complained, "I should have undertaken this trip had I been able to march, from the rageing fury of a tumer on my anckle musle."[29] Lewis, who set out down an Indian road leading to the point where the river entered the mountains, quickly surmised that their water journey was about to end, at least temporarily, inasmuch as the once mighty Missouri had become a rivulet small enough to stand astride. He left behind a note advising his partner not to proceed until he returned. That message must have come as music to the ears of the weary crew members, who were already urging Clark to abandon the river. Drawing ever closer to the Continental Divide, Lewis eagerly anticipated seeing the fabled passage to the Pacific stretching before him. But on August 12 when he and his party crested Lemhi Pass and became the first U.S. citizens to cross that great dividing ridge, they were shocked to behold a series of immense ranges of high mountains blocking their path. The Rockies were far greater than anyone had dared imagine. This unexpected revelation dashed all hopes for an easy portage to the Columbia and doomed the centuries-old dream of discovering a Northwest Passage that had become Jefferson's guiding vision.[30]

The stark new realities unveiled at Lemhi Pass made Indian assistance even more essential for the expedition's survival. Not long before, Lewis with the aid of his telescope had sighted a mounted Indian whom he determined was likely a Shoshone. His efforts to signal friendship using a blanket, offering beads and other trinkets, and rolling up his sleeve to reveal his white skin failed to have the desired effect, as the Indian turned and rode off, apparently believing that Lewis was affiliated with the enemy Blackfeet. Two days after Lewis and his party had crossed the Continental Divide and entered into Idaho, they again observed Indians in the distance, but as before they fled. Just when prospects for establishing contact with the apprehensive Shoshones, known to the Americans as the Snake Indians, seemed bleak, Lewis unexpectedly made contact with three Shoshone women before they could escape. His nonthreatening demeanor, gifts and trinkets, and application of vermilion to their tawny cheeks gradually diminished their fears. With the assistance of Drouillard's sign language he conveyed his wish to meet their chiefs and warriors. The women were by then sufficiently reassured to lead Lewis and his band down a road to their camp, where a short time later a party of sixty mounted warriors rode out to meet them.[31]

Eager to avoid a repeat of the previous ill-fated encounters with the Shoshones, Lewis laid down his gun and approached carrying only a U.S. flag. The women rushed forward proudly displaying the presents they had received, after which Cameahwait, the band's leader, and two other headmen advanced to embrace these strangers, who were the first white persons they had ever seen. A round of hugs in their traditional fashion left the Americans smeared with Indian grease and paint, but no less gleeful about finally having made contact with the Shoshones.

In a further gesture of friendship, the Indians removed their moccasins when they joined the white strangers for a ritual smoke. Lewis followed suit and afterward presented his hosts with some blue beads, vermilion, and an American flag. The scene was subsequently repeated at the Shoshone camp on the Lemhi, where curious native people crowded around for a glimpse of their unexpected guests. Only later would the Americans make the serendipitous discovery that the obliging Cameahwait who had first welcomed Lewis was in fact the brother of their traveling companion Sacagawea.[32]

In the conversations that followed, Lewis attempted to explain his mission, and Cameahwait conveyed the disappointing news that it would be impossible for them to follow the Salmon River to the Pacific by land or by water. That was not the news Lewis had wanted to hear, so he consoled himself with the possibility that this might simply be a ruse to detain him. He then retired for the evening, leaving the others to continue their dancing and celebrating. The next day when Lewis pressed his hosts for more exact geographic information, they drew maps on the ground using a stick to mark the rivers and employing piles of sand to represent the mountains. Their graphic demonstration showed why the Shoshones had never attempted to proceed across the high mountains. Lewis learned that Nez Perce hunting bands regularly made the crossing via a route to the north and west. That news kept alive the possibility that the mountain barrier might still be easily breached, and Drouillard's estimate that he had seen at least four hundred horses grazing nearby suggested the animals required for any such crossing were available.[33]

Because more than a few of Lewis's Shoshone hosts suspected that he intended to lead them into an ambush at the hands of their enemies, his pleas that they return with him to help Clark and the expedition's main body make the crossing through Lemhi Pass elicited stiff resistance. They relented and agreed to make the trip only after he shamed them by intimating they were afraid to accompany him. When they reached the fork of the Jefferson River Lewis had designated to rendezvous with Clark, he discovered that his partner had not yet arrived. Sensing that his justifiably skittish Shoshone companions might bolt and leave the Americans to make their way on their own without the benefit of horses, Lewis took the initiative and handed his party's guns over to Cameahwait and the others, saying that if he betrayed them, they could use the weapons to defend themselves and use them against him. For the moment Lewis had placed himself at the mercy of the very "savages" he considered so far beneath him.[34]

To his great relief, Clark showed up a short time later with the interpreters Sacagawea and Charbonneau. He had traveled ahead of the canoes after correctly surmising that the Shoshones might be waiting for the expedition. When Clark and his companions first sighted the mounted Indian party approaching them, Sacagawea joyfully signaled that they were Shoshone. When he saw that Drouillard was with them, Clark rushed forward to join them for the trip to their camp. When they arrived, Lewis watched in amusement as the Shoshone tribal leaders embraced his partner with their traditional hugs and tied shells to his red hair. The unflappable Clark, by then a veteran of such encounters, seems to have taken it all in stride, but even he must have been moved by the tearful reunion between Sacagawea and her brother Cameahwait.[35]

Such sentimentality soon gave way to hard bargaining as Lewis and Clark entered into negotiations to procure the horses now viewed as essential for what promised to be an extended portage through the mountains. In return for his promises to provide horses and other kinds of support, Cameahwait extracted assurances that in the future the Americans would supply his people with firearms—an important matter for a tribe surrounded by enemies who already had acquired such weapons from Canadian-based British traders. The American commanders agreed that while Lewis directed the transport of the expedition's cargoes across the Continental Divide with Shoshone assistance, Clark would travel ahead with a party of eleven men to check out their prospects for crossing the mountains. Before he departed, Clark, ever the diplomat, mollified two lesser chiefs who believed they had been shortchanged in the gift-giving rituals by offering them a couple of his well-worn officer's coats.[36]

When he reached the main Shoshone encampment on the Lemhi River, Clark was careful once again to take part in the all-important ceremonial welcoming rituals that Lewis referred to as the national hug. He then outlined his plans for traveling down the river, asked for someone to guide them, and urged the Shoshones to send additional horses and men to assist Captain Lewis with his crossing through the Lemhi Pass. Even though this was the season of scarcity, Clark's generous and obliging hosts shared their meager stores of salmon and dried chokecherries before his party proceeded along the Lemhi to the Salmon River. His reconnaissance in search of navigable waters took his party through the exceedingly harsh and difficult terrain in eastern Idaho. When they reached the Salmon River, they followed its course along a trail so rugged that horses could navigate its steep slopes only with the greatest risk and difficulty. The rapids-filled river was no better option, and the region's only potential food sources appeared to be seasonal chokecherries and red haws. It was a scenic wonder, but a traveler's nightmare. Their Indian guide, whom they nicknamed "Old Toby," advised Clark that the route along the river only became worse ahead. Even though the Salmon River eventually flowed into the Columbia, it was clearly not a viable course for them to follow.[37]

Clark had seen enough to recommend to his partner that the entire party should travel overland via the northerly trail used by the Nez Perce until they reached a navigable stream. They would need more horses—preferably one for each man—and someone to show them the way across the Lolo Trail. Clark suggested that they employ "Old Toby" to guide them. The trek had alerted Clark's men to the probable danger they faced, and as they retraced their steps back to the Lemhi River encampment more than a few fretted that they might be doomed to starve in this country devoid of all game except a few fish.[38]

Lewis signed off on Clark's proposal for the entire company to proceed via the northern route. With only twenty-nine horses at their disposal, far short of the number they had hoped for, Lewis and Clark were ready to depart on August 30. Food was scarce, and the rough traveling conditions soon took a toll on men, animals, and equipment alike. The expedition's last thermometer broke when the box it was in was thrown against a tree, and a short time later Clark's much-used writing desk suffered a similar fate. When they crossed the Lost Trail Pass and entered the Bitterroot Valley, the first whites to do so according to Clark, the corps came upon a large encampment of Salish Indians. The Flatheads, as the Americans called the Salish, were then on their way to join the Shoshones for a hunting expedition at the Three Forks. Those friendly natives, whose distinctive guttural intonations Clark likened to gurgling sounds spoken through the throat, offered the pale-skinned strangers some better horses.[39]

According to Salish historical tradition, William Clark fathered a son by a Flathead woman during his stay in the Bitterroot Valley. Known as Joseph Clark, the lad was baptized sometime after the first Catholic missionaries arrived in western Montana and lived until circa 1884. There are equally strong Nez Perce oral traditions that Clark likewise fathered a son by one of their women during the return journey in 1806. Clark never acknowledged any such liaisons, and the journals are mute on the subject, though they do include frequent references to sexual relations between other corps members and native women.

While many historians have been quick to dismiss the tribal accounts on the grounds that there is no proof to substantiate them, the absence of any corroborating evidence from nonnative sources does not necessarily negate their validity. Clark was a healthy, single young man with normal sexual appetites, so such a dalliance hardly seems unthinkable. Those who doubt that Clark chose to indulge himself contend that Joseph Clark could have been sired by another member of the party but chose to identify himself with the Redhead because of his greater prestige in both societies. They also insist that as an officer Clark would not have violated the ban on sexual activity he and Lewis had imposed to counter venereal disease. Barring the unlikely possibility of establishing a link through DNA, the debate seems destined to continue.[40]

Following their brief respite at Traveler's Rest, the exploring party headed westward on the Lolo Trail across the Bitterroot Mountains for what proved to be the most difficult and challenging portion of the entire journey. In their attempts to ascend the steep mountain slopes, the horses sometimes lost their footing and tumbled down the rugged hillsides, which Clark, not surprisingly, noted "hurt them very much." The view from the snow-covered peaks provided little reassurance, for as Clark wrote, "From this mountain I could observe high ruged mountains in every direction as far as I could See." Having failed to find any game, the weary sojourners slaughtered one of their colts and dined on its flesh. A storm that deposited between six and eight inches of new snow further hindered progress as they struggled to follow the now hidden Lolo Trail through the pine-covered Bitterroots. Clark, no stranger to wilderness travel, remarked, "I have been wet and as cold in every part as I ever was in my life, indeed I was at one time fearful my feet would freeze in the thin mockersons which I wore, after a Short delay in the middle of the Day." He and one of his men pushed ahead of the others and thoughtfully had blazing campfires waiting to warm the "verry cold and much fatigued" travelers when they arrived at dusk. A second colt provided their supper.[41]

Clark's concern for his troops was real. Sensing that the lack of provisions and the difficulties of mountain travel had caused morale to plummet, the captains agreed that Clark should lead a hunting party ahead in search of fresh game to send back to the hungry corps, still struggling to advance along the treacherous Lolo Trail and reduced to subsisting on the inadequate and unpalatable portable soup rations Lewis had procured in the East. Clark stopped briefly with his men beside a mountain stream he dubbed Hungry Creek because while there, they had nothing to eat. After two more days of tough going, they descended into northern Idaho's Weippe Prairie, a small, grass-covered, upland plain dotted with scattered pine trees where the Nez Perce Indians came during late summer to harvest camas roots, an essential ingredient of the native diet in the interior Pacific Northwest.[42]

A sighting of some Indian lodges in the distance gave reason for them to hope that the worst of their ordeal was about to end. Not long thereafter an elderly man hesitantly approached them, notwithstanding his fear that they might be enemy raiders. Clark soon learned that recently the tribe's younger men had left the women, children, and older men behind and headed out on a war party. Reassured by Clark's actions, more and more of the curious Nez Perce gathered around for a closer look at these hungry visitors who eagerly feasted on the small piece of buffalo meat and the more ample quantities of dried salmon, berries, and camas bread placed before them, totally oblivious to the potential side effects of their hearty repast. Before day's end Clark declared that his generous meal of fish and roots had left him feeling unwell. The others also discovered that these foods produced heaviness of the stomach and diarrhea, but after their lengthy period of deprivation they found it difficult to resist the temptation to indulge.[43]

In response to Clark's queries, one of his Nez Perce hosts drew a crude chart locating the Clearwater and Snake rivers and the Indian nations that resided along them. His informant also told him about the great falls on the Columbia, below which there were white traders with beads, cloth, and brass. After sending Reuben Field back to the Lolo with fish and roots for the others, Clark proceeded up the Clearwater in search of Twisted Hair, a tribal leader whom he hoped would be able to provide him with additional information. His reception there was less tentative, thanks in part to the intercessions of Watkuweis, an elderly Nez Perce woman who lived among whites in Canada after the Blackfeet had taken her captive and sold her to a Plains Indian tribe. During her captivity she had met Euro-Americans whose kind treatment she sought to repay by urging her people not to harm these strangers from the east. Yet again, Native Americans reached out in friendship to assist them. The old woman's words persuaded Twisted Hair and his son to join Clark as he doubled back to find Lewis.[44]

On the way Clark met John Shields, who gave him a small piece of venison from one of the three deer that he had killed. After exchanging horses with Shields, Clark set off on a fresh but skittish mount that threw him three times before he was able to secure a replacement. It was dark when they eventually made it to the first of the Nez Perce villages, where Clark found his partner and the others partaking plentifully of fish and roots. He hastened to warn them to eat sparingly, but his admonition did not come in time to save them from the adverse effects of the local diet and bacteria. Despite the lateness of the hour, Lewis and Clark pressed Twisted Hair for more geographic details as they attempted to converse via sign language. The accommodating chief drew a map on a piece of white elk skin locating the rivers that would take the American travelers to the Columbia. The methodical Clark sought to verify Twisted Hair's cartographic rendition by securing similar drawings "from Several men of note Seperately which varied verey little." The following day they rewarded Twisted Hair and the other chiefs with an assortment of presents.[45]

The fish and roots diet exacted a toll on Lewis and more than a few of his men, and Clark prescribed the standard remedy for complaints of the stomach and bowels, a dose of Dr. Rush's pills. Unfortunately, Lewis's condition persisted for several days, causing Clark to switch his treatment to salts, tartar emetic, and jalap. Meanwhile, in preparation for the expedition's return to the rivers, the captains assigned all remaining able-bodied men to begin building new canoes. Even though he continued to suffer from the effects of the same malady that had sidelined so many of the men, Clark persevered.[46]

Lewis's more serious indisposition, compounded perhaps by a temporary relapse into one of his periodic bouts of melancholia, required Clark to take the lead in superintending the final preparations for their departure. Those tasks included branding the horses that they planned to leave under the care of the Nez Perces until they returned from the Pacific the following year. They also buried their saddles along with an extra canister of powder and bag of shot that they hoped to retrieve on the return trip. Once again Lewis had abandoned his regular journal writing, leaving that chore solely to Clark until year's end. As they prepared to set off on October 7, Clark grumbled what may have been a rare and oblique censure of his friend and partner: "I continue verry unwell but obliged to attend every thing." Perhaps it is too much to suggest that he believed that Lewis had fallen down on the job, but he clearly felt harried as the expedition resumed its journey down the Pacific slope. Time was fleeting, and there was not a moment to waste. Fortunately, two days later Clark was able to report, "Capt. Lewis recovering fast."[47]

The fast-running Clearwater and Snake rivers once again tested the skills of the expedition's now seasoned watermen as they guided their canoes through one rapid after another, taking chances that they normally would have avoided. Sometimes all went well, as on October 13 when Clark reported candidly, "Capt Lewis with two Canoes Set out & passed down the rapid[.] The others Soon followed and we passed over this bad rapid Safe. We Should make more portages if the Season was not So far advanced and time precious with us." Lewis's improvement obviously had continued apace. A short time earlier he had barely been able to walk or even to ride a gentle horse, and now he was successfully maneuvering boats through the white water. Things, of course, did not always go so well. Canoes occasionally capsized, leaving the nonswimmers clinging to their sides until they could be rescued, and jagged rocks sometimes poked holes in the hulls, allowing the water to rush in and dampen both passengers and cargo. More than a little merchandise was lost in these accidents.[48]

In an effort to vary the monotonous and often disagreeable diet of dried fish and roots, they frequently purchased dogs from the local Indians, but in contrast with his messmates, poor Clark could never develop a taste for canine flesh. When complaining about the sameness of their diet he wrote, "all the Party have greatly the advantage of me, in as much as they all relish the flesh of the dogs." Sadly for Clark, there were few other options. Wild game, like firewood, was a scarce commodity in this barren country.[49]

Along the way they encountered new Indian tribes, among them the Wanapams, Yakima, and Walula, who all spoke languages unknown to the expedition's regular interpreters or to the Nez Perce guide traveling with them. Even though Sacagawea was no longer able to assist with the translations, Clark made it clear that her presence continued to be a great benefit: "The wife of Shabono our interpetr we find reconciles all the Indians, as to our friendly intentions[.] a woman with a party of men is a token of peace[.]" At the junction where the Snake intersected with the Columbia, two hundred singing and dancing Wanapam men, beating on drums and keeping time to the music with sticks, encircled the American exploring party in a boisterous welcoming ceremony equal to any they had witnessed during the course of their now lengthening journey.[50]

They were in fishing country, with scaffolds of drying fish beside every lodge, and piles of dead salmon everywhere. Inside the mat lodges Clark reported seeing nets, gigs, and fishing tackle of various sorts. On October 18 Clark caught a glimpse of Mount Hood in the distance, although he did not then know its name, and the following day he saw yet another snow-covered peak that he mistook for Mount St. Helens, which he had read about in British explorer George Vancouver's *A Voyage of Discovery*. Clark unexpectedly sent residents of a nearby Umatilla village scurrying to take refuge in their mat-covered lodges when he shot a crane while waiting for Lewis to arrive with the canoes. As he later learned, they believed that these strangers had come from the clouds and were not men. Fortunately, once again Sacagawea's presence calmed their fears and confirmed the friendly intentions of this band of sojourners.[51]

While the crews prepared to portage around Celilo Falls, John Collins transformed the molded and sour remnants of the camas bread they had acquired at Weippe Prairie into a mash that he used for making what Clark described as "some excellent beer." Perhaps the one-time delinquent had finally redeemed himself in the eyes of his fellow soldiers. Having long since exhausted their liquor cabinet, Collins's brew must have come as a welcome treat. Over the next several days they portaged around the Columbia's Great Falls and traveled through the Dalles, a stretch where the river's narrowing channel made for difficult travel but simultaneously afforded an ideal place for catching fish, the local economic mainstay. Clark's precise and beautifully drafted sketches of the river's many features in that vicinity reveal just how difficult the passage through this area must have been.[52]

Lewis and Clark felt it necessary to take added precautions to guard against pilfering and stealing by the very Indians who had assisted them with their portage, for as Clark stated, they feared the natives' thievery more than their arrows. A rumor overheard by one of the older Nez Perce chiefs traveling with them suggesting that the tribes from below might attempt to kill expedition members did prompt the captains to order an inspection of their arms to ensure that all would be in readiness in the event of an attack. Always on guard, the veteran explorers seemed to take it all very much in stride, with Clark noting that they were "under no greater apprehention than is common." An infestation of fleas that obliged nearly every man in the party "to Strip naked . . . that they might have an opportunity of brushing the flees of[f] their legs and bodies" seems to have been their paramount concern for the moment.[53]

The Dalles was crowded at this time of the year with Indians who congregated there to fish and to exchange goods. Evidence of their links with the Pacific coastal trade was not hard to find. When Clark entered one of the houses along the river he saw "a British musket, a cutlash [cutlass] and Several brass Teas kittles of which they appeared verry fond." He also puzzled over the "figures of animals & men Cut & painted on boards in one Side of the house which they appeared to prize, but for what purpose I will not ventur to say." Clark continued to ponder the meaning of these ubiquitous images and subsequently concluded: "I cannot Say certainly that those natives worship those wooden idols as I have every reason to believe they do not; as they are Set up in the most conspicuous parts of their houses and treated more like ornaments than objects of aderation."[54]

In contrast with the impoverished tribes they recently had encountered, these people appeared to possess "a great deel of property and possessions." As experienced traders, they knew how to drive a hard bargain. Clark was unable to ascertain if they trafficked directly with white traders lower down the river, or if they secured their goods via Indian intermediaries. While their knowledge of white people seemed imperfect and the goods they traded—fish, roots, and Indian basket grass—would have been of little interest to the foreign merchants, these tribes clearly had access to large quantities of beads, tea kettles, brass arm bands, scarlet and blue robes, and European-style clothing.[55]

Put off by both their personal conduct and their physical appearance, Clark found the native people along the Columbia much less to his liking than the Missouri River and Plains tribes. To his way of thinking they were little more than petty thieves, dirty in the extreme, poorly dressed, and physically unattractive with rotten teeth, weak eyes, flattened heads, and swollen legs and thighs, but in truth the people of these inland river tribes were numerous and lived well thanks to a mild climate, an abundant food supply, and ready access to trade goods supplied by seaborne traders from distant places.[56] The expedition reached the Cascades of the Columbia River, or as Lewis and Clark called it, the "Great Shute," at the end of October, and once they cleared that final barrier, they moved rapidly toward the Pacific Ocean that they had been "so long anxious to see."[57]

On November 7, 1805, William Clark jubilantly proclaimed, "Ocian in view! O! the Joy." In truth the sights and sounds that he observed that morning when the fog finally lifted were those of the Columbia's broad estuary and not the Pacific, but it was clear to all that the Corps of Discovery's grand trek across the continent was nearing its end. According to Clark's final calculation, the exploring party had traveled 4,142 miles since it began its ascent of the Missouri eighteen months earlier. Lewis became the first of the partners to reach the Pacific coast, but it was Clark who first put pen to paper to record the momentous occasion. When Clark finally took in the panoramic view of the great western seascape on November 18, he pronounced the immense ocean and its high waves dashing against the coastal rocks an astonishing scene. And indeed it was. He marked the historic event by carving his name, the date, and the words "by land" on a nearby tree as Captain Lewis had done before him.[58]

Unfortunately, the monotonous realities of their dreary daily existence soon supplanted wonder and awe of such grand spectacles. On November 8, only a day after uttering his initial joyful proclamation, Clark scribbled what was soon to become a familiar refrain, "we are all wet and disagreeable." Indeed, the immediate prospect of passing the winter in what seemed to them such an unpleasant place quickly tempered the momentary euphoria that members of the Corps of Discovery had experienced upon reaching their destination. While Clark camped on the ocean shore with the small party that had accompanied him to view the sea for the first time, several of the men declared themselves in favor of returning to the falls for the duration of the winter.[59]

It already seemed clear that the exploring party's stay on the Pacific shore was not apt to be a repeat of its idyllic winter sojourn at Fort Mandan. For complex reasons, neither the Americans nor their Indian neighbors formed a very favorable impression of each other. The prices demanded by the hard-bargaining Chinooks, Clatsops, and Tillamooks irritated Lewis and Clark nearly as much as their pilfering. The American explorers quickly figured out that they would be hard put to compete with the well-stocked trading vessels that annually called at the mouth of the Columbia, and they likewise understood that if they were not careful, they might easily deplete the stores of merchandise essential for their return trip. Indeed, near the end of their stay on the Pacific coast, the now impoverished American travelers would soon be reduced to surrendering Captain Lewis's best officer's coat in exchange for a much-needed canoe. For their part, the coastal Indians had grave misgivings about the bedraggled overland travelers who seemed so unlike their seaborne counterparts. By comparison with the seafarers, Meriwether Lewis and William Clark appeared more standoffish, stingier, and less well supplied. Still more puzzling was their preference for foodstuffs over furs and their seeming indifference to the amatory advances of the native women. It was little wonder that both chose to keep their distance.

A tenuous relationship with the neighboring Indians was only one of the problems facing the Americans as they prepared to settle in for the winter. What they perceived as the dreariness of the place added to their discontent, and while they were eager to see friends and relatives once again, the journey homeward promised to be somewhat anticlimactic, for in the minds of most they had already attained their primary objective. Undoubtedly, Sergeant Patrick Gass spoke for many members of the corps when he wrote in his journal on November 16, 1805, "We are now at the end of our voyage, which has been completely accomplished according to the intention of the expedition."[60] It would remain for the captains to explain to Mr. Jefferson that the hoped-for easy passage to the Pacific by way of the Missouri and Columbia rivers was nonexistent.

Their most urgent need was to locate a suitable site for their winter quarters. They had pitched camp on the northern side of the Columbia, but that location soon proved unbearable. A November rainstorm accompanied by intense winds threw the river's waters out of its banks with such force that the resulting waves and breakers drenched the campsite and split apart one of the canoes. Clark captured the prevailing mood in his usual succinct manner, "O! how horriable is the day."[61] Two days later the commanding officers polled members of the corps to ascertain their preferences concerning the best location for a winter camp. Lewis and Clark took the unprecedented step of recording the individual opinions registered by each member of the exploring party, including, remarkably, those of York and Sacagawea, but it would be somewhat far off the mark to suggest that the U.S. military had gone so far as to embrace democracy. As Gass notes, most of them believed that they should cross over to the southern side of the river and determine if they could locate a good hunting ground in that general vicinity. It was hardly surprising that the preferred choice was the plan that Lewis and Clark favored. Even so, the willingness of the captains to consult with their men on such an important matter was a sign of their mutual respect for one another, and when Captain Lewis found a promising location, Clark and the other corps members did not hesitate to ratify his recommendation.[62]

Lewis selected a site on a small river, now called the Lewis and Clark River, that fell into a small bay on the Columbia's south bank a few miles upriver from the ocean. It was close enough to the Columbia's mouth to allow them to make contact with any trading vessels that might call there—none did during their stay—and accessible by overland trek to an Oregon beach, where they could boil salt from the ocean's waters. Even better, Lewis reported that there appeared to be sufficient elk in that vicinity to satisfy their need for food and for clothing. A driving rain prevented the corps from relocating immediately, and when they finally set out for their new campsite on December 7 they had to battle high waves and a surging tide.[63]

In a change from the proceedings at Camp River Dubois and Fort Mandan, Captain Lewis took charge of the construction of their winter fortification, while Captain Clark set out with five men seeking to locate the most convenient route from their new home to the sea and also to find a suitable place for making salt. During his trip Clark encountered the neighboring Clatsops, whom he judged to be both friendly and neater in their personal and dietary habits than the native people they recently encountered, noting that they frequently washed their faces and hands. The Clatsops treated their American guests to syrup made from dried berries and soup made from breadroots and berries served in trenchers with conch shells as spoons. Clark noted with interest their games, including one employing pieces similar in size and shape to those used in backgammon, but the veteran backgammon player failed to understand the intricacies of the Indian equivalent. The stay was pleasant enough save for the pesky fleas that continued to pester him.[64]

When Clark returned to the camp, Lewis and all of the hands were busily engaged in felling trees for their new fort, which they decided to call Fort Clatsop in honor of their neighbors. They completed the meat house first, in order to provide a dry place to hang and smoke freshly killed game to prevent spoilage in the mild and damp climate. When the perpetual rains briefly changed to snow, work on the installation slowed down because the men lacked socks to wear with their moccasins. They salvaged some boards from an abandoned Indian house in an effort to accelerate the project's completion. On December 22 four of the cabins had been roofed and provided with puncheon floors and bunks, and the following day Captains Lewis and Clark occupied their as yet unfinished quarters.[65]

By Christmas most of the ill-clad troops were at least under a roof and out of the weather. Their dilapidated tents and garments full of tears and holes had long since failed to offer much protection from the elements. Aside from the relative comfort afforded by their new accommodations, there was little cause for merriment on this particular holiday morn. At the crack of dawn the men assembled under the windows of the captains' quarters, fired a salute, and

Fort Clatsop. Courtesy of the National Park Service. This historic re-creation of the expedition's 1806 winter quarters is located in the Fort Clatsop National Historic Park.

followed it with a shout and a song. There was no grog to enliven this year's festivities, and the troops had to settle for a half carrot each of tobacco. Those who did not use tobacco received a small handkerchief in its stead. As usual it rained all day, and their "bad Christmas dinner" as Clark styled it consisted of tainted elk and fish and some roots that they only ate out of necessity. The game in their meat house spoiled despite efforts to preserve it with constant smoking.[66]

Clark exchanged gifts with some members of the corps. Captain Lewis gave him fleece hosiery, a shirt, drawers, and socks. Clark did not record what he gave his "particular friend" in return. Clark received some other presents as well. Joseph Whitehouse provided a pair of moccasins, Silas Goodrich gave a small Indian basket, and Sacagawea presented her good friend with two dozen white weasel tails. Even under these adverse conditions, members of the corps found ways to make the best of their third Yuletide together. With Christmas over, it was back to work putting the finishing touches on Fort Clatsop. By year's end the fortress was finally completed, and the officers issued a new set of orders stating that its gates would be closed daily at sunset, and unless they received special permission all Indians would be required to vacate the premises. It was a far cry from the largely unregulated coming and going that had prevailed at Fort Mandan. There were also new rules governing the daily military routines.[67]

The troops ushered in New Year's Day in 1806 with a volley of small arms at the crack of dawn, fired in front of the officer's quarters. It was the only mark of respect they had in their power to pay to this honored day. Drouillard had brought in some fresh meat, so at least the day's repast was a major improvement over their Christmas meal. For his part, Clark feasted on a fine marrowbone and an elk tongue. Otherwise, he and the others were left to spend the day looking forward to January 1, 1807, when they might enjoy the mirth and hilarity of another New Year in the bosom of family and friends. On this day, however, any toasts would have required the use of "pure water," their only beverage.[68]

The fresh game brought in by the party's hunters supplemented with whale blubber the captains purchased from visiting Indians had improved their diet, but to Clark's chagrin dog meat continued to be their primary fare. It was the same old story. The men seemed to thrive on it, but he lamented that "as for my own part I have not become reconciled to the taste of this animal as yet." Lewis, who found it more palatable, likened it to beaver. Lewis and the others also welcomed the flavoring provided by the salt produced at the party's coastal saltworks, but Clark remained curiously indifferent to that particular condiment as a seasoning for meat.[69]

Reports that a whale had been beached on the ocean shore interrupted the monotonous daily routines at Fort Clatsop and sent Clark and a party of men downriver in two canoes in search of the dead animal with an expectation that they might acquire some of its tasty flesh. Sacagawea, who had not yet seen the ocean, pressed the captains to allow her to accompany the expedition. She argued that after traveling so far she deserved to have an opportunity to see the great waters and this monstrous fish. Her pleas fell on receptive ears, and she was allowed to join the others with, as always, her babe in arms. While en route their little party stopped at the salt maker's camp, where they basked in the glow of moonlight on the first clear night in two months. Clark employed an Indian to guide them along a tortuous mountain trail in the direction of the whale carcass.[70] When they finally crossed over the peak of the coastal mountain range, Clark declared the boundless ocean before him one of the grandest and most pleasing sights his eyes had ever surveyed. Sacagawea must have been equally pleased by what she saw. After descending to the shore Clark discovered that the whale's bones had been picked clean and only the skeleton remained. The Tillamooks had beaten him to the punch.[71]

At a nearby village Clark struck a deal to purchase about three hundred pounds of blubber and a few gallons of oil from the savvy Tillamook traders that he chose to label as "close and capricious." That night several of the men in Clark's party stole away to seek the companionship of native women at a nearby encampment, and in an incident rare in the expedition's annals, an Indian from another town bent on stealing Hugh McNeal's clothing and blanket plot-ted to slit his throat. Only the persistent importuning of McNeal's sympathetic female companion saved the hapless soldier from death at the hands of his would-be assailant. After the excitement had settled down and the men re-turned safely to their camp, Clark posted a guard.[72]

With that situation resolved, Clark contemplated the difficult return trip across the rugged pine- and fir-covered hills to Fort Clatsop. After fretting about their prospects, he reassured himself that determined persistence would see him through this ordeal as it always had in the past. He took added comfort in the assurance of divine providence: "[I] thank providence for directing the whale to us; and think him much more kind to us than he was to jonah, having Sent his monster to be *Swallowed by us* in Sted of *Swallowing of us* as jonah's did."[73]

Clark and the other corps members passed much of the remainder of the winter dealing with matters far more mundane than their quest for the great fish. "Nothing worthy of notice occurred today," was a recurring phrase in the journal entries written at Fort Clatsop. When their supply of candles gave out, Lewis and Clark improvised by using elk tallow to fashion new ones with the help of the candle molds and wicks that they had hauled across the continent—yet another example of their resourcefulness and careful planning. Candles must have burned almost continuously during the dank Pacific North-west winter days and nights while the captains huddled over writing tables in their dim and gloomy quarters. The primary focus of Clark's winter labors seems to have been his map of the country from the mouth of the Missouri to the Pacific based upon firsthand observations, information supplied by native in-formants, and a dash of conjecture. As he labored to incorporate their unex-pected discoveries of the past year, he and Lewis faced the difficult challenge of reinterpreting old and inaccurate notions about western geography and com-ing to grips with the new reality that there was no continuous water route across the continent. After announcing the completion of his map of their jour-ney, Clark rationalized, "We now discover that we have found the most practi-cable and navigable passage across the Continent of North America," albeit one that required an extended overland trek.[74]

While Clark worked on his maps, Lewis devoted countless hours to the preparation of scientific descriptions and drawings of the unfamiliar plants and animals they had discovered. At the beginning of 1806 Lewis had once again taken up his pen and resumed writing lengthy and detailed daily entries in his journal. Clark, busily engaged in mapping and drawing, took advantage of his partner's renewed efforts and temporarily abandoned the tedious chore of recording daily events. Then or perhaps later he simply copied Lewis's work, with only minor modifications, into his own journal. He did provide his own drawings of various plants and animals along with some interesting sketches of the head flattening and skull deformation employed by Indians in the region.

Lewis also wrote ethnographic descriptions of the various tribes sure to interest the president. His observation that the coastal Indians frequently employed English words gave added evidence of the extent of British influence in that region. The phrases, picked up from visiting sailors, included nautical terms like "heave the lead," and saltier expressions such as "sun of a pitch."[75] The fact that Lewis and Clark had passed beyond the bounds of the United States placed them in a diplomatic limbo that left them uncertain about how far they should go in their negotiations with the region's native people. Their failure to make contact with any of the European coastal traders eliminated the need to weigh the possibility of returning by sea—an option that Jefferson had originally posited for them.

The rank-and-file corps members occupied themselves with their assigned military duties, hunting, and occasional dalliances with the local damsels, from whom several contracted venereal diseases. Perhaps the prevalence of sexually transmitted afflictions had helped dampen Captain Clark's ardor. In his 1810 conversation with Nicholas Biddle he related that after he had successfully treated a Clatsop man for some disorder, the grateful patient had sent his sister to pleasure him. The woman whom he described as anxious to join her brother's good intentions stayed two or three nights in the next room at Fort Clatsop with Sacagawea. She left, according to Clark, quite mortified by his rejection.

Colds, fevers, and influenza were common medical complaints. The men spent considerable time dressing skins, tanning leather, and making new clothing for their homeward journey. A shortage of animal brains and soap, both used in the tanning process, slowed the process, but near the end of February Lewis reported that the men had "provided themselves very amply with mockersons and leather clothing much more so indeed than they ever have since they have been on this voige [voyage]."[76]

Members of the Clatsop and Chinook tribes occasionally came calling at Fort Clatsop to trade, but they were seldom permitted to stay overnight. Their offers to sell sturgeon, cured anchovies, and wapato roots indicated that they had learned to accommodate their commerce to the American needs and tastes. The Clatsop chief Coboway was the most popular of their visitors. Lewis called him "the most decent and friendly savage that we have met with in the neighborhood," and on one occasion Clark presented him with a pair of old gloves and his sons with a twisted wire to wear around their necks.[77] Despite their generally positive experiences with native people throughout the course of their journey and their good feelings toward this particular amiable Clatsop

"[G]rouse, the feathers about it's head are pointed." Entry of March 2, 1806. Voorhis Journal #2. Courtesy of the Missouri Historical Society. Clark's drawing of the Cock of the Plains (sage grouse, *Centrocercus urophasianus*) is one of the numerous artistic representations he sketched in his journals.

leader, Lewis and Clark held fast to their deep-seated distrust of Indians, which they had learned long before. In admonishing the men to remain on their guard, they spelled out their not so latent suspicions with clarity: "we well know, that the treachery of the aborigines of America and the too great confidence of our countrymen in their sincerity and friendship, has caused the distruction of many hundreds of us."[78]

Lewis and Clark, and no doubt their men as well, had begun counting the days until their departure for home from the moment they had settled in at Fort Clatsop, but the leafing of the huckleberry told them that spring was at hand and it was time for them to depart. In looking back on their experiences of the past several months, the captains concluded that while they may not have lived sumptuously, they had fared quite as comfortably as they had any reason to expect and had accomplished every object they had set out for them- selves save for making contact with one of the trading vessels that frequented the Columbia River. In a last-minute gesture Lewis and Clark gave the houses and furniture they had built at Fort Clatsop to their friend Coboway after post- ing on the wall of their cabin a listing of the names of every member of the Corps of Discovery, along with a brief description of their voyage as a re- minder of their presence. They had distributed similar lists among local tribal leaders to ensure that others would know of their exploits. It was now time to head home.[79]

Six

Homeward Bound to Blaze New Trails

THE WINTER HAD BEEN long and dreary, but as Captain William Clark and his traveling companions prepared to abandon Fort Clatsop on March 23, 1806, he chose to put the best face on their experiences of the past few months. His journal entry for that date was predictably upbeat: "at this place we have wintered and remained from the 7th of Decr. 1805 to this day and have lived as well as we had any right to expect, and we can Say that we were never one day without 3 meals of Some kind a day either pore Elk meat or roots, not withstanding the repeeted fall of rain which has fallen almost Constantly Since we passed the long narrows [of the Columbia River] on [26 October] Last."[1] Clark was not prone to dwell on the negative, nor was he inclined to live in the past. He was already looking forward to returning home to family and friends and to capitalizing on any opportunities that might come his way following the successful completion of their tour to the Pacific. Short one canoe and unwilling to pay the price that the Clatsops demanded, members of the expedition decided to appropriate one, after rationalizing that it would be just compensation for six elk that the neighboring tribe had taken from them earlier. Whatever their justification, this theft from the "kind and hospitable" Coboway was nothing less than a shameful betrayal.[2]

It somehow seems fitting that the Corps of Discovery's final day at Fort Clatsop, like so many before it, began with rain. The downpour and the rising river

134

momentarily stayed the expedition's departure, but at midday when the skies finally cleared the homeward-bound travelers hastily loaded their canoes and embarked on their long anticipated return trip. Upon learning that their American neighbors had departed, a party of Chinooks set out in hot pursuit, hoping to strike one final bargain. The following day, during a brief stopover at a Cathlamet village, two shell-adorned canoes prompted the observant Clark to conjecture that Captain James Cook had likely mistaken similar decorations for human teeth. It was the kind of scholarly aside that one normally would have expected to come from the pen of his better-schooled partner.[3]

The depletion of the expedition's stores of tobacco did not ease the rigors of travel for the nicotine-starved crewmen, who Clark reported "suffer much" from its absence. Wild crab and red willow bark and a traditional Indian smoking mixture, saccacommis, all proved poor substitutes, and to make matters worse, the troublesome mosquitoes had returned. Knowing that they were heading home undoubtedly made such annoyances more bearable for the wilderness travelers, but other concerns, not so easily dismissed, soon clouded their happy visions of comfortable reunions around the family hearth.[4]

Indians descending the river in search of food ominously reported a scarcity of provisions upstream. That was hardly welcome news to the Americans, who feared they might have difficulty restocking their larders and worried that delays occasioned by inadequate provisions might prevent them from reaching their destination before the Missouri River would once again freeze over late in the year. After putting their heads together on April 2, Captains Lewis and Clark chose to stay put long enough to procure and dry a sufficient quantity of meat to see them through to the Nez Perce villages.[5]

While the expedition's most experienced hunters were on the prowl, a visiting Watala piqued Clark's interest with his mention of a great river flowing into the Columbia from the south that somehow had eluded the mapmaker's notice. In response to Clark's determined questioning aimed at discovering how he could have overlooked such an important geographic feature both times he had passed it by, his Indian informant told him that a large island obscured it from the view of travelers following the north bank. Guided by a pilot whom he hired for the price of a sunglass used for starting fires, Clark returned downriver for a firsthand look at the river the Indians called the Multnomah.[6]

He stopped at a Watala village on the Columbia's south bank hoping that he might barter for some wappato. When the American captain entered one of the dwellings he encountered several "sulkey" natives who balked at his demands for a parcel of the nutritious roots. Uncharacteristically, Clark resorted to trickery to force a sale. He cut off a piece of a cannon fuse and threw it into their fire, causing it to flame and change colors. With the aid of a magnet he also made the needle of his compass spin briskly as if by magic. His antics frightened and alarmed several female bystanders, who threw bundles of the roots at his feet while imploring him to take away the bad fire. Only then did he offer them compensation and agree to smoke his pipe with the men. It was not Clark's finest hour, but his certitude that these were in his parlance "bad Indians," coupled with his concern that members of the corps might perish in the wilderness without additional provisions, no doubt salved his conscience.[7]

With the wappato in hand, Clark proceeded to the Multnomah River, today known as the Willamette River. He ascended it for about ten miles until mist and fog forced him to turn back, but he already had seen enough to conclude that a man-of-war could easily ply its waters. With the measurements he took and the information he gained by interviewing some of the river's inhabitants, he returned to the camp the following day, picked up his pen, and resumed his drawing. In this rare instance, his extrapolations concerning the river and its course proved to be highly inaccurate and contributed to the most glaring mis-representation on the master map of the West that he drafted in 1810.[8]

Preparatory to their leaving for the Nez Perce towns on the Clearwater, the commanding officers ordered the soldiers to practice their slightly rusty shoot-ing skills and to make sure that their firearms were in good working order. John Shields, the expedition's gunsmith, busied himself repairing and adjust-ing weapons. His skilled reboring of Captain Clark's small Kentucky rifle won him high praise from the gun's owner: "the party owes much to the injenuity of this man, by whome their guns are repared when they get out of order which is very often."[9]

Once under way again, the little band encountered rough going on the Co-lumbia's fast-flowing waters. It was a familiar story as large rocks and rapid currents forced weary crewmen to portage around some of the river's most treacherous stretches. Indian thievery and pilfering were serious enough mat-ters for the captains to instruct the men hauling baggage along the slippery Columbia portage to carry their shorter rifles as a precautionary measure. The theft of an ax drew an angry response from Clark's sometimes-intemperate partner, but it was the loss of his Newfoundland dog Seaman that most ran-kled Captain Lewis. He sent three men to retrieve his faithful watchdog and hunting companion with orders to fire on the thieves if they refused to return the animal. Fortunately that did not prove necessary.[10]

The destruction of a large pirogue during an attempt to haul it over some rapids reduced their fleet to two pirogues and two smaller canoes, an insuffi-cient number of vessels to accommodate the travelers and their baggage. After they managed to cram the extra baggage into their remaining canoes, Lewis scurried to find replacements. He successfully negotiated the purchase of two

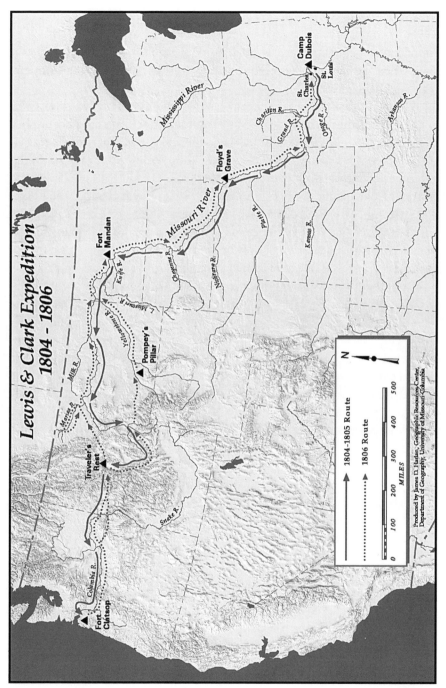

Route Map of the Lewis and Clark Expedition.

canoes, four paddles, and two dogs to boot. Dog meat continued to be a dietary staple, and Clark, who still did not like the stuff, was at least by then willing to acknowledge that it "is a healthy strong diet." Even so, he was no doubt pleased when the hunters delivered four deer brought down by the company marksman Drouillard.[11]

As the time when they would again have to abandon the river drew ever closer, the expedition's leaders turned their attention to acquiring horses, but Clark initially came up empty-handed when the savvy Indian bargainers turned up their noses at his paltry offers. Even the amusement of Cruzatte's fiddling failed to budge them. Clark had gone to the Dalles–Celilo Falls area in search of horses. Native people from far and wide came to buy fish and trade horses and buffalo robes for beads and assorted goods at the place Clark called "the Great Mart of all this country." There were to be sure horses to be had, but the merchandise-strapped Clark had only limited success in striking a deal on the terms he was prepared to offer. To make matters worse, the crawling rodents and vermin that infested his quarters kept him awake most of the night. When Lewis learned of his partner's poor showing he authorized him to up the ante.[12]

In the end Clark's medical chest proved a greater inducement to trade than his depleted stock of wares. After Clark dressed the sores of a principal Nez Perce chief and applied camphor and warm flannel to his grumpy wife's aching back, the tribal leader agreed to sell him two horses at a bargain price. The following day Clark successfully bartered two of the expedition's mess kettles for four additional horses. With his supply of surplus pots exhausted, he resorted to offering his coat, sword, plume, and large blue blanket, none of which attracted any takers. It was time to move on.[13]

With only enough horses to carry the expedition's baggage and equipment, they proceeded on foot. When a party of Indian families, unacquainted with the military regimen, joined the American travelers, the annoyed commanders complained their horses raised too much dust and interrupted the line of march. Sore feet and legs were a common complaint as the fatigued soldiers trekked through deep sand and across rough ground. Clark, who suffered along with his men, obtained temporary relief by bathing his lower extremities in cold water. Their persistent efforts to secure more horses finally bore fruit, and the captains were the first in the company to enjoy again the luxury of a mount. In the military, rank has its privileges, and Clark and his tired and aching feet no doubt welcomed the reprieve from walking.[14]

Mindful of the toll that their lengthy march had taken on both men and animals, the sympathetic commanders readily accepted an invitation from their old friend the Walla Walla chief Yelleppit to spend three or four days at his village. While sharing a meal of roasted mullet and roots, Yelleppit told the captains about an overland route to the Nez Perce towns that would shave eighty miles from their journey. During the course of their friendly get-together the obliging Walla Walla leader presented Clark with an elegant white horse. More often than not their native hosts singled out Clark to accept their special gifts.[15]

Clark's efforts to minister to the Indians' medical needs contributed to his popularity. Word of the treatments he and Lewis had dispensed during their westward journey had spread far and wide, and when they returned a year later, eager patients flocked to their camps seeking medical care. During his brief sojourn among the Walla Wallas Clark tended to fevers, broken limbs, sore eyes, and other assorted pains which he said he "administered as well as I could." The scene was soon repeated when they reached Nez Perce country. A short distance up the Clearwater River, one of the principal chiefs gifted Clark with a "very elegant" gray mare, asking only for eye water in return. "Dr." Clark recalled having treated him and another patient in that vicinity the previous year, and as he noted "those two cures has raised my reputation and given those natives an exolted opinion of my Skill as a phician. I have already received maney applications." Clark quickly became as his friend Lewis noted, "their favorite physician."[16]

Clark's ministrations were not totally altruistic, and he candidly acknowledged that he consciously had elected not to downplay his medical skills because "in our present situation I think it pardonable to continue this deception for they will not give us any provisions without Compensation in merchendize, and our Stock is now reduced to a mear handful." To his credit, Clark pledged to render his patients no harm, and while he did exact a price in food and horses for his services, his treatments appear to have brought at least momentary relief to many of his clients.[17] Hippocrates would have been proud. During his month-long stay at Camp Chopunnish, as the corps dubbed their camp near Twisted Hair's village, the Nez Perce's favorite physician seldom wanted for patients.

As the Corps of Discovery progressed eastward, its leaders quickly discerned that it would be impossible for them to pass through the mountains until some of the snow melted. Their Indian friends informed them that would not occur for at least another month, or as they phrased it not until the next full moon. That was unwelcome news for a homesick band of travelers subsisting on horseflesh and roots. Any doubts about the accuracy of the native predictions evaporated on May 10 when an eight-inch snowfall caused their horses to stumble and slide as they made their way across the relatively level plateau situated well below the towering ranges looming ahead.[18]

Following their arrival in Nez Perce country, Lewis and Clark had taken steps to reclaim the horses and saddles they had left with Twisted Hair the previous fall, but those efforts quickly ensnared them in a tangle of intratribal misunderstandings and hurt feelings that they unknowingly helped precipitate. It seems as if their decision to place the animals in the custody of the lesser chief Twisted Hair had irked his higher-ranking rival, Cutnose. The latter had wasted no time in making his unhappiness known to the Americans and in advising them that their protégé had failed to properly care for the animals during their absence. To their great relief the captains were able to sort things out and in the process to retrieve twenty-one of their horses, a majority of them in good shape. By the time they reached the residence of Broken Arm, the most prominent of the Nez Perce chiefs, they had managed to smooth things over between Cutnose and Twisted Hair.[19]

The snowfall had stopped when the U.S. military expedition entered Broken Arm's village on the banks of Idaho's Lawyer Creek, with William Clark in the lead. He stepped forward to greet the savvy tribal leader who had cleverly placed himself beneath the U.S. flag he had been given the previous year. It was all quite cordial, as the accommodating Broken Arm offered his guests two bushels of roots, four cakes of bread, and a dried salmon. Recalling the digestive disorders that diet had brought on during their earlier visit there, the captains asked to exchange one of their bad horses for a young colt they might kill for food. The chief immediately sent for two young colts, which he provided gratis. Red Grizzly Bear, another important Nez Perce leader, arrived a short time later.[20]

Broken Arm ordered a leather tipi erected to accommodate the visiting Americans and directed that a parcel of firewood be placed at the door. Once all was in readiness, the large assembly that had turned out to greet them crowded into the dwelling to partake of the freshly cooked horsemeat before resuming their council and smoking the pipe. With all of the principal Nez Perce chiefs in attendance, the American military officers took advantage of the occasion to explain once more the U.S. government's plans for establishing trading houses and for restoring peace and harmony among the region's various tribes. To demonstrate the nation's strength and wealth, Lewis and Clark drew a map of the United States showing its immense size. The task of interpreting proved somewhat tedious and took the better part of the day as the words were translated successively from English to French, to Hidatsa, to Shoshone, and finally to the Nez Perce tongue. At times Clark excused himself from the deliberations to treat the steady stream of ailing patients who had come seeking his cures. He had returned in time to receive another token of appreciation from Broken Arm, who literally gave Clark the shirt off of his back.[21]

Not since their winter among the Mandans had the Americans seemed so at ease with their Indian hosts. Both of the American commanders commended the Nez Perce hospitality and praised their cleanliness. Their friend Clark declared them to be "more clenly in their persons and habitations than any nation we have Seen Sence we left the Illinois." In his 1810 interview with Nicholas Biddle, he stated that those nations with few previous white contacts were generally more agreeable and hospitable. Clark's favorable view of the Nez Perce lends credence to that tribe's tradition that he fathered a son by Red Grizzly Bear's sister during his 1806 stay. The woman's son, who always called himself Clark, died sometime after the famous Nez Perce War in 1877. If Clark ever found out about him, he, like his St. Louis friend Pierre Chouteau, chose not to publicly acknowledge his wilderness progeny.[22]

With several weeks remaining before the melting snows would permit the expedition to head into the mountains, the captains established an encampment on the east bank of the Clearwater near present-day Kamiah, Idaho, within a circular depression that once had been the site of an underground Indian dwelling. Lewis and Clark directed the erection of a bowery to shade them from the sun's rays while they continued writing. Their leaky tent was so porous that during one nighttime downpour Lewis's chronometer got wet for the first time during their travels. He immediately attempted to dry out the delicate instrument and lubricate its parts with bear's oil to prevent rusting, but when the problems with the tent persisted, they replaced it with a lodge constructed with willow poles and grass mats that proved to be their most comfortable shelter since Fort Clatsop.[23]

The rising waters of the Clearwater finally signaled that the mountain snows had begun to thaw. For some time an anxious Clark had daily eyed the icy barrier separating him from family and friends and repeatedly pressed to learn when they might safely proceed. Clark's growing medical practice afforded him breaks from the tedium of the writing desk and drawing board. Acting on a suggestion from John Shields, Lewis and Clark experimented with the use of a traditional Indian sweat lodge in their treatment of William Bratton's chronic back ailment that left him virtually immobilized. The procedure worked wonders for the soldier and persuaded Clark to give it a try in the case of a paralyzed tribesman whose relatives had brought him to the Americans seeking a cure for his strange malady. Clark justifiably was less optimistic about the efficacy of this treatment for his severely disabled Indian patient, but to his surprise and astonishment, the heat of the sweat lodge alternated with a dousing in cold water and a few spoonfuls of laudanum appeared to restore partial use of the paralyzed man's limbs. Such successes only enhanced Clark's reputation as a medical practitioner.[24]

While at Camp Choponnish, Pompey came down with a swollen jaw and throat severe enough to produce an abscess on his neck and to place his very survival in doubt. Lewis took the lead in his treatment using wild onion poultices, cream of tartar and sulfur among other things, but Clark also tended to the young boy he had become so fond of. Under their watchful eyes, the lad was nearly recovered by the time they were ready to depart. Given the arduous conditions of their lengthy journey, Sacagawea's unheralded daily care and nurturing of a newborn infant with no obvious assistance from her traveling companions must rank as one of the more remarkable feats of the entire enterprise. It seems probable that more than any of the others, William Clark appreciated her motherly efforts, but he never chose to comment about them in his journal.[25]

It was a familiar refrain as members of the corps prepared for their return to the Lolo Trail. Captains Lewis and Clark struggled to acquire enough provisions to see them through the expected ordeal, and with their stores of merchandise virtually exhausted, they found themselves reduced to trading with empty tin boxes and buttons they had cut from their coats. The three bushels of roots and bread that those trinkets yielded prompted the grateful captains to liken the arrival of those few morsels to the return of an East India merchant's cargo. Obviously at this juncture the representatives of the great American Republic were sensing their vulnerability. Little wonder they were so eager to return to the comforts of home.[26]

During their month-long respite at Camp Chopunnish the horses had reverted to their old ways and become so wild that the Americans had to enlist the assistance of the dexterous natives skilled in roping them. Pilfering had been a less serious problem there, but the theft of a tomahawk belonging to the late Sergeant Charles Floyd produced considerable consternation in camp and prompted a successful effort to recover it. The loss had especially distressed Clark, who had intended to return the weapon to the deceased soldier's Kentucky relatives.[27]

When Lewis and Clark learned on June 3 that the Indians had sent an express across the mountains to Traveler's Rest seeking news from the Salish, the American captains sensed that the time to begin their crossing might be near at hand. Their native consultants cautioned them against a premature departure. Doubtful that the salmon run would begin before they left, Lewis and Clark determined to move closer to the mountains so they would be ready when the time to leave finally arrived. There were final talks with Broken Arm, Cutnose, Red Grizzly Bear, and other Nez Perce leaders, during which Broken Arm presented Clark with some roots and two pipes, one for the Shoshones and the other for their favorite redhead. Clark chose the Nez Perce pipe "made in the fashion of the country" for himself. He had a keen eye for interesting Indian objects and later displayed some of his collection at the museum he opened in St. Louis.[28]

To get their out-of-shape men back in top form, the captains organized foot races, pitting them against their Indian hosts. Lewis seemed rather surprised that one of the native lads was as fleet as the expedition's premier runners Drouillard and Reuben Field. When the races ended, members of the corps divided themselves into two groups for a game of prisoner's base, a contest in which each side attempted to make prisoners of members of the opposing team when they ran outside of their base area. After dark Cruzatte took out his fiddle, and the dancing began. The following day the games resumed with the addition of pitching quoits—flattened rings tossed at a pin. Everyone seemed in a good mood as they contemplated moving on.[29]

On June 10 they headed for the Weippe Prairie where they planned to hunt for a few days while allowing more time for the mountain snows to melt. Thanks to their Nez Perce hosts, there were enough horses to provide each person in the hearty band with a mount and a packhorse for carrying the gear. William Clark spent the bulk of his time at Weippe Prairie updating his list of Indian nations with its accompanying information about location and probable numbers. The temptation was mounting to chance an assault on the snow-clogged route leading to Traveler's Rest on the other side of the Lolo Pass, even though the prospect of crossing those "tremendous mountains" made Clark shudder as he contemplated the deep snows and scarcity of animal fodder they were likely to encounter.[30]

He soon discovered that those fears were not unfounded as the expedition made its way up the steep rocky slopes along a snowy, slippery road. Clark, who was in the lead, had increasing difficulty locating the trail, and by the time he reached the top of the mountain the snow drifts measured between twelve and fifteen feet. Realizing that they were still at least four days from Traveler's Rest, and alarmed that they might easily get lost in the mountains without an Indian guide, Lewis and Clark agreed that they should turn back. Yet again the American explorers found themselves wholly dependent on the very natives whose lands they sought to claim. This marked the first time on the entire trip that they had been forced to retreat, but the prospect of risking their lives and the reports of their discoveries seemed too great a chance for them to take after having come so far. They placed their baggage and valuable papers on scaffolds after deciding that it would be too dangerous to attempt to transport those articles back down the treacherous mountain road they had just scaled.[31]

At the foot of the mountain they sent Drouillard and Shannon in pursuit of assistance from the Nez Perce. After securing three experienced guides, they resumed their trek with their "most admirable pilots" leading the way up and down the mountain slopes along a barely perceptible trail. The native traveling companions broke the monotony of the trail by torching some of the fir trees lining their path and creating a fiery display that the men likened to fireworks.

At the top of the mountain the members of the corps took the property they had left there down from the scaffolds, while Clark took advantage of the elevated view to survey the stupendous mountains surrounding him on all sides. They were far more extensive than geographers had expected, and Clark no doubt was eager to report this along with the expedition's other equally important discoveries.[32]

Once they were safely on the other side of the mountain, they left the snowy trails behind them and took time out to plunge into a hot springs that Clark judged to be as hot as the warmest of the baths at Hot Springs in Virginia. Clark could stand the steamy waters for only ten minutes, but his partner, perhaps eager to show up his good friend, remained in them for nearly twice as long. Lewis and Clark reached their old camp at Traveler's Rest on July 30 and finalized plans for dividing the party to allow the commanders to explore separate routes. They agreed that Lewis would ascend the Marias River to learn more about that stream and its northern reaches, while Clark would investigate the Yellowstone River.[33]

For the first time since their departure from St. Charles more than two years earlier, the captains prepared to part company for an extended period. Lewis's comments suggest that he had some trepidation about dividing the corps: "I took leave of my worthy friend and companion Capt. Clark and the party that accompanied him. I could not avoid feeling much concern on this occasion although I hoped this separation was only momentary." Clark, for his part, plunged ahead after noting only that he had taken leave of Captain Lewis and the Indian guides. Two days later Clark followed his normal custom and paused to observe the anniversary of American independence. He ordered the best fare he could muster—a fat saddle of venison and mush made from Indian roots. Now traveling through familiar country, Clark and his party returned to Camp Fortunate at the forks of the Beaver River, where they paused long enough to retrieve the merchandise and canoes that they had left there. As soon as the men dismounted, the chewers and smokers within their ranks made a headlong dash to uncover the buried cache with its tobacco stash. With a plug or a pipe in their mouths, they were ready to begin raising, washing, and repairing the canoes they had left behind.[34]

They moved through the game-rich country by horse, canoe, and on foot. The hunters killed six deer and a grizzly bear as Clark's band headed for Three Forks, where it set up camp on July 13. After dispatching Sergeant Ordway and his crew downriver to the Great Falls with the canoes, Clark headed for the Yellowstone overland with a party of twelve, including his usual traveling companions York, Charbonneau, Sacagawea, and Pomp. Sacagawea, whom he called "the Indian woman who has been of great service to me as a pilot through this country," recommended an alternate route through a mountain gap, at present-day Bozeman, Montana, and with her advice they were on the Yellowstone only two days later. They continued on horseback in spite of the tenderness of the animals' feet. To help alleviate the problem, the resourceful Clark ordered the hooves of the lame horses covered with specially made moccasins fashioned from green elk hide, even as he launched the building of new canoes so they could resume their journey by water. The injuries George Gibson sustained while attempting to mount his horse added to the urgency of that task, since Clark believed that Gibson would be unable to continue on horseback. When they paused to build the new canoes, Clark took advantage of the hiatus to write some letters and to draft a message to the Crow nation, whose representatives he expected to encounter farther down the Yellowstone.[35]

Clark never had an opportunity to deliver that address, but it provides an early example of the rhetorical style he adopted in his Indian negotiations. In that carefully constructed document, he advised the "red children" inhabiting the Yellowstone that "the great chief of all the white people towards the rising sun" was their new great father. As his representative, Clark had not come to harm them but to do them good. The people of his country were as numerous as the grass on the plains and had sufficient goods to supply all of the red children between the rising sun and the Great Lake of the West. No doubt eastern U.S. tribes long under siege would have been surprised to hear Clark's assurances that "the red children of your great father who live near him and have opened their ears to his counsels are rich and hapy[,] have plenty of horses cows & Hogs fowls bread &c. &c. live in good houses, and sleep sound." His patronizing tone typified the approach U.S. government officials regularly employed in the ritualized world of Indian diplomacy.[36]

He also wrote a letter seeking Nor'Wester Hugh Heney's assistance in arranging for a Sioux delegation to travel with the returning explorers to the federal capital. He entrusted the delivery of that letter to Sergeant Pryor, whom he was sending ahead to the Mandan villages with their remaining horses. The theft of twenty-four horses, taken, Clark surmised, by a Crow raiding party, had halved the size of their herd. Pryor with the assistance of three men set out for the Mandan towns with the animals while the remnant of Clark's dwindling party boarded the canoes and headed down the Yellowstone.[37]

The only impediments to their otherwise peaceful journey downriver were the omnipresent swarms of mosquitoes whose bites were severe enough to produce excessive puffiness and swelling on the baby Pompey's face, the incessant sounds of grunting and bellowing buffalo that often kept wilderness travelers awake at night, and a menacing grizzly in hot pursuit of their meat-laden boats. They made some interesting discoveries along the way, notably the remarkable two-hundred-foot-high geological formation that Clark dubbed Pompy's Tower, now known by the more elegant sounding name Pompey's Pillar (courtesy of Nicholas Biddle), where on July 25, 1806, Clark carefully inscribed his name and the date. They also came across a three-foot-long fossilized rib that Clark retrieved from a formation along the riverbank. He speculated that it had belonged to a fish and probably had in mind the whale they had seen on the Pacific shore. He was wrong, of course, for it was in all likelihood a bone from one of the terrestrial dinosaurs whose remains have since been found in that vicinity. But he cannot be faulted since scientists had not yet identified those prehistoric creatures, nor had they even coined the term "dinosaur." Jefferson after all had urged them to be on the lookout for mastodons and mammoths, who some suspected still roamed the American wilds.[38]

When Clark's party reached the Yellowstone's junction with the Missouri, they pitched camp to await the arrival of Captain Lewis and his men. The mosquitoes, as bad as any they had ever seen, eventually drove them from their river encampment, and as they made a hasty retreat Clark posted a note on a stick advising his partner that they had gone ahead. Four days later Clark was startled to see Sergeant Pryor and his contingent approaching from upriver in a Mandan-style buffalo boat. Clearly Pryor's plan to travel overland to the Mandan villages had gone awry. When he caught up with them, Pryor explained that two days after they parted company, Indian raiders had stolen their horses and left them stranded. Faced with the prospect of traversing the long distance to the Mandan villages on foot, the adaptable woodsmen killed a buffalo and used its hide to fashion a leather boat similar to those used by the village tribes on the upper Missouri.[39]

On August 11, Clark and his contingent hailed down Joseph Dickson and Forest Hancock, the first nonnatives outside of their party they had laid eyes on since April of 1805. The two trappers returning from the Yellowstone had been in Indian country since the summer of 1804 and had little recent news to relate other than reports of continuing warfare among the Upper Missouri tribes. This disappointing intelligence suggested that Lewis and Clark's efforts to promote peace among those nations two years earlier had accomplished little and prompted Clark to surmise correctly that those hostilities would complicate any plans for escorting a combined delegation of Hidatsa, Mandan, and Arikara leaders to the federal city.[40]

Clark barely had time to ponder the implications of those sobering reports before he spotted the boats carrying Captain Lewis's party heading in his direction. As the vessels drew closer, he looked in vain for a welcoming gesture from his good friend, who to his surprise was nowhere to be seen. Moments later one of Lewis's men informed him that the captain had accidentally been injured on the previous day. Alarmed at the news, Clark rushed to the boats, where he found his partner stretched out in the pirogue. Though still very much in pain from the recent mishap, Lewis hastened to reassure his friend that his wound was not mortal and that he expected to fully recover within a month. Clark must have heaved a sigh of relief when he discovered that his friend was fully lucid and able to explain matter-of-factly that Pierre Cruzatte had shot him in the thigh and buttocks after mistaking his leather-clad figure for an elk in a thicket of brush.[41] Both Lewis and Clark seemed ready to forgive the one-eyed Cruzatte, who was notoriously nearsighted. Undoubtedly his otherwise unblemished record of conduct had helped spare him their wrath.[42]

But notwithstanding his pain and discomfort, Captain Lewis had other harrowing tales to relate. While on the Marias, an encounter with a party of Blackfeet had ended violently after the tribesmen tried to make off with the Americans' weapons and horses. During that fray Reuben Field had stabbed one of the Indians to death, and Lewis had shot and possibly killed another before his small squad hightailed it out of the area as speedily as it could. Remarkably, the incident on the Marias was the only violent encounter with Indians during the entire western tour, a record that virtually no one except possibly an idealistic president might have believed possible.[43]

Reunited for the first time since they had parted company at Traveler's Rest, Captains Lewis and Clark headed down the river with all deliberate speed, eager to complete a mission whose end was now in sight. With his partner sidelined by injury, Clark yet again became the expedition's sole journal keeper, a role that he was to occupy for the remainder of the journey. Clark soon filled another of his copybooks, and before beginning the next one, the methodical record keeper made a notation outlining several unfinished tasks that remained to be accomplished to complete his record of the expedition.[44]

The Corps of Discovery's arrival at the Hidatsa and Mandan villages on August 14 marked a homecoming of sorts. The villagers seemed genuinely pleased to see these familiar faces, but to his great disappointment, Clark failed to persuade any influential tribal leaders to accompany him eastward to visit their Great Father the president. It was clearly an offer that both Black Cat and One Eye could and would decline. They made their excuses, primarily that their enemies downriver might seek to harm them, but in the end it seems clear that neither saw any compelling reason to leave their homelands and subject themselves to more American lectures.[45]

Clark tried every imaginable ploy to effect a change of mind, including the decision to give Le Borgne the swivel cannon that they had retrieved from their cache at the Great Falls. The influential Hidatsa chief proudly hauled the weapon away to his village, but he remained firm in his determination not to join the

Shahaka (Shehekshote or White Coyote), by Charles B. J. F. de St. Memin. Following the Corps of Discovery's return from the Pacific, the Mandan tribal leader, who first met Lewis and Clark during the winter of 1804–1805, agreed to accompany them to Washington, D.C. Clark subsequently helped organize the U.S. government's attempts to return the tribal leader safely to his Upper Missouri village. Courtesy of the American Philosophical Society.

American expedition on its trip downriver. When neither his assurances of protection nor his promises of gifts succeeded in overcoming resistance to his overtures, Clark approached the Mandan interpreter René Jusseaume with a promise to continue his employment if he could convince one of that tribe's leaders to accompany them. The Frenchman reported shortly thereafter that White Coyote had agreed to go providing they would also take his wife and son and Jusseaume's wife and children along with them. The deal was struck, and White Coyote hurriedly prepared to take leave of his village, Mitutanka. At the time, it seemed a victory for the American captains, who had been determined to have a representative from this important tribe visit the president, but had they known about the troubles that they would face in securing the Mandan leader's safe return home at the end of his visit, they might well have canceled their offer.[46]

Clark clearly would have preferred to employ Charbonneau rather than the wily Jusseaume, but he could not justify keeping a Hidatsa interpreter on the payroll when no one from that tribe consented to accompany them. Clark, who by then had grown quite fond of Charbonneau and his family, offered to convey them to St. Louis, but the Frenchman declined going for the present because he had neither acquaintances nor any prospects for making a living downriver. He reasoned he would be better off living as he always had. It is unlikely that Sacagawea shed any tears over his decision to remain upriver. Clark next volunteered to take "his little son a butifull promising child who is 19 months old," and while both Charbonneau and Sacagawea declared themselves willing to have Clark raise Jean Baptiste, they advised him that he was still too young to be separated from his mother, no doubt at her insistence. Preoccupied with completing the necessary arrangements for White Coyote's departure, Clark failed to press the issue and afterward regretted that he had not been more persistent on the subject.[47]

Only three days after their departure, already missing "my little dancing boy Baptiest," his mother, Janey, and even the rascally interpreter, Clark jotted a letter to Charbonneau urging him to reconsider his decision not to go to St. Louis. Clark reiterated his offer to educate the boy and to treat him as his own son. He promised Charbonneau a piece of land and livestock if he chose to reside in the Illinois country or if he preferred to travel to Montreal, and he offered to provide him with a horse and look after his family during his absence. This rather poignant missive clearly reveals the degree of Clark's attachment to the Charbonneau family.[48]

Clark settled the accounts with Charbonneau and with John Colter, who was formally discharged after electing to stay upriver in order to join Hancock and Dickson's trapping party heading back up the Missouri. With those matters out of the way, and with Shehekshote safely on board, the corps said its goodbyes and fired a final salute before departing. On their way downriver Clark briefly went ashore at Fort Mandan to inspect the old structure, which had burned during their absence. Its charred remains failed to evoke any obvious nostalgia, for Clark, like his companions, was looking forward, not backward.

Back on the boat, the loquacious White Coyote gave Clark a lesson in Mandan history. Drawing upon his own Biblical frame of reference, Clark seems to have likened the Indian leader's tale of tribal origins to the creation story in Genesis. Perhaps those similarities persuaded him to accord White Coyote's oral traditions greater respect than he gave the stories told him two years earlier by the Arikara leader Eagle Feather, whose village they were then approaching.[49]

Sadly, shortly thereafter three traders heading upriver carried the unhappy news that Eagle Feather had died before returning home. Their report proved to be true, though the details they provided about the time and place were inaccurate. When the corps reached the Arikara villages a party of Cheyenne camped nearby joined the Arikara in welcoming them back. As he had at the Mandan and Hidatsa villages, the recuperating senior partner chose not to leave the boats and left it to Captain Clark to handle the proceedings on shore.

The reception was quite friendly, and for the first time Clark met Grey Eyes, a principal Arikara chief, who had been away when they passed upriver in 1804. Clark gave him a stern lecture about their decision to support the Sioux against the Mandan and Hidatsas, but he provided nary a hint about the absentee Eagle Feather's likely fate. From the Arikara's perspective their chief's continued absence offered reason enough for them to decline Clark's invitation to send another delegate eastward.[50] The Cheyennes also attended the proceedings, and it fell to Clark to prepare a description of that tribe for the record.

On August 22, eleven days following his accidental shooting, Lewis was able to take his first halting steps. As they continued downstream, the American captains kept their eyes peeled for the troublesome Teton Sioux. Clark reported on August 26 that their arms were in good repair and that they would not tolerate any insults at the hands of those bands. There were buffalo everywhere. After climbing a high rise overlooking a great expanse of the plains, Clark estimated that he saw nearly twenty thousand of the shaggy animals grazing on the prairie grasses in a single view. The plentiful supply of meat and a bountiful harvest of sweet-tasting plums made the hunger they once had experienced seem a distant memory.[51]

The plum juice was still dripping from their faces when they spotted a party of about twenty Indians standing with a trader attired in French Creole garb on a high hill overlooking the river, and immediately below them on the opposite bank they observed another party of eighty or ninety additional well-armed men who fired their guns as a salute. Clark directed his men to respond with two rounds. Unable to identify their tribal affiliation, he hoped that they might be representatives of the friendly Yanktons, Poncas, or Omaha. But their menacing appearance suggested otherwise. Clark immediately set out in a canoe with the three Frenchmen who could interpret the various languages in an effort to determine their identity.[52]

Upon discovering that they were members of the infamous Black Buffalo's Brulé band, Clark delivered some of the toughest talk that he had used to date in his dealings with native people. He advised them that he considered them bad people because they had abused his party two years earlier and other white travelers since then. He said he had not forgotten their mistreatment and warned that if they persisted in their misdeeds, the whites would return with enough soldiers to whip any villainous people who dared oppose the United States. He also let it be known that they had supplied the Mandans and Hidatsas with guns, powder, and a cannon to defend themselves. He finished with a stark warning that if they persisted in their bad conduct, the Americans would kill every one of them. It was payback time, and Clark refused to listen to their complaints as he cast off in his canoe and headed across the river, leaving them with his harsh words still ringing in their ears.[53]

There was yet another scare a short time later when they mistook a friendly Yankton band for more Tetons. The sound of shots in the distance led Clark to deduce they had been directed at one of the expedition's lagging canoes. With a party of fifteen men he set out in pursuit of the supposed culprits, while Captain Lewis hobbled up the bank to direct the defense of the remaining men and their boats against an assault. When Clark discovered that the supposed miscreants were actually Yanktons firing at an empty keg the Americans had discarded in the river, there were sighs of relief all around. They sat down for a smoke while Clark explained about his earlier tense encounter with the Tetons.[54]

On September 3 the returning party met James Aird, a longtime trader at Mackinac who was then on his way upriver to trade with the Sioux. The Scotsman had recently spent some time in St. Louis, and Clark pressed him for the latest news from the United States. To their great satisfaction Lewis and Clark learned that all was well with their commander-in-chief Thomas Jefferson, whose political party remained firmly in control of the government. There was some shocking news, however. Aaron Burr, lately the vice president, had shot and killed his Federalist archenemy Alexander Hamilton in a duel, and in St. Louis their friend Pierre Chouteau's house and furnishings had been damaged by fire. They also found out that Clark's onetime Kentucky friend and military superior General James Wilkinson now resided in St. Louis, where he served as governor of the Louisiana Territory, but rumors were already afoot that he was about to be redeployed to lower Louisiana to counter possible Spanish movements against the United States from the southwest. The recent hanging of two Kickapoo Indians in St. Louis was another prime topic of discussion. Lewis, by then sufficiently recovered to walk about on his own, must also have joined his partner in quizzing Aird.[55]

At Floyd's Bluff, both captains and several of the men climbed the hill to inspect the burial site of their fallen comrade. To their dismay, they discovered that the grave had been disturbed. In 1810 Clark told Nicholas Biddle that he had been told that a Sioux chief had ordered his deceased son buried with Floyd so that he could accompany him to the next world, but that seems unlikely. It may simply have been the work of an animal. The commanders ordered the grave filled in before they returned to the river.

When they met a boat outfitted by their old friend Auguste Chouteau, his agent sold them a gallon of whiskey, which was soon dispensed among the men, giving them their first taste of real liquor for well over a year. In anticipation of their return to the white man's world, several of the men exchanged leather hides with the river trader for linen shirts. A second vessel belonging to Chouteau carried Joseph Gravelines, the interpreter who had traveled with Eagle Feather to Washington. He confirmed for the captains that the Arikara leader had died in the federal capital, and explained that he had in his possession a personal message from the American president expressing his sorrow along with the gifts that Jefferson had presented to the visiting tribal leader prior to his death. Lewis, now nearly recovered, was able to walk and run almost as well as ever.[56]

Meanwhile, the men gorged themselves on the ripening pawpaws found on-shore; unknown to them, the fruit may have contributed to an outbreak of sore eyes that plagued more than a few of them. The sighting of cows grazing near the settlement of La Charette sent up a shout of joy among corps members, and their arrival at the French river settlement set off a celebration among both French and American settlers, who were all quite shocked to see them after having long since given them up for dead. Their astonishment only confirmed what Captain John McClallan, another river traveler and old army buddy of Lewis, had told them a couple of days earlier—most Americans had long since presumed them deceased. Only a faithful few, including the president, held out any hope for their safe return. Such news only hastened their desire to be home.[57]

The Corps of Discovery reached St. Charles on September 21, where it received a rousing welcome. Local inhabitants invited the returning travelers into their homes to escape the rain and spend the night in dry quarters, hoping no doubt to learn something about their adventure. Those continuing showers prevented an early departure the following morning, and Clark used the time to work on letters informing relatives in Kentucky that he was safe and sound. The corps spent the following night at Cantonment Belle Fontaine, chatting with the officers and soldiers and purchasing some clothing for White Coyote at the public store. The combined fort and trading factory, established in 1805 by General Wilkinson at Coldwater Creek near the mouth of the Missouri, was the first U.S. military installation constructed west of the Mississippi. It was yet another sign of the many changes that had occurred while they were away.[58]

They departed bright and early the following morning—September 23. Word of their pending arrival had preceded them to St. Louis, and when they put ashore there at noon a large crowd lined the riverbank shouting its approval. In the by then well-rehearsed ritual, the returning corpsmen saluted the gathering by firing a volley of shots into the air. A slight shower failed to dampen either the turnout or the mood as the eager townspeople rushed to the river to greet the expedition's return. There were many familiar faces in the welcoming party. Clark spotted his former Kentucky neighbor William Christy, who had since moved to St. Louis and opened a tavern, and during a brief exchange he arranged to have their baggage placed in Christy's storerooms. The Chouteau brothers were there, of course, and Pierre immediately invited Lewis and Clark to take a room in his refurbished home, now restored from the ravages of the fire that had damaged it during their absence.[59]

Later in the day they adjourned to Auguste Chouteau's stately stone mansion where they passed the evening exchanging news with old friends. It must have been an exhilarating occasion where words and liquor both flowed freely and kept the interpreters busy. Lewis and Clark brought with them new facts and figures. Specific distances could now be assigned to the vast western spaces. In twenty-eight months the intrepid explorers had traveled more than eight thousand miles. No doubt the American commanders enthralled their listeners with stories about the Great Falls of the Missouri, the tense confrontation with the Tetons at Bad River, the dreary winter at Fort Clatsop, and their encounters with grizzlies, but for St. Louis's merchant princes it was the shining otter skins and other luxurious furs they brought back that gained attention.[60] Theirs was a two-way conversation, and for their part Lewis and Clark must have inquired about Pierre Chouteau's trip to Washington, Aaron Burr's troubles, and General Wilkinson's alleged machinations. It was a late night for Clark, who "sleped but little," but he was at his desk bright and early the next morning eager to finish his correspondence before the post departed. Lewis had sent a note to John Hay, the postmaster at Cahokia, requesting that he hold the mail until noon so that he and his partner could include letters announcing their safe return.[61]

Both men recognized the importance of these initial dispatches and were careful to put the best face on the disappointing news that Jefferson's water passage to the Pacific was nonexistent. No doubt they had given this matter considerable thought long before they reached St. Louis. Today's political spin doctors would find much to applaud in the way Lewis broke the news to the president. Clark employed quite similar phraseology in the letter he sent to his brother Jonathan. He also dashed off a note to his army friend William Henry Harrison, then governor of the Indiana Territory. Their claims to have "discovered the best rout which does exist across the continent of north America in that direction" proved to be somewhat inflated, a fact that became fully evident only after the later detection of an alternate route through the South Pass.[62]

Historian Donald Jackson credits Meriwether Lewis with the authorship of these important communications containing the summary sketch of their journey. Indeed, there is a draft of Clark's letter to his brother written in Lewis's hand, and Jackson surmises that Clark simply copied it. Lewis undeniably was the better literary stylist, and on previous occasions he had written letters for his partner. But as historian James Holmberg has recently pointed out, Clark was hardly a slacker when it came to writing, and a close reading of the letter in question suggests that it clearly bears evidence of his imprint as well. Moreover, Clark's journal indicates that during their layover in St. Charles he was already at work on letters to friends in Kentucky. In truth the available sources make it impossible to determine with certainty the precise process or sequencing involved in the construction of these communications, but it seems reasonable to conclude that they were in fact a joint effort for which the junior partner deserves at least partial credit.[63]

These missives were written to inform the public of the expedition's successful outcome and to disseminate the first information about its discoveries. In an accompanying letter Clark removed any doubt about the purpose of his report by specifically authorizing Jonathan to have it published. In the second communication he also promised to give his brother a personal briefing as soon as he reached Louisville, which he guessed would be in about three weeks. Unsure after his long absence which of his friends and relatives were living or dead, he simply instructed Jonathan to remember him to all. Jonathan heeded his brother's suggestion and submitted the letter to the editor of the *Frankfort Palladium,* where it appeared on October 9. Newspapers across the land soon reprinted this welcome report, and Lewis and Clark's spreading fame enabled them to bask in the reflected glory of their remarkable accomplishments.[64]

Once their letters were in the mail, Captains Lewis and Clark dined with the Chouteaus, and then went shopping for some new clothes to replace the few threadbare garments in their now nearly empty wardrobes. A trip to the tailors completed the process. When he settled his accounts in St. Louis early the next month, Clark paid for a coat, two flannel shirts, and two pair of drawers. Undoubtedly he acquired other articles of clothing as well. One can safely assume that he saw to it that he was suitably attired the following evening when the citizens of St. Louis staged a gala celebration in their honor.[65]

St. Louis's leading lights turned out in force for the sumptuous dinner and ball held at Christy's Tavern, during which the happy revelers drank no fewer than eighteen toasts. No doubt to the great satisfaction of the honored guests they began with a salute to the expedition's architect: "The president of the United States—The friend of science, the polar star of discovery, the philosopher and the patriot." Seventeen toasts and more than a few glassfuls later the happy celebrants concluded the festivities by raising their glasses one final time and hailing "Captains Lewis and Clark—Their perilous services endear them to every American heart." It was little wonder that Silas Bent, a recent arrival in St. Louis, reported that "all parties have joined here in expressing their high sence of the great merit of these Gentlemen."[66]

The morning after the bash at Christy's, William Clark, recovering from yet another late night, recorded the understandably abbreviated final entry in his daily journal: "a fine morning we commenced wrighting &c." During the course of the next few weeks he and Lewis occupied themselves writing reports, discharging members from the corps, settling accounts, arranging to escort Indian delegations to the federal city, and disposing of the expedition's leftover equipment and property. The sale of rifles, muskets, powder horns, shot pouches, powder, lead, kettles, and axes at a public auction in St. Louis raised $408.62 for the federal treasury, a sum to which Clark contributed with his purchase of a gun. But Clark, normally not one to hold a grudge, still had a score to settle. On October 10, the same day that the corps members were formally discharged from military service, he fired off a letter to Henry Dearborn containing his lieutenant's commission and a cryptic note stating, "the enclosed commission having answered the purpose for which it was intended I take the liberty of returning it to you." Now flush with success and confident that a better job awaited him, he felt emboldened to use the occasion to make a point about his failure to receive the captain's commission he had been promised at the outset of the expedition. Dearborn surely got the message, but he chose to ignore the very human gesture and allowed Clark to remain in service until February 28 when he resigned preparatory to taking on a new assignment for the U.S. government.[67]

Wrapping up the loose ends in St. Louis took far longer than Clark had anticipated, and he and Lewis did not depart from the territorial capital until late in October. Joining them on their trek eastward were the Mandan chief Shehekshote and his entourage, Pierre Chouteau and an Osage delegation, John Ordway, François Labiche, and Clark's constant companion York. They traveled overland by way of Vincennes and arrived at the Falls of the Ohio on November 5, where Clark had a happy reunion with family members. He and York remained in Louisville while all of the others continued their journey to the seat of government. Clark stayed in Kentucky until December 13, when he and his slave departed for Virginia, making several stops along the way, including one to visit his nephew and ward John O'Fallon who was then attending school in Danville, Kentucky. Following his long separation from his wife, York must have regretted having to part from her so soon. Traveling along the Wilderness Road and through the Cumberland Gap, William Clark was in Fincastle, Virginia, on January 8 in time to receive an effusive tribute from the local citizens. Clark received their flattering accolades with humility, suggesting that the interposition of providence may have had as much to do with the expedition's safe return as the wisdom of its leaders. He also acknowledged his partner, who was by then in Washington, D.C., and promised to see that he received a copy of their address.[68]

Pleased though he might have been by such an outpouring, he had a far more important reason for visiting the historic town in southwestern Virginia. Encouraged by his old army pal Major William Preston, Jr., Clark paid a call at Santillane, the impressive new residence of George Hancock, a prominent citizen of Botetourt County who had served two terms in the U.S. Congress. The

Julia Hancock, portrait by John Wesley Jarvis. Julia, who wed William Clark in 1808, bore him five children prior to her untimely death in 1820. Courtesy of the Missouri Historical Society.

reason was Hancock's flaxen-haired daughter Judith, better known to her family as Judy or Julia. Clark in all likelihood had first met her before the expedition while visiting his friend Preston, who in 1802 had married Judith's older sister Caroline. Despite the difference in their ages—Clark was thirty-six and Judith only fifteen—the attraction seems to have been mutual. No doubt the young girl was drawn to the handsome blue-eyed soldier just returned from a triumphal tour of the West, and he, long desirous of marrying, was finally financially able to court someone from a proper social circle. The obviously smitten suitor's attempts to woo the young Virginia beauty caused him to tarry at Fincastle far longer than he had intended.[69]

The resulting delay forced Washington's city fathers to postpone the gala celebration they had planned as a tribute to the returning heroes. When Clark had not reached the capital city by the second week in January, the event's sponsors decided to proceed with only one of the honored guests in attendance. Meriwether Lewis was present at the elegant dinner on January 14, 1807, as were

Shehekshote, Pierre Chouteau, and a host of governmental dignitaries. Any regrets Clark may have had about missing the grand event were quickly forgotten as his thoughts constantly harkened back to the fair lass at Santillane.[70]

When William Clark finally reached the capital on January 18, he found himself caught up in the swirl of Washington politics and society. Meetings with the president, heads of the executive departments, and members of Congress proved to be a heady experience for the ambitious westerner who at long last had reason to believe that his fortunes were looking up. He proudly boasted to his brother that "my old western friends do not forsake me and [appear] happy that they have it in their power to pay me much respect which [appears] to be the general disposition of every member of Congress with whome I have become acquainted."[71]

There was also a reunion with his friend Lewis, who was still basking in the limelight of the post-expedition celebrations. Poet Joel Barlow had even proposed renaming the Columbia River in Lewis's honor. Clark, of course, wasted no time in telling his partner about Julia. His joyful anticipation of returning to Virginia to continue his courtship was perhaps tinged with a bit of sadness as Lewis recounted his frantic and thus far unsuccessful efforts in pursuit of true love. They also discussed Lewis's plans for the publication of their journals, something that the president clearly was eager to see happen.

Clark's conversations with Jefferson went well. The chief executive listened intently to the disturbing reports about Aaron Burr's western expedition that Clark's brother Jonathan had provided from his listening post in Louisville. They also chatted about the fossils at Big Bone Lick, Kentucky, and Clark volunteered to assist the president in securing some new specimens from there. Jefferson signaled his intent to find suitable positions for both Lewis and Clark and to see to it that they were properly compensated for the valiant services they had rendered their country. To his credit Lewis continued to press for equal recognition and compensation for his friend, fellow officer, and traveling companion, whom he still considered to have been ill-treated in the matter of his commission. In his very first post-expedition communication to the president, Lewis left no room for doubt about Clark's role in the enterprise: "With respect to the exertions and services rendered by that esteemable man Capt. William Clark in the course of late voyage I cannot say too much; if sir any credit be due for the success of that arduous enterprise in which we have been mutually engaged, he is equally with myself entitled to your consideration and that of our common country."[72]

In his recommendations to the House committee appointed "to inquire what compensation ought to be made to Messrs. Lewis and Clarke, and their brave companions," Secretary Dearborn, whom Clark dubbed the "God of

War," chose to follow standard military protocol and proposed that Lewis be granted fifteen hundred acres of land and Clark one thousand, but he also informed the committee chair of Lewis's sentiments in the matter. In the end Congress chose to honor Lewis's wishes, which the president also supported. Even as the compensation bill worked its way through the legislative process, Secretary Dearborn took steps to make amends and properly reward Clark by proposing that Lieutenant Clark be promoted to the rank of lieutenant colonel in the Second Regiment of Infantry. Jefferson included that recommendation along with the nomination of Meriwether Lewis to be governor of the Louisiana Territory in the list of appointments he submitted to the Senate on February 28. Lewis's nomination sailed through, but some of the senators balked at advancing Clark over the heads of officers with greater seniority and declined to approve his promotion.[73]

Clark, by then confident that he would be taken care of, took it all in stride, advising his brother Edmund, "The President thought proper to nominate me as Lt. Col. To one of the regiments which was rejected by the Senate on the Grounds of braking through a Principal. I am truly gratified to find that in this decision of the Senate they as I am told unanimously agreed that they would confirm any other nomonation in the gift of the government." Congress did grant Captains Lewis and Clark each sixteen hundred acres of public land west of the Mississippi, more than Clark had expected, and double pay as well. The army also awarded him an extra ration for his "black waiter" York. In addition, at the order of the president, Clark was subsequently granted an extra sum "for difference of Pay & Subsistence between a Lieut. & Captn. During the Expedition." With various adjustments and additions, Clark's total compensation package eventually exceeded four thousand dollars, a handsome sum by any standard.[74]

True to their promises, federal officials also found Clark a suitable position in government service. At Lewis's urging, President Jefferson and Secretary Dearborn signed off on Clark's appointment as U.S. Indian agent for all tribes in the Louisiana Territory excepting the Osages, who remained under the purview of Pierre Chouteau. They set Clark's salary for that post at fifteen hundred dollars per year. This assignment meant that he and Lewis would continue to work together in St. Louis, and it may have crossed Jefferson's mind that the arrangement might allow Clark to assist his partner with the final editing of the journals, particularly those he had written.[75]

With a new job in federal service and his handsome expedition pay, Clark was ready to return to Fincastle to pop the question. He had already advised Jonathan's wife, Sarah, who had been urging him to marry, to begin fattening the chickens and ducks and preparing sugar and plumbs for pies to make good on her promise of a wedding feast. Since Lewis planned to remain in the East for a time to confer with publishers about the journals, he assigned Clark the task of distributing the land warrants and payments to the members of the corps in St. Louis. After hastily completing the necessary arrangements, Clark bade his friend and colleague good-bye and headed back to Virginia on March 11.[76]

More good news followed when Robert Frazer arrived at Fincastle carrying Clark's commission as a brigadier general in Louisiana's territorial militia, making him the third of the Clark boys to attain that elevated rank. This added position was simply icing on the cake. Things went equally well at Santillane, where Clark received George Hancock's blessing to marry his daughter Judith the following January and of course the bride-to-be's consent as well. Clark sent off a note informing Lewis of his engagement and even tried his hand at matchmaking for his old friend. He cautioned the governor that his forthcoming marriage would require him to absent himself from the territory late in the year. He also confided the dark secret that his soon-to-be father-in-law had Federalist leanings, but he promised to introduce some "sincere republicanism" into a branch of the family in January. Not long thereafter William Clark set off for St. Louis to take up his new duties.[77]

Seven

Soldier, Diplomat, and Businessman

NEWLY COMMISSIONED BRIGADIER General William Clark arrived in St. Louis in May of 1807 and took a room formerly occupied by the Spanish lieutenant governors in a residence at the corner of Main and Walnut. During his previous stays in the river settlement he had often attended special functions there, but however familiar his new quarters may have seemed, the city was a far different place from the French Creole village he first visited a decade earlier. The introduction of U.S. authority following the Louisiana Purchase had produced visible changes in the culturally diverse community of nearly fifteen hundred residents. New two-story brick and frame buildings with symmetrical windows and gable roofs interspersed among the older French-style structures with their galleries and steep-hipped roofs were beginning to give the territorial capital a decidedly American look.

Businessmen, lawyers, and land speculators pouring in from the United States clamored for an end to practices and procedures left over from the French and Spanish regimes. Their attempts to challenge the legality of Spanish land titles and mining concessions alarmed members of the territory's powerful French Creole establishment, who sought to press the legitimacy of those claims with the new U.S. officials. During his tenure as Louisiana's territorial governor, the self-serving James Wilkinson had cast his lot with the wealthy and influential Francophones. His barely disguised partisanship only intensified the rift between the ancient inhabitants and the American newcomers. Clark first learned about those controversies while returning from the Pacific in the fall of 1806. Even before he reached St. Louis, American settlers living a short distance above St. Charles complained to him about Governor Wilkinson's bias in favor of old-timers who had used large concessions from the former Spanish authorities to grab up the territory's best lands.[1]

But partisan squabbling was not the only problem facing American officials in the Louisiana Territory. The escalating dangers from abroad triggered by Europe's Napoleonic Wars made a conflict with Great Britain seem entirely possible. Rumors abounded in St. Louis that British agents in Canada intended to foment a bloody assault against America's exposed western frontier, and speculation about the treasonous designs of Aaron Burr's alleged western conspiracy added to the volatile mix. Concerned that military action might become necessary in the western provinces, President Jefferson and Secretary Dearborn rushed to place the experienced Clark in command of Louisiana's territorial militia.[2] Such were the diverse challenges that awaited Governor Lewis and General Clark as they prepared to take up their duties in the turbulent territory in the aftermath of Wilkinson's departure. Jefferson believed that their military backgrounds, coupled with their previous dealings with native people, made them the ideal pair to tackle Louisiana's daunting problems. He would have no cause to regret Clark's appointment, but the same could not be said for Lewis, who for complex reasons never quite measured up to the task and in despair soon chose to take his own life.

Clark's first years as a resident of St. Louis proved eventful. He embarked upon what was to be a lengthy career in the Indian service, helped organize Louisiana's territorial defenses, dabbled in private business ventures, acquired real estate, and perhaps most important of all married and started his family. As the amiable redhead slipped comfortably into his new post-expedition life, his close friend and associate Meriwether Lewis began drinking heavily and descended ever further into despondency. The unhappy governor's subsequent suicide left his former partner profoundly saddened and facing the formidable and unwanted task of superintending the long-delayed publication of the expedition's journals.

During Clark's 1807 visit to the national capital, the president, secretary of war, and Governor Lewis gave him extensive briefings about his new responsibilities. Since Lewis intended to remain in the East to work on his book, he counted on his "dear friend" to be his eyes and ears in Louisiana. Lewis allowed Clark to read the confidential instructions he prepared for Territorial Secretary Frederick Bates, the official charged with acting as chief executive in the governor's absence, before they were sealed.[3]

Bates preceded Clark to the territory by about a month, and his lack of

Frederick Bates. Clark was often at odds with Bates, the longtime territorial secretary and later governor of Missouri. Courtesy of the Missouri Historical Society.

experience in Indian diplomacy caused him to turn to the veteran negotiator for assistance as soon as he arrived. At the time, the town was crowded with visiting tribesmen. Pierre Chouteau was holding talks with an Osage delegation that had come there to protest the U.S. government's failure to deliver on the president's promises to provide a gristmill and blacksmith shop. In a not so veiled threat, the Osages let it be known that Spanish emissaries recently had visited their villages for the purpose of enlisting their support. Clark chose not to involve himself in Chouteau's domain, but he made it a point to mention the Osage complaints in communications with his superiors in Washington.[4]

Clark's first order of business was to mount a military expedition to conduct the Mandan leader Shehekshote (White Coyote) to his Upper Missouri village. After visiting the president and completing a grand eastern tour, the homesick Mandan chief longed to return to his lodge at Mitutanka. Acting in conformity with Secretary Dearborn's instructions, Clark assigned Pacific tour veteran Ensign Nathaniel Pryor and a detachment of soldiers from nearby Cantonment Belle Fontaine to see White Coyote and his party safely home, and to augment their numbers, he arranged for them to travel with a private trading party led by Pierre Chouteau's son Auguste Pierre. A graduate of the U.S. Military Academy, young Chouteau recently had resigned from regular military service to join the family business. His outfit was the third such venture to head upriver in 1807, a sure sign that Lewis and Clark's stories about the region's untapped commercial potential had encouraged St. Louis fur merchants to move farther into the Indian Country.[5]

Certain that military force would be required to curtail Spanish and British influence in those distant regions and to enforce the laws regulating trade with the Indian tribes, Clark urged Secretary of War Dearborn to deploy troops in the Indian Country. Taking his cue from Jefferson, Clark believed that commerce was a crucial mechanism for controlling the Indians. In his view, the well-entrenched foreign traders constituted a serious threat to U.S. interests on the Upper Missouri. In September he warned Dearborn, "the Indians high up the Mississippi and towards the Lakes Shew Some hostile Simptons, and that British Subjects are the Cause of their discontent."[6]

While Clark was finalizing plans for sending Shehekshote home, fifteen influential Sioux leaders showed up in St. Louis seeking authorization to travel eastward for an audience with the president. His memory of their exchange at the Bad River was still fresh, but the pragmatic agent, charged with bringing peace to the western frontier, wisely chose to let bygones be bygones. Careful not to exceed his authority, Clark declined to allow the Sioux visitors to continue on to Washington without prior authorization, but eager not to miss an opportunity for improved relations, he sent them back to their villages with a military escort, a supply of U.S. medals and flags, and nearly fifteen hundred dollars' worth of merchandise as pledges of future American protection and trade. White Coyote, fearful that his enemies might try to prevent him from passing upriver, made a last-minute plea to combine the two military convoys. Clark agreed to permit both groups to travel together as far as the Sioux villages. Unfortunately, the attack that White Coyote feared occurred farther upriver after the extra troops from the Sioux escort already had headed back to St. Louis.[7]

Closer at hand, a Sac and Fox party had murdered trader Antoine Le Page during a drunken encounter at Portage des Sioux, the alluvial tongue of land between the Mississippi and Missouri rivers in St. Charles County, but tribal leaders stalled when Clark demanded they surrender the murderers to U.S. authorities. While General Clark attributed the heightened native unrest to the machinations of British and Spanish agents, he also recognized that the escalating white encroachment on Indian lands posed an equally serious obstacle to harmonious relations. His refusal to remove a peaceful Kickapoo family that had planted corn on Indian land claimed by a white settler in the district of St. Charles clearly irritated Bates, who showed no concern for the displaced natives and their futile attempts to heed Jefferson's call for gradual assimilation.[8]

Clark did find common ground with Bates on other subjects, such as the necessity of removing suspected Burrites from local civil and military offices and the need for a revision of the territory's defective militia laws. With Bates's help, General Clark prodded the territorial legislature to rewrite the existing regulations governing the militia. In the works for nearly six months, the revised statutes were not ready for submission to the secretary of war until September. Even with the force of the new laws, Clark estimated that half of the territory's widely scattered 2,433 militiamen were still unarmed. Should an Indian war erupt, he confided to Jefferson, "they would be in a very defenceless State." His concerns were legitimate. In addition to the shortage of weapons, many of the independent backwoodsmen resented being summoned for compulsory military duty. Christian Schultz observed that many inhabitants "do not relish the idea of traveling sixty or a hundred miles, to attend to other people's quarrels; or of carrying a gun and cartouch-box the same distance for *one man to look at,* and then bring it home again."[9]

The demands on Clark's time were considerable during the two and a half months he spent in St. Louis in 1807, but his diligent attention to official duties did not keep his thoughts from wandering back to Fincastle and to Julia. In almost schoolboyish fashion he scribbled the names "Julia Hancock" and "Julia Clark" on the back of the draft copy of a memo he had started to Secretary Dearborn, looking forward no doubt to their reunion and forthcoming marriage in the Old Dominion. Having taken care of his principal assignments in St. Louis, Clark departed in midsummer for Kentucky's Big Bone Lick, where he had promised the president that he would superintend a search for bones to enhance the American Philosophical Society's fossil collection.

Clark's exit from the territory placed Bates in charge of Indian affairs at a time when reports of growing native discontent along the Upper Mississippi were the talk of the town in St. Louis. The most ominous accounts predicted that the Shawnee leader Tecumseh was poised to unleash an attack at any moment. Although Bates considered the rumors exaggerated, in Clark's absence he ordered all men in the territory to arm themselves in compliance with the new militia law.[10]

Clark was careful to shield himself from criticism for having left his post. From Louisville he regularly updated his superiors in Washington on current conditions in the western territories. Most important, he kept the president informed about his activities at Big Bone Lick. He reported in early September that his hired hands had uncovered an assortment of bones, but with the exception of a nearly ten-foot-long tusk, he did not consider their finds particularly consequential. Slogging about in the muddy pits in the chilly fall weather was not especially pleasant work, and Clark asked Jonathan to send him his greatcoat and the latest newspapers. Brother George, still much addicted to drink and a continuing source of concern to his younger brother, had accompanied him to the site.[11]

The amateur paleontologists unearthed a jawbone with teeth but failed to locate the remainder of the creature's head. After an additional week on the job, Clark sent the president a detailed summary of the excavation complete with an inventory of the fossils that his crews had collected. As usual, the methodical Clark had done his homework. After consulting the *Encyclopedia,* the only treatise on zoology available to him, the self-taught natural historian produced a remarkably informed assessment of his discoveries. Jefferson's friend, the renowned French scholar Bernard Lacépède, subsequently confirmed Clark's supposition that the fossilized bones he uncovered came from two distinct animals, a mammoth *(Mastodon americanus)* and an elephant *(Elephas primegenius* or Siberian mammoth). Jefferson was so delighted with the three boxes of fossils that he asked Clark to forward the smaller bone pieces which George had retained. The assortment was large enough to allow Jefferson to divide its contents between the American Philosophical Society and the Museum of Natural History in Paris.[12]

While Clark was wrapping up his final report to Jefferson, he received some disturbing news from another quarter. Pryor's expedition to the Mandan towns had been turned back after coming under hostile fire from an Arikara war party. White Coyote understandably declined Pryor's offer to continue by an overland route and returned to Cantonment Belle Fontaine until the U.S. government could deliver on its promise to see him home safely. This unexpected turn underscored how precarious things had become in the Upper Missouri country. After notifying Secretary Dearborn about the failed expedition, William Clark headed for Virginia to usher in 1808.[13]

Five days into the new year the dashing redhead, attired no doubt in the new coat and pantaloons that he had recently ordered from a Louisville tailor, married the attractive Judith (Julia) Hancock at Santillane, the elegant home of her parents. The newlyweds honeymooned in the East before continuing to Kentucky, where the proud husband introduced his bride to family and friends. Preparatory to setting up housekeeping in St. Louis, Julia went shopping for furniture and housewares. Her husband undoubtedly advised her that the Kentucky emporiums offered larger selections and cheaper prices than she would find in St. Louis. Having anticipated that a considerable expense would be required to settle his wife comfortably, Clark had taken the precaution of securing an eleven-hundred-dollar advance against his salary from the secretary of war.[14]

A perusal of the Clarks' Louisville purchases suggests that their St. Louis abode was to be more than adequately furnished: their acquisitions included two bedsteads, ticking, feathers for mattresses and pillows, bed cords, a table, a dozen chairs, plates, cups, saucers, a sugar dish and cream pot, bowls, salt stands, wooden trays, knives, forks, spoons, a cake roller and board, flannel and linen, a quart bottle, and various hardware and tools. Their pantry was to be equally well stocked. Clark bought 1,000 pounds of bacon, 437½ pounds of biscuit, half a gallon of whiskey, a gallon of wine, 20 pounds of tallow and 20½ pounds of butter. Along with these personal stores, Clark had contracted with a Louisville blacksmith to build a horse mill, no doubt intended to fulfill Jefferson's promise to the Osage.[15]

Once he secured a flatboat to transport his party and goods down the Ohio, all was in readiness for the couple to proceed to the Mississippi River settlement. Clark's unmarried niece Ann Clark Anderson, who was about Julia's age, had agreed to take up residence with the newlyweds in St. Louis. Joseph Charless, a printer hired by Lewis to establish a newspaper in the Louisiana Territory, was also joining them as a passenger. Had Clark known that the feisty Irishman would one day spearhead a concerted campaign to discredit him, he might not have been so accommodating. In addition, several of their Kentucky friends planned to accompany them as far as the Cumberland.[16] Not all members of the Clark entourage were so eager or willing to make the journey. York, Clark's slave since childhood, understandably resentful at being compelled to take leave of his wife and family in Louisville, went under protest. Similarly, the nine or so other Clark slaves who likewise found themselves compelled to move to a strange place could not have been any happier about their forced separation from friends and loved ones in Louisville.

When William and Julia Clark finally embarked for St. Louis on June 2, friends and family trekked down to the river landing, where they exchanged tearful good-byes. During their journey down the Ohio, Julia and Ann complained about the pesky mosquitoes that were the bane of river travelers, but all else went smoothly. Along the way Clark received a letter from his friend Lewis, who finally had taken up his gubernatorial duties in St. Louis, a full year after his appointment. He had arranged for a military escort to meet Clark at the mouth of the Ohio, where he had also engaged two keelboats to transport his "goods" upriver. The musty, fusty, rusty old bachelor, as Lewis now styled himself, jokingly threatened to expose his partner's shortcomings and declared his eagerness to make the acquaintance of Miss Anderson.[17]

Accommodations were scarce in the river town, and Lewis had taken the liberty of renting a home on Main Street with the intent that he would share it with them. Julia must have pored over his detailed description of the dwelling's layout, but she may have been worried if it would be large enough to accommodate the three of them comfortably along with Ann Anderson and the Clarks' numerous slaves. Lewis apparently had doubts on that score as well, for he had hastened to add "Should we find on experiment that we have not sufficient room in this house, I can obtain an Office somewhere in the neighbourhood and still consider myself your messmate." He cautioned Clark that he had been able to procure only a little furniture, most of which was not of very good quality, and expressed a hope that he and Julia would be bringing a good stock of household apparatuses with them. Clark's decision to purchase those items in Kentucky obviously had been a wise one.[18]

Lewis's somewhat poignant letter suggests that the lonely bachelor was somehow hoping that he and his former partner might be able to pick up where they had left off at the end of their Pacific journey. But Clark was now married and prepared to move on to a new life, while Lewis sadly seemed more focused on recapturing the "most perfect harmony" that he had once shared with Clark and their little traveling family. While the two old friends would once again have an opportunity to work together, it was never to be quite the same.

The dwelling that Lewis had rented proved to be, as suspected, too small. Not long after their arrival in late June, Clark informed his brother Jonathan that he had hired out most of his Negroes and "Shall if possible live in a little Snug way." Lewis soon took quarters elsewhere, but seems to have continued to have his meals with the Clarks. Within three months Clark had leased their original dwelling for use as a tavern and moved his family into a larger house. The general's beautiful and accomplished niece reportedly had the town's bachelors agog, but even in the more spacious accommodations she soon tired of the frontier town and longed to return home. At the time Ann was preparing to set out for Kentucky, Governor Lewis had announced his intent to go eastward to work on his book. Although his partner procrastinated for several months longer, Clark had contemplated that once Meriwether and Ann were gone, he and Julia would for the first time be "alone, without any white person in the house except our Selves." But that too would soon change, because Julia was by then seven months pregnant.[19]

The expectant mother could always count on the family's domestic servants to tend to her needs, but the Clarks' relationship with their slaves was anything but placid. William Clark's insistence that York abandon his family and take up residence in St. Louis, his willingness to place his surplus slaves in the service of strangers as soon as they hit town, and his casual remark to Jonathan that "on our way we lost Nan[c]ys Child, and Bens horse," equating the death of a slave child with the loss of a horse, all speak volumes to his callous indifference. Priscilla, Aleck, Tenar, Juba, and the grieving mother Nancy all found themselves hired out to other masters, while Ben was put to work making hay and York assigned to prune trees, tend garden, and look after the horses. Influenced perhaps by army procedures that made flogging the prescribed method for disciplining insubordinate soldiers, William Clark had few qualms about using the whip on his slaves. After giving his cook Venos fifty lashes, he declared that the punishment had transformed her into "a very good wench." As he confided to Jonathan, "I have been obliged [to] whip almost all my people. And they are now beginning to think that it is best to do better and not Cry hard when I am compelled to use the whip. They have been troublesome but are not at all so now."[20]

Early the following year he gave his pregnant slave Easter a "genteel whipping" even though she was ready to deliver any day. Fearful that his brother might label him a severe master, he hastened to justify his actions: "I find it absolutely necessary to have business done, and to Check a Slanderrous desposition, which has for a long time Suffered to rage, in nancy and Sillo I have but little trouble, but Easter & venos much, and have only Chastised E-3 times & V twice, and they appear Something better fer it." Clark also repeatedly threatened to sell his recalcitrant slaves down the river. After bullying Scipio in that manner, he relented only when the frightened slave begged stoutly to continue with him. Ten years later the same poor fellow shot and killed himself after Clark once again threatened to ship him to the infamous New Orleans slave markets.[21]

But it was York who seems to have vexed Clark most. He viewed his lifelong companion's refusal to heed his will without complaint as an act of disloyalty and betrayal. York, missing his family in Louisville, repeatedly pressed his owner to allow him to return to Kentucky and hire himself out. Failing that, the long-suffering servant even suggested that he be sold to someone in Louisville. York persisted, and Clark eventually relented and agreed to allow him to return to the Falls of the Ohio for a few weeks, but the obviously irritated master vowed to teach his slave a lesson by sending him downriver if he gave any hint of refusing to perform his duties or attempted to run away.[22]

To Clark's chagrin, York never completely bowed to his wishes. Having once tasted a degree of freedom seldom accorded a slave, the veteran of the Pacific expedition was not prepared to turn back. Clark protested that he wanted to do well by his servant, but lamented that York "has got Such a notion about freedom and his emence Services, that I do not expect he will be of much Service to me again." To Clark's way of thinking, York's refusal to fulfill his lawful obligations violated slave codes and promised to extract a financial cost. Money seems always to have been the critical consideration with Clark, who seldom if ever deviated from the central precept that slaves were first and foremost property. When York returned to St. Louis after an absence of several months, his master complained that he was sulky and gave him a trouncing. Not long thereafter he once again threatened to put York on the auction block. Relations between the two were clearly at low ebb, and that is where they were to remain.[23]

William Clark eventually sent York back to Louisville for good, where he hired him out in various capacities, typically as a wagoner and deliveryman. In the ensuing years he turned York's care over to his brothers and seldom bothered to inquire about him. In 1811, after discovering that Clark's once boon companion was ill clad and in a generally wretched state, John O'Fallon urged his uncle to mend fences with York, but the general apparently took his time. When the writer Washington Irving asked about the expedition's only African American member, Clark informed him that he had freed his former slave and set him up in a drayage business that had failed not long before he fell victim to cholera and died in Tennessee. There seems no reason to doubt the accuracy of those remarks, but Clark's belated decision to grant York his freedom had come grudgingly and far too late to excuse his shabby treatment.[24]

William Clark's slaves bore the scars of the peculiar institution both literally and figuratively, but so too in his own tragic way did their owner. He was undeniably a product of his age, and his views about slavery and race were not unique. But the amiable redhead who was in most other ways a kind and decent man seems always to have known intuitively that his actions were indefensible. One suspects that his repeated denials that he was a severe master and his frequent attempts to justify his conduct were symptoms of an underlying sense of guilt that he never quite managed to shake. Clark did on rare occasions allow his humanity to break through, as evidenced by his commitment to care for his aged and infirm slaves. When preparations were under way to sell his old farm at Clarksville in 1810, he instructed his brother, "I must draw you attention a little to the old negrows at the point, they must not Suffer when they have become infirm, may I beg of you to doo the best you Can with them So that they may not Suffer I will with much pleasure pay for expences which may be incured by them under your directions."[25] That seemingly contradictory impulse simply reflected Clark's notion of an owner's obligations under the slave codes that he clung to as a justification for his other actions. Clark's children appear to have become genuinely fond of some of the family slaves and when they were away from home almost always made it a point to inquire about their welfare, but their concern did not extend far enough to award them their freedom.

Clark's official duties demanded much of his time after he returned to St. Louis in the early summer of 1808. Lacking an assistant in the Indian office, it fell to him to settle all accounts with the numerous subagents and interpreters in his employ. Governor Lewis, who had launched a number of initiatives designed to curtail the growing threats of Indian hostilities, also called on him for advice and assistance. An attempt to bring to justice three Indians charged with killing three French traders in two separate incidents culminated with some sensational murder trials in St. Louis during July and August that revealed their starkly contrasting notions of justice. More than one hundred members from the Sac and Ioway tribes came to the territorial capital to witness those proceedings, and as the cases dragged on endlessly, the thoroughly befuddled tribal representatives beat a regular path to Clark's door beseeching him to pardon the defendants, who insisted that the killings had either been justified or accidental. Clark complained to his brother that he had been "much pestered" by their constant importuning. It was little wonder that Julia was moved to declare that she now resided in a "wild country."[26]

The local juries had no difficulty finding the Indians guilty and sentencing them to hang, but in the case of the Ioways, a territorial judge set aside their verdicts on the grounds that the local courts lacked jurisdiction to hear cases involving crimes committed in Indian country. It took well over a year to finally resolve the complex legal issues. Because the Ioways eventually went free on a legal technicality, Clark determined that it would be unwise to proceed with the execution of the Sac prisoner Little Crow, who had been languishing in the St. Louis jail for well over a year. His recommendation that the president grant clemency was dictated as much by practical necessity as by humanitarian impulse, but during his 1820 gubernatorial campaign, Clark's critics cited the pardon as an example of his pro-Indian leanings.[27]

While Clark may have demonstrated a greater solicitude for the plight of Native Americans than for the traumas experienced by his own slaves, the dutiful soldier and bureaucrat never wavered in his commitment to an expansionist national agenda that expected Indians to surrender their lands and abandon their traditional ways. The 1808 Osage land cession he engineered made that abundantly clear. The powerful Osage, long considered the scourge of the prairies, had shown remarkable forbearance as eastern tribes resettled west of the Mississippi steadily encroached on their traditional tribal lands, but by 1808 many of their members had become increasingly restive. Dissidents within the ranks of the normally pro-American Missouri Osages had embarked on a campaign of stealing horses, killing cattle, and harassing isolated territorial settlers. They rejected the leadership of White Hair, the compliant Chouteau protégé, who seemed too willing to take orders from his nonnative allies. In an effort to reign in the hostile Osage factions, Governor Lewis ordered a cessation of trade with the once commercially dominant tribe and invited enemy tribes to wage war on them.[28]

President Jefferson cautioned Lewis that military force should be employed only as a last resort, holding that "commerce is the great engine by which we are to coerce them & not war." The Jeffersonian strategy sought to cultivate commercial dependency and indebtedness as mechanisms for controlling native peoples and extracting land concessions from them. It was a plan that William Clark fully embraced. As early as the winter of 1805 he had called for the creation of a chain of new federally run government trading posts or "factories" in the Indian country. In choosing to support the controversial factory system, Clark broke ranks with his trader friends who saw the government-owned establishments as a threat to their economic livelihoods. The factory system's critics failed to dissuade officials in the War Department, who in 1808 ordered that new government trading factories be built near the Osage villages on the Osage River and on the Upper Mississippi at the mouth of the Des Moines River. Secretary Dearborn instructed the commander at Belle Fontaine to establish military forts adjacent to each of the new trading stations, to be manned by enough soldiers to protect them.[29]

General Clark suggested that the proposed site for the factory on the Osage River would be inaccessible, and at his urging the secretary of war agreed to shift its location to a point on the Missouri River approximately three hundred miles upstream from the Mississippi. In early August 1808, a keelboat expedition under the command of Captain Eli Clemson set out from Cantonment Belle Fontaine carrying men and supplies to launch the new Missouri River installation. A short time later, General Clark traveled overland with Captain Nathan Boone's company of mounted dragoons from the St. Charles district to join Clemson's force at the Missouri River site.[30]

Clark had selected a spot for the fort that he first sighted while traveling upriver with the Corps of Discovery in 1804. Its elevated location and its unobstructed view of the river and the surrounding countryside were exactly as he remembered. Ignoring the severe discomfort of a recurring bout of dysentery, Clark drew up plans for an upright log palisade and four blockhouses, a connected two-cabin factory store with a cellar, barracks for the soldiers, and other assorted buildings. He set aside time for writing letters to his wife and to Lewis before sending the contractor's boat back downriver. For Julia, already suffering from homesickness, her husband's absence must have added to the loneliness, but while his letter to her is no longer extant, he undoubtedly used it to reassure and encourage her. Like countless military spouses before and since, Julia had to learn that frequent absences went with the job.[31]

Even before work was under way on the log structures, Clark dispatched Captain Boone and an interpreter to the Osage towns to inform them of his arrival and invite them to take up residence nearby. He and Lewis had decided to employ a carrot-and-stick strategy with the momentarily out-of-favor Osages.

Fort Osage in present-day Jackson County, Missouri. This historic reconstruction is an authentic replica of the original fort built under Clark's superintendence in 1808 on the Missouri River bluff that he had identified in his expedition journal as a suitable site for such an installation. Courtesy of the Jackson County Parks Department.

While threatening the errant tribesmen with war, they simultaneously tried to lure them back into the American fold with a promise to build a U.S. trading factory in their midst. White Hair, his supporters, and a band of Little Osages accepted Clark's invitation and rushed to the site known to them as Fire Prairie.[32]

Clark's instructions directed him to build the fort and to secure Osage agreement to relocate their villages nearby. But acting on his own initiative, he used White Hair's obvious eagerness to retain the favor of his American benefactors to extract a land cession from the compliant chief. No doubt, Clark believed that such a bold stroke would be well received by his superiors. The so-called "land purchases" were a crucial component of Jeffersonian Indian policy, and Clark was destined to become a key figure in the implementation of that scheme. Playing to the fears of the acquiescent White Hair and his followers, he persuaded them that such an agreement would assure them U.S. protection against their enemies. According to Clark, "what pleased most was the idea I segusted that it was better that they should be on the lands of the U.S. where they Could Hunt without the fear of other Indians attacking them for their Country, than being in continual dread of all the eastern Tribes whom they knew wished to distroy them & possess their Country." The agreement, as he proudly informed Secretary Dearborn, ceded to the United States "near 50,000 Squar Miles of excellent Country—for which I have promised the Osage protection under the guns of the Fort at Fire prarie, to keep a Store at that place to trade with them, to furnish them with a Blacksmith, a Mill, Plows, to build them two houses of logs, and to pay for the Horses and property they have taken from the Citizens of the U: States since the accession of Louisiana." They had, he hastened to add, cheerfully assented to those terms. It was, to his way of thinking, quite a bargain.[33]

Having secured the approbation of White Hair and his minions, Clark showered them with more gifts. In celebration, the Osages applied paint and joined together in singing and dancing for most of the night. General Clark, who continued to feel unwell, turned in early, well pleased with what he had accomplished. By the time that Clark departed on September 16, the outlines of his "butifull fort," which some had begun to call Fort Clark, were clearly visible. Six days later he was back home reporting to Julia and the governor about his successes and taking a dose of medicine to relieve his vexatious intestinal disorder.[34]

The ink on the treaty Clark had negotiated was barely dry when an Osage delegation came to the territorial capital to express its displeasure with the terms. The angry Indians protested that the compliant White Hair was a "government chief" without authority to bind the tribe to such an agreement. It was little wonder that they would take exception with what proved to be a land grab of monumental proportions. Their objections irritated Clark, who insisted that he and the interpreters had carefully reviewed every provision with the Osage leaders before they signed the treaty. Lewis believed that the treaty had been accurately represented to the tribesmen but sensed the anger White Hair's actions provoked among competing tribal leaders.[35]

Lewis personally drew up a new treaty designed to eliminate some of the specific objections to the previous agreement and then directed Osage agent Pierre Chouteau to see that they signed it. The disgruntled Osage leaders gritted their teeth and affixed their signatures to the revised document in November to avoid further angering the U.S. "gun-men." Clark faulted jealous individuals who had not been a party to the negotiations for the original agreement's rejection and especially blamed Pierre Chouteau for having instigated the opposition. He believed that the Chouteaus had helped orchestrate the Osage protests in an effort to secure the inclusion of a provision recognizing the validity of a large grant the Osages had given them in 1792. Clark privately conceded to his brother that he probably should not have acted without any sort of instructions because as he facetiously put it, "it is too much for one man like me to do and the pie must have a new Crust and more plumbs put in by partcular fingers to be engraved to make it palaleable." The U.S. Senate had enough questions about the Osage treaty to delay final ratification until April 28, 1810.[36]

When the dust finally settled, Clark's admittedly rash action had dispossessed the Osages of an immense tract of land. But as historian J. Frederick Fausz asserts, the 1808 Treaty of Fort Osage proved even more costly in terms of tribal sovereignty and independence and threatened to transform the once proud commercial hunters into lowly plowmen. Years later, with the benefit of hindsight, a wiser and more reflective Clark seems to have developed second thoughts about the terms he had extracted from the Osages. In his diary, Major Ethan Allen Hitchcock, who briefly served as an aide in Clark's St. Louis office, recorded what must have been some of the redhead's final observations about the treaty: "he said at the time that it was the hardest treaty on the Indians he ever made and that if he was to be damned hereafter it would be for making that treaty. It really seemed to weigh upon his conscience and he was the kindest man in the world to any Osages who might visit St. Louis, but then he was kind to everybody."[37]

Following his return from Fort Osage in 1808, Clark once again found himself swamped with the demands of public business. The oversight of numerous and scattered Indian agents and interpreters commanded a great deal of his time and energy, as did the visiting Indian delegations, jobseekers, and assorted others who showed up at his doorstep looking for advice or assistance. Only the arrival of the traditional wintertime hiatus in Indian business freed him to devote more time and attention to his personal and private affairs.[38]

The soon-to-be father confessed that the married state made him more mindful of his needs and those of his family. His deeply rooted belief in the benefits of property ownership set him in search of potentially valuable pieces of land in the Louisiana Territory. One of his first purchases was a fourteen-hundred-acre tract located about six miles outside St. Louis that he acquired from Pierre Chouteau in August of 1808. Initially known as the Marais Castor tract, it later was referred to as Council Grove because General Clark on occasion conducted negotiations with visiting Indian tribes there. He wasted precious little time before putting his slaves to work making improvements at the site. Their strenuous efforts gradually transformed the property into a well-ordered farm and a country retreat for the Clark family. In 1809 Clark also purchased a town lot at Main and Pine. Situated between the river and Main Street, he viewed it as an ideal location for the business establishment that he planned to open in the city, but his family did not occupy the residence on that site until they returned from the East in the summer of 1810.[39]

Clark's fleeting attempts to break into the world of commerce during the

1790s alerted him to the capriciousness of the marketplace, but his business aspirations never went away. His frontier experiences taught him that merchant
capitalists were the driving force in a developing economy, and he longed for a
piece of the action. As he considered his future prospects, Clark sought to entice his nephew, Louisville merchant John Hite Clark, and his brother Edmund
to join him in a business partnership aimed at taking advantage of St. Louis's
untapped economic potential. His carefully thought-out proposition called for
them to open a store offering goods designed to appeal to common folk. Noting
the scarcity of items for this "country trade," he observed that the "whole Town
of St. Louis has not as many Goods as John has in his Store at Louisville." He
proposed that they should stock meal, bacon, meat, potatoes, apples, turnips,
salt, cider, tobacco, soap, furniture, planks, bar iron, and lead. He made it clear
that by focusing on the sale of these ordinary wares, he had no intention of attempting "to run with the rich French merchants of this place."[40]

Clark had no qualms about the propriety of mixing public duty with private
pursuit. Noting that his Indian agency dispersed large sums and that the other
governmental offices and the troops stationed there also put much cash in cir-
culation, he confided to his brother, "we may as well as others Ceatch a little."
He proposed to use the often idle public boats he maintained for transporting
government merchandise to haul his own goods and intended to throw a little
public business his own way as well.[41]

John Hite Clark came to St. Louis to check out his uncle's plans, but in the
end the venture never got off the ground, in large measure because the cash-
strapped, would-be merchant, still in debt for his moving expenses and recent
land acquisitions, could not come up with the ready funds required to get the
store up and running. Though they elected not to join his little venture, William Clark remained on close terms with his brothers Jonathan and Edmund
and Jonathan's son John Hite, always adhering to his admonition, "If there is
any objections or Dificultes prey let us not risque our happiness and love fer
each other."[42]

Such was not the case with other branches of the Clark family. Financial dis-
agreements growing out of William Clark's handling of the estate of his sister
Fanny's second husband, Charles Thruston, resulted in strained relations with
some of the unhappy heirs who questioned the terms of the settlement. Clark,
who always had been solicitous of Fanny's interests, had assumed guardianship
of John and Benjamin O'Fallon, her sons by her first marriage. He placed John,
the older and more studious of the two, at a school in Kentucky, and took the
more volatile Ben into his own home. The O'Fallon boys did not always welcome his fatherly guidance, but he remained an enduring presence in both of
their lives for as long as he lived. The thrice-married Fanny's finances were

complicated, and some of the interested parties claimed that the executor had not done right by her children. Exasperated by their allegations and short of cash, Clark rationalized claiming his fees as the estate's administrator on grounds that the compensation would help him bear the sneers of the ungrateful. While Clark may have chosen to put his own interests first, he seems to have been on firm ground legally. Even though the disgruntled O'Fallon boys often grumbled in private, they chose not to publicly air their alleged grievances because they continued to believe that their influential mentor might prove helpful to them in the future.[43]

Of greater concern to William Clark was his brother George's continued decline. The architect of the Revolutionary War's western campaign had severely burned his right leg after falling into a fire at his Clarksville home in March of 1809. Some blamed the accident on a stroke, but the rumors that inebriation had been the cause seem entirely credible. The leg became gangrenous and had to be amputated, and his worried little brother monitored his progress from St. Louis and lamented that he was not in a position to be of greater assistance. Following his recovery, George moved in with his sister and brother-in-law Lucy and William Croghan at their home east of Louisville, Locust Grove, where he was confined to a wheelchair until his death in 1818.[44]

The 1808–1809 St. Louis winter was long, cold, and a time that Julia Clark was not soon apt to forget. Housebound and expecting her first child, the teenage Julia was miserable. Lonesome, homesick, and unable to enjoy the normal wintertime diversions, she had to stay indoors and fill her hours with household chores. Her largely clueless older husband sensed her unhappiness, but he seems not to have curtailed his activities. He told his brother Jonathan that she stayed at home and worked, and when she found herself thinking of old friends she had a cry and then tried to amuse herself with her domestic concerns. She may also have leafed through the pages of her four-volume set of Shakespeare's works that tradition suggests had been a wedding gift from Meriwether Lewis.[45] On January 10, 1809, Julia gave birth to the couple's first child, a son whom no doubt to the governor's delight they proudly named Meriwether Lewis Clark. His father described him as "a Stout portly fellow with Strong longues [lungs] and well formed." Julia had come through the delivery relatively well thanks to the assistance of the local midwife, whose rates her husband complained about to no avail.[46]

Like many new parents, the couple found themselves forced to endure more than a few sleepless nights. Notwithstanding his occasional sleep deprivation, the doting father delighted in watching his son being bathed and also saw to it that he was inoculated with the cowpox as a preventive measure. Julia was soon thinking about planting her garden and looking forward to the time when she would be able to show off her firstborn to family and friends in Kentucky and Virginia. Meanwhile, following his decision to become a partner in the newly formed St. Louis Missouri Fur Company, her husband seemed busier than ever.[47]

The venture, a brainchild of the bold and audacious fur merchant Manuel Lisa, attracted a host of notable investors who joined together to forge a powerful alliance linking business and government. The firm's list of subscribers read like a who's who of Upper Louisiana's commercial and political power brokers. In addition to Lisa and Clark, Pierre Chouteau and his son Auguste Pierre; William Morrison; Pierre Menard; Reuben Lewis, the governor's brother; Benjamin Wilkinson, the general's nephew; Sylvestre Labbadie; and Andrew Henry were all partners. Clark, who had reconciled his differences with the Chouteaus, jumped at the chance to participate in the enterprise and offered to take two full shares with the expectation that he would be able to persuade his brother-in-law Dennis Fitzhugh, his brother Edmund, and/or his nephew John Hite Clark to come on board with him.[48]

Governor Lewis, with clearance from his superiors, seemed to have eliminated any impediment to Clark's participation. Eager to break the British hold on the Upper Missouri trade and mindful that a U.S. government–run venture there would not be feasible in the near future, Lewis turned to his friends in the St. Louis mercantile community for assistance in promoting U.S. interests along the Missouri's upper reaches. To entice them to enter those markets, he agreed to give them free rein in the region by suspending all trading restrictions there. That decision removed the firm from Clark's superintendence as U.S. Indian agent and paved the way from him to join the Missouri Fur Company with a clear conscience. Lewis, in all likelihood, was a secret partner in the new firm.[49]

Clark's rush to capitalize on the economic opportunities the burgeoning fur trade offered private investors seems not to have decreased his support for the U.S. government's factory system, and he readily accepted an appointment to act as St. Louis agent for U.S. Superintendent of Indian Trade John Mason, the official charged with operating the government-run trading stores. Notwithstanding Governor Lewis's decision to exempt the upper river trade from governmental regulation, Clark's obligations to receive, transport, and sell merchandise and furs for the western U.S. trading factories at Forts Osage and Madison clearly had the potential to create a conflict of interest, but his government superiors seem never to have questioned the propriety of his dual involvement.[50]

Organized during the winter of 1808–1809 for the purpose of exploiting the beaver-rich streams on the Missouri's upper reaches, the St. Louis Missouri Fur

Company's Articles of Association and Co-Partnership stipulated that each partner would go on the first expedition planned for the spring of 1809 or provide an acceptable substitute. William Clark, whose official duties precluded him from going upriver, was designated to act as the firm's resident St. Louis agent. He soon demonstrated his value by helping his new partners negotiate a lucrative government contract for returning the stranded Mandan chief White Coyote to his village on the Upper Missouri.

That deal, struck even before the company's final Articles of Agreement had been signed, was undeniably a boon to the new venture. Under its terms, the firm agreed to raise and equip 125 militiamen to escort the chief to his village. Pierre Chouteau was placed in command of the unit, which was to include forty expert American riflemen. By stipulating that the group's military commissions would expire when they reached the Mandan nation, the agreement gave the Missouri Fur Company a ready-made trading party in the Indian country. The agreement obligated the U.S. government to pay the company seven thousand dollars for its services. As an added incentive, the governor promised not to grant any licenses for trading in the area above the Platte River until after the company's scheduled departure date, thereby assuring the Missouri Company's traders a head start.[51]

Both Governor Lewis and General Clark believed the contract served the national interest. From their perspective, the joint expedition provided a sensible and economical way to resolve the embarrassing problem caused by the U.S. government's initial failure to secure the safe return of White Coyote, and the new company also promised to increase the American trading presence along the Upper Missouri. It was a view widely shared in St. Louis. The *Missouri Gazette* editorialized, "The Missouri Fur Company, lately formed here, has every prospect of becoming a source of incalculable advantage, not only to the individuals engaged in the enterprise, but the community at large."[52]

During the early months of 1809 Clark's duties as the new company's St. Louis agent kept him engaged purchasing supplies, signing notes, and keeping the books. Altogether, the Missouri Fur Company dispatched approximately 350 men up the river in May and June 1809, but the mounting costs associated with those ventures forced Clark to relinquish one of his shares in the company after he failed to persuade any of his Louisville relatives to help underwrite his investment. While still predicting success, the prudent but overextended venture capitalist decided that he could not afford to carry more than a single share on his own. His partners were disappointed that he had been unable to enlist the Kentuckians, but they chose not to hold it against him. They still believed that Clark's influence "would do them no harm" and very much wanted the conscientious public servant to continue in his post as company agent.[53]

Two hundred miles upriver, several trappers outfitted by the company absconded with the firm's goods and equipment and set out on their own. It fell to Clark, acting in his capacity as company agent, to prefer formal charges against the deserters. The star-crossed enterprise never lived up to original expectations, and within a year Clark privately lamented to his brother that the returns were not even sufficient to cover its costs. Fearful that he might soon be required to pony up an additional twenty-four hundred dollars, he took steps to tighten his belt financially and attempted unsuccessfully to unload his remaining share. In 1813, with war raging with Great Britain, the directors authorized William Clark, then the company's president, to sell the merchandise at the firm's Omaha post and initiate action to settle accounts and collect the monies due it. On December 5 the firm's board authorized a division of its remaining assets, and at a January 17, 1814, meeting the firm's partners voted to formally dissolve the company. The dependable Clark continued to initiate legal actions on the company's behalf for several more years. Once more financial disappointment stalked William Clark as he struggled to make ends meet on his government salary.[54]

The optimism surrounding the launching of the St. Louis Missouri Fur Company flew in the face of the reports of worsening relations between the United States and Great Britain. In St. Louis the situation seemed more ominous than ever. Fort Madison, the newly constructed outpost on the Mississippi near the mouth of the Des Moines River, was in danger. Reports persisted that the Shawnee Prophet Tenskwatawa was again inciting various tribes to wage war on the United States. Governor Lewis attempted to shore up territorial defenses by dispatching two volunteer companies of militia to relieve the beleaguered garrison at Fort Madison and place territorial militia companies on alert. General Clark reported that the troop movements had frustrated British plans for the moment, but he urged the secretary of war to keep troops on patrol in the Indian country to observe their movements. He also called for a larger garrison of regular troops at St. Louis.[55]

The news from the federal capital was equally unsettling, now that President James Madison's new administration was in place. Although both Lewis and Clark were on friendly terms with the incoming president, their relationship was destined to be far different from the one they had enjoyed with Jefferson. Madison's advisers seemed likely to be less accommodating than their predecessors, especially his secretary of war, William Eustis. The tightfisted New Englander had taken an especially dim view of the contract Governor Lewis signed with the St. Louis Missouri Fur Company for escorting White Coyote home. He faulted the plan for its costs and its quasi-commercial character. Eustis agreed to honor the seven-thousand-dollar sum stipulated in the agreement, but he declined to allow an additional five-hundred-dollar payment Governor Lewis had authorized for Indian gifts. The bureaucratic Eustis censured Lewis for having failed to secure advance authorization for this costly project and also refused to reimburse him for several of his other expenditures.[56]

Clark rushed to the defense of his already troubled friend. He wrote to his brother Jonathan, "I assure you that he has done nothing dis honourable, and all he has done will Come out to be much to his Credit," but he was clearly anxious about the governor's mental state. These latest blows simply added to the stresses caused by Lewis's growing differences with Frederick Bates. The two men disagreed about everything, and their mutual dislike for one another kept them from reconciling their misunderstandings amicably. Lewis's habit of ignoring Bates and turning to Clark and others for advice regarding significant territorial matters especially rankled the jealous secretary, who made no effort to disguise his disdain for the governor. Bates, still smarting from Jefferson's decision to appoint Lewis and not his brother Tartleton as his personal secretary in 1801, attributed many of the governor's problems to his military habits, and accused him of having acted like "an overgrown baby."[57]

Clark tried to mediate and managed to forestall a duel between the two combatants following an incident at a public ball in St. Louis when Bates refused to speak to the governor and then walked away to underscore his contempt. An angry Lewis, clearly intent on issuing a challenge, retired to an adjacent room and summoned his friend Clark, who declined to send for Bates, even though his agitated associate insisted that he could not allow this latest insult to pass. Clark wisely persuaded his friend to go home, and then used his good offices to effect reconciliation between the two men. Bates demurred after advising Clark, "you come . . . as *my* friend, but I cannot separate you from Gov Lewis—You have trodden the *Ups* & the *Downs* of life with him and it appears to me that these proposals are made solely for *his* convenience." When the demands of their offices forced the feuding officials to meet not long before Lewis departed from the territory, their tempers had cooled sufficiently to enable them to reach a truce of sorts. Once again Lewis's steady friend Clark had come to his rescue.[58]

These regrettable encounters contributed to the governor's growing mental depression, as did his inability to deliver on his promises to the president to prepare the expedition's journals for publication. His inaction on that score had even frustrated Clark, who at one point privately complained that his procrastination had likely lessened their chances for profiting from the sales of their journals. When the governor headed east to seek a rehearing for his protested accounts and belatedly initiate work on the book, Clark reflected on the situation of his beleaguered partner, who was in his judgment an honest man with the purest of motives. When they parted, Clark confided to his brother, "if his mind had been at ease I Should have parted Cherefully." While he sensed that all was not well, William Clark did not realize that he would never again see this truest of all friends. As someone who had shared endless hours in pleasant conversation about all matter of things with this man he had come to love and admire, it seems tragic that Clark found their final words so unsettling.[59]

While clearly bothered by Lewis's troubles, Clark did not have time to dwell on them. He was also settling his personal and private affairs in preparation for a trip to Kentucky, Virginia, and the federal city. Not long after the governor's departure, a harried Clark received notice that the secretary of war had pared the Indian agency's proposed budget, after chiding him that his recommended expenditures for Indian affairs in the Louisiana Territory amounted to four times the sum allotted for civil administration. Prior to his leaving he faced the disagreeable task of dismissing several agents, interpreters, and smiths in his employ, though defensively he hastened to add that they had all been Lewis's appointees. He turned the Missouri Fur Company's ledgers over to Pierre Chouteau, Jr., who had been designated to keep the books during his absence from the territory. Before leaving, Clark also had to tend to the shipment of furs from the U.S. government trading factories and the closing of those accounts as well. It was little wonder that he reported a room full of people waiting to see him a few days before he left St. Louis. He also took time to attend his initiation into the rites of the Masonic order. It seems curious that he delayed taking this step until after Lewis's departure, inasmuch as Lewis was Grand Master of the St. Louis lodge, but no doubt he recognized that membership in the fraternal order would be beneficial for his career path.[60]

Julia Clark, who planned to accompany her husband eastward, was ecstatic at the prospect of escaping her lonely confines and having an opportunity to show off her new son to family and friends in Kentucky and Virginia. She filled her hours packing both for their trip and for a move into the residence they recently had purchased. A few days before their departure, her equally occupied spouse reported that all of their furniture with the exception of a bed, a few chairs, and his writing desk had been sent to their new house. Following a round of farewell visits in St. Louis on September 21, the Clark entourage crossed the Mississippi and headed for Cahokia, where they spent the night while the general attended to some loose ends involving his public duties. The next day they set out for Kaskaskia and a visit with Clark's Missouri Fur Company partner William Morrison.[61]

Traveling overland was seldom easy, and making the journey with an eight-month-old baby was even more trying. The experience may have given even the seasoned explorer pause to reconsider the difficulties that his friend "Janey" must have encountered traveling with an infant during the Pacific expedition. On this particular trip poor roads filled with stumps, stream crossings, lame horses, and broken carriage straps all slowed their progress. Public accommodations along the route were routinely poor, and when there were only scant provisions at one lodging the resourceful Julia and a slave killed two chickens and prepared a breakfast with what they had on hand. Their party reached brother Jonathan's Kentucky residence on October 12, where no doubt they found the food and lodgings a cut above the fare they had encountered along the way. They stayed at Trough Spring for two weeks, giving the baby, who was under the weather, a few days to recuperate and also allowing William time for the confidential chats he had so longed to have with Jonathan.[62]

They proceeded from Trough Springs to Soldier's Rest, the home of Clark's brother-in-law Colonel Richard Anderson, where Julia must have reminisced with his daughter Ann, who had spent many hours with her in St. Louis. No doubt she quizzed Ann about her pending nuptials with John Logan. At every stop the proud parents took the opportunity to show off their son. But shortly after leaving Soldier's Rest, Clark experienced a jolting shock when he read in the Frankfort *Argus of Western America* that Governor Lewis had killed himself by slitting his throat while traveling between the Chickasaw Bluff and Nashville. The report had too much of a ring of truth to allow Clark to reject it out of hand, though he continued to hope against hope that it was unfounded. A recent letter from Lewis had not been reassuring, and in a hasty note that Clark wrote to Jonathan from a crowded tavern room filled with drunks, he expressed his worst fears: "I fear O! I fear the waight of his mind has over come him, what will be the Consequence?" And then as an afterthought he expressed a personal concern about the fate of the journals and expedition notes that Lewis had in his possession. The following day Clark met Dennis Fitzhugh, who confirmed what he had suspected. Lewis was dead, from a self-inflicted gunshot wound.[63]

Meriwether Lewis's tragic death cast a pall over Clark and his young wife. He seems never to have doubted that it was suicide, and one suspects that he asked himself what, if anything, he might have done to prevent this terrible tragedy. But if nothing else, William Clark was a practical man, and he immediately focused on the unwanted responsibilities that he had just inherited of overseeing the publication of their long-delayed book and settling Lewis's financial affairs and property. With such thoughts swirling about in his head, he headed on to Virginia with Julia and little Lewis, as they called the baby. The roads were bad and the child's severe cold seemed no better. As the news of the governor's passing spread, friends along the way began urging Clark to seek the appointment to replace his deceased partner. But even in his grief, he seemed certain about his likely response, having already concluded, "to have a green pompous new england[e]r imedeately over my head will not do for me." Clark no doubt held the penurious Yankee William Eustis partially to blame for hastening his friend's demise.[64]

Clark did in fact decline to be considered for the appointment that eventually was awarded to Kentucky Congressman Benjamin Howard, whom he met briefly during one of his stops on the way to Virginia. The Clarks spent their last night on the road at the home of George Hancock's neighbor William Lewis. The family's children all had whooping cough, and in an effort to protect little Lewis from contracting the dreaded disease, his worried father tied a string around the tot's nose. The next morning they hurried on to Santillane, where a warm welcome and hugs all around quickly dispelled the chill of that cold and snowy evening. Julia's return home with her baby, then broken out in sores but otherwise healthy, provided a happy ending to an otherwise troubled journey. While Julia regaled her family with stories about her life in the wilderness capital, including no doubt accounts of the numerous Indians who called upon her husband at his office, the general made preparations to sally forth to Washington, D.C.[65]

He had received word that the War Department had declined to pay some expenses for his Indian agency, and that news had greatly alarmed him, coming as it did on the heels of the rejection of various of Governor Lewis's vouchers. He was eager to settle those accounts and no doubt to clear his deceased partner's name. He also desired to follow up on his efforts to secure the return of the expedition journals and papers. And of course there was the matter of his book. These things needed immediate attention, and he set out for the capital city in a quest to resolve them. While making his way to Washington, Clark stopped by the residence of Lewis's mother, Mrs. Lucy Marks, to convey his condolences, but she was away at the time. He did have an opportunity to speak with other family members, whom he found understandably distressed. In Charlottesville he encountered Thomas Jefferson, who invited him to spend the night at Monticello.[66]

The former president undoubtedly thanked Clark in person for the Rocky Mountain sheepskin and the Indian blanket that he had recently forwarded for inclusion in the collection of Indian curiosities on display in Monticello's Entrance Hall, but their mutual friend Lewis was foremost in their thoughts. His affairs were the principal topic of conversation that night. Both men considered it very likely that Lewis had taken his own life. Their discussions also turned to the publication of the expedition journals, long a subject of paramount interest for Jefferson, and now one very much on Clark's mind. The sage of Monticello had already advised Philadelphia publishers C. and A. Conrad and

Company that Clark was the proper person to now take charge of the project. But the heir apparent doubted his suitability for the task and was more forthcoming in expressing his reservations than his partner had been. When he first sent Jefferson an early draft of his journal from Fort Mandan, Clark had worried that his writing was not sufficiently polished for general viewing, and five years later he harbored the same misgivings. Jefferson sensed Clark's diffidence, and the two of them seem to have settled upon a plan for hiring a good writer to prepare a narrative of the journals and a competent scientist to organize and analyze the scientific data. Clark would do what he was best equipped to do—draw the map. It seemed a workable strategy for advancing the long-stalled project.[67]

In Richmond Clark met with William D. Meriwether, who had responsibilities for settling Lewis's estate, and they talked over matters related to Lewis's finances, the settlement of his estate, and the publication of the journals. When he finally arrived in the capital city, things went very well. Lewis's trunks had been sent there, and Clark took possession of the expedition journals and maps. All was accounted for, save the botanical specimens and the celestial calculations, which he expected to find in Philadelphia. President Madison took time to meet with the western official even though he was much preoccupied with finding a way to maneuver around the maze of European blockades and counter-blockades that threatened to embroil the young American Republic in Europe's stormy conflicts.[68]

A meeting with Secretary Eustis produced agreement on western defense measures and an amicable settlement of Clark's accounts. The top-ranking officials seem to have recognized Clark's growing command of issues involving the Indians. It was all quite reassuring for the territorial officer, who informed his brother, "I find the president & Secty. Of war reather favourably disposed towards me & in place of my having lost Confidence, I feel flattered from their attention & refurences that I am reather a faverite." No doubt he hurried off a note to reassure his "dear angel," who had just written to express her worries about the unfavorable reports about Lewis and by inference Clark that had begun to circulate in Virginia. The expressions of trust and confidence from his superiors in Washington would have tempted a lesser man to change his mind about accepting a gubernatorial appointment in the Louisiana Territory, but Clark's sure instincts correctly told him it would be a mistake.[69]

Clark was a conciliator who found controversy and discord distasteful. As he candidly acknowledged, "I do not think mySelf Calculated to meet the Storms which might be expected." In contrast with Lewis, Clark had avoided a direct confrontation with Frederick Bates, even though truth be known he was no fonder of the acerbic official than his friend had been. Clark sensed that his appointment would not be kindly received by Bates, who had already launched a campaign to discredit him along with the late governor, and he resolved that given the current circumstances he would be happier remaining where he was. Clark was ambitious without being power-hungry, and unlike many public figures he tended to underestimate his own abilities.[70]

Perplexed and perhaps a little angry with his deceased partner for having failed to initiate work on a published account of the expedition, Clark set out for Philadelphia to work out an agreement with the publishers along the lines that he and Jefferson had settled upon. While in the City of Brotherly Love he entered an agreement with A. Conrad and Company Booksellers to publish the work and to pay all expenses. He secured Dr. Benjamin Barton's agreement to write the volume reporting their scientific findings and took time out to pose for a portrait painted by Charles Willson Peale. The confident countenance that Peale portrayed in his painting belied the uncertainties that Clark expressed in their private conversations.

While sitting for the artist in his museum, perhaps under the gaze of the portrait of Lewis that Peale had done three years earlier, Clark shared his plans for publishing the expedition journals with the illustrious painter and natural historian. Peale came away from the discussion convinced that his subject "was far too diffident of his abilities." In his estimation, General Clark's rich store of knowledge about "the different Nations of Savages & things" offered a wealth of information not to be found in Captain Lewis's notes. It was high praise indeed for the reluctant Clark, who shortly thereafter settled upon Nicholas Biddle to write the narrative for him. The general had made the correct decision. The demands on his time were already very great, and he was in no financial shape to give up any of his income-producing positions.[71]

Biddle had doubts about undertaking the project and did not make himself available to Clark while he was in Philadelphia. Only the intercession of the publisher and Dr. Barton persuaded the young litterateur to reconsider, and once on board he traveled to Fincastle, where he spent nearly three weeks interviewing Clark and going over the journals preparatory to beginning work on his narrative. Biddle's copious notes of Clark's responses to his questions are an added source of information concerning the expedition and Clark's personal views. The publisher wasted little time in issuing a prospectus announcing Biddle's forthcoming history, but despite the author's diligent efforts it was still four years away. All was now in readiness for Clark, anxious to get back to the place he now called home, to leave for St. Louis. Julia was not so eager to abandon Virginia again.[72]

They arrived back in St. Louis on July 7, 1810. Julia and Lewis were suffering from mosquito bites that had festered into sores on her legs severe enough to

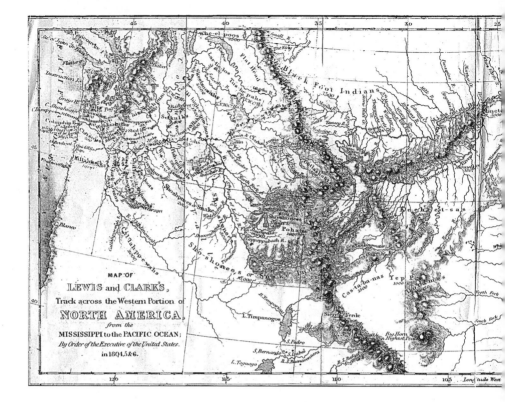

cause her to limp. They occupied the house they had purchased the preceding year only to discover that it had a leaky roof, which the new homeowner arranged to have repaired. As if that were not enough, British traders had stepped up their activities among tribes east of the Mississippi; those actions, in combination with the ongoing work of the Shawnee Prophet and Tecumseh, were threatening to turn the principal tribes of the Old Northwest against the United States. Major segments of the Shawnee, Potawatomi, Winnebago, Kickapoo, and Sac nations seemed ready to defy the American authorities, and the spreading unrest brought leaders from undecided neighboring tribes scurrying to St. Louis to confer with General Clark and take the measure of the American government's intentions.[73]

In July a band of renegade Potawatomis had stolen a number of horses from settlers at Loutre Island on the Missouri and then murdered four members of the party sent to retrieve them. When incoming Governor Benjamin Howard finally arrived in the territory in September, the situation in the capital was tense. Fortunately, Clark found himself in complete agreement with the new governor concerning the policies they should follow. The same could not be

A Map of Lewis and Clark's Track, drawn by cartographer Samuel Lewis from William Clark's 1810 map, was first published in Nicholas Biddle's history of the Lewis and Clark expedition. This landmark map altered long-held notions about North American geography and launched a new generation of American maps. Courtesy of the Library of Congress.

said for Bates, who had spread disparaging reports about the conduct of both the deceased former governor and Clark. Clark was obviously furious about the conduct of someone he once considered a friend but now viewed as "a contemptible little animal." Unlike Lewis, Clark chose to ignore Bates's insults, confident that he was in good standing with the new governor and with officials in Washington. Always one to get along, he managed to work with Bates, but they were never again friends.[74]

The candles and lamps burned late at the Clark residence. The press of public and private affairs often kept him up until nearly midnight. He devoted many of his waking hours to the completion of the master map of the West that he promised to furnish for Nicholas Biddle's edition of the Lewis and Clark journals. On December 7, 1810, Clark dashed off a letter to Biddle reporting, "I have nearly finished a large Connected Map which I shall send on by the next mail. I wish the whole or such part of it annexed as you think proper in such a way as you, think best, the map is made on a scale which I think will please you . . . The map will not be Corrected by Celestial observations, but I think verry correct."[75]

In preparing his 1810 map Clark also incorporated additional geographic data obtained from various explorers, traders, and trappers who passed through his St. Louis office. The result was what geographer John Logan Allen has called "an item of superlative craftsmanship and analysis" that launched a new generation of American maps. Unlike its predecessors, Clark's map showed the West's topographical diversity, including the tangled ranges of the formidable Rockies, along with more accurate depictions of western waterways, many of which were not navigable. Absent was any attempt to link the sources of the Missouri River with those of the Columbia River.[76]

Good as his map was, Clark did perpetuate one great error based upon a misinterpretation of information from his Indian sources and the persistence of the geographic theory of continental symmetry. His depiction of the mythical Multnomah River (his attempt to represent the Willamette River) kept explorers searching for a Passage to India for another generation. When Biddle finally received Clark's manuscript map, he turned it over to Philadelphia cartographer Samuel Lewis, who made a slightly truncated copy for engraving and printing. It first appeared in Biddle's 1814 history of the expedition under the title "A Map of Lewis and Clark's Track." Sometime afterward, Biddle returned the manuscript map to Clark, who kept it on the wall of his St. Louis office, adding new details from time to time.[77]

Beyond its geographic importance, William Clark's cartographic masterpiece presented the West as a region. His visual depiction helped forge a link in the popular imagination between the West's vast expanses and the American Republic's future destiny. It was, in the words of James Ronda, "an act of political imagination . . . [that] advanced an American imperial agenda—one that acknowledged an Indian presence while ignoring Spanish and British claims in the West. In the largest sense the 1814 map is Manifest Destiny visualized."[78]

Numerous other responsibilities also required Clark's attention. Following his return to St. Louis, he resumed his duties with the floundering St. Louis Missouri Fur Company, even as he continued to act as the agent for the U.S. trading factories at Fort Osage and Fort Madison. An assault by a party of hostile Blackfeet at the Three Forks on the Upper Missouri and several other mishaps had proven costly to the Missouri Fur Company, and as he had earlier feared as a partner, he was being called upon to pay twenty-four hundred dollars to cover his share of the expenses. Clark found himself in debt, and to cover the demands of his creditors he sold some of his Clarksville lots and may also have disposed of the sixteen-hundred-acre land warrant he had received as compensation for the expedition.[79]

There had been a surprise following Clark's arrival back in St. Louis. His former traveling companions Toussaint Charbonneau, Sacagawea, and little Pompey—now five years old—were in the city. The family had journeyed to St. Louis late in 1809 no doubt to take advantage of their red-haired friend's promises to provide the French interpreter with a plot of land and to see to the boy's education. At the time that Clark was making his rounds in the national capital in late December, Father Urbain Guillet had baptized Jean Baptiste in St. Louis's vertical-log Catholic church. Since the Charbonneaus' benefactor was out of the city, St. Louis's venerable cofounder Auguste Chouteau and his daughter Eulalie served as the lad's godparents. When the Charbonneaus learned of Clark's return, they made their presence known, and true to his word, in October 1810 Clark arranged for the transfer of a tract of land in the St. Ferdinand township to the Frenchman. A farmer's life does not seem to have been the trapper's calling, and less than six months later he sold the land back to Clark for one hundred dollars and headed back upriver with Sacagawea, leaving the child behind under Clark's care. Sacagawea died the following year (1812) at Fort Manuel on the Upper Missouri, but Clark saw to it that Charbonneau found regular employment in the Indian service. The Frenchman lived on until about 1843.[80]

Entries in Clark's account books indicate that he paid tuition and board for Jean Baptiste, who took classes in St. Louis. In 1823 the well-schooled eighteen-year-old met Paul Wilhelm Prince of Wurttemberg, then on a grand tour of the American West. With the elder Charbonneau's consent, Jean Baptiste accompanied the German prince back to his homeland and for the next six years lived and studied in the royal household. The man whom Clark once called "my little dancing boy" lived on in the far West until he died in Oregon in 1866.[81]

For Clark the year 1810 literally ended with a bang—one produced by several gunshots exchanged during a duel that he helped facilitate. When the smoke cleared on Bloody Island, as the sandy Mississippi River isle that often served as St. Louis's dueling grounds came to be known, St. Louis attorney James Graham lay mortally wounded at the hand of Clark's friend and frequent houseguest Dr. Bernard Farrar. The complicated affair began during a card game when Graham accused Lieutenant John Campbell of cheating. Campbell felt honor-bound to demand satisfaction for this insult and asked his friend Dr. Farrar to deliver the challenge. Graham refused to accept on grounds that Lieutenant Campbell was a liar and cheater and thus not entitled to fight in the manner of a gentleman.

Under the bizarre rules of the code duello, Dr. Farrar, who had presented Campbell's demand, now became the aggrieved party and considered it his duty to take to the field of honor against Graham. He summoned Clark to make the necessary arrangements and the general consented. Graham and Clark met in the general's office on Christmas Day and agreed upon the time, place, and terms for the engagement. The duelists met at the appointed hour with pistols at the ready. Three exchanges at close range left both men bleeding, but Graham's injuries were the more life-threatening. The regretful Dr. Farrar ignored his own wounds and rushed to treat his opponent. Though initially it seemed likely that Graham would survive, a ball lodged in his spine took his life a few days later.[82]

In the meantime, a report passed through the town by word of mouth that Clark had given Farrar private signals that enabled him to get the first shot. An obviously vexed Clark called upon the wounded Graham to exonerate him from those false accusations. The gallant Graham obliged from his deathbed with a declaration stating that the entire duel had been conducted in a fair and honorable manner and branding the charges leveled against Clark and Farrar malicious and false. Shortly thereafter his statement was published in the *Louisiana Gazette*. With the matter settled in proper form, Graham was free to die a short time later. William Clark never recorded his thoughts about Graham's death, but Dick Steward, the author of a recent study of dueling in Missouri, concluded that Clark was more often than not a calming influence who frequently mediated efforts to curb the political violence.[83]

Clark's struggle to pay his debts and make ends meet persisted. His letters to brother Jonathan in 1811 suggest that he had opened a store in an effort to alleviate his pecuniary problems. In the spring he wrote that John Luttig had been his storekeeper for some time and was well acquainted with his financial affairs, and a few months later he reported, "I am getting a little tired of mercantile business and if I do not get Such a person to join as I wish Shall Sell out. Not withstanding money is to be made at it." With the approval of its other shareholders, Clark sold goods and merchandise worth $1,405.51½ to the Missouri Fur Company in September of 1810. St. Louis's newest storekeeper seems finally to have realized his ambition to become a man of business, but his distinct roles as merchant, Missouri Fur Company agent, and U.S. factory agent make it exceedingly difficult to sort out his complex mercantile transactions. Unfortunately, the returns from those varied ventures always fell far short of his expectations.[84]

The financially strapped official with a growing family welcomed a modest $150 increase in his federal salary as factory agent. On September 10 Julia had delivered their second-born, "a rough red headed fellow" whom they named William Preston Clark after his proud father's longtime Virginia friend. Scarcely three months later distressing news from Louisville tempered that joy. William Clark's beloved brother Jonathan, his friend, confidant, and adviser, had died at his Trough Springs home on November 25, 1811. It was a blow equal to the one he had suffered with the passing of his trusted companion Meriwether Lewis.[85]

The obligations of his Indian agency showed no signs of abatement. To the contrary, the secretary of war had extended his responsibilities to both sides of the Mississippi and placed agents Pierre Chouteau and Nicholas Boilvin under his supervision, even though his remuneration for that position remained unchanged. British interference and the Shawnee Prophet's messianic message seemed to foment perpetual unrest in the territories east of the Mississippi. To keep things in check on the west bank, Governor Howard and General Clark directed the organization of additional militia companies and superintended the construction of several blockhouses in the trans-Mississippi territory's remote stretches.[86]

The persistent intrusions of white interlopers on Indian lands still threatened to imperil the peaceful relations west of the Mississippi. A community of emigrant Shawnee and Delaware Indians on the Meramec River in a settlement known as Rogerstown was especially at risk. When its inhabitants petitioned the president to allow them to mine lead on lands around their town because wild game was becoming so scarce they could no longer feed and clothe their families, General Clark described them as "a peaceable and well disposed people, and have been of great service to our frontier settlements in that quarter, in preventing the robberies of the Osage and in bringing in horses which had either Strayed or had been Stolen from the frontiers." His strong endorsement persuaded federal officials, who approved the request and instructed him to expel any white intruders from the Indian lands accorded by law. It was at best a futile gesture, but one sufficient to prevent the Missouri Shawnee bands from joining the powerful, anti-American coalition headed by their tribal brother Tecumseh.[87]

The end of 1811 brought added terrors to the inhabitants of the Louisiana Territory. A series of earthquakes centered at New Madrid, 160 miles south of St. Louis, rattled dishes, toppled chimneys, and unnerved residents in the capital city until the tremors finally subsided in early February. The fretful Frederick Bates openly worried that with all the adverse publicity about earthquakes, Indians, and epidemics, Missouri would in a few years "be nothing but a place of exile for Robbers & Outlaws." Clark failed to take public notice of the earthquakes, but the increased threat from hostile Indians prompted his calls for stronger defensive measures, including a proposal that companies of mounted rangers should be kept perpetually in motion patrolling the exposed countryside.[88]

Eager to remove his own little family from harm's way, he conveniently arranged to conduct a delegation of Osage, Sac, Fox, and Shawnee leaders to the federal city for a conference in the summer of 1812. That trip afforded him an opportunity to settle Julia and the boys safely at her parents' home in Virginia.

They left St. Louis on May 5 and headed for Louisville, where they passed some time before proceeding on to the East Coast. Somewhere along the way he learned that Congress had declared war on Great Britain. Clark separated from his family at Hagerstown, and they continued on to Fincastle while he headed for Washington with his Indian traveling companions. When the general finally arrived at the seat of government in early August, the nation seemed ill prepared to challenge Great Britain. Federalist opponents openly questioned Mr. Madison's War, and a recently launched campaign to invade Canada was already in disarray. It was hardly an optimal time for Clark to arrive with his Indian visitors.[89]

There was also bad news of another sort awaiting Clark when he reached Washington. A letter from Nicholas Biddle informed him that their book's publisher had gone out of business and the publication was once again stalled. As soon as he had completed his official business in the capital, Clark detoured with his Indian entourage to Philadelphia, where he waited impatiently for four days to confer with Biddle. When the author failed to show, Clark fired off a note expressing his displeasure at the prospect that the young writer had decided to abandon the project. He pleaded, "Can't I purswade you to become *Interested* in Lewis & Clarks work [?]" And to sweeten the pot he offered him half of all profits if he would attend to the final details for publication. The frontier was already in flames, and the general had precious little time to devote to a book. As he prepared to depart from the City of Brotherly Love, he reminded Biddle of his obligations: "I am a public officer and must move with a parcel of people (Indians) who are placed under my charge."[90]

On his way down the Ohio with his Indian charges, Clark traveled under the protection of two companies of raw recruits then on their way to join the army of the Northwest. Back in St. Louis, unsubstantiated reports circulated that angry Kentuckians planned to kill the Indians in Clark's party in retaliation for some recent murders near Louisville. During a pause at the Falls of the Ohio in late October, Clark felt it necessary to broach the subject of his prolonged absences from the territory. He sent Secretary Eustis a letter from Louisville reminding him that he had found it necessary to leave his family in Virginia because the frequent alarms precluded them from returning to the frontier. He requested permission to go back to Virginia at the end of the year to tend to his family and from there to Philadelphia to iron out the difficulties with his now stalled book project. While acknowledging that government employees had an obligation to be at their posts, he noted that the winter season was a slack time in his offices.[91]

After a seven-month absence, Clark arrived back in St. Louis on November 21 with his well-traveled Indian companions, who were in all likelihood sporting the new boots that a Washington boot maker had fashioned especially for them. His stay in the territorial capital was to be a brief one. After sending the Indians back to their respective tribes with what he described as a plain and pointed talk, arranging to initiate some reconnaissance patrols once the weather improved, and recommending the construction of gunboats to defend the Mississippi and Illinois rivers, he set out on December 14 to retrace his steps eastward. Prior to his departure, Clark was chosen to preside at a public meeting convened for the purpose of drafting a series of resolutions addressed to Governor Howard, who like Clark had been away from the territory much of the time. After expressing their high regard for the governor, the citizens tactfully pressed Howard to advise them about his future plans. Their intent undoubtedly was to put an end to speculation that he had decided not to return in the spring. The governor's noncommittal reply simply stated that he would have to await the government's instructions. Neither Clark nor Howard tarried long in St. Louis, but they did find time for an extended conversation about possible military operations the following spring. If the governor confided that he intended to step down from his current office, Clark chose not to betray his confidence.[92]

William Clark rejoined his family at the Hancocks in January. Shortly thereafter he and Mrs. Clark traveled to Washington for a round of visits and from there went to Philadelphia, where Julia made the acquaintance of the socially prominent Biddles and perhaps consulted with a local physician about her medical problems. Clark and Biddle finally had an opportunity to confer about their book. Interest in Lewis and Clark's travels had waned, and Philadelphia booksellers, sensing that there was little profit to be made, were reluctant to become involved with the project. Eager to be done with it, Clark granted his power of attorney to Biddle, who engaged Paul Allen as an editorial assistant to complete the manuscript that he had begun. His *History of the expedition under the command of Captains Lewis and Clark* . . . was finally ready for distribution in 1814, nearly eight years after they had returned to St. Louis. The sales proved disappointing, the publisher went out of business, and Clark never received a single cent from the publication. By then he had become accustomed to financial disappointment.[93]

But the country was at war and General Clark, soon to become Governor Clark, had more urgent matters on his plate. Following the outbreak of the War of 1812, the Madison administration implemented a number of changes that directly affected him. Secretary Eustis's unpopularity had made it necessary for the president to remove the punctilious clerk from that office. His replacement and Clark's new superior, John Armstrong, was much better versed in military matters, but he was at the same time abrasive, indolent, and desirous of becoming

194 *Wilderness Journey*

the next president. Even so, Clark considered him an improvement. There were other changes afoot as well, including plans for a reorganized army command structure that divided the United States into nine military districts. The eighth department, which encompassed the states of Kentucky and Ohio and the territories of Indiana, Illinois, Michigan, and Missouri, was to be placed under the command of Clark's friend General William H. Harrison. Because of that district's size, the War Department agreed to create a new position in the regular army for a brigadier general who would direct military operations in the Illinois and Missouri territories.

Concerned about how the proposed changes would affect his duties, Clark sent the secretary of war a detailed list of questions regarding the Missouri Territory's defenses. In his response, delivered on the eve of Clark's departure for St. Louis, Secretary Armstrong advised him that under the new arrangement the office of agent for Indian Affairs west of the Mississippi would be eliminated and those duties assigned to the governor of the Missouri Territory. From his sources in the capital city, Clark must have learned about President Madison's plan for offering Governor Howard the option of either accepting the special brigadier general's commission or retaining his current position as governor, with the understanding that he would offer whichever post Howard declined to General Clark. Either way, Clark was assured of a key assignment.[94]

William Clark left Washington to make his way back to St. Louis, unaware that Governor Howard had already written to inform Secretary of State James Monroe that he intended to decline reappointment as the territorial chief executive. When he reached Louisville in mid-June, Clark advised his nephew John O'Fallon to direct his mail to St. Louis, where he would "be planted either in civil or military." In either case, William Clark was about to open another chapter in his storied life.[95]

Eight

Mr. Governor

WILLIAM CLARK APPEARED before Superior Court Judge John B. C. Lucas in St. Louis on July 6, 1813, to take the oath of office as governor of the Missouri Territory. For him, the path to the governor's chair had been circuitous. He had declined a gubernatorial appointment following Meriwether Lewis's death in 1809, and landed the position four years later only after Benjamin Howard had ruled out a second term. When he discussed his possible options for continuing in government service with President Madison and Secretary Armstrong, Clark apparently made it clear that he no longer had any qualms about serving as governor. Secretary Eustis had departed, and Clark's familiarity with the Missouri Territory's dire problems emboldened him to believe that he was now up to the job. The unorthodox procedure of allowing Howard to choose between the governorship and a brigadier generalship in the U.S. Army and then offer whichever one he declined to Clark seems not to have bothered the popular redhead, whose appointment drew applause all around. In contrast with his two immediate predecessors who had cared for neither the office nor the place, William Clark relished being governor and came to think of Missouri as his home.[1]

He vacated the governor's office in 1820 only after voters in the new state of Missouri rejected his bid to continue in that position. Even so, his seven-year tenure made him the territory's longest-serving chief executive and arguably its best. Long before he became governor, Clark had formed strong personal and business attachments with some of the most influential members of Missouri's social and economic establishment. His unwavering loyalty to their interests opened him to the charges of elitism and favoritism that eroded his prospects for winning elective office. Flawed though his political instincts may have been, William Clark's administrative, diplomatic, and military skills and his commitment to public service enabled him to compile an impressive record while serving as the territory's top official.

Clark assumed office during what he later termed to have been the worst of times. Bands of hostile Indians roamed along the territory's northern and eastern borders, held in check only by the rangers, militia units, and armed gunboats patrolling the countryside and the rivers. Under the circumstances, the incoming governor elected to leave his young family in Kentucky temporarily. With the nation at war, the redheaded chief had to devote the bulk of his time and energy to defensive measures and Indian affairs. General Howard and Colonel Daniel Bissell previously had ordered the evacuation of Fort Osage and the construction of a fortified base camp for territorial military operations at Portage des Sioux, but the shortened line of defenses did not prevent a stealthy Sac war party from attacking several men and boys working in their fields north of St. Louis only a few weeks after Clark took up the reins of government.[2]

The Sac raiders fled across the Mississippi, and General Howard, long an advocate of a campaign against the eastern tribes, was soon in hot pursuit. Clark concurred wholeheartedly with Howard's offensive and was confident that the general's handsome little army of thirteen hundred men would curtail the threat posed by the marauding bands. In a move calculated to make a statement of his own, Missouri's new chief executive arranged for the army's next armed gunboat to be built at St. Louis in full view of the Indians who regularly came there to confer with him. Beyond that he took the unconventional step of inviting several hundred Sac and Fox Indians to vacate their villages along the Mississippi and take up winter quarters on the south bank of the Missouri in present-day Moniteau County. In relocating these friendly Indians in the heart of the Missouri Territory, he hoped to sequester them from the influence of designing British agents and belligerent tribes. To assuage the Osages and reward the transplanted Sacs, Clark also authorized the opening of new trading factories in mid-Missouri as a replacement for the now closed Fort Osage.[3]

Across the Mississippi, when the Sac raiding parties managed to elude General Howard's advancing troops, the American soldiers burned several Indian towns and built a fort on the Illinois River that they called Fort Clark in honor of the Missouri governor's famed Indian-fighting brother George Rogers Clark. Meanwhile, the welcome news of Oliver Hazard Perry's great naval victory on Lake Erie in September 1813 triggered a spontaneous celebration in St. Louis.

The happy revelers set a canoe on fire and drew the blazing craft through the city's streets in a torchlight procession. On the heels of Perry's triumph came word that General Harrison's troops had killed the Shawnee organizer Tecumseh at the Battle of the Thames in Canada. For a moment even Governor Clark dared hope that the wars in his quarter were about to be at an end, a sentiment echoed in the pages of the *Missouri Gazette* by "An Old Man" who proposed the governor and Colonel Auguste Chouteau as candidates to conduct peace negotiations with the vanquished tribesmen.[4]

The man at the helm of the Missouri Territory used the lull in fighting to meet with legislators, decide on territorial appointments, and tend to routine administrative matters. In his opening remarks to the General Assembly the new governor stressed the need for unity and cooperation. His old republican values came to the fore as he urged the legislators to exercise caution and prudence in writing new laws, reminding them that frequent changes in the territorial codes rendered the statutes perplexing to magistrates and jurors and encouraged litigation. There were areas that he believed required the legislature's attention, and before year's end he called upon the territorial assembly to revise the statutes governing the militia and public roads. As his parents had so often done in difficult times, Clark admonished the assemblymen in his closing remarks to "invoke the aid and guidance of divine providence which can alone conduct us free from error in the discharge of our important functions."[5]

The governor was not timid when it came to political matters. He made a daring though unsuccessful effort to have Frederick Bates replaced as territorial secretary. In recommending his friend Edward Hempstead for the post, Clark suggested that Bates's obligations as recorder of land titles required his undivided attention. Bates still had sufficient political clout to retain both positions, and Clark wisely bowed to the inevitable and maintained a professional though distant relationship with his fellow officeholder. In most other instances Clark's efforts as a political broker were more successful. John G. Heath, an early Clark critic, angrily protested when President Madison, no doubt on the advice of the governor and his supporters, passed him over for an appointment to the territorial Legislative Council and named instead Benjamin Cooper, who Heath claimed "can neither read nor write, [and is] a very Ignorant old man in his dotage." Never hesitant to tout friends or relatives for governmental appointments, Clark recommended Clement Biddle Penrose, a controversial champion of the Spanish land claimants, James Wilkinson's nephew, and also a kinsman of Nicholas Biddle, to fill a vacancy on the territorial superior court. He likewise was instrumental in securing government jobs for his relatives the O'Fallons and the Kennerlys, and in making his gubernatorial appointments, Clark saw to it that his supporters were well represented.[6]

A steady stream of petitions and special pleadings routinely crossed the governor's desk. Secretary of State Monroe forwarded a complaint from the French minister concerning one of his countrymen, then in Ste. Genevieve, who claimed exemption from militia duty, and John Gates, a soldier who had enlisted as a sergeant during a "drunken frolick," petitioned the governor to grant him a discharge from the military service on the grounds that his absence from home would work a hardship on his poor children. Clark dutifully handled such matters, though not always to the satisfaction of the individuals seeking relief. In the case of the French national, the governor had determined that he was unfit for service anyway, but Clark the army man showed little sympathy for Gates and declined to intercede on his behalf.[7]

With tensions in the Missouri Territory temporarily on the wane, Clark returned to Louisville in mid-October to escort his family to St. Louis. The unsettled weather conditions and "the clumsy state of part of my family" (Julia was pregnant again) caused him to decide that they should travel by boat. For his family's comfort he secured a vessel with a room and a good fireplace. During Julia's separation from her husband that summer and fall, she had kept busy drying fruit, making preserves, barreling apples, preserving flour, and making thirty gallons of excellent bounce—a favorite Virginia liqueur made from cherries, brandy, and perhaps a touch of sugar. The governor was clearly pleased with his wife's developing domestic and culinary skills and her contributions to the family's provisions. She swapped recipes with friends and neighbors and carefully recorded her favorites in a household memo book alongside home remedies for common ailments. Julia also liked to set a good table. In advising his brother that they should stock a one-hundred-dollar set of blue printed queens ware and a fine china tea set, St. Louis merchant Christian Wilt invoked his friend Julia Clark's observation that such pieces were in the long run much the cheapest crockery because people took better care of them.[8]

The Clarks arrived home on November 13, and Julia delivered Mary Margaret Clark, their third child and only daughter, on New Year's Day in 1814. The happy mother boasted to her brother George Hancock that the newest member of her expanding family was a beauty. As for the boys, the sickly Lewis was already showing signs of artistic talent, and William was thriving. But the daughter of gentrified Virginia quickly discovered how unpredictable life was in the volatile world she now inhabited. By February the optimistic predictions of the previous fall seemed only a distant memory as she fretted that the return of good weather was sure to bring more trouble with the Indians. Reflecting no doubt her husband's renewed concerns, Julia exclaimed to her brother, "God only knows what our fate is to be."[9]

General William Henry Harrison's unexpected decision to transfer General

Howard's first regiment from St. Louis for deployment in the Canadian campaign set off alarm bells throughout the territory. General Harrison assured the secretary of war that Governor Clark's military talents and his superb knowledge of Indians qualified him to direct operations there, thus making it possible to reassign General Howard and his forces elsewhere. Clark may have felt complimented by Harrison's expression of confidence, but General Howard's departure now placed the primary burden for defending the territory on his shoulders. In February the governor issued general orders summoning both independent volunteer and regular militia companies to muster and put themselves in readiness to defend the territory, but he also decided that the current state of affairs called for more aggressive measures.[10]

Never one to sit idly by, Governor Clark proposed going on the offensive. Acting on his own authority, he initiated a plan for sending a military expedition up the Mississippi to occupy Prairie du Chien, a British outpost about five hundred miles upriver from St. Louis. The governor believed that an American military garrison at that site would effectively isolate the Indians on the Lower Mississippi from their British allies in Canada and forestall renewed hostilities the following spring. In outlining his proposal, Clark informed Secretary Armstrong that he already had most of the necessary provisions on hand and any remaining expenses could be paid for out of the Indian fund. When a response from his superiors was not soon forthcoming, Clark opted to launch the expedition without formal approval. It normally took between four and eight weeks for dispatches from St. Louis to reach the capital, and officials in the War Department seldom acted quickly on such matters. In the governor's judgment there was not time to wait for official word. Upon learning of Clark's plan, the secretary of war questioned the advisability of establishing a post in the heart of enemy country, but he made no move to recall the expedition, which by then had departed from St. Louis.[11]

Given the high stakes of his gamble, Governor Clark took personal charge of the campaign. A convoy of three armed boats and approximately two hundred men set out for Prairie du Chien on May 1, and Clark joined it a few days later. When they arrived at the Upper Mississippi outpost on June 2, 1814, Clark's forces took possession of the site without incident. Lieutenant Joseph Perkins and his sixty regulars temporarily occupied a recently abandoned British trading house, while militiamen manned the gunboats that stood watch nearby. Work was soon under way on a new log fortification they dubbed Fort Shelby in honor of Kentucky's governor. Once the fortress had begun to take shape, Governor Clark transferred command to Lieutenant Perkins and headed back downriver for St. Louis, where the grateful citizens saluted his speedy return and hailed his victory. During a banquet held in his honor at the Missouri Hotel, the assembled guests toasted Clark and his Missouri volunteers, whom they prematurely credited with cleansing the outpost of British spies and traitors.[12]

During Governor Clark's brief absence the news had been anything but reassuring. The pages of the *Missouri Gazette* were sprinkled with stories of Indian atrocities and mayhem. Neomite, a Sac leader, had crossed the Mississippi to entice the Missouri River Sacs to join in the war against the United States, after planting a British flag in front of their council lodge and demanding several bottles of whiskey as his price for taking it down. General Howard, who had been ordered back to St. Louis with his troops following a great public outcry, retroactively lent his support to Governor Clark's plan for the establishment at Prairie du Chien, but he doubted that the small detachment currently there would be adequate to defend it. He requested immediate authorization to send reinforcements to guarantee the safety of the troops, but his actions came too late to save the besieged northern outpost, which was overrun by a combined British-Indian force numbering nearly twelve hundred on July 19.[13]

Clark's bold move had failed, but he continued to defend his course of action. Claiming that he had successfully executed his part of the plan, he blamed Fort Shelby's subsequent surrender on the failure of the United States to capture Mackinac as a consequence of a decision to withdraw troops from the Great Lakes for deployment elsewhere. Had that post been taken, Clark hypothesized, Prairie du Chien would have remained in U.S. hands and the Indian threat in the Mississippi Valley would have been largely eliminated. By the time the reports of Fort Shelby's surrender reached his desk, the secretary of war paid only scant heed to news of the remote northern outpost's fall. He was still attempting to pick up the pieces in the aftermath of the British assault on Washington, D.C., and the torching of government buildings there. Meanwhile, in the Missouri Territory, residents continued to voice strong support for Governor Clark's aggressive actions. Serious public criticism of the northern expedition did not surface until his political opponents belatedly chose to make the military campaign an issue in the 1820 gubernatorial contest.[14]

Personal matters frequently intruded on William Clark's already crowded schedule. As a family man with a sickly wife and three children, the oldest of whom was five, Clark often had his hands full at home as well. In March of 1814, while juggling efforts to arrange for the Prairie du Chien expedition and to apprehend the renegade Osages responsible for murdering Abraham Eastwood on the Gasconade River, Clark advised George Sibley, "I write you in haist [haste] as my family is calling my attention every moment. Mrs C. & my son Lewis now in bead [bed] sick & four others also Sick with measles & plursey."[15]

The Clarks were communicants of the Protestant Episcopal Church, but since there was as yet no regular Protestant clergyman in residence in St. Louis, the governor had prevailed on an old friend from Kentucky then in St. Louis, Catholic Bishop Benedict Flaget, to baptize his children. The bishop administered the rites of baptism to Meriwether Lewis Clark, William Preston Clark, and Mary Margaret Clark on August 8, 1814, in the log church where St. Louis Catholics had long held their services. The proud parents witnessed the christening, but since members of their immediate family and many of their friends were not Catholics, others had to serve as godparents. The obliging bishop agreed to act in that capacity, as did prominent St. Louisan Anne Lucas Hunt. This arrangement seems to have been fine with Clark, who was religious but not narrowly sectarian. When two Presbyterian ministers came calling in St. Louis to solicit funds for the establishment of a society to distribute Bibles and religious tracts, they proudly announced that Governor Clark had been one of their first subscribers.[16]

A few days after the baptisms, Julia traveled eastward in search of treatment for a sore and enlarged breast that her husband feared might become cancerous. Clark informed Nicholas Biddle that his wife had spent several weeks that fall at Virginia's mineral springs, but she was at home in St. Louis with her family at Christmas. Her plans for traveling to Philadelphia to consult a physician apparently had been shelved because of the uncertainties that followed the British invasion of the Chesapeake. With the prospect of Indian war as likely as it had ever been, by year's end Governor Clark once again contemplated returning his family to the relative safety of Kentucky or Tennessee.[17]

When Manuel Lisa passed through the Boonslick settlements along the Missouri River in August 1814, he sent word that the Indians were still on a rampage, roaming the countryside and killing isolated settlers, stealing horses, and shooting cattle for food. The settlers, he reported, were barricaded in their forts. With only limited forces at his disposal, Governor Clark resorted to enlisting the Shawnee, Delaware, and Osage Indians to wage war against the hostile eastern tribes menacing Missouri settlements. Pitting the tribes against one another ran counter to the governor's natural instincts, but he considered it his best available option.[18]

With the exposed frontiers again in flames, General Howard launched a three-pronged attack against the marauding Indians with the assistance of three militia companies he requisitioned from Governor Clark. Howard sent the main body up the Mississippi while dispatching the two smaller parties up the Missouri and the Illinois rivers. The results were disappointing on all fronts, but most territorial residents chose not to hold Clark culpable. The *Missouri Gazette* editorialized: "Some blame Governor Clark for the manifold disasters which have occurred, we would ask in the name of common sense how can he be liable to answer who has nothing more to do in the defence of the country than to order out such portions of the militia as may be demanded of him?"[19]

General Howard's unexpected death in September from a sudden illness added to the gloom. In making a plea for added military assistance, Governor Clark warned that the British seemed intent on using their Indian allies to drive away the Missouri Territory's American settlers. He had reason for concern. With each passing year, it was becoming increasingly difficult to raise a fighting force locally. The repeated calls to arms had taken a toll compounded by the U.S. government's failure to pay many of the rangers and militia for services rendered in 1812 and 1813. Yet again the governor pressed territorial legislators to strengthen the militia laws and empower local officials to punish slackers who refused to respond to the call of duty.[20]

The tumultuous events of 1814 overshadowed the long delayed publication of Nicholas Biddle's two-volume *History of the expedition under the command of Captains Lewis and Clark . . .* The publisher even failed to send Clark his copies, but it was of little immediate consequence since he had not yet found time to read a set loaned to him by one of the few people who actually purchased the books. Despite the disappointing sales, the publication drew sufficient notice in U.S. scientific and literary circles to secure Clark's election to membership in the American Antiquarian Society, an organization dedicated to the collection and preservation of the arts and sciences in America. Curiously, Biddle's narrative attracted almost as much attention in Europe as it did in the United States, but to Clark's disappointment, in neither place did it become a bestseller. When Biddle advised him the following year that their publishers Bradford and Inskeep had declared insolvency, Clark authorized him to do what he could to claim his share of the books, papers, and sales receipts.[21]

Clark had little time for such matters, and as 1815 dawned the demands on him were about to increase. While he enjoyed the holidays with his family in St. Louis, diplomats in the faraway Belgian town of Ghent plotted a future course for the remote North American frontier under his jurisdiction. On Christmas Eve in 1814, U.S. peace commissioners signed the Treaty of Ghent, an agreement terminating all hostilities with Great Britain. The treaty may have officially concluded the War of 1812, but on the other side of the Atlantic, in places like New Orleans and the Missouri Territory, there were battles yet to be fought. Unaware of what had transpired abroad, General Andrew Jackson and his Tennessee and Kentucky riflemen routed a larger British force at New Orleans fully two weeks after the treaty signing. Word of Jackson's splendid victory triggered an impromptu celebration in St. Louis. The joyful residents fired a salute and placed lighted candles in their windows. The Clark windowpanes on Main Street no doubt shone brightly that night.[22]

The disclosure of the fine print in the Treaty of Ghent left more than a few Missourians outraged. Article nine, which called for an immediate cessation of hostilities against the Indians and a return of the rights and privileges to which the Indians had been entitled before the war—providing that they also refrained from any further belligerence—was especially galling. The idea of suspending military operations against the Indians enjoyed little support within either the military or civilian sectors. Christian Wilt gave voice to local sentiment: "it is the Opinion of the People here that we shall not have peace with the Indians until we drub them soundly into it."[23]

The close of the conflict left the warring Indian tribes equally angry and bewildered. They had expected their British allies to continue to fight until the Americans had been driven back to their earlier boundaries. Britain's sudden withdrawal from the contest greatly increased their vulnerability. In their confused state, the tribes debated what course to follow. Some remained determined to push ahead with the battle against their American adversaries; others displayed uncertainty.

Governor William Clark, who had just received word of his brother Edmund's death in Louisville, found himself in the eye of a storm when the president assigned him the onerous task of negotiating peace accords with the numerous Missouri and Mississippi river tribes in accordance with the controversial stipulations agreed to at Ghent. Madison also appointed Governor Ninian Edwards of the Illinois Territory and St. Louis fur merchant Auguste Chouteau to join Clark as peace commissioners. Alexander McNair, a popular militia officer and army sutler, wisely declined a seat on the commission when the president offered it to him. McNair, who snagged the lucrative post of register of the St. Louis land office, astutely surmised that among rank-and-file Missourians, dispensing land would make him more popular than would giving gifts to Indians. His friend Clark would belatedly discover that truth when the two men squared off against each other in Missouri's 1820 gubernatorial contest.[24]

But Governor Clark's position did not afford him the luxury of a choice, as he set about to bring an end to the hostilities at a time when few combatants on either side seemed eager to lay down their arms. Neither the planners in Europe nor those in the federal capital for that matter fully appreciated the difficulty of the assignment they had given the peace commissioners. In mid-April Clark warned the secretary of war that the Indians had killed ten people on the frontiers during the past month and showed no sign that they intended to alter their present course. With warfare continuing to rage around them,

Governors Clark and Edwards and Commissioner Chouteau met in St. Louis on May 11 to initiate plans for a general peace conference at Portage des Sioux in early July that they hoped would help rein in the violence. They dispatched experienced Indian agents, army officers, and fur traders into the Indian country bearing "talks" addressed to thirty-seven different tribal bands advising them that the United States and Great Britain had buried the tomahawk and summoning their leaders to Portage des Sioux to negotiate peace treaties with the United States. Unlike most U.S.-Indian deliberations, land cessions and trade agreements were not on the table. Secretary Monroe had specifically instructed the commissioners "to confine this treaty to the sole object of peace."[25]

Understandably, the commissioners were not particularly sanguine about their prospects for success. The gathering of such a large assembly of disenchanted Indians so close to settled areas gave them added pause. They called upon the War Department to provide a military force sufficient to maintain order and protect the nearby settlements, even before a band of Rock River renegades brutally murdered five members of a St. Charles County family or territorial militia units clashed with belligerent warriors in a bloody battle near the Cuivre River.

While pledging to work for peace, William Clark and his associates cautioned their superiors to prepare for war. True to their calling, the commissioners did their best. They counseled local citizens not to harm the Indians, who would soon be arriving to participate in the peace talks, after reminding them that the U.S. government had pledged to ensure the safety of the visiting tribesmen. Such words did not play well in the Missouri Territory, and reports that federal officials had ordered twenty thousand dollars' worth of merchandise to help grease the wheels of the diplomatic machinery did little to sustain Clark's popularity locally. Critics lambasted the peace policy, asking, "Shall we allow so sacred a thing as a treaty to be a passport to conduct the murderers into our houses and towns?[26]

To forestall possible trouble, General Daniel Bissell deployed 275 regulars under the command of Colonel John Miller to Portage des Sioux and assigned two fully manned gunboats, the *General Clark* and the *Commodore Perry,* to patrol the nearby waters. As an added precaution he called upon Governors Clark and Edwards to provide one militia company from each of their respective territories to stand guard. As the time appointed for the Portage des Sioux peace council drew near, Governor Clark met with General Bissell to select a site for a council house. Early arriving tribal leaders, some of whom had already conferred with Clark in St. Louis, set up camp, while canoes bearing additional tribal representatives, more than a few of whom appeared contemptuous of U.S. authority, daily descended on the tiny French settlement already

Auguste Chouteau. William Clark frequently called upon the venerable St. Louis businessman and cofounder of St. Louis for assistance in conducting Indian negotiations. From the Collections of the St. Louis Mercantile Library at the University of Missouri–St. Louis.

overrun with Indians and soldiers. This was clearly a situation that would require Governor Clark to demonstrate the full range of his diplomatic skills.[27]

When Clark returned with the other commissioners on July 6, they found several hundred Piankashaw, Potawatomi, Omaha, Sioux, Ioway, Shawnee, Delaware, Kickapoo, Sac, and Fox encamped at Portage des Sioux in lodges of every description. Nearby, Colonel Miller's troops pitched their army tents in neatly lined rows. The brush arbor that Miller's men erected to serve as a council house stood ready and waiting. Peddlers, gamblers, and idle curiosity seekers ambled about hoping to make a buck or simply to take in the colorful spectacle. Reports that representatives from other tribes were still en route caused the commissioners to postpone the opening ceremonies until July 10, 1815.[28]

As Governor Clark mingled among the crowds, he recognized many familiar faces. The Teton leaders Black Buffalo and the Partisan who had caused him so much grief at the Bad River were there, considerably more chastened than they had been during their encounter eleven years earlier. Several lesser Sac and Fox chiefs strutted about as defiant as ever, but the notorious dissidents Black Hawk and Lemoite were notably absent. When the formal proceedings finally got under way, Governor Clark, who was well versed in the pageantry of Indian diplomacy, ordered the uniformed troops to parade before the assembled delegates. The regular cadence of the military drumbeat supplied the requisite aura of formality, and Governor Clark, attired in his dark suit and white ruffled shirt, cut an impressive figure as he stood to address the tribal leaders who crowded around the council house. Nearby stacks of blankets, strouds, calicoes, handkerchiefs, ribands, frock coats, flags, silver medals, paints, wampum, looking-glasses, knives, fire-steels, rifles, fusils, flints, powder, tobacco, pipes, and other assorted articles stood ready for all who proved obliging. After reviewing the previous conduct of the various tribes, Clark advised his hearers that their great father in Washington was willing to forget their past transgressions in return for an agreement to bury the hatchet.[29]

Clark reserved his harshest remarks for the Sac, Fox, and Kickapoo, whom he chastised for their continuing misdeeds and for having sent only minor chiefs to this gathering. Clark warned them that they could no longer rely on their British fathers who had been forced to withdraw from the region, and he ordered their principal chiefs to appear in person at Portage des Sioux within thirty days or face the consequences. When the interpreters translated his remarks, his tough talk drew applause and shouts of approval from the sworn enemies of the Sac and Fox in the audience. Sensing possible trouble, the commissioners ordered a party to guard the unpopular Rock River tribesmen against a possible assault from one of their numerous foes, but under cover of darkness the delegates representing the still defiant Mississippi River tribes slipped off to complain about the insults they had endured.[30]

During the next several days the commissioners held separate talks with each of the remaining tribes, carefully going over the proposed treaty terms and listening to their special concerns and complaints. Clark's son Lewis, who was not quite six years old, sat by his father's side during some of the sessions and recalled years later that one of the chiefs had placed a hand on his head and proudly proclaimed that they were both Clark's sons. The Teton chief Black Buffalo's sudden death brought the proceedings to an abrupt halt, and the commissioners ordered him interred with full military honors. Governor Edwards and Colonel Chouteau were present for the burial ceremony during which the Omaha chief Big Elk rendered an elegant funeral oration, but Clark did not attend, perhaps in order to escort Lewis home and to check on others in his family.[31]

Missouri's governor was back at Portage des Sioux on July 18 when the commissioners affixed their signatures to treaties with the Potawatomi of the Illinois River and the Piankashaw. Over the next two days Clark and his colleagues reached peace accords with the Teton Sioux, Sioux of the Lakes, Sioux of St. Peters River, Yankton Sioux, and the Omaha, many of whom expressed a willingness to join the Americans in a war against their Sac and Fox rivals. Having completed the initial phase of their deliberations, the commissioners adjourned to await the expiration of the thirty-day ultimatum Governor Clark had issued leaders of the Rock River Sacs and other absent tribes. When he reconvened the proceedings at the end of August, Governor Clark reported that about four hundred Indians representing diverse tribes were still in the vicinity. During the course of the next three weeks the commissioners secured additional signed agreements with the Kickapoo, Osage, and Missouri River Sacs, as well as the Fox and Ioway prior to declaring the Portage des Sioux deliberations officially adjourned. Back in St. Louis the commissioners wrapped things up and advised the secretary of war that the last of the Indian negotiators finally had headed homeward. Shortly thereafter a Kansa delegation belatedly showed up in St. Louis and huddled briefly with Commissioners Edwards and Chouteau before signing a treaty on October 28. Clark had already departed for Kentucky to tend to family matters.[32]

Following the conclusion of the Portage des Sioux negotiations, Clark replied to a series of interrogatories posed in a U.S. Senate report designed to address the larger issues of postwar Indian relations. He began his response with an unequivocal assertion: "our Indian relations ought to be materially altered." Among other things, the governor and ex-officio Indian superintendent called upon federal officials to grant U.S. agents greater authority to manage operations in the field. On the thorny subject of Indian trade, he proposed a continuation of the current U.S. factory system, but in a bolder move he also suggested the creation of a large, well-capitalized firm capable of furnishing tribes in remote regions with trade goods and driving British operatives from the country with government support and backing. Speaking from firsthand knowledge, the onetime president of the Missouri Fur Company observed that "small companies are found, from experience, to produce no valuable change, and are soon compelled to give up the Indian trade."[33]

While Clark pondered these broader policy matters, the commissioners learned that the recent construction of a string of U.S. forts from the Great Lakes to the Mississippi had caused the Rock River Sacs and several other holdouts among the Upper Mississippi tribes to have second thoughts. Long before his foray to Prairie du Chien, Clark had been a proponent of the establishment of military/trading installations in the Indian country, and several of the fortifications currently under construction had been placed at strategic sites he first identified on a chart he prepared during his 1805 winter stay at Fort Mandan. Though federal planners seldom adopted William Clark's brash schemes in toto, the U.S. government's postwar defensive strategy and Indian policy nevertheless bore his indelible imprint.[34]

Having been deserted by their former British allies, the once defiant tribes had no place to turn, and well before the springtime thaw their envoys began streaming into St. Louis. Given this apparent change of heart, the War Department directed the commissioners to reopen negotiations. By May, Missouri's territorial capital was once again crowded with Indians seeking to make peace. Black Hawk had not come, but Lemoite had. Initially the Sac leader stalked out of the talks, but Clark held firm and the unhappy chief returned on May 13, 1816, to place his mark on a treaty for the Rock River Sacs. Similar agreements with the Winnebago, Ottawa, Chippewa, and Potawatomi were inked on parchment by midsummer. Clark's policy of accommodating tribes willing to come to terms while holding to a hard line with the recalcitrant nations clearly had the desired effect. Between July 1815 and August 1816 William Clark was a signatory to sixteen treaties concluded at Portage des Sioux and St. Louis.[35]

As historian Jay Buckley has aptly noted, the standard diplomatic phrases in those treaties belied the complicated negotiations that had been required to secure tribal consent. Clark's willingness to seek accommodation with those tribes that showed evidence of being sufficiently chastened contributed materially to the restoration of peaceful conditions along America's extended western frontiers. Not everyone in the Euro-American community applauded his handling of the negotiations. Many Missourians continued to press for forcible coercion to chastise the errant tribes properly for past misdeeds, and they openly complained about the government's alleged lavish spending on the Indians and the "Indian treaty-men." It was a message that would come back to haunt the diligent diplomat, but an unbiased assessment suggests that Clark's diplomacy helped open the way for the settlement of Missouri's vast interior spaces.[36]

After 1815 immigrants flooded into the Missouri Territory in unprecedented numbers. According to U.S. census figures, the territory's nonnative population swelled from 19,783 in 1810 to 66,586 a decade later, and in 1816 Governor Clark estimated that nearly 5,000 Native Americans still resided within the confines of present-day Missouri, with at least twice that number occupying close-by areas. During the deliberations at Portage des Sioux, Missouri's Shawnee and Delaware inhabitants voiced concerns about white settlement on their lands. The commissioners advised officials in the War Department that the complaints appeared well founded and commended the aggrieved Indians as deserving of the U.S. government's benevolence and justice. Before year's end Governor Clark, who once before had interceded in behalf of these "sober and well behaved" natives, issued an order requiring "all white persons who have intruded and are settled upon the lands of the Indians within this territory, depart therefrom without delay—Should they neglect this last and peaceful warning the military power will be called upon to compel their removal." President Madison followed it up with a broader pronouncement calling for the ejection of squatters from both public lands and Indian lands.[37]

In separate memorials to Congress, members of the territorial assembly took exception with both edicts. They questioned the validity of Indian claims to such extensive tracts of "the richest and most fertile parts" of an area surrounded by flourishing settlements and suggested that the removal of the Shawnee and Delaware to unsettled parts of the territory would boost development and bring tranquility to the territory. The territorial legislature's call for Indian removal and ethnic cleansing represented a departure from the more tolerant attitudes prevalent under the French and Spanish regimes. Prior to the War of 1812, pockets of native peoples had coexisted peaceably beside white neighbors in a multiethnic society, but the torrents of Indian-hating newcomers to the Missouri Territory were far less inclined to permit a continued native presence in their midst. These new realities only complicated William Clark's tasks as Indian superintendent.[38]

The editor of the *Missouri Gazette* opined that Clark's federal superiors had assigned him a task far more difficult to perform than they could possibly have imagined, and Colonel Alexander McNair flatly stated that the territorial militia would refuse to march against the intruders. The president quickly retreated from his initial order and approved a law on March 25, 1816, permitting settlers to remain on the public lands until they were offered for sale, and Clark set about to obtain agreements for the removal of Shawnee and Delaware to more secure locations farther west. Though William Clark was an ardent proponent of the divestiture of Indian lands, he favored adhering to the law and protecting peaceable Indians sympathetic to the United States until that could be accomplished.[39]

Indian tracts were not the only contested lands in the Missouri Territory. In January of 1815 the territorial assembly petitioned Congress to grant New Madrid earthquake sufferers relief by allowing them to exchange their damaged lands for comparable tracts in other sections of the Missouri Territory. When federal legislators enacted a law authorizing individuals with destroyed lands in the affected area to relocate, at no cost, the same quantity of land, not to exceed 640 acres, on any U.S. public lands approved for sale, New Madrid fever gripped the territory as eager land speculators rushed to buy up titles to ruined tracts at bargain prices. Shortly after the bill became law, William Clark, ever mindful of his own economic interests, contracted with Theodore Hunt and Charles Lucas to purchase titles to damaged lands for him. When subsequent abuses roused public ire, Missouri's territorial delegate Rufus Easton tried to tarnish Clark's reputation by circulating documents tying his political foe to the controversial New Madrid speculations.[40]

The dustup between Easton and Clark was emblematic of the Missouri Territory's intensely personal political culture. Individual feuds and personal grudges were the order of the day. The first hint of trouble between the pair surfaced in 1815 when Governor Clark queried his friend Secretary of State James Monroe about a report that Nicholas Boilvin, the Indian agent at Prairie du Chien, had allegedly distributed in the federal capital accusing him of improperly using Indian goods and public property for the benefit of his nephew Benjamin O'Fallon—a document that Clark believed Easton had helped frame, but if so, it had little effect. Monroe advised him that he had no recollection of any such charges having been called to his attention, and added that, if they had, he would have made Clark aware of them.[41]

But the fat was already in the fire, and Clark joined forces with a coalition led by influential St. Louis Creole leaders and several rising lawyer-politicians including Edward Hempstead, Thomas Hart Benton, and John Scott—a group that Joseph Charless, editor of the *Missouri Gazette*, dubbed the "little junto"— in an effort to unseat Easton in the 1816 election for territorial delegate. Easton's supporters rallied to his cause. Joseph Charless, William Russell, John B. C. Lucas, his son Charles, Frederick Bates, and David Barton were among those to be found in his corner.[42]

In an effort to neutralize Easton's strength in the southern counties and defuse the anti–St. Louis bias of voters outside the territorial capital, the members of the junto selected Ste. Genevieve attorney John Scott as their candidate. A fundamental disagreement over policies for the confirmation of Spanish land titles was the campaign's defining issue, but the race quickly degenerated into a name-calling slugfest. Scott's supporters portrayed the incumbent Easton as a do-nothing who had accomplished little for his constituents and charged him with consistently opposing the legitimate interests of Missouri's land claimants. Easton's backers portrayed Scott as a profane gambler aligned with a faction of lawyers, colonels, and majors in St. Louis bent on dominating the territory and fleecing the public of its money, goods, and offices.[43]

The hotly contested 1816 election proved to be a real cliffhanger that was not finally decided until Governor Clark declared Scott the winner by a margin of fifteen votes. However, in certifying the Ste. Genevieve attorney's election, Clark, who had made no secret of his preference, included a set of contested returns from Cote sans Dessein in St. Charles County, personally delivered to St. Louis by the victorious candidate, before they had been certified by the local election judges. Election procedures were considerably less prescriptive then, but Clark's certification of those votes at the last minute opened him to charges of favoritism.[44]

The polls had scarcely closed when Scott stormed into the offices of the *Missouri Gazette* demanding to know the identity of the author of an unflattering handbill that had cast him in a bad light. Charless reluctantly pointed a finger at Charles Lucas, whereupon Scott threw down the gauntlet and demanded satisfaction from him and four of his other critics for having called his honor into question. Only the young firebrand Lucas accepted Scott's challenge, and in the blink of an eye preparations were under way for the two of them to meet on the field of honor. Governor Clark, perhaps remembering all too well the tragic duel that had taken the life of James Graham, proposed mediation as an alternative to bloodshed. Bernard Pratte and Auguste Chouteau joined him in urging that course of action, but when the arbiters appointed to seek a peaceful resolution met, Lucas rejected their proposed terms. At the last minute Colonel Scott thought better of his impulsive act and rescinded his challenge, no doubt after considerable prompting from his friend the governor. Lucas, who afterward taunted Scott for withdrawing, foolishly got himself killed the following year on the field of honor following a similar election-day imbroglio.[45]

Scott headed off to Washington to take his seat as a territorial delegate, and Easton also showed up to urge his former congressional colleagues to reject Governor Clark's official tally. Armed with a lengthy report detailing various alleged irregularities and inaccuracies in the returns submitted by Clark, he presented his case before the House Committee on Elections. After protracted debates in the committee and in the full House, the representatives voted in January of 1817 to declare the seat vacant and order a new election on the grounds that the original one had been conducted illegally.[46]

While the political maneuvering in the capital city ran its course, William Clark went about his normal routines in St. Louis. His little family was getting larger. On May 6, 1816, Julia delivered their fourth child, a son whom they named George Rogers Hancock Clark in a nod to both sides of the family. Since both the public and private spaces in the building William Clark currently occupied at the corner of Main and Pine fell short of his needs, he had added to his Main Street holdings with the acquisition of another lot at Main and Vine and ordered the old stone structure at that site demolished preparatory to constructing a handsome new two-story brick residence that was ready for his family in the fall of 1818.[47]

The expiration of Clark's three-year term prompted President Madison to issue an interim appointment continuing him in his gubernatorial post until Congress reconvened and the Senate could confirm him for another full three-year term. The governor must have taken comfort in knowing that the recent territorial squabbles had in no way diminished the administration's confidence in him. In his spare moments Clark looked after family properties in Kentucky and Indiana, including several that he had acquired from George Rogers Clark. In the fall he lobbied Speaker of the House Henry Clay to support an increase in the government pension for Pacific tour veteran George Shannon, who had lost a leg in the line of duty while serving with the Pryor expedition during its unsuccessful attempt to convey the Mandan leader White Coyote to his Upper Missouri village. Following the amputation of his leg, the youthful invalid had at Clark's behest aided Nicholas Biddle with the preparation of his two-volume narrative. Thanks to Clark's intervention, the young pensioner received an increase that made it possible for him to study law in Kentucky and later become a Missouri judge.[48]

Not long thereafter a letter arrived from Monticello seeking Clark's assistance for Jefferson's effort to secure publication of the scientific data that Biddle had not included in his volumes. The former president remained eager to see the astronomical observations, geographical charts, and Indian vocabularies compiled by Lewis and Clark made available to the public. Flattered by his distinguished former Virginia neighbor's continuing interest, Clark lamented his own failure to give "to the world all the Results of that expedition." After promising to arrange for the transfer of those materials to the care of the sage of Monticello, Clark briefed him on the latest western developments. He shared his proposal for the creation of a great company to keep British operatives out of the Upper Missouri country, and exuded a quiet confidence as he recounted his success in managing the territory under very difficult circumstances, noting only that "Laterly a Small and disappointed party has spring up determined to vex & Tease the executive."[49]

Those vexations persisted as the governor found himself embroiled in yet another controversy in early 1817. Following a heated debate, members of the territorial assembly voted to grant the newly formed Bank of Missouri a charter over the strenuous objections of the officers and shareholders of the territory's only financial institution, the Bank of St. Louis. When the president of the Legislative Council, an opponent of the new bank, refused to sign the bill and attempted to block further legislative action by resigning his post, the new bank's legislative supporters seized the bill from the upper chamber and delivered it directly to Governor Clark, who promptly signed it into law.[50]

Clark's detractors protested the unorthodox manner in which the bill had been handled, but the measure stood. For his part, the governor may have come to regret signing off on the new bank, on whose board of directors he later served. Like so many of his investments, the Bank of Missouri did not live up to his expectations, and its eventual collapse put him at risk financially. Despite his involvement in the territorial political feuds, Clark remained much in demand for civic and social functions. When the citizens of St. Louis turned out for an elaborate dinner marking George Washington's birthday in 1817, they accorded him the honor of presiding over the festivities, and members of the General Assembly did not hesitate to place his name at the top of the list of individuals they designated for service on a board of trustees for superintending schools in St. Louis.[51]

Governor Clark convened the school board at his office in April 1817, and his colleagues unanimously elected him chair, a position that he continued to hold as late as 1824. He proved a wise choice. His contacts with federal officials facilitated the board's attempts to claim the abandoned federal property that Congress had made available for use in supporting public education. The St. Louis board successfully claimed the original courthouse and several abandoned military fortifications built under the auspices of the Spanish government, once Clark helped persuade federal authorities that they no longer had any strategic value.[52]

When reports reached the territory in late February that the U.S. House of Representatives had unseated John Scott as Missouri's delegate and ordered a special election, the warring political factions prepared to resume combat. After some initial debate, both sides elected to stick with the candidates they had put forward a year earlier. Easton's supporters attempted to make the governor a campaign issue this time around. William Russell predicted that many of Scott's supporters in the southern counties would desert his candidacy because of his associations with the governor. Clark was, he said, "as unpopular as it is possible for a man to be," thanks to his exertions in support of the Bank of Missouri. For his part Clark openly campaigned for Scott, sending copies of the candidate's circulars to some of his political appointees for distribution.[53]

In St. Louis on election day Clark's sometimes rowdy nephews John and Benjamin O'Fallon, with assistance from a few friends, fashioned a tent from a canvas sail outside the door of the polls as a gathering place for candidate Scott's friends. Benjamin, feeling flush thanks to the recent appointment that his uncle had secured for him as U.S. Indian agent, joined his cohorts at the refreshment table, dispensing food and whiskey to waiting voters. They engaged in friendly banter with the Scott supporters and taunted Easton men as they entered the courthouse. A nearby military recruiting band struck up a tune, and a few well-armed soldiers paraded by wearing labels in their hats proclaiming their support for Scott. To no one's surprise, when Governor Clark arrived at the polls he declared his intent to vote for Scott. Such antics were standard fare for frontier elections, but the high-profile presence of the governor and members of his family especially rankled the opposition.[54]

With tempers at or near the boiling point, the situation was ripe for trouble. Captain John O'Fallon engaged Dr. Robert Simpson, the author of several letters attacking Governor Clark, in a shouting and shoving match inside the courthouse on election day and continued the fray a few days later when he pummeled the physician during a heated exchange in the streets. Another election-day altercation had more tragic consequences. When Charles Lucas challenged Thomas Hart Benton to prove that he had paid his taxes before he voted, Benton disdainfully dismissed Lucas as a "puppy." Both men were hypersensitive, and their disagreement ended in a duel on Bloody Island that left young Lucas dead. Clark, whose political differences with Lucas were well known, had nonetheless on occasion employed the able young lawyer and no doubt regretted his premature death at the hands of his friend Benton. Clark also mourned the passing of his ally and political confidant Edward Hempstead, who had died only days before the Benton-Lucas affair after sustaining injuries in a fall from his horse.[55]

When the election tallies showed that Scott had soundly defeated Easton in the 1817 rematch, the anti-junto faction again cried foul. Russell attributed Scott's margin in the southern counties to the fact that "nearly every devil in the county that now holds or wants to hold a commission under the governor supported Scott actively," and in St. Louis Joseph Charless charged military interference, alleging, "On Monday last an election for delegate to congress took place in the several districts of this territory. In this town, the election was conducted in the most violent, turbulent and savage manner." A military court of inquiry exonerated the soldiers of official misconduct, but the election had intensified the personal animosities even more.[56]

Despite the turmoil, Scott took his seat in Congress without incident, and the St. Louis–based junto temporarily reclaimed its dominant position in the local political arena. Clark kept as busy as ever. During the October term of the St. Louis Circuit Court he filed a suit in behalf of his partners in the defunct Missouri Fur Company seeking to collect on a promissory note signed by their former employee Charles Tibeau, and during the same session he also initiated action to force the removal of a smelly slaughterhouse that Louis and Auguste Brazeau had constructed illegally on a town lot that he owned in St. Louis. In the latter case Rufus Easton, to no one's surprise, rushed to defend the Brazeaus against Clark's action.[57]

A war raging between the Osage and the Cherokee occupied much of the governor's attention during the summer and fall months, though he privately doubted that there was much he could do to curb the violence in the short run. Attempts by the emigrant Cherokee to claim traditional Osage hunting grounds was at the heart of the matter. As the winter season neared, Clark made preparations for yet another pilgrimage to the federal capital to ensure that he remained in good stead. On the eve of his departure a member of the Chouteau clan provided him with details about the latest bloody encounter involving the two tribes. It was a subject that he undoubtedly intended to pursue with officials in the War Department when he reached Washington. Clark embarked on November 27, leaving his family behind in St. Louis. Julia elected not to make the journey with four small children, who according to a family friend chattered incessantly about their father during his absence. Once again left to keep the home fires burning, Julia complained of an occasional pain in the face, but she was feeling well enough to attend a dance at the Masonic Lodge near the end of December. Julia and the children were not the only ones who missed Clark's congenial presence. His card-playing buddies lamented his empty seat at the local whist tables.[58]

On his way eastward Clark stopped in Louisville, where he no doubt discovered that his brother George was failing rapidly. Their brief reunion was destined to be their final earthly encounter. He reached the national capital in mid-December and spent the next two months politicking, socializing, and conferring about Indian matters and other official business. No doubt he was at pains to counter any unfavorable reports about his conduct as governor or his involvement in the recent elections, particularly since the curmudgeonly Judge Lucas was making the rounds there as well. Clark completed arrangements with Nicholas Biddle for transferring his journals and expedition notes to the American Philosophical Society, with the stipulation that he would always retain personal access. He took time out to take in a circus and make a number of purchases including several books, a new pair of spectacles, an inkstand, quills, and writing paper.[59]

On his return trip he paid his in-laws at Fincastle a visit and made another stopover in Louisville, where he rushed to the post office hoping to find word from his "dear wife and little family." To his disappointment there was no letter awaiting him, but his nephew Temple Gwathmey had received a letter from Julia, the contents of which lowered Clark's spirits. When he arrived at the Preston's the following day, the letter he had been looking for was there, and it contained some "astonishing news"—no doubt the report that Julia was again pregnant. He conferred with Dennis Fitzhugh and others concerning the estate of George Rogers Clark, who had died at Locust Grove on February 13. Of all his siblings, William had been closest to his oldest brothers, Jonathan and George, and now both were gone.[60]

He hurried back to St. Louis, and while passing through Vincennes received a distressing report suggesting that Julia was not well. To his great relief, the anxious husband and father found her somewhat better when he finally returned to the embrace of his family on April 8. No doubt the public reception Thomas Hart Benton organized to quash reports of the governor's ebbing popularity in St. Louis buoyed his spirits, but his mood soon turned somber when Julia's health took another turn for the worse. In mid-May Clark advised George Sibley that he was only able to absent himself from her side for a few minutes at a time. On July 7 the couple's fifth child, Julius John Clark, was born after a very difficult delivery that left the infant physically impaired and Julia in a declining state from which she never fully recovered.[61]

The governor's official duties provided the primary respite from his woes at home. With Auguste Chouteau's assistance, he concluded treaties with three Pawnee bands in June, but President Monroe placed a higher priority on ending the conflict between the Cherokee and the Osage as a first step in the larger design for a wholesale Cherokee relocation west of the Mississippi. In July Clark advised Secretary Calhoun that he was encountering greater difficulty than he had anticipated in securing an agreement because both tribes had successfully recruited other Indian nations to join their respective causes. Not until late September was Clark able to report success. On the twenty-fifth of that month delegates representing the Cherokee and Osage bands affixed their marks to a treaty in Governor Clark's presence in St. Louis. The truce once again came at a price for the Osages, who under pressure conceded hunting rights to the Cherokee in the lands south of the Arkansas River.[62]

At home there was a faint glimmer of hope in late September when Julia seemed well enough to travel to Louisville to spend the winter with her sister and brother-in-law Caroline and William Preston. The week before their departure, the Clarks moved their belongings into their handsome new two-story brick residence at the corner of Main and Vine Street. Tragically, Julia never had a chance to live in the fine new home that her husband had built especially for her and their now sizable brood. With the Cherokee-Osage deal inked, William and Julia Clark set out with their children for the Falls of the Ohio, where they arrived on November 7. The governor remained at Julia's side in Louisville until March, when with the encouragement of his brother-in-law he returned to St. Louis to tend to official business.[63]

In June 1819 he went back to Louisville to accompany his family eastward for a reunion with Julia's parents in Virginia. Concerned that Julia was not up to a long bumpy coach ride, Clark arranged for them to travel by steamboat to New Orleans and from there to the East Coast by sailing ship. In the federal capital Clark conferred with President Monroe about public business. The president,

Mrs. Monroe, and several other fashionable ladies were especially kind to Julia, who was largely confined to her hotel room. She heeded their advice to seek treatment at a nearby warm springs, but the therapeutic waters failed to have the desired effect, and the young mother, who was not yet thirty, had to be transported on a bed to her parents' plantation, Fotheringay, where all hoped she would recuperate under the care of close relatives. Still attempting to juggle personal affairs with public duties, William Clark made another hasty trip late in the year to Washington, where a congressional impasse over slavery had stalled Missouri's bid for statehood, but he was back in Virginia with his family for Christmas. It was to be the last one that he would share with Julia.[64]

Governor Clark's extended absences from St. Louis produced a storm of criticism from political enemies who suggested that if he could not tend to public business, he should resign. Early in 1820 Clark received a letter from Dr. Bernard Farrar urging him to enter the governor's race and stressing the need for him to come to the territory as soon as possible. Heeding his friend's advice, Clark arrived in St. Louis on March 19, where he received an "affectionate welcome" according to the sympathetic editor of the *St. Louis Enquirer*. In the flurry of activity surrounding his homecoming, Clark found time to assist Chester Harding, a sign painter turned aspiring portraitist, in hanging out his shingle in the city. According to the young artist, the governor "kindly helped me about getting a suitable room for a studio and then offered himself as a sitter. This was an auspicious and cheerful beginning." It was a kind gesture on the part of a busy man who already had had his likeness captured on canvas by C. B. J. Fevret de Saint-Memin, Charles Willson Peale, John Wesley Jarvis, and Joseph Henry Bush. Harding's full-length portrait of Clark showed the young artist's inexperience, but the visage of his illustrious subject was good enough to entice a steady stream of patrons to his St. Louis studio. When James Otto Lewis, a local engraver, prepared a lithograph of Harding's portrait of Daniel Boone, Clark lent added support by purchasing three copies.[65]

Within a week of Clark's return to the territorial capital in March, word reached the city that Congress had finally approved a compromise authorizing Missouri's admission to the Union. Clark no doubt joined in the spontaneous celebrations that erupted throughout the territory, but he also understood that the agreement meant that he was about to be out of a job and soon would need to make new arrangements for his future. Meanwhile, planning for the transition to statehood proceeded apace. In early May Missourians went to the polls to elect delegates to a constitutional convention. Members of the conservative, commercially oriented territorial establishment with which Clark was affiliated successfully fended off the opposition by seizing upon largely unfounded fears that yet another attempt might be made to restrict slavery in Missouri.

William Clark portrait by Chester Harding. This 1820 painting helped
launch Harding on a successful career as a professional artist. From
the Collections of the St. Louis Mercantile Library at the University of
Missouri–St. Louis.

The newly elected convention delegates convened at St. Louis's Mansion House Hotel on June 19 and immediately began drafting a framework of government for the new state. While members of the convention debated the constitution's provisions, leaders of the triumphant old guard caucused behind-the-scenes to settle on a slate of candidates for the new state offices that would include Clark at the top of the ticket.[66]

Initially, William Clark appeared to be the odds-on favorite to lead Missouri once it crossed the threshold into statehood. His friends and political allies believed that his lengthy years of public service made him the most qualified prospective candidate in the field. Even with such warm encouragement, Clark's decision to stand for office did not come easily. In the spring of 1819 he had signaled his willingness to become a candidate for the state's highest office, but a year later his wife's deteriorating health had given him second thoughts. By then predisposed not to enter the race, Clark drafted a letter addressed to a local editor announcing with regret "that the particular situation of my family now in the state of Virginia demand my immediate attention & will deprive me of the satisfaction of tendering my services in execution of the duties of chief magistrate of the new state of Missouri." The unfinished letter was never sent.[67]

With Clark seemingly out of contention, several local politicos bandied about the name of Clark's friend and constitutional convention member Alexander McNair as a possible alternative, but his increasingly populist views and the opposition *Missouri Gazette*'s endorsement of his candidacy made him unacceptable to the governor's staunchest allies. Clark remained their preferred choice, and when they failed to find a suitable replacement, he relented and agreed to allow his name to be put forward as a candidate for governor. In late June of 1820, John O'Fallon reported the good news to junto member General Thomas Smith in Franklin, and Clark himself informed Indian Agent Thomas Forsyth, "I have become a candidate for the place of governor, and so has Colonel McNair."[68]

Friendly pressure was not the sole reason for Clark's change of mind. Reports from Virginia via Louisville suggested that Julia had not improved, and the sobering prospect of being on his own and caring for five children, all under the age of eleven, forced him to take stock of his situation. Missouri's pending statehood placed his continued federal employment at risk at the very moment that he most needed a steady income. The proposed 1820 Constitution established the governor's salary at two thousand dollars per year, the same amount that he currently received for his combined duties as territorial governor and superintendent of Indian affairs, and that surely provided added incentive for him to reconsider. Along with his many other woes, Clark constantly worried about his finances. His private ventures had not fared well. The Missouri Fur Company had discontinued its operations and the Bank of Missouri was in serious trouble. As if to remind himself that financial gain was not meant to be the primary measure of a man, he inscribed in the back pages of his journal the maxims "who lives to nature never can be poor, who lives to fancy never can be rich," and "riches and honour are seldom the reward of merit."[69]

But it was Julia who remained foremost in his thoughts and prayers. In June Clark's brother-in-law Dennis Fitzhugh passed along to John O'Fallon the latest word from Virginia: "I fear your poor Aunt Clark is no more. The last advises inform us that she was not expected to live many days. Remember me affectionately to him [William Clark]." Clark knew that Julia was not improving, but he seems to have been unaware of how rapidly her condition had deteriorated and still talked of bringing her home to St. Louis. In preparation for his return to Virginia, he informed Indian Agent Thomas Forsyth, "I set out to try and get Mrs. Clark to this place if she is able to be moved. I fear her health is worse," but his departure on July 3 came too late even to allow him to comfort his dying wife. Unbeknownst to him, six days earlier on June 27 his beloved Julia had expired, in all likelihood from the ravages of breast cancer.[70]

Clark received word of Julia's death in mid-July somewhere on the road between Louisville and Fincastle. When he arrived at Fotheringay on July 27, he found a household shrouded in grief. Julia's death had been followed three weeks later by the passing of her father, George Hancock. Father and daughter were buried side by side in a nearby family plot. Two years later the Hancocks moved their remains to a mausoleum constructed on the hill overlooking Fotheringay. The somber Clark embraced his stricken children and sought to comfort his anguished and heartbroken mother-in-law, Margaret Hancock. His wife had been dead for a month by the time he joined his family, but there were many matters that required his attention. In his journal, he recorded making payments for the medical care Julia had received during her final days and the twenty dollars her coffin had cost.[71]

There was also the question of how to care for his young children. In conversations during the ensuing days, a plan was worked out. Two-year-old Julius, a child with significant disabilities, was to remain with his grandmother in Virginia for the present. Six-year-old Mary Margaret would stay with her Aunt Caroline in Louisville. The three remaining boys, Meriwether Lewis, William Preston, and George Rogers Hancock, would return with their father to the familiar environs of St. Louis and to the new home that their mother had so looked forward to occupying.

During William Clark's absence, Missouri voters chose the new state's first governor. On July 2, the day before he departed for Virginia, Clark drafted a

Alexander McNair. The popular militia officer and businessman handily defeated William Clark in Missouri's 1820 gubernatorial contest and gained the distinction of being the new state's first governor. Courtesy of the State Historical Society of Missouri.

statement addressed to the People of Missouri formally announcing his candidacy for that office. Desirous not to appear overly eager, he asked the printer to hold his message until the state's new constitution had been officially adopted. Word soon leaked out, and McNair, who had not yet publicly declared, told friends privately that he would remain in the race even though "he would regret to mortify an old friend." In its July 5 issue the *Missouri Gazette* broke the news and informed its readers that both men had consented to serve as governor if elected.[72]

Three days after the Constitutional Convention adjourned, the *St. Louis Enquirer* published Clark's formal announcement. Backers of the opposing candidates immediately mobilized their forces for what promised to be a contentious contest between two onetime political allies. Until recently both Clark and McNair had been affiliated with the little junto, but as statehood approached McNair gradually distanced himself from the St. Louis–based group. During the constitutional convention McNair broke ranks with his former friends to embrace the tide of democratic reform sweeping the country. The new political imperative required candidates to affect a common touch, and McNair got the message and cast his lot with the legions of farmers and mechanics among whose ranks he already claimed considerable support. As adjutant general and inspector general of the territorial militia, Colonel McNair lobbied the federal government to pay Missouri militiamen and rangers for their wartime services, and as federal register of lands in St. Louis he championed squatters' rights and pre-emption. These actions greatly enhanced his popularity in Missouri's rapidly growing out-state regions. Clark, true to his principles and oblivious to the emerging populist dynamic, remained steadfast in his loyalty to the coterie of French Creole merchants and U.S. political and military leaders and professionals who had effectively dominated territorial affairs.[73]

But as the combatants squared off to battle for control of the new state, they knew that the hordes of newcomers flooding into Missouri in search of a better life would be the final arbiters of their destiny. Clark's backers confidently believed that their esteemed candidate's renown and his extensive administrative experience would propel him to victory, even as McNair and his supporters took to the hustings to wage a campaign to win over the hearts and minds of the state's ordinary working folk. From the outset, it was clear that their campaigns would be very different.

Clark seemed unbothered that his personal situation would prevent him from taking part in the campaign. In announcing his candidacy to the people of Missouri he acknowledged the necessity for his absence from the state but hastened to add: "this circumstance does not give me uneasiness, except as it might be construed by some into an indifference for your good will. Otherwise I think it of no importance for me to be present. The choice of a Governor is your business and not mine; and so far as my fitness for that place may be the subject of enquiry, that matter may be discussed as well in my absence as in my presence. I should take no part in the discussion even if I remained at home, but should leave it to those whose business it is to decide upon my pretensions." Clark took his lead from the well-honed techniques of political canvassing that he first witnessed during his boyhood days in Virginia, no doubt confident in the knowledge that the tried and true system had produced the likes of Washington, Jefferson, Madison, and Monroe.[74]

In his message Clark briefly outlined his qualifications and his record of public service. He declared himself a republican and invoked the principles of his Virginia mentors. Beyond that he simply pledged to "bring with me a fervent wish to contribute to your prosperity, and to maintain the honor of a State whose name must forever be dear to me." Clark's decision to adopt a hands-off approach to campaigning and to refer enquiries concerning his character to the territory's "old inhabitants and early settlers" played into the hands of political enemies who sought to portray him as aloof, out of touch with ordinary voters, and a captive of the old guard.[75]

William Clark was a congenial man, usually affable and agreeable, but his bearing was clearly that of a gentleman. Noah Ludlow, an actor and theatrical entrepreneur who first met Governor Clark in St. Louis in 1820, remembered him as "the finest specimen of the old Virginia gentleman" and a patron of the arts. Ludlow considered the illustrious westerner's gentlemanly demeanor charming, but Clark's political opponents claimed that in the matter of gubernatorial dignity he excelled McNair "only in stiffness and formality." John B. C. Lucas, a bitter foe of Clark and his outspoken champion Thomas Hart Benton, entered the fray by publishing a series of letters in the *Missouri Gazette & Public Advertiser* under the signature of An Elector. In some hastily scrawled rough notes the wealthy and irascible Lucas portrayed McNair as a decent and plain Pennsylvania farmer while he styled Clark as possessing the borrowed manners of a Virginia overseer.[76]

Lucas cast McNair as a man of the people whose candidacy originated not in a political caucus "but in the cabins among the farmers, the mechanics and the multitude, which all popular government ought and must govern." McNair, eager to place himself on the side of the people and to distance himself from the political squabbling, condemned the politics of an entrenched establishment, but left it to others to attack his opponent directly. He pledged, "to do that which would result to the benefit of this country, and its citizens . . . with an eye to the present and future prosperity of our country, without respect to friends or party."[77]

Those noble words moved a McNair partisan to suggest: "If Wm Clark were to make another tour to the Pacific Ocean, build another boat and go to Prairie du Chien; if he were to be a general of militia . . . a governor seven years longer, and spend his whole time at Washington City, and in Virginia, he never would learn to utter so dignified—so republican—and so liberal a sentiment as that." Perhaps the opposition's most telling salvo against Clark was the charge that while acting in his official capacities as governor and superintendent of Indian affairs he often favored his Indian charges at the expense of his white constituents. These charges infuriated Clark's supporters, as did the allegations that their candidate had failed to properly defend the territory's exposed settlements during the War of 1812, because they considered them unfair, but even more because they seemed to strike a responsive chord with ordinary voters. Especially galling was an attempt to question the propriety of Clark's 1814 expedition to Prairie du Chien on grounds that the hapless excursion had unnecessarily extended the lines of defense and diminished the number of troops available in the territory.[78]

The published allegations that Clark was partial to the Indians paled by comparison with the even more egregious rumors circulating by word of mouth. A letter in the *Enquirer* chronicled numerous "villainous and contemptible" falsehoods that were being given credence in the state's outlying regions, including reports that Governor Clark traded with the Indians during the war, recently authorized the resettlement of a Kickapoo band on the Osage River, kept an Indian wife, had his Indian children educated at public expense, and loved Indians more than white people.[79]

Clark's supporters rushed to his defense in the columns of local newspapers with slight effect. They allowed that Clark had sometimes treated the unfortunate Indians with mildness and humanity, noting that it was his duty to do so, but they suggested that his humane actions were also the impulses of a magnanimous heart. More important, they argued that he understood native peoples and how to control them. They credited his mildness of manner and firmness of purpose with creating the relatively peaceful conditions that prevailed on the Missouri frontier at the same time that neighboring regions found themselves subjected to far bloodier scenes. But reasoned words in Clark's defense were no match for neighborhood gossip or tavern talk.[80]

In fact, General Clark's friends seemed at a loss to figure out how to counter McNair's electioneering in tippling shops and along back streets. It all appeared quite unseemly to them, but they also sensed its effectiveness. Clark's friends railed against McNair's populist campaign and accused him of pitting recently arrived farmers and the poor against Missouri's old inhabitants. And they fumed that the honest candidate who stayed at home attending to his ordinary business was stigmatized as a proud man and enemy of the people. While a majority of the territory's American voters seemed ready to embrace McNair's candidacy, Clark's longtime French Creole allies remained steadfast in their support.[81]

As election day drew near, it was clear to Clark's friends that all was lost. John O'Fallon advised members of the Clark family in Louisville, "Uncle William will not be elected. His opponent will have a handsome majority." In a last-ditch effort to salvage his absentee uncle's candidacy, O'Fallon put pen to paper and drafted a lengthy campaign biography designed to remind newcomers to the state of William Clark's past glories. Among other things, O'Fallon lamented that his fellow countrymen had failed to grasp the value and importance of America's scientific expedition, but alas, his detailed recounting of the Corps of Discovery's actions and of William Clark's numerous other accomplishments fell largely on deaf ears. The official canvass gave McNair 6,576 votes and Clark only 2,656. In seeking to explain away Clark's loss, Thomas Hart Benton protested that the endless predictions of a McNair victory had caused many Clark supporters to jump on the McNair bandwagon at the last minute. But Benton knew better, and he would soon follow McNair's lead and embrace the new populist political realities. It was too late politically for William Clark, who had fallen victim to changing times.[82]

Clark was on his way back to Missouri with the boys when he learned of his electoral defeat. The political setback was mortifying for the veteran soldier and public servant, but he did not allow his disappointment to show. His wife's death and his decisive loss at the polls seemed a lot to bear. As always, the steadfast Clark persevered in the face of tragedy and adversity. He and the boys arrived in St. Louis on September 19, the day after the state's newly elected General Assembly had convened in the Missouri Hotel, but the devoted and doting father's priorities were now with his young sons, for whom he purchased an assortment of apples, nuts, and toys.[83]

The 1820 election marked the end of William Clark's political career, but it did not terminate his role as a public servant. He put the loss behind him and decided to remain in St. Louis, the place he now considered home. His past service would soon bring him a new federal appointment as the superintendent of Indian affairs in that city, which enabled him to play a prominent role in the administration of U.S. Indian policy until his death in 1838. Missouri voters may have failed to appreciate William Clark's crucial role in guiding their exposed and culturally diverse frontier territory through its fractious prestatehood years, but with his steady hand at the helm, the Missouri Territory successfully weathered the storms of political and economic transformation that prepared it for membership in the American Union.

Nine

The Graying of the Redheaded Chief

T HE YEAR 1820 HAD BEEN a trying one for the careworn William Clark, and events during the ensuing year gave him little reason to believe that his spate of troubles was about to end. He was grieving from the loss of his wife, separated from two of his children, and faced with the possibility of losing his job during an economic downturn that threatened him with financial ruin. Protective of the three sons in his care, he attempted to keep them entertained and busy lest they dwell on the death of their mother and the absence of their siblings. There were shiny apples awaiting them on Christmas Day along with a celebration for members of the Clark household that even included the distribution of small sums to the family slaves as a holiday gift. For the boys' diversion, and for his own as well, he often took the older lads to theatrical productions and saw to it that they were treated to cake afterward. For George, too young to attend the plays, there was a new rocking horse, and when the windy days of early spring approached the attentive father purchased some fish line and a kite to introduce his sons to that playful sport. Mindful of the children's studies, he enrolled William and Lewis in classes at the Roman Catholic school that Father Francis Niel had recently opened in St. Louis.[1]

In the Indian superintendent's office, things went along as usual. Secretary of War John C. Calhoun instructed Clark to carry on with his duties as before, but the prolonged silence from Washington about future plans for the Missouri agency prompted him to ask Missouri Representative John Scott to seek a clarification from the War Department about his status now that statehood was at hand. When the answer arrived, it was not what the veteran public servant had hoped for or perhaps expected. Secretary Calhoun advised him that Congress had halved the appropriations for the Indian Department and eliminated his position as superintendent. In an effort to let him down gently, the secretary stressed that Clark's experience and assistance would be required to implement the changes and instruct the remaining agents who henceforth would report directly to the War Department. Clark was to be kept on the federal payroll until June 1.[2]

Faced with this loss of income, the financially pressed Clark sought an extension on his four-thousand-dollar loan from the Bank of Missouri at a time when the value of the fifty shares of the bank's capital stock he had pledged as security seemed in doubt. The Panic of 1819's belated arrival in Missouri unleashed worsening economic conditions that threatened to bring down the Bank of Missouri. Its aging president, Auguste Chouteau, resigned in January of 1821 amidst mounting signs of trouble, and the directors turned to Clark, who declined the presidency but did agree to serve on the board. After suspending specie payment in August, the Bank of Missouri limped along, creating fiscal stress for the outgoing governor and a host of other clients and investors.[3]

While Clark struggled to sort out his personal finances and those of the bank as well, daughter Mary Margaret's letters from Louisville warmed his heart and underscored how much he missed her cheerful presence. On July 13 he opened one of her first efforts and began reading, "Dear papa. I hope you are well. I want to see you, and my Brothers. kiss them for me. I am a good Girl, and will learn my book. your affectionate Daughter Mary, M, Clark." Two months later, using the same bold script, she told her father about attending a tea party with little cups and saucers and assured him that she read and wrote something every day. The seven-year-old eagerly anticipated his forthcoming visit and hoped that her brothers would be joining him, but by the time he and the boys reached Kentucky, she had fallen seriously ill. The only hint about the cause of her malady was her father's remark that he had found the place very sickly and planned to take his children back to St. Louis as soon as possible.[4]

Mary Margaret did not live to return to the place of her birth. Her death at Middleton, Kentucky, on October 15 was yet another heartbreak for the stalwart soldier to bear. When informed of this latest bit of bad news, John O'Fallon summed up his uncle's plight: "I sympathize most sensibly for the irreparable loss of uncle Wm. I am gratified to hear that he bears it so well. I fear

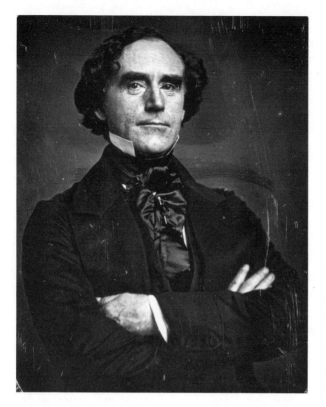

Meriwether Lewis Clark. William Clark named his firstborn son after his partner in discovery. Lewis Clark, as the family called him, was especially close to his father. Courtesy of the Missouri Historical Society.

he will not spend the evening of his life as serenely as he desires. The failure of the Bank and the embarrassments here will I apprehend hurt him more than he is aware of; I wish he could get something from the Genl. Govt. to contribute to his support."[5]

O'Fallon, a perpetual worrier, underestimated William Clark's resilience and his perseverance in the face of adversity. Back in St. Louis, the grieving husband and father found solace in the company of Julia's cousin and girlhood friend Harriet Kennerly Radford. A widow with three children, she had come to St. Louis to live with her brother James Kennerly following her husband's death. Comely like Julia, the thirty-three-year-old Harriet was eighteen years younger than Clark. When he asked her to become his wife, she accepted, and the Reverend Salmon Giddings, the father of Presbyterianism in Missouri, married the couple at the Kennerly residence on November 28, 1821. Blending families is never easy, and Harriet's eldest son, William, then fourteen, balked at moving in with his new stepfather, preferring to remain at the home of his uncle. Not long thereafter, the Clarks shipped him off to a boarding school in

Harriet Kennerly Clark, from a portrait by Chester Harding. William Clark's second wife was a native of Fincastle, Virginia, and a cousin and girlhood friend of Julia Hancock Clark. From *Persimmon Hill: A Narrative of Old St. Louis and the Far West* by William Clark Kennerly (University of Oklahoma Press, 1948).

the East where he developed a fondness for the sea, and when he was of age, Clark, with whom he had long since reconciled, helped secure him a naval appointment.[6]

Harriet and her two younger children, Mary and John, joined the Clark household, where the Clark boys readily embraced them. O'Fallon, never hesitant to bear tales, reported that Clark's new bride was only a tolerable economist and housekeeper devoid in the arts of arrangement and economy, but he hastened to add that she was an affectionate and good wife and mother. The former governor was, he noted, in very good spirits, and O'Fallon believed that this union would indeed contribute much to his uncle's comfort and happiness. No doubt Harriet helped nurse her new spouse through a painful attack caused by "gravel" or kidney stones. Not long thereafter a letter from Margaret Hancock, Julia's mother, reported that John Julius, the son he had been forced to leave behind, was growing, able to run about, and speaking much better, though she was quick to add that she did not mean to imply that he was or ever would be fully recovered. Even that guarded outlook gave cause

Mary Margaret Clark. This miniature portrait of William Clark's only daughter was painted shortly before her premature death in 1821. Courtesy of the Missouri Historical Society.

for hope, and by year's end, things at long last appeared to be looking up for long-suffering Clark.[7]

With his ties to the Indian service now severed, he watched from the sidelines as agent Richard Graham attempted to resolve a dispute over Ozark hunting grounds between the recently transplanted Delaware and the Osage. No doubt the redheaded chief's absence from the negotiations puzzled his Indian friends, but in early summer there was good news for them and their benefactor. New congressional legislation had established a St. Louis–based superintendency, and without a moment's hesitation Secretary Calhoun dashed off word to the highly regarded official that he was to be offered the position. David Barton, a U.S. senator not among Clark's supporters, subsequently carped that the office had been created as a special sinecure for the aging explorer, and in truth it probably had.[8]

The new law assigned him jurisdiction over all trans-Mississippi tribes as well as others in the Illinois Territory and along the Upper Mississippi, making his superintendency the largest both in area and in the number of Indians within its boundaries. Clark's duties were numerous and wide-ranging: the various agents, subagents, interpreters, and other officials within his district reported to him; he was also charged with keeping track of accounts and maintaining records, handling treaty negotiations, distributing annuities, issuing li-

censes and passports for traders and travelers in the Indian country, and order-
ing the removal of interlopers or unauthorized persons from those areas. Best
of all for Clark, the position carried an annual stipend of fifteen hundred dollars, less than his governor's salary but welcome nonetheless.[9]

Along with the routine duties of office, several new challenges awaited the
superintendent's immediate attention. Under intense lobbying from John Jacob
Astor and other American fur moguls, Thomas Hart Benton successfully pushed
legislation through Congress abolishing all U.S. trading factories and ending a
social experiment intended to protect the Indians from exploitation by greedy
private traders. Clark, who had supported the old system over the protests of
some of his St. Louis allies, quickly fell into line and forwarded instructions to
his agents for liquidating the government stores. Private traders eager to fill the
gap created by the factory closings flocked to the superintendent's office seeking trading licenses.

St. Louis–based fur merchants had every reason to believe that their friend
Superintendent Clark could be counted on to lend them a helping hand, and
they were not wrong. He viewed them as agents of empire and key players in
the struggle to reduce British influence in the Indian country and promote harmonious relations with its Native inhabitants. When one of his agents voiced
concern about the propriety of licensing General William H. Ashley and Major
Andrew Henry to trade along the Upper Missouri, Clark rushed to the St.
Louis traders' defense. On the heels of the announcement that Ashley and
Henry intended to open a trading establishment at the mouth of the Yellowstone River, the St. Louis superintendent encouraged the expansionist-minded
Secretary of War John C. Calhoun to consider the creation of a U.S. military
post there, arguing that such an installation would be beneficial for all parties
in the upper country. Shortly thereafter Clark granted Ashley and Henry a five-
year license authorizing them to operate not only on the Upper Missouri but
also westward into the Rockies.[10]

The infamous Arikara attack on Ashley's 1823 expedition and its heavy toll
(fourteen dead and nine wounded) underscored the need for increased fortification in the heart of the Indian country. U.S. authorities promptly dispatched
a military expedition under the command of Colonel Henry Leavenworth to
chastise the errant Arikara, but absent a larger military presence, the threat
along the Upper Missouri remained largely unchecked. Eager to avoid a repeat of the bloody episode, Ashley pioneered the rendezvous system, allowing
independent traders and trappers to operate in the interior away from the
more exposed rivers. His innovations revolutionized western fur operations
and unleashed an enterprising breed of expectant capitalists known in the
popular parlance as mountain men. Meanwhile, from his St. Louis post, Clark

continued lobbying for an increased military presence to support the expanding western operations of U.S. traders and trappers and to no avail submitted Ashley and Henry's claim seeking federal reimbursement for the losses that they had sustained at the hands of the Indians.[11]

Sidelined once again with kidney stones, Clark turned to folk medicine for relief. He consumed several quarts of a tea brewed from wild carrot stalks and seeds and watermelon seeds, a concoction he declared to be as tasty as China tea when sweetened with honey or sugar. Undoubtedly the passage of an exceedingly large stone had made the unusual beverage seem more palatable. Back on his feet, the former governor was feeling fit enough to confer with Father Charles Van Quickenborne and the newly arrived contingent of Jesuit missionaries who had made their way to St. Louis from Belgium. He encouraged their plans for opening an Indian school at Florissant, and helped facilitate a five-hundred-dollar federal subvention for its support. Such schools were a part of Clark's grand but chimerical vision for the gradual assimilation of native people by teaching them "to live in houses, to raise grain and stock, to plant orchards, to set up land marks, to get the rudiments of common learning, such as reading, writing and cyphering . . . the first steps towards improving their condition."[12]

On most days the redheaded chief could be found tending to business at the Indian office housed in the Main Street residence he had built in 1818 or in the adjoining chamber that served as a combined Indian council room and museum. Along with the steady stream of tribal delegations, traders, Indian agents, subagents, and interpreters who routinely passed through the agency's door on official business, visiting dignitaries, travelers, scientists, and artists regularly stopped by seeking Clark's advice and assistance. Anyone desirous of visiting Indian country had to secure the superintendent's permission, and his renowned master map of the West, prominently displayed on his office wall, was a must-see for all western travelers.

More often than not, he invited his callers to inspect the large collection of curiosities on display in the Indian council chamber. Clark had adorned its walls with the articles of Indian clothing and decorative arts, native weapons and battle instruments, animal skins, hides and horns, geological specimens, Indian portraits, and assorted oddities that he had collected. His little museum, already touted as a St. Louis showplace, seldom failed to fascinate or enthrall those who viewed its exhibits. When Paul Wilhelm, Duke of Wurttemberg first visited St. Louis in 1823, the German scientist was so taken with the beautifully embroidered animal skins in Clark's collection that he urged that they should be painted and described before vermin had a chance to ruin them.[13]

To the duke's delight, Clark also invited him to attend a council with a

Potawatomi contingent then in St. Louis. Eager not to miss anything, the young aristocrat traveled to their camp on the city's outskirts, where he observed the Indians painting their faces and bodies and donning their finest tribal regalia in preparation for their session with General Clark. He followed along as they paraded through town carrying a well-worn banner bearing the U.S. insignia and then witnessed the thirty-minute session Clark conducted with them in his council chamber. At the conclusion of those talks, the Indian superintendent presented the delegation's leader with various presents, including a red-collared blue uniform coat that he promptly donned to the amusement of the duke, who observed that it contrasted ridiculously with his native clothing. When the chief stepped forward to offer his hand to General Clark and his European guests, the Potawatomi Indian women and children, waiting impatiently outside the council room for the deliberations to conclude, rushed into the chamber to collect their gifts. With Clark's help, Prince Paul subsequently launched the first of two trips up the Missouri to collect plant and animal specimens.[14]

Two years later, in May of 1825, the renowned veteran of the American Revolution, the Marquis de Lafayette, passed through St. Louis while on a return visit to the United States. The Frenchman made a point of asking his hosts in the river city to include a stop at Clark's museum on his crowded itinerary. Lafayette's decision to honor the American explorer with a personal call during his one-day stay in St. Louis was a sign of his regard for the western patriarch. Clark returned the favor by presenting the hero of two worlds with a buffalo-skin garment made in the fashion of a Russian riding coat.

While escorting Lafayette and his entourage through his museum, he regaled them with entertaining anecdotes pertaining to the objects on display. Four necklaces made from grizzly bear claws caught the eye of the French dignitary, who informed his host that the London Cabinet of Natural History had only a single claw from the American continent's most terrible animal in its collection. Lafayette's offhand observation did not escape the notice of Clark, who subsequently dispatched a live grizzly cub to France as a gift for the French aristocrat. After failing to make a pet of the animal, which developed a vile and ferocious temper, Lafayette donated it to the zoo at the Jardin des Plantes in Paris, where the wild creature became an international sensation.[15]

General Clark also lent a helping hand to artists and writers interested in the West. During the summer of 1830 he befriended George Catlin, an aspiring artist who dreamed of recording and preserving the history of North America's Indians through a series of paintings and a collection of artifacts. Convinced that the Indians were doomed to perish, Catlin took up the cause of documenting the appearance, costume, and customs of the Plains Indians. Clark encouraged the ambitious scheme and conducted its author on a guided tour of his museum. Suitably impressed with what he saw, Catlin later used Clark's little exhibit as a model for his own famed traveling Indian gallery that drew crowds in America and Europe. To help him realize his wish to capture Indian images on canvas, Clark invited Catlin to accompany him to Prairie du Chien to witness a council with members of various northern tribes. Assured by his host that tribal leaders, decked out for the gathering in their finest attire, would afford an abundance of subjects for his portraiture, the eager painter readily signed on for the trip. Catlin's professional peers found little to admire in his paintings. His sketches were hastily drawn and not very exacting, but his portrayals of Native Americans and the landscape of the Great Plains were among the first to call attention to those subjects. Grateful to the great explorer for advice and assistance in arranging his western tours, Catlin painted his portrait. Unfortunately, the stiff and formal rendition of his esteemed subject failed to capture the lighthearted jest and jocularity that the artist so aptly attributed to Clark in his writings.[16]

Swiss painter Karl Bodmer and his patron Maximilian, Prince of Wied, were similarly indebted to Clark. Biddle's narrative of Lewis and Clark's journey had inspired the German naturalist to undertake a scientific expedition across North America. Before coming to America, he hired the young draftsman Bodmer to join his tour as an illustrator. When Maximilian arrived in St. Louis in 1833, he immediately turned to Clark for guidance in organizing his western trip. Among other things, the accommodating Clark authorized his nephew Benjamin O'Fallon to allow his foreign guests to copy his famed Missouri River maps then in O'Fallon's possession. Yet again Clark's assistance yielded wonderful dividends, including, in this instance, Bodmer's masterful sketches and watercolors of early-nineteenth-century western scenes.[17]

At about the same time, Clark also hosted the famed American writer and western traveler Washington Irving and the Scottish adventurer and sportsman Captain William Drummond Stewart. The valuable services Clark rendered each of his illustrious guests earned him their gratitude and a well-deserved reputation as a patron of western exploration and art. For his part, the aging western patriarch, while never a glory seeker, basked in the glow of the attention accorded him by a parade of distinguished visitors.

Clark's Indian diplomacy earned him equal notice. After years of trying to resolve differences between Indians and whites, the veteran diplomat had concluded that removal was the best option available to his Native American clients. He believed that their relocation in the territories west of present-day Missouri and Arkansas offered potential benefits for them and for his Euro-American constituents. The strategy would complete the transfer of tribal lands

William Clark, portrait by George Catlin. Renowned for his efforts to record and preserve the history of North America's Indian inhabitants, Catlin painted this portrait in 1832. Like many other artists fascinated by the American West, he was indebted to William Clark for the assistance and encouragement he provided. Courtesy of the Smithsonian Institution National Portrait Gallery.

in the East to the U.S. government and open them to settlement by the nation's expanding Euro-American populace. As for the Indians, Clark suggested that resettlement would afford them an opportunity to retain their own laws and regulations, help shield them from the temptations of ardent spirits so readily available in areas populated by whites, and allow them to make a transition from hunting to agriculture and thereby enjoy the same blessings available to whites. The grassy prairie lands they were being offered in exchange for their ancestral homelands and hunting grounds were, from his perspective, ideally suited for their needs. It was a scheme filtered through the lens of Clark's Jeffersonian vision of gradual assimilation. Notwithstanding his long years of association with native people, the thought that they might prefer to retain their traditional ways never seems to have seriously entered his mind.

Clark's reputation for honesty and fairness in his dealings with the Indians and his sensitivity to their plight were products of his philanthropic views, but the well-intentioned and paternalistic redhead failed to fully grasp the magnitude of the sacrifices that he urged upon his "red children." When the peaceable Kickapoo Prophet Kenekuk continued to resist removal from his ancestral homelands and hunting grounds, Clark chose to believe that intratribal rivalries were the primary cause for his hesitancy to relocate in the Ozarks. Richard Graham, an agent assigned to Clark's superintendence, was closer to the mark when he opined that the Kickapoo's strong attachment to the land of their fathers would make it difficult to eject them. Clark was quick to acknowledge that as often as not the Indians had more grounds for complaint than their white neighbors, but his long-term solution to their predicament remained constant— they should sell their lands and move westward. In his efforts to impress tribal leaders with America's might and reward their cooperation, the St. Louis superintendent continued the firmly established custom of escorting selected chiefs on a grand tour to Washington.[18]

In 1824, when Keokuk showed a willingness to accede to U.S. demands for more land concessions, Clark set in motion plans for the compliant Sac leader to visit the U.S. capital and meet his Great Father, the president. A blessed event momentarily interrupted arrangements for the trip when William Clark welcomed another addition to his still growing brood. On February 29, 1824, Harriet delivered a fine bouncing boy. Unable to agree upon a name for the lad, his proud parents simply called him Pomp. Two years later when they finally settled on Thomas Jefferson Kearny for the boy's given name (perhaps as a compromise), they were not quick to abandon the by-then firmly fixed moniker Pomp. That usage led some latter-day historians to confuse young Jeff Clark with the by then grown Jean Baptiste Charbonneau, who years earlier Clark had affectionately referred to as "my boy Pomp." The year that Jefferson

Clark was born, Sacagawea's eighteen-year-old son accompanied the Duke of Wurttemberg to Europe, where he remained for several years.

By mid-1824 William Clark was in Washington showing the sights to his son Lewis and his stepson William Radford. Lewis, an artistic lad, sketched some of the city landmarks while his father made the rounds with Keokuk and other members of the Sac, Fox, and Ioway delegation traveling with them. The Indians had gone there to affix their marks to treaties relinquishing all claims to their lands within Missouri. The "smooth tongued" Keokuk, as Black Hawk once called him, took advantage of his audience with federal officials to press for a peace conference for the purpose of settling boundary disputes among tribes along the Upper Mississippi. Clark used the successful completion of yet another land deal to press his case for a salary increase that would compensate him for the added duties he had inherited under the Indian Department's latest reorganization. Federal officials demurred from granting him a raise and offered him instead an interim appointment as surveyor for the states of Missouri and Illinois and the territory of Arkansas. He had surveyed enough land in his day to oversee those operations, and after some initial hesitation he accepted the temporary assignment for the extra income it promised to provide.[19]

With his business accomplished in Washington, Clark headed to New York and Philadelphia to entertain his Indian guests and to tend to some private matters. After dispatching the Indians homeward from Philadelphia via a northerly route, Clark enrolled Lewis and William Radford at an Elizabethtown, New Jersey, academy. With the boys settled at school, Clark headed for home by way of Virginia and Kentucky, in part with the intent of relieving Julia's aging mother of the burden of caring for his six-year-old son Julius. General Clark arrived in Missouri in time to learn that in Missouri's 1824 U.S. senatorial contest he had polled fifteen votes in the General Assembly, even though his friends had declined to formally place his name in nomination against the incumbent Barton.[20]

Early the next year Clark once again set out along the well-worn road to the nation's capital. His avowed purpose was to tend to his accounts and resolve matters affecting the St. Louis superintendency, but if the truth were known, his primary objective was to check on his sons. While in Washington he was able to secure confirmation of Lewis's pending appointment to the U.S. Military Academy at West Point and finalize arrangements for getting him to the New York school before classes began in the fall. No doubt Clark's long deceased partner Meriwether Lewis would have been pleased to know that his namesake had chosen to pursue a military career. Clark's second son, William Preston, also away at school, was not doing as well, and his father urged his older brother, Lewis to write him a few words of encouragement.[21]

Following the elder Clark's return to St. Louis in late spring of 1825, it was

Keokuk, portrait by George Catlin. Keokuk accompanied William Clark in 1824 to Washington, D.C., where the accommodating Sac leader and members of his delegation met the president and signed a treaty ceding tribal lands to the United States. Courtesy of the Smithsonian American Art Museum.

back to business as usual at the Indian Office. Federal officials approved his plan for "purchasing" more land in the Ozark highlands from the Osage and Kansas Indians to make room for the incoming eastern tribes, and gave him the order to proceed. It would not be an easy sell. Neither tribe was eager to part with more of its shrinking territory, but in the end the Red Head persuaded them that the larger annuities they would receive as payment for their lands would enable them to better feed their families, now that game was becoming scarcer, and the land cessions would produce peace and quiet with the other tribes and with whites as well. It was another bitter pill for them to swallow, but Clark sweetened the deal with increased payments, and in June both tribes agreed to relinquish what he described in a letter to his son Lewis as an immense country.[22]

As his father had done, Clark regularly corresponded with his children when they were apart. Clark, a typical parent, was eager to hear how Lewis was faring at the military school. He assured his son that the entire family sorely missed him but hastened to add that they found consolation in their belief that one day his accomplishments would make them all proud. He worried that the one hundred dollars he had given Lewis might have fallen short of his actual needs, and he urged him to write frequently, advising him to "keep nothing from me let it be what it may either good or bad and recollect that no person now living can be as much your friends and devoted to your true interest as your father." There was bad news to report: Lewis's mother was in poor health, his baby brother Pompey was ill, and his Aunt Fitzhugh (Clark's youngest sister Fanny) had died. That left William and older sister Lucy Croghan as the only surviving members of John and Ann Clark's ten children. Once his letters had been posted, Clark could again turn his attention to pressing matters in the Indian country.[23]

A decade after Clark had first attempted to assert U.S. authority in the vicinity of Prairie du Chien, the situation there had improved only marginally. Intertribal warfare and white intrusions on Indian lands and lead mines kept the region in a state of perpetual turmoil. In early July of 1825, Clark set out for the Upper Mississippi outpost to preside, with Governor Lewis Cass of the Michigan Territory, at a grand council called for the purpose of restoring peace to the area—an idea that Keokuk had touted the previous year in the federal capital. Temperatures were unseasonably warm as the huge gathering assembled, and to make matters worse Clark was feeling unwell when he arrived. In his opening remarks before a throng of nearly two thousand tribal representatives, the Redheaded Chief informed them that he and Governor Cass had traveled a great distance to help end the incessant conflict and strife that ravaged their land. That was their sole purpose, and the American officials proposed to achieve that objective by assisting the warring parties reach agreement on fixed boundaries delineating their respective territories. The often tense and tedious negotiations lasted for nearly a month, as the rival bands one by one came to terms with one another.

During one session convened by Clark for the purpose of arranging a boundary between the Sac and Sioux territories, even the normally mild-mannered Keokuk defiantly shook his lance in the faces of the enemy Sioux. When all of the final lines had been drawn, the delegates departed with their share of the guns, powder, lead, tobacco, salt, sugar, and as always firewater that General Clark and Governor Cass had specially ordered for the occasion. Exhausted but pleased with what they had wrought, Clark boasted to a Louisville friend that "after some trouble and patience all the objects have been most happily accomplished."[24]

Back in St. Louis, and still somewhat indisposed, he took a few days off to recuperate and enjoy a break with his family. William and the younger boys, now enrolled in classes with a local teacher, each received six thousand dollars, mostly

View of Great Treaty at Prairie du Chien. In 1825 William Clark superintended treaty negotiations with northern Indian tribes at the Upper Mississippi site he had first visited a decade earlier. Courtesy of the Library of Congress.

in Kentucky lands following the final settlement of their grandfather Hancock's estate, which included a similar amount for Lewis and a one-thousand-dollar bequest for their father. At about the same time, word reached Clark that his lengthy dispute with the Thruston heirs in Louisville had finally been resolved. In 1823 they had filed a lawsuit in the Kentucky courts charging him with malfeasance in the administration of the estates of Charles Thruston and George Rogers Clark. Determined to thwart their "rascally actions," Clark provided his attorneys with a detailed accounting of his actions as executor for the two estates. Two years later the court-imposed settlement cost him twenty-five hundred dollars, but he must have heaved a sigh of relief finally to be done with the unpleasantness after years of wrangling.[25]

In November fire accidentally destroyed the old Indian office at Main and Pine that Clark had vacated when his new quarters had been completed seven years earlier. The government had leased the structure to Thornton Grimsley, a local saddle maker, but after the conflagration only the four exterior walls remained. The Indian agency's blacksmith and gun shops, located on the back of the lot, were unscathed. Clark inquired at the War Department if he could have the structure rebuilt to provide his agency with rental income to help offset office expenses, and the response was affirmative.[26]

That fall Clark attempted to tackle the Indian depredation claims filed by

Missourians, seeking damages for losses they claimed to have suffered at the hands of the Indians. Responding to local pressures, the St. Louis official urged Secretary Barbour to address the delinquent claims, some of which went back as far as 1804. In many instances the amounts seemed paltry, but as one hapless Missouri petitioner asking for seventy dollars as compensation for a stolen horse pointed out, the amount was not trivial to him. Barbour tossed the political hot potato back to Clark, instructing him to first seek recompense from the culprits accused of the misdeeds, and failing that to provide him with a report on the merits of each individual case in accordance with the law. In some of the more recent cases the superintendent was able to secure restitution, but tribal leaders shook their heads in disbelief when asked to respond to incidents that had occurred twenty years earlier. Clark completed a final report in time to take it with him when he traveled to Washington early in 1826, but despite his efforts and congressional involvement, the claims continued to languish unresolved amidst a lot of buck passing.[27]

It had been a long and arduous year for the harried superintendent, and an unexpected reprimand for having exceeded his initial cost estimates for the recent land acquisitions from the Kansas and Missouri tribes clearly irritated the veteran official. He fired back a letter complaining that the appropriations for his agency had not been increased to reflect the added obligations imposed on his superintendency by recent treaty arrangements and by the addition of new subagencies. Clark advised Secretary Barbour that he believed it would be desirable for him to communicate his views in person before U.S. officials adopted any more changes affecting his agency. Sensing the St. Louis official's frustrations, Barbour rushed to reassure him that he enjoyed his full confidence. Clark expressed his appreciation for the support, but he could not resist making a point about the personal and financial sacrifices he had suffered in discharging his governmental duties. And with that off of his chest, he prepared to go to Washington to state his case.[28]

When Clark arrived in the federal city in February of 1826, Secretary Barbour sought to smooth ruffled feathers by asking him to provide his candid assessment of the various legislative proposals for addressing the nation's Indian problems then under consideration in Congress. Three decades of dealing with native people from the trans-Appalachian region to the Pacific had left him with definite ideas on the subject. Clark held firm in his commitment to the expansionist national agenda that expected Indians to surrender their lands and abandon their traditional ways, but unlike most nonnatives he also appreciated the devastation that those very policies had visited upon America's indigenous peoples. Without intervention to alter the present course, he warned Secretary Barbour, they seemed doomed to extinction:

> The obligation which is imposed upon this government to save them [the Indian tribes] from extinction . . . and to make persevering exertions to improve their condition, is equally the dictate of magnanimity and justice. The events of the last two or three wars, from Genl. Wayne's campaign in '94 to the end of the operations against the southern tribes in 1818, have entirely changed our position with regard to the Indians. Before these events, they were a formidiable and a terrible enemy; since then their power has been broken, their warlike spirit subdued, and themselves sink into objects of pity and commisseration. While strong and hostile it was our policy and duty to weaken them; now that they are weak and harmless, and most of their lands fallen into our hands, justice and humanity require us to cherish and befriend them.[29]

Clark went on to lay out for the secretary a series of precise proposals for implementing federal removal policies and providing assistance to the beleaguered tribes. His recommendations included calls for the employment of commissioners personally acquainted with the Indians; the creation of specific territories for each of the tribes to occupy; the creation of programs to assist Indians during a transitional period; the establishment of common schools in the villages; the formation of governments designed to inculcate the idea of submission to the authority of a civil government; the establishment of military posts adjacent to the Euro-American settlement frontier; and the replacement of smaller permanent annuities with larger temporary payments to encourage the abandonment of old tribal ways, avoid the creation of a permanent dependency, and rescue the U.S. treasury from a long-term financial burden.[30]

Clark predicated his plan on the assumption that the Indians had to choose either assimilation or extinction. But he also acknowledged that previous attempts to promote assimilation had failed, in large measure because the Indians had not been provided with the wherewithal they needed to succeed. After describing the pitiable state of many of the trans-Mississippi tribes, he cautioned Secretary Barbour, "It is vain to talk to people in this condition about learning and religion; they want a regular supply of food, and until that is obtained the operations of the mind must, like the instinct of mere animals, be confined to warding off hunger and cold." Clark's proposed benevolence came with a price. The Indians must submit to U.S. authority and abandon their old ways, but tragically the terms he proposed were among the best that were on the table.[31]

By the time that Clark had returned home in April, Indian removal was all the talk in Missouri. The *Missouri Intelligencer* heralded the expected deployment of additional troops in Missouri, preparatory to the pending removal of Indians to territories west of Missouri and Arkansas, and in the same issue they carried a separate account from a sister publication saluting Clark's role in facilitating these relocations.[32]

Back at his desk in the Indian Office, the superintendent directed his clerks to begin logging daily weather and river conditions, steamboat arrivals and departures, and other activities of interest. Only rarely did he make the actual entries himself, but the riverfront location of his offices afforded him a ready view of the growing number of vessels that tied up along the city's waterfront. Steamboat travel was not without risks, and when the *Liberator* ran aground on some rocks opposite the city in June, the boat's owners summoned the old riverman Clark and several other local citizens to help them assess the damage.[33]

Increased river traffic was only one indicator of the city's growing importance as a commercial hub and the revival of its economic fortunes. During the late 1820s new buildings and fine houses were springing up all over town, and many of the city's streets were being graded and paved. In describing the changes for Lewis, who was at West Point, Clark wrote, "this town improves astonishing in building & population and will unquestionably grow to be a large city," and at about the same time his mother reported, "you have no idea of the number of stores and vast emigration to this place." In 1826 the St. Louis superintendent oversaw the construction of a two-story brick building, with eight rooms, on the Main Street lot where the burned-out Indian Office had once stood. When the new structure was completed the following year he moved his offices and the Indian council room into the new building, and rented out the remaining rooms. The government's refusal to give him an added rental allowance for the quarters his agency had been occupying at his private residence seems to have prompted Clark's decision to relocate his offices in a publicly owned space. He quickly renovated the spaces vacated by the removal of the government offices, including the old council chamber, and leased them to private tenants, taking advantage of the higher rental rates in the booming city. Clark had to borrow money to make those changes, but he considered it a worthwhile investment and optimistically predicted that income from the property combined with economical living would make him debt-free within four years.[34]

The U.S. Army's new infantry school of instruction at nearby Carondelet gave the local economy an added boost. When the War Department announced its decision to abandon the deteriorating structures at Fort Bellefontaine and replace them with a new facility, Clark had joined Generals Edmund Gaines and Henry Atkinson and Missouri's Governor John Miller in recommending that the new installation known as Jefferson Barracks should be built at Carondelet, just south of St. Louis. By September of 1826, Clark informed his son that several splendid brick and stone quarters were taking shape at that location.[35]

Harriet, expecting another child, was barely able to walk around the house

View of St. Louis by J.C. Wild. This 1840 sketch of St. Louis depicts the burgeoning river entrepôt as it appeared during William Clark's last years. Courtesy of the State Historical Society of Missouri.

and prone to burst into tears, fearful that she was not likely to survive. To the relief of everyone, she delivered a black-haired, dark-eyed boy on September 9, 1826. After debating whether to call him Richard or Edmund, in honor of one of his father's now deceased brothers, they settled on Edmund. Harriet ordered the child of one of her slaves sent to the farm so that its mother could suckle young Edmund. Like her husband, she viewed their slaves as chattel, and suggested that they might have to sell Henry because of his thievish ways. Even so, Clark wrote to his son Lewis that the Negroes were every bit as interested in his success as were his other friends.[36]

Clark's travels and his busy schedule did not allow him much time to oversee the family farm at Marias Castor. Left to the care of "an indifferent white man" and Ben, one of the family slaves, Harriet Clark worried that it had been a good deal neglected while her husband attended to the steady stream of Indians passing through his office that summer, many on their way westward. The influx of eastern emigrant tribes led to renewed conflict as the Osage sought to block Delaware and Kickapoo encroachments on their territories. In late September Clark brought representatives of the feuding tribes together in St. Louis for a council that concluded on October 7 with the signing of a treaty of friendship.[37]

Clark's success in negotiating removal agreements with the northern and western tribes prompted officials in the War Department to dispatch him to Alabama and Mississippi for talks with leaders of the Choctaw and Chickasaw nations, but even he could not persuade the sedentary southeastern agriculturalists to sell their lands and move westward. The weary official who had spent much of the year away from home returned to join his family for a Christmas celebration. The stationing of two hundred married officers at nearby Jefferson Barracks had brightened the social scene, especially for the Clarks, who were almost always included on the guest list for special functions there. Harriet Clark felt well enough to reciprocate with a party at which she provided piano accompaniment for the dancing.[38]

Tragedy again struck the Clark household early the next year, when a gun carried by George Rogers Hancock Clark's hunting companion Henry accidentally discharged, wounding the Clarks' ten-year-old son as he returned from an excursion to the farm. The shot entered below George's right eye and opened a gaping hole in the roof of his mouth. The incident left the poor slave Henry distraught and frightened, but he seemed blameless, and the Clarks chose not to hold him personally responsible for the terrible mishap. George's father described the outpouring of grief and concern that had followed the accident: "You never saw so much grief as was shown by all white & black when they thought he would not live, it had like to have killed your mama, . . . at least 500 persons visited him the night & day after he was wounded of all classes and not less than four have set up with him ever since he was shot." Within a few days the boy's fever abated and he was able to speak well enough to be understood, though the damage his mouth sustained caused him problems for years to come.[39]

The accident forced Harriet Clark to cancel her planned trip to the East, and the family suggested that Lewis request a furlough so that he could come home for a visit. Young George was sufficiently recovered to accompany his father to the scene of his mishap in late April for a look at a bridge under construction over a creek, but the gap in the top of his mouth still made it difficult for him to speak plainly. There were other family problems. William, unhappy in school, seemed determined to return home. Apprehensive that Julius's deformity was getting worse and becoming a greater burden for him to bear, his father sensed that he would not live to enjoy a long life. A diligent student, Julius attended classes with George at a nearby school and refused to allow his disabilities to interfere with his studies. Pompey, who curiously still had not been given a formal name, was according to his father a noisy wild fellow, but he was in his mother's eyes the finest boy ever.[40]

With young George's survival no longer in doubt, the senior Clark set out in May of 1827 for the mouth of the Tennessee River, where he had platted a new town known as Paducah on a portion of the large tract that George Rogers Clark had conveyed to him in 1803. In naming his town, Clark had chosen to honor the Plains Apache band known to early explorers as the Padouca. At a time when the declining state of Indian people was very much on his mind, he advised his son Lewis, "I have laid out a town there and intend to sell some lots [in] it, the name is Pa-du-cah once the largest Nation of Indians known in this Country, and now almost forgotten." Clark's promotional handbill, announcing the availability of 150 building lots for sale, declared that "Few, if any points on the western waters, present so many advantages to the merchant, mechanic and capitalist, as does Paducah." One of his more profitable entrepreneurial ventures, Clark lobbied successfully to make the town the county seat of McCracken County.[41]

The Indian traffic at his new offices showed no signs of abating. A large Shawnee party migrating from Ohio to occupy new homes in Kansas came calling on August 6 and 7, 1827, but yet another family tragedy forced Clark to turn their care over to his assistants. On August 12 the distressed superintendent personally recorded two poignant lines in his diary: "Edmund Clark (my Infant Son) died at 8 ½ A.M. (10 mo. 3 days old)." It was one more heartache for the fifty-seven-year-old husband and father to bear. The baby's death took a special toll on Harriet, whose health was, according to her husband, already "delicate." Lewis continued his studies at West Point, despite his parents' growing concerns about his poor eyesight. A talented artist, the youthful cadet sent his mother some drawings that she proudly showed off to everyone who came to call. William, who had returned home and opened a store in partnership with George Kennerly in his father's new building, was learning to play the fiddle and the flute, no doubt with some encouragement from his musical mother. George, still recuperating from his injuries, went off to Kentucky, where he enrolled at Augusta College to study Greek and Latin. His distressed parents chided him for failing to notify them once he was settled in. Never hesitant to offer fatherly advice, Clark counseled his third son to be obedient and respectful to his teachers, friendly to fellow students, polite to the citizens, to avoid the company of bad boys and cultivate the friendship of worthy ones. Julius, increasingly deaf and experiencing difficulty breathing, struggled with few complaints, even as his prognosis worsened. Pompey, whom they had finally named Thomas Jefferson Kearney Clark (and later called Jeff), was a healthy four-year-old sprite who already had declared his intent to enroll in the same school as his brother George.[42]

The elder Clark spent more time at the farm with his family, staying there at least two nights a week. During winters, the younger boys invited their friends from school to join them there for hunting and skating. As he grew older, Clark was content to leave more of the routine Indian Office business to his clerks and assistants. Things did not always go smoothly in the St. Louis superintendency. The amiable and easygoing official expected his employees to show proper respect, and as agents Nicholas Boilvin, William Lovely, and Thomas Forsyth could attest, the old army man did not take kindly to criticism from subordinates. His disputes with the able but outspoken Sac agent Forsyth serve as a case in point. For reasons that are unclear given his own record, Clark reproved Forsyth for his absenteeism, and he failed to lift a finger in the capable agent's defense when a U.S. senator maneuvered to award Forsyth's post to an influential supporter. Following his removal from office, the disgruntled Forsyth held Clark responsible for his downfall and labeled him "a perfect ignoramus" who "can do no wrong." In 1830 Tennessee's former governor Sam Houston (better known later for his role in securing Texas independence) blamed Clark's inattention for the mishandling of some accounts involving his Osage clients. As the years passed William Clark may have experienced lapses in judgment and committed administrative blunders, but his lengthy record of distinguished service in Indian affairs was noteworthy by any standard.[43]

During most of the summer and early fall of 1828 Clark hosted Chickasaw, Cherokee, and Creek Indians who had been sent west to explore the country northwest and southwest of Missouri in search of a permanent home. In September former President James Monroe sent a portion of the memoirs he was writing for Clark's perusal, along with a request that he do whatever he could to assist his brother-in-law who recently had taken up residence in Missouri. After seeing off the southern tribes and closing out his accounts for the year, Clark prepared to return to Washington, where he and Lewis Cass had been summoned by officials in the War Department to assist with a revision of U.S. Indian and trade policies. Harriet was still not feeling well, but her husband believed that the exercise required by overland travel would do her good. Having been advised that his services would be required for several weeks, he arranged to close up the house in St. Louis, which was to be left under the care of two slaves. Son Julius was to stay with his Aunt Kennerly, and son William would continue to operate his store. The slaves were parceled out. Anthony was placed in charge of the farm, Henry assigned to work at the Indian Office blacksmith shop, and Ben assigned to haul wood into town for sale. The remaining slaves were hired out for the duration of the Clarks' absence to keep them gainfully employed and help offset the expenses of the trip. With those matters taken care of, in late October the Clarks and their son Pomp boarded a stage that bounced along the National Road on its way to the federal capital.[44]

William Clark arrived in Washington in late November as members of

Congress prepared to come back into session. Andrew Jackson's victory in the recent elections had the city abuzz with rumors about the likely changes the unpredictable new president intended to initiate. Politicians of all stripes maneuvered to place themselves in good stead with Old Hickory and his cronies. As an appointed official, Clark worried that his job might be at risk thanks to the likes of George Strother, a St. Louis businessman then in Washington who seemed bent on doing him harm. Bracing himself for any such eventuality, Clark wrote his nephew John O'Fallon, "I get along tolerably well, having but little to expect from any government." He wanted his salary raised, but sensed that the time was not right for him to make his pitch, so he resolved to get along as well as he could on what seemed to him a pittance.[45]

His family traveled ahead to New York while he and Governor Cass continued the laborious task of rearranging the voluminous federal statutes governing Indians and trade. Alone in his Washington quarters, laid low with a bout of influenza, Clark was left to ponder his future. If his enemies should succeed in injuring him, he consoled himself with the thought that the nation would be the poorer for having lost the services of a faithful agent. In a flight of fancy the old explorer hinted that if he lost his position he just might migrate to Oregon or any other part of the world to escape his enemies.[46]

His worries were for naught. Clark's standing was to be as solid with the new administration as it had been with previous ones. In the meantime, he and Cass plugged away at their assigned task. In December they sent Senator Benton a report outlining their views on the fur trade. They pointed out the fur industry's economic importance, noting that $290,052.39 worth of goods had been sent into the Indian country in 1827, but they hastened to add that the traffic in furs was more essential for Indian relations than for national industry and enterprise. Clark's anti-British bias, something he held in common with the new president, dated to his boyhood days in Revolutionary Virginia and made it easy for him to blame Canadian-based British operatives for many of the current problems. In making their recommendations to Congress, Clark and Cass chose to play it safe. Clark's assistant, John F. A. Sanford, better known today as the plaintiff in the infamous Dred Scott case, took note of their cautious approach: "I have been diligently engaged in assisting Govrs. Clark & Cass in their Indian business. They have made no changes nor have they recommended any I believe or but few. They have merely condensed all the laws regulating intercourse with the Indians into one general law & rendered more definite and positive others." In fairness, their lengthy report contained some valuable suggestions, based on firsthand experience, for regularizing procedures and providing more prescribed rules for operations in the Indian Department. Beyond that, the Cass-Clark report paved the way for an important 1834 congressional overhaul of federal statutes governing Indian policy and trade.[47]

The Clark family remained in Washington long enough to attend Andrew Jackson's inauguration, but none of them said much about the raucous affair, except to mention the large number of strangers who had descended upon the federal city to witness the popular general take the oath of office. In the days immediately preceding the official ceremonies, Old Hickory and the Red Head seem to have had an opportunity to exchange a few pleasantries. They were staying in the same hotel, and according to George Kennerly their two families attended the Catholic Fair, an annual bazaar offering various kinds of merchandise for sale.[48]

Before leaving the city, General Clark, who decided not to press for a salary increase, asked to be reimbursed for various Indian Office expenses. He submitted his request to Thomas McKenney in the Office of Indian Affairs, who then forwarded it with an explanatory note to John Eaton, the new secretary of war. Clark claimed a balance of $7,125.37 was due him for office rent, clerk hire, fuel, and other contingencies, but Eaton denied the claim and referred the matter to Congress. From St. Louis Clark acknowledged that the forty thousand dollars allowed for the St. Louis superintendency was as much as could have been expected, but he cautioned Secretary Eaton to expect cost overruns that would have to be paid from the department's contingency fund.[49]

Once again Clark found himself compelled to urge prudence and economy on members of his family, explaining that they had to live on his paltry salary since his debts swallowed up every other means of obtaining funds. His pleas were not always heeded. His wife, who found it difficult to pinch pennies, had upon their return given a grand party for the citizens and officers large enough to require that she throw open four rooms to accommodate the guests who stayed until three o'clock in the morning. Less than a month later the family purse keeper sounded a familiar refrain: "my house is as usual a place of resort but more respectful and less expense than formerly as my means lesson my expenses must necessarily be curtailed."[50]

Clark's oldest son, about to begin his final year at West Point, now looked to his father for advice. In assessing his son's future prospects, Clark reminded the soon-to-be academy graduate that "a farmer requires means, a politician also requires means, and if the army is preferred a home is necessary & I hope will always be found with or near me. A farmer or politician would be preferred as the one is independent & the other would likely be more pleasing to you as it has more honours in the road of preformance of the days." But he was more equivocal in his response to what clearly had been a bombshell. Lewis had confided to his father that he was smitten with his stepsister Mary Radford and wanted to ask her to marry him. Lewis had made his feelings known to Mary, but he worried because she was still seeing others. After advising his son that there was no legal impediment or societal impropriety precluding such a union, he wisely suggested that since they were both young they would do well to take a year or two to discover their true feelings and preferences. He placed Lewis's letter under lock and key and chose to keep the matter to himself, apparently preferring not to worry Harriet about it. It was just as well, for Mary, who obviously did not share Lewis's feelings, married Major Stephen Watts Kearny at the Clark farm in September of the following year.[51]

Harriet Clark made a brief trip to visit family in Fincastle in the fall of 1829, but her husband, who was always ready to hit the road, found it necessary to stay behind in St. Louis. He was knee-deep in what had come to be known as the Big Neck Affair. It began in the fall of 1828 when an Ioway hunting party illegally entered Missouri in pursuit of game. Big Neck, one of the tribe's headmen, remained in the area with a handful of followers in violation of an 1824 agreement ceding the land in question to the United States. The Ioway intrusions raised howls of protest from settlers who accused the nearly destitute Indians of stealing their hogs. During an angry encounter the whites unleashed a series of volleys at the Indians, who then returned the fire, killing three of the settlers. Reports of the incident had the citizens of central Missouri up in arms and demanding retribution.[52]

Clark's initial investigation determined that only a small party of renegade Ioways had been involved and the circumstances surrounding the firefight were very much in dispute, but the military authorities required the tribe to provide hostages for detention at Jefferson Barracks until Big Neck and his followers surrendered themselves. By fall Big Neck and his cohorts were in custody, and preparations were under way to try them. After conducting his own investigation of the case, James Birch, editor of the Fayette *Western Monitor,* concluded that the attack on the Indians had been unprovoked, and he urged Clark to spare the accused tribesmen from the hangman's noose. When Clark's sources corroborated Birch's findings, he forwarded a copy of the journalist's letter to Secretary Eaton with his endorsement. The true facts came out during the ensuing trial, and remarkably a white jury declared Big Neck and the other defendants not guilty and ordered them released. The Ioways' wretched state confirmed Clark's 1826 portrayal of the rapid decline of America's native people, and his decision to come to the aid of Big Neck helps explain why many Indians viewed him as their friend even as he continued to prod them westward.[53]

Clark, who was not feeling particularly well, often retreated to his cottage at the farm during the spring of 1830. In years past the vigorous and active westerner's recurring health problems had been more of an annoyance than a hindrance, but at age sixty he was finding it necessary to slow down his pace. His red locks had turned to white, but he retained his good nature and sense of humor according to George Catlin, who joined Clark, his wife, young son, and several members of the Indian Office staff when they departed for Prairie du Chien in late June to attend a general conference of the northern tribes. Clark returned to the familiar outpost on the Upper Mississippi in yet another effort to bring peace to the troubled area. He convened the immense gathering of tribes on July 4, and during the next ten days the two sides hammered out yet another agreement to cede land to the United States. The pace of land transfers was accelerating as a consequence of Andrew Jackson's ethnic cleansing policies. As Senator Thomas Hart Benton noted, Clark had been complicit in the adoption of the 1830 Removal Act, compelling the relocation of all eastern Indians to lands west of the Mississippi.[54]

The deliberations at Prairie du Chien had precluded William Clark from attending Meriwether Lewis Clark's graduation from West Point. It was a proud moment for the Clark family. To the delight of his father, the newly commissioned lieutenant was temporarily assigned to the Sixth Infantry at Jefferson Barracks. He arrived in St. Louis on August 31, but his homecoming was a bittersweet occasion because a few short days following his return, Lewis's first love, Mary Radford, wed Stephen Watts Kearny at the Clark cottage outside of town. The next year William Preston, who had toyed with the idea of following his brother to West Point, enrolled instead at the University of Virginia to prepare for legal studies.

The return of cold weather signaled it was time for William Clark to begin his annual trek to the federal capital. It was a damp and disagreeable November day, and recent rains had turned many of the city's streets to mud when he set out with his family for Washington with the Indian Office accounts and the Prairie du Chien treaties in his valise.[55] Following his arrival in the capital city, Clark made the obligatory rounds with members of Congress and officials in the War Department, stressing to all who would listen that he needed additional funding to assist the westward-moving tribes and to implement his most recent Indian treaties. Because he had viewed firsthand the appalling condition of many of the emigrating Indians, he made a compelling witness.

Though his own circumstances were not so dire, he did not hesitate to point out that his government allowance was insufficient for his family's needs. Privately he complained that in the crowded capital city they were living in a "wretched situation," but the acclaim he was receiving quickly overshadowed any such unpleasantness. Obviously flattered, he reported that he was "crowded with attention, and in demand before the committees." His business took far longer than he had expected, and Harriet was growing restless, perhaps in part because of their unsatisfactory accommodations. The lengthy impeachment trial of Judge James Hawkins Peck, a federal district judge from Missouri, interrupted the regular flow of congressional business. While he waited for members to complete the sensational trial, Clark followed the proceedings against the Missouri jurist with great interest. Clark's sympathies clearly were with those seeking to remove Peck from the bench, but in the end the Jacksonians leading that cause failed to muster the two-thirds majority in the Senate required for conviction.[56]

During his own appearances before congressional committees, Clark encountered little opposition to the treaties that he had negotiated with the northern tribes, but he reported such was not the case with the arrangements that his counterparts had made with the southern tribes. He persisted in his efforts to persuade the tight-fisted Congress to authorize supplemental appropriations to cover the mounting expenses for Indian removal and delayed his departure until those measures had been adopted. Meanwhile, John O'Fallon covered a twelve-thousand-dollar note for funds Clark had borrowed to pay unreimbursed expenses in the Indian Office. Clark was grateful for the assistance from his nephew, the president of the St. Louis branch of the Bank of the United States, but he was miffed to discover that during his absence in the East he had lost his seat on the bank's board of directors.[57]

Son Lewis joined his family in Washington in 1831 to investigate his prospects for employment prospects outside the army. He declined an appointment in the capital city and opted to continue with his regiment at Jefferson Barracks, perhaps in deference to his aging parents, who liked the idea of having the most dependable of their boys nearby. With his lengthy business in Washington finally at an end, the weary Indian superintendent returned home to St. Louis. That summer William Preston Clark began his studies at the University of Virginia, where he advised his father he expected to remain until his education was sufficiently complete to get into some business. After so many false starts, he had finally settled upon law as his chosen profession. Concerned about his parents' health, William urged them to exercise more frequently: "I hope my dear Father you take more exercise than when I left. Nothing would be more conducive to your health than a walk or ride every morning & evening. Also ma her health would become better by active exercise." He likewise cautioned his mother against her overreliance on magnesia, which he warned many considered the perfect poison when used in such quantities.[58]

The second-born son also expressed concern about his brother Julius, and with good reason. Fortunately, the Clarks were back in St. Louis when the thirteen-year-old lad, who had struggled against so much adversity, passed away quietly at home in their presence on September 5, 1831. He was, his grief-

Rabbit's Skin Leggings, portrait by George Catlin. A member of the Nez Perce tribe, he and three companions traveled to St. Louis from their villages in present-day Idaho in 1831 to confer with William Clark, who had met their people twenty-five years earlier during his voyage of discovery. Courtesy of the Smithsonian American Art Museum.

stricken father reported, alert to the end and had actually begun a letter to his older brother Lewis that he was unable to finish. For a third time, one of William Clark's children had predeceased him.[59]

Getting back to work was his best tonic. Sometime in October four Nez Perce men, Black Eagle, Man of the Morning, Rabbit's Skin Leggings, and No Horns on His Head, arrived in St. Louis in search of the redheaded chief who had visited their eastern Idaho village twenty-five years earlier. The precise purpose of their lengthy journey has become a subject for considerable debate. With no one in St. Louis able to converse in the Nez Perce tongue, they were forced to communicate using sign language, which helps explain why so much confusion still exists about their reasons for making the trip. According to one tradition, they came seeking a book of knowledge, which Christians of various persuasions chose to mean they were in search of religious conversion. Modern tribal leaders believe that it was not that simple and equate their quest not with a desire to become Christian converts but with a broader quest for knowledge and technology that might lighten their burdens. What is incontrovertible is that two of the sojourners, Black Eagle and Man of the Morning, died while in St. Louis, where they were buried with Catholic rites.[60]

There can be little doubt that they would have sought out Clark, but the meticulous record keeper's failure to register even the briefest mention of their presence in the city is puzzling. Perhaps it simply was a matter of his preoccupation with Julius's recent death and Harriet's deteriorating health. His only reference to the Nez Perce travelers came later in response to a query from George Catlin about the journey's purpose. Modern Nez Perce historians assert that in their conversations with Clark the visitors would not have failed to mention his Nez Perce son, Daytime Smoker, who represented a direct physical link to the admired redhead and his culture. If they did, he chose to keep that information to himself.[61]

Preoccupied with his domestic situation, Clark exhibited more than a little irritation with the constant bombardment of requests from Washington for official reports. In a letter to his old friend Lewis Cass, now secretary of war, he complained that a lack of cooperation from some of the traders had made it difficult for him to secure the information he had been called upon to provide. He noted the report he and Cass wrote three years earlier addressed many of the same issues, and suggested that he had learned nothing since that might substantially alter those views. In response to questions regarding the use of liquor in the fur trade, he acknowledged that some traders took excessive quantities of whiskey into the Indian country, allegedly for the use of boatmen but in truth with the intent of watering it down and dispensing it by the gallon and keg to their thirsty Indian customers. His solution was direct and to the point: "As those Traders have evinced so little good faith, such disrespect to the Government as to violate its most imperative laws, & so little humanity toward the Indians themselves, as to disregard the most sacred provision for their protection, I shall conceive it my bounden duty to recommend the total & entire prohibition of this article in the Indian country, under any pretence, or for any purpose whatever." This represented a departure from his earlier position that agents in the field should be empowered to make decisions regarding the importation of the controversial commodity. It was a thorny problem. The superintendent had seen firsthand the adverse effects caused by the introduction of liquor into the Indian country, but U.S. officials, including Clark, had long employed alcohol in their deliberations with those same tribes.[62]

After so many years of wrestling with this and other issues, the seasoned government official undoubtedly sensed that these latest efforts to control the flow of spirits was doomed to fail. His thoughts understandably were focused elsewhere. His dear wife, Harriet, had been steadily declining, and on Christmas morning, she breathed her last gasp. "She is gone, I hope to a better world," he advised his son Lewis, who was then serving as an aide-de-camp to General Gaines in Memphis. This latest blow left the aging warrior in an understandable but uncharacteristic state of despair. "My spirits are low and my course indecisive," he told his firstborn. Harriet Kennerly Radford Clark was buried in St. Louis and sometime afterward removed to the burial vault at Colonel John O'Fallon's country home.[63]

Clark's preoccupation with personal cares complicated by his dispute with Forsyth no doubt contributed to his failure to launch a diplomatic initiative to stave off the Black Hawk War, but the principal reason for his course of action was in all likelihood his frustration and anger with the defiant and warlike band of pro-British Sacs that had tested his patience for nearly three decades. Those "blood thirsty and ferocious savages," as he called them, represented a serious obstacle to the U.S. government and its designs for the nation's future. Clark's bitter critic Thomas Forsyth charged him with mishandling the situation and missing an opportunity for a peaceful resolution in 1830 when he chose to disregard his advice. Forsyth clearly had an ax to grind, but by all accounts, he enjoyed unquestioned standing among the Sac and Fox people, and any intelligence he gathered was apt to have been accurate. After the war had concluded Forsyth went so far as to assert, "if I had remained at Rocky Island as Indian agent no troubles would have ever taken place between the white people and Indians, and all the lives lost and money expended in the troubles with Black Hawk and his party would have been saved and no other person is to blame but General William Clark."[64]

By the spring of 1832 the situation had deteriorated to the point that both sides seemed to have ruled out a peaceful settlement. It had become a contest of wills between two proud and aging warriors with starkly contrasting visions of what was meant to be. In April of that year Black Hawk led a band of five hundred mounted fighters across the Mississippi intent on reclaiming tribal lands on the river's east side, in direct violation of previous agreements with the United States that the Sac leader defiantly refused to recognize. Their return incurred the wrath of white settlers who had staked out those lands for themselves. Fearing for their safety, Black Hawk and his followers sought refuge and assistance at a Winnebago village on Rock River. After learning of these latest intrusions and related hostilities, the Sac warrior's irritated nemesis, General Clark, recommended the deployment of a combined force of federal troops and Illinois militia to drive out the interlopers. In a letter to General Henry Atkinson, he stated that "those fellows must be punished severely, otherwise others will be encouraged to prosue [pursue] the same course."[65]

Three weeks later the seemingly dormant, anti-Indian impulses William Clark had learned at the knee of his brother George Rogers Clark suddenly reared their ugly head. The benevolent benefactor of besieged and oppressed Indian people pressed a far different cause on Secretary of War Lewis Cass: "The faithless and treacherous character of those at the head of our Indian enemies appears now to be so well known & understood, as to permit an expression of the hope that . . . a Ware of *Extermination* should be waged against them. The honor & respectability of the Government requires this:—the peace & quiet of the frontier, the lives & safety of its inhabitants *demand it.*"[66]

How does one reconcile this seeming dichotomy? In truth, in William Clark's world, there were two categories of Indians—good and bad. The champion of "sober and well-behaved" native people held a far different view of belligerent Indians resistant to American progress and a threat to its peace. The latter, representing the darker side of the American dream, momentarily overwhelmed Clark's humanitarian impulses as this struggle unfolded in 1832.[67]

During that summer U.S. military forces ranged over northern Illinois and southern Wisconsin in pursuit of the errant bands. Among those summoned to duty there was Lieutenant Meriwether Lewis Clark, now engaged for the first time in military combat. The senior Clark worried about his son's safety, counseling him to "take care of yourself and do not unnecessarily expose yourself either to climate or the enemy. I wish you had one or two howitzers to rout those fellows from the strong hole." Lewis replied that the Indians had taken to the swamps with his men in hot pursuit. The war ended when General Atkinson's combined force of regulars and volunteers virtually annihilated the remnant of Black Hawk's band as it attempted to flee back across the Mississippi at the mouth of the Bad Axe River, wantonly slaughtering men, women, and children in what was a sorry spectacle. Black Hawk, who abandoned his forces and retreated across the river, survived the massacre. He subsequently surrendered to U.S. forces at Prairie du Chien, and they dispatched him downriver to Jefferson Barracks to await his fate.[68]

One of the first accounts of the battle at Bad Axe to reach St. Louis included a report that Lewis Clark's horse had been shot from under him, causing his anxious father to fear the worst. A letter from Lewis soon laid that worry to rest, and shortly thereafter the Clark family embraced the young lieutenant when he arrived in St. Louis "ragged & durty with a long beard, much tanned." In gratitude for his son's safe return, for second son William's recovery from fever in a city ravaged with cholera, and no doubt for the war's outcome, the now white-haired patriarch of the Clark clan led his sons Lewis, William Preston, William Radford, and Pompey to the family pew at St. Louis's Christ Episcopal Church the following Sunday morning. William Clark had been a founding member of St. Louis's first Episcopal parish when it was established in 1819, but he also retained his own pew in St. Louis's Catholic cathedral.[69]

His other surviving son, George Rogers Hancock, away at the time in Lexington, Kentucky, seemed headed on the right path, having put his youthful

Black Hawk, portrait by George Catlin. William Clark's angry response to Black Hawk's incursion contributed to what his critics called an unnecessary tragedy. Courtesy of the Smithsonian American Art Museum.

follies behind him. His father was especially pleased that the lad had visited his aging relatives at Locust Grove. William, having completed his studies at the University of Virginia, headed off to Harvard shortly afterward to read law under the tutelage of some of the country's top legal scholars. Clark urged his children to write him, and took delight in their accomplishments. To George he wrote, "My children are now my first consideration and to see them do well will be a consolation in my old age not to be equaled by any other events."[70]

With cholera raging in St. Louis, Clark sought refuge at his cottage in the country. When Washington Irving visited the old general there on a fresh September day, he provided one of the few actual descriptions of the rustic dwelling's interior. In its cozy sitting room he observed that its owner had placed a calumet over the fireplace and stood his rifle and game bag in a corner of the room. Nearby Lewis had built a small house on a hill overlooking the pond, and a new stable stood in close proximity. Irving and the venerable Clark lunched outdoors at tables laden with fried chicken, bacon and grouse, roast beef, roasted potatoes, tomatoes, excellent cake, bread, and butter carefully prepared by the family slaves and served under the shade of the trees. The setting with its well-cultivated fields, orchards, and vineyards, a shady walnut grove, chirping insects, bee hives, dove cotes, canoe by the pond, and surrounding prairies thoroughly captivated the romantic writer, as did his amiable host with his shoulder-length gray locks.[71]

The conversation was engaging, particularly the general's discourses about the Indians. They also talked about slavery, and Clark informed his guest that he had granted three of his servants their freedom, but they had much preferred slavery, or so he thought. One of those slaves was York, who according to Irving's notes had decided to return to Clark in St. Louis after going bust in his drayage business in Tennessee, but he contracted cholera and died before he made it back to Missouri. There is no reason to doubt that Clark had eventually given York his freedom or that he had died from cholera, but given their stormy relationship the story about his desire to return to Clark's care seems dubious.[72]

At Clark's invitation the Indians often camped at his farm when visiting St. Louis, but given the unhealthy conditions in the city in 1832 he opted to conduct his negotiations there as well, causing the site afterward to be known as Council Grove. He informed his son George "the last two months I have been at the farm, and have concluded treaties with about 400 Indians." He went on to explain that about three hundred had died from cholera in St. Louis, but only one Indian and a "Dutch" general had succumbed during the gathering at the farm. He recommended that George and John Radford stay in Kentucky with their friends when classes were finished.[73]

More and more Clark was content to leave the affairs of his office in the hands of his underlings, and his diminished oversight dimmed the luster of a once efficient operation. His letters now were frequently written in another hand with only his signature affixed below. The changes did not go unnoticed, but no one was prepared to publicly challenge the competence of the proud western patriarch now entering his dotage. In assessing the situation that he inherited, Joshua Pilcher, Clark's eventual successor as the St. Louis superintendent, advised the commissioner of Indian Affairs that during his final years in office the venerable Clark's "infirmities and good ness of heart [had] induced an implicit reliance upon every thing recommended by his subordinates," and even Clark's longtime friend Senator Benton acknowledged that near the end of his life the office had become "nearly useless."[74]

The superintendent's growing inattention was apparent in his mishandling of the issuance of liquor licenses following the congressional enactment of a total ban on liquor shipments into the Indian country in July of 1832. That fall Clark, preoccupied perhaps with the aftereffects of the Black Hawk War, licensed fur companies to import whiskey in accordance with the previous laws, and the resulting contretemps set off a battle between rival fur companies that raised eyebrows in Washington as officials rushed to finesse the flap over the stiff new law that Clark had endorsed. The entire affair took up a great deal of the careworn superintendent's time.[75]

Meanwhile, that winter Black Hawk and his fellow prisoners languished in chains in their Jefferson Barracks cells. At Clark's invitation a parade of visitors, including Irving, Maximilian, Bodmer, and Catlin traveled downriver to the military post for a firsthand look at the famed warrior and his companions. Catlin spent some time drawing them, and at their urging he made a sketch showing them with their balls and chains. Hesitant to release the captives back into the Indian country, Secretary of War Cass ordered them transferred to the East, where they had an audience with President Jackson before being confined at Fortress Monroe in Virginia. Cass soon had second thoughts about the wisdom of detaining the now hapless prisoners and recommended that they be returned to Iowa and placed under the custody of tribal leaders. When Indian Commissioner Elbert Herring asked Clark for his thoughts about the wisdom of releasing the prisoners, he gave the proposal an approving nod. In his view, because the tribal dissidents were properly chastened and fully reconciled to the futility of trying to resist U.S. authority, they no longer posed a threat. Once they had dutifully acknowledged the U.S. government's sovereignty, Clark again felt secure in allowing the better side of his nature to take charge.[76]

In the waning days of Clark's career tributes poured in from old friends and colleagues. Pierre Menard's warm and complimentary letter of resignation as Delaware Indian agent must have been especially gratifying. The prominent Creole entrepreneur expressed appreciation for Clark's uniform kindness and courtesy even under the most difficult of circumstances and for his wise and unwavering advice and assistance. He hastened to add: "nor can I refrain from an expression of the opinion that 'the poor remnant' . . . of those who once covered the greatest portion of our quarter of the Globe, are more indebted to your active and humane exertions, for the comparative happiness which they have in prospect, than to any other individual within my knowledge."[77]

In the loneliness of widowerhood, Clark continued to focus his attention on his children. Lewis, now torn in his affections between two young women, pressed his father for advice, but the savvy parent declined to intervene in what he termed one of the most important decisions of life. "Make your choice and I will be satisfied," he told Lewis, adding, "I never suffered any one after I came to an advanced age, say over 30 to interfere with my love matters, and I don't think a parent should say anything unless an evident defect or unworthiness was known, which I do not believe anyone can state in relation to those ladies." The following January Lewis married Abigail Prather Churchill of Spring Grove, Kentucky. Cold weather and short notice prevented his

Black Hawk and Five Other Saukie Prisoners, by George Catlin. When William Clark escorted Catlin to Jefferson Barracks to sketch Black Hawk and his fellow prisoners, the languishing Indian captives insisted that the painter include their balls and chains in his drawing. Courtesy of the National Gallery of Art.

father from attending the nuptials, but he expressed the greatest satisfaction over his son's choice and invited the young couple to reside with him in St. Louis until they found a more suitable place. Their arrival a few short weeks later buoyed the old man's spirits on the eve of his departure for the U.S. capital for yet another go at collecting the monies he believed the federal government still owed him. According to his calculations he was due an additional $36,077.[78]

Still in debt, he looked to a federal payment to help rescue the bottom line of his financial ledger. Clark's properties had appreciated in value, but he remained cash-poor. Finances continued to be a sensitive subject for the proud man who was reticent to discuss his pecuniary affairs with any but his closest family members. From Washington, he complained about the slow way of doing government business and the necessity for explaining everything in writing, but his efforts persuaded War Department auditors to reconsider at least some of his previously disallowed expenses. Even so, when Lewis and Abby asked him to purchase a floor cloth and various other items, he said he only promised to acquire as many as his small means would allow. After two and a half months, he was eager to head homeward, along a northerly route via New York, the Great Lakes, and Chicago. Back in St. Louis he had to address a problem with his ten-year-old son Pompey, who had run away from school during his absence.[79]

The old gentleman, as John O'Fallon now called him, was becoming frailer with each passing year. Still struggling to pay off his obligations to the bank, he sold some of his properties and again dared to hope that he would soon be debt-free, though now he had to worry about the profligate habits of his sons, especially Lewis. He occasionally lent his name to civic causes. In 1835 he was a subscriber to a campaign for the construction of a new theater that his son Lewis had helped spearhead. The Clarks were longtime playgoers who believed that their city, which now exceeded eight thousand inhabitants, needed a comfortable theater. He was also forward-looking enough to throw his support behind business and civil leaders seeking to promote the construction of a railroad linking St. Louis and Fayette in Howard County.[80]

Tragically, the passage of years had done nothing to ameliorate William Clark's racism or to lessen his commitment to slavery. Not surprisingly, he authorized a citizens' group formed in St. Louis for the purpose of ridding the town of its expanding free black community to list his name as a corresponding member. According to a newspaper account the organization had several goals, including the compilation of a list of the city's free people of color and the establishment of a fund to transport them to Liberia. The committee also called for an end to the practice of allowing slaves to hire themselves out because the pernicious practice gave them too much freedom and threatened to undermine the slave system.[81]

When a campaign by Missourians to annex the fertile strip of land between the state's western boundary and the Missouri River in Missouri's northwest corner gained congressional approval in 1836, contingent upon the extinguishment of all Indian claims in the region, Clark inherited the task of making the necessary arrangements. He traveled to Fort Leavenworth, where he negotiated a treaty with the Ioway, and the Sac and Fox of Missouri, relinquishing their rights in the Platte Country. It was the thirty-seventh treaty that he had arranged over the course of his three decades in the Indian service, and it was to be his last. Not up to traveling farther upriver to secure similar concessions from other tribes with similar claims, he dispatched John Dougherty and Joshua Pilcher to handle that chore. Ratification of those agreements paved the way for the addition of the Platte Purchase to Missouri in 1837 and was to be one of Clark's final acts as Indian superintendent.[82]

The negotiations at Fort Leavenworth, the stress resulting from a dispute involving some of his property at Clarksville, Indiana, across the river from Louisville, and new concerns about his children left the old soldier worn out and bedridden at the beginning of 1837. John O'Fallon worried that the old man might not survive many months and made it a point to visit him every day while Lewis and William were in Jefferson City, where Lewis was serving in the Missouri General Assembly. Sensing his mortality, William Clark executed a new will in April, making some minor alterations in the bequests for each of his children.[83]

By early summer he had rallied sufficiently to travel eastward in the company of Lewis and his family and William. He was in New York City on the Fourth of July, and local civic leaders invited him to participate in a dinner honoring the sixty-first anniversary of American independence, an event that, unlike most of those in attendance, he could recall from firsthand experience. The bustle tired him out, but he took time to advise his son George in St. Louis that though fatigued he was feeling better. To conserve his strength he announced that he did not intend to leave his New York boardinghouse until he departed for Washington. He was clearly worried about William, who had suffered three of the mysterious attacks that now plagued him. Six weeks later the elder Clark was in Warm Springs, Virginia, after traveling by way of Philadelphia, Washington, and Fredericksburg. Illness had detained him in Philadelphia for three weeks, and he had also been unwell when he was in Washington. He hoped that the springs might facilitate his recovery, but he was clearly eager to get home to St. Louis. By early November he had finally made it back to the comfort of his own bed.[84]

Early in 1838 Clark was well enough to respond to a request from James Herring for information about the Clark family. His short but informative account of each of his brothers and their military service during the Revolutionary War showed that his memories of those now long-ago years had not dimmed appreciably. Not long thereafter word came from Louisville that his last surviving sibling, Lucy Croghan, had passed away at Locust Grove. Now he alone remained.[85]

Lewis and Abby were occupying their grand new house, and Lewis's envious cousin John O'Fallon fretted endlessly about his extravagant spending in anticipation of his inheritance. William Preston Clark's mysterious malady had grown steadily worse. References to his dissipation suggest that he had become a chronic alcoholic. Hard drinking was commonplace, and his uncle George suffered from the debilitation of alcoholism, but there were hints that an underlying problem may have triggered William Preston Clark's drinking bouts.

The most explicit discussion of his problems appeared in a letter that Sarah Mason wrote to her sister Rosalie von Phul in St. Louis describing his condition: "William is in very bad health, besides the attacks he had in the west, he was quite ill here & again at West Point. I think it may be owing to the fall he got before we left. I think too he is imprudent, he has a predisposition to something like vertigo & he pays no attention to his diet." Finding someone to care for him was becoming a problem, and O'Fallon suggested that he believed the only alternative was a lunatic asylum. In fact the family had him briefly committed to such an institution in Kentucky, but that did not happen until after his father's death. It seems unlikely that the family patriarch would have sanctioned such a drastic measure. In an act of desperation shortly before his father's death, William headed west under the care of his brother George and stepbrother John Radford, but his debilitating attacks persisted.[86]

William Clark had converted his old council house and museum into rental space with offices below and apartments above and leased the property to Dr. William Beaumont, the army doctor whose experiments with human digestion had garnered him considerable renown. The Beaumonts initially took their meals with Clark and whatever family members were present. He welcomed their company and was no doubt comforted to have a physician so close at hand. Another tenant and guest at the Clark table was Lieutenant Robert E. Lee, then in St. Louis to supervise harbor improvements. The elder Clark was failing rapidly, and in late February Lewis and Abby moved him into quarters in their home at the corner of Fifth and Olive where they could keep a closer eye on him. His unsteady hand prompted him to ask his brother-in-law James Kennerly to inform his son Jeff that he had been unable to write him a letter, a sure sign of his decline. Sometime in May when John O'Fallon and his cousin George Gwathmey visited Clark, the old man experienced difficulty in recognizing Gwathmey.[87]

The end came quietly at the home of his son Lewis on the evening of September 1, 1838. William Clark was sixty-eight years old. With William, George, and John Radford still away in Indian country, and Jeff attending classes at the Jesuit College in Bardstown, Kentucky, with his cousin Clark Kennerly, Lewis was left to bury his father. But he was not to be alone. The morning after his passing, Major Ethan Allen Hitchcock, Clark's deputy in the Indian Office, dispatched the following message to Washington: "The venerable General William Clark died between the hours of 7 and 8 last evening at the house of his son, Lewis, in this city. I think proper to communicate this intelligence officially for although the event will be immediately known over the whole country and will throw a gloom over this section of the union and be received with mourning everywhere, I deem it my duty thus to make a record of the date from the office so lately under his superintendence."[88]

As word spread, tributes began pouring in while family, friends, and even those who knew him only by reputation mourned his loss. Flowery and lengthy obituaries celebrated his virtues and his accomplishments, but Noah Ludlow, the actor, wrote to his wife simply, "Old General Clark died here last night—another good man gone—And the world has none to spare. I shall attend his funeral tomorrow. It has thrown a gloom over the whole city." Ludlow was not alone as hosts of the residents of Clark's adopted city prepared to join him for what turned out to be the largest funeral St. Louisans had ever witnessed.[89]

Epilogue

A LARGE CROWD quietly assembled outside Meriwether Lewis Clark's St. Louis residence on the morning of September 3, 1838. Persons of all descriptions had come to pay their final respects to the famed western patriarch William Clark. By all accounts, St. Louis was a city in mourning. Sensing that the elder Clark's passing marked an important historical milestone, many individuals not personally acquainted with him had turned out to witness the somber proceedings.

At 11 a.m. a band playing a solemn dirge stepped out to lead the funeral procession bearing the old soldier's body to John O'Fallon's country estate for burial. The St. Louis Grays, a volunteer militia company attired in their distinctive gray uniforms trimmed in black with silver buttons and braid, bell-shaped black patent leather caps, and red sashes, marched in military precision close behind the musicians with their banner furled as a sign of respect. Next in line, the deceased's Masonic brothers wearing the symbols of their ancient order walked slowly ahead of a hearse drawn by four white horses draped in black with black feathers attached to their heads. One of Clark's longtime African American slaves outfitted in mourning garb followed, leading the general's riderless mount with his sword and military cap fastened to the empty saddle and his boots fixed in the stirrups. Scores of family members and friends rode in sixty or so carriages trailed by well over one hundred mounted riders. The procession stretched out for nearly a mile as it wound its way to the O'Fallon farm four miles outside the city.[1]

When the first units drew near to the cemetery, a cannon began firing at one-minute intervals and continued until the last of the mourners reached the grave site. As the final echoes of the military salute died away, the Masons conducted their final rituals. Immediately afterward the Right Reverend Peter Minard solemnly intoned the familiar words, "I am the resurrection and the life, saith the Lord . . ." that open the traditional Episcopalian burial rite from the *Book of Common Prayer*. The brief service included a eulogy and concluded with a benediction, after which Clark's body was laid to rest in the family vault, while the honor guard fired a final volley.[2]

Henry B. Miller, a young tradesman relatively new to the city, was among those who joined the throng that autumn day to honor a man whom he called "a departed hero, venerable sage, hardy pioneer, amiable father and respected citizen." It was unlikely that Miller had ever met Clark, but the young stranger's final thoughts recorded in his diary came closer than he perhaps realized to capturing the true measure of William Clark's greatness: "If eccessive [excessive] toil and Peril, and a life of Laborious Servitude spent in the service of his country entitle a man to honours, there are none more deserving than Gen. Clark."[3]

Today, nearly two centuries later, William Clark stands as a national icon representing American exploration and discovery, even though he was neither a pathfinder nor a trailblazer in the truest sense. He and Meriwether Lewis had not been the first to traverse the North American continent, nor did they discover the most practicable route westward. Moreover, they could not have completed their journey without assistance from countless Native Americans along their route of march. Those realities do not diminish the value of Clark's endeavors, nor do they render him any less historically significant. His daring and remarkable voyage to the Pacific with his friend and partner Lewis laid open the American West to exploitation and occupation by later generations of westering Americans, and his cartographic masterpiece, depicting North America's vast trans-Mississippi expanses as a single region, enabled the American people to visualize the West as crucial to their national fortunes. Clark's actions helped sow the seeds of Manifest Destiny and the bittersweet harvest it yielded.

While his map and the journals of his western tour with Lewis acknowledged a large-scale Indian presence throughout the sprawling domains he had traversed they also inspired expansionist designs that consigned the West's native inhabitants to a far different and less promising destiny. William Clark's role in that unfolding drama did not end with his return from the Pacific. His post-1806 labors as a soldier, diplomat, territorial governor, head of the largest western U.S. Indian agency, and patron of western exploration and travel facilitated the opening of America's vast western hinterland to an avalanche of white settlement that forever altered the western landscape. A loyal and dependable public servant, Clark worked tirelessly to secure the region's peaceful incorporation within the American Republic and to advance its political and economic

William Clark's tomb at Bellefontaine Cemetery in St. Louis. Following the opening of St. Louis's Bellefontaine Cemetery, William Clark's descendants had his remains moved there and reinterred on a grassy knoll in sight of the Mississippi River. In 1904 family members erected this stately monument to mark his grave, with its impressive granite obelisk and bust of the renowned explorer under the constant gaze of the decorative heads of a grizzly bear and a buffalo. HABS photograph, courtesy of the Library of Congress.

transformation. Mindful that however beneficial those changes might be for national development, they had exacted a heavy toll on Native Americans, Clark also struggled unsuccessfully to rescue his beleagured Indian friends from the tragic consequences of the very forces he had helped unleash. More than most of his contemporaries Clark exhibited a bona fide compassion for besieged Indian people threatened with extinction, but his benevolence came with strings attached. He expected and demanded acquiescence to U.S. authority as the price for his support. Strange as it may seem today, the Pacific expedition was simply a prologue to Clark's most enduring legacies.

In a larger sense, William Clark's story mirrors the youthful and restless beginnings of the United States of America. His sixty-eight-year life spanned an era of relentless change. He entered the world in time to witness the birth of the American Republic, and he lived long enough to observe its transformation from thirteen rustic and struggling states along the Atlantic seaboard into a sprawling and far-flung nation encompassing a significant part of the North American continent poised on the threshold of a new industrial age. During most of those years Clark inhabited a world of racial and cultural diversity that foreshadowed the makeup of modern America, but his upbringing and cultural biases blinded him to his own prejudice and intolerance.

William Clark in many ways reflected the virtues and the vices of the rising young Republic and its restless citizenry. His devotion to family and to country, his commitment to republican principles, his determination, energy, and enterprise, his ability to face and overcome adversity, and his willingness to come to the aid of downtrodden Indians personified many of the noblest attributes of the nation he loved and served. At the same time, his adherence to slavery and racial prejudice, his support for policies of exploitation and conquest, unmasked the ugly faces of discrimination, abuse, and injustice also abroad in the land.

The privileges of birth and inheritance presented Clark with special advantages and opportunities, but his life was never easy. It is not difficult to identify William Clark's shortcomings, but his modern critics would do well to remember that he lived in a time and place far removed from their own. Even though the core issues he struggled to address may not be so very different, the setting was. In the final analysis, those toils defined who he was and guided him along the way during his wilderness journey. Only at life's end had he achieved the economic success that he had so long coveted. In his last will and testament William Clark was able to bequeath slightly more than thirty thousand dollars to each of his surviving sons, in addition to the various properties that they had previously received, but the family patriarch had long before learned the fleeting nature of fame and fortune.[4]

Clark would likely not be particularly surprised to discover that within a few short years after his death, his attainments had been all but forgotten, the celebrated artifacts and curiosities he spent a lifetime collecting had been lost or dispersed, and even the wealth he worked all of his life to accumulate gradually had been dissipated in the hands of his sometimes-profligate progeny. To the contrary, he undoubtedly would be astounded to learn that twenty-first-century Americans have rescued him from obscurity and awarded him a celebrity unlike anything he ever experienced. All of the fuss surrounding the bicentennial of his voyage to the Pacific would no doubt please him, but he might choose to caution his modern devotees that honor and distinction seldom come quickly or easily.

As he entered the twilight years of his life, William Clark sought to convey that message to his own children. Six years before his death, Clark advised his sixteen-year-old son George: "You have capacity and can make of yourself any thing you please, do not suffer yourself to be unhappy from misfortune or disappointment; we all have to meet them and should bear them with firmness, resolved to use every exertion to better our situation and gain the good will of our fellow creatures." And in many ways those words represent the sum of William Clark's life and provide a fitting epitaph for him.[5]

Notes

One *The West Beckons*

1. Jonathan Clark Diary, October 29, 1784, Filson Historical Society (FHS).

2. See David Hackett Fischer and James C. Kelly, *Bound Away: Virginia and the Westward Movement,* 202–5.

3. Robert E. Gatten, Jr., "Clark Land in Virginia and the Birthplace of William Clark," 6–11, and Draper Mss., 1J37, State Historical Society of Wisconsin, Madison. Many accounts state that the Clark forebears were English, but according to Meriwether Lewis Clark, his father said that the original Clark ancestors had come from the southwestern part of Scotland. Draper Mss., 7J110–120.

4. C. Ballard Thurston, "Some Recent Finds Regarding the Ancestry of George Rogers Clark," 1–27.

5. Gatten, "Clark Land in Virginia," 6–11, and Dumas Malone, *Jefferson: The Virginian,* 3–4, 26–27. There is some confusion concerning the uncle from whom John Clark inherited the Caroline County property. In the Draper Mss. Lucy Temple Green, a cousin of John Clark, identified his bachelor uncle as Edward. See Draper Mss., 7J145.

6. Draper Mss., 7J147, 7J150, 7J152; Gatten, "Clark Land in Virginia," 6–9.

7. John Clark to Jonathan Clark, September 23, 1773, Draper Mss., 1L12. Ann Clark and Owen Gwathmey were married on October 22, 1773.

8. John Clark to Jonathan Clark, March 12, 1780, Draper Mss., 2L4.

9. Draper Mss., 7J147.

10. John Clark to Jonathan Clark, August 10, 1772, Draper Mss., 1L7.

11. Draper Mss., 7J146.

12. Clark Family Mathematics Copy Book, Missouri Historical Society (MHS), St. Louis.

13. John and Ann Clark to Jonathan Clark, April 1777, Draper Mss., 1L35.

14. The closeness of William and Jonathan is well documented in James Holmberg, ed., *Dear Brother: Letters of William Clark to Jonathan Clark.* John Clark to Jonathan Clark, August 10, 1772, Draper Mss., 1L7.

15. Journal of Reverend David Jones as quoted in Temple Bodley, *George Rogers*

Clark: His Life and Public Services, 8; John H. Roy to Jonathan Clark, November 22, 1772, in James Alton James, ed., *George Rogers Clark Papers, 1771–1781,* 1–2. Near the end of his life, William Clark recalled the exploring journey that George Rogers had made with his father, though his recollection that it was in about the year 1769 was off by three years. William Clark to James Herring, January 7, 1838, George Rogers Hancock Clark Papers, MHS, St. Louis.

16. George Rogers Clark to Jonathan Clark, April 1 and July 6, 1775, in James, ed., *George Rogers Clark Papers,* 9–10.

17. George Rogers Clark to Jonathan Clark, July 6, 1775, in ibid., 10.

18. Stephen Aron, *How the West Was Lost: The Transformation of Kentucky from Daniel Boone to Henry Clay;* petition from the committee of West Fincastle, June 20, 1776, in James, ed., *George Rogers Clark Papers,* 14–16. Bodley, *George Rogers Clark,* 33–34.

19. Jonathan Clark Diaries, February 18, March 20–27, April 25, and July 18–August 17, 1775, FHS.

20. Obituary of Jonathan Clark in Draper Mss., 10J341; William Clark to James Herring, January 7, 1838, George Rogers Hancock Clark Papers, MHS.

21. John Clark, Jr., to Capt. Jonathan Clark, November 5 and December 8, 1777, May 16 and July 3, 1778, all in Draper Mss., 1L37, 1L39, 1L42, and 1L46; William Clark to James Herring, January 7, 1838, George Rogers Hancock Clark Papers, MHS; Draper Mss., 10J38, 10J114.

22. Draper Mss., 10J38, 10J114, 34J16.

23. John Clark to Col. Jonathan Clark, March 12, 1780, Draper Mss., 2L4; Certificate, July 22, 1781, in ibid., 2L16; William Clark to James Herring, January 7, 1838, George Rogers Hancock Clark Papers, MHS.

24. Journal of the Executive Department, August 23, 1776; George Rogers Clark Diary, December 1776, and Patrick Henry to George Rogers Clark, January 2, 1778, all in James, ed., *George Rogers Clark Papers,* 18–19, 20, 34.

25. Mary Ellen Rowe, *Bulwark of the Republic: The American Militia in the Antebellum West,* 2–3, 5.

26. Hugh F. Rankin, *George Rogers Clark and the Winning of the West,* 9–16, 24–31.

27. Andrew R. L. Cayton, *Frontier Indiana,* 70–75; Rankin, *George Rogers Clark and the Winning of the West,* 32–51.

28. Rowe, *Bulwark of the Republic,* 4.

29. Draper Mss., 12J53; Bodley, *George Rogers Clark,* 338.

30. Jonathan Clark Diaries, April 29, 1783, FHS.

31. George Rogers Clark to Governor Benjamin Harrison, June 16, 1783, and Harrison to Clark, July 2, 1783, in Bodley, *George Rogers Clark,* 234–37.

32. Thomas Jefferson to George Rogers Clark, December 4, 1783, in Donald Jackson, ed., *Letters of the Lewis and Clark Expedition with Related Documents, 1783–1854,* vol. 2, 654–55.

33. George Rogers Clark to Jefferson, February 8, 1784, in ibid., 655–56.

34. Jonathan Clark Diaries, October 1783–May 1784, FHS.

35. Ibid., September 14, 1784.

36. Hazel Dicken-Garcia, *To Western Woods: The Breckinridge Family Moves to Kentucky in 1793,* 32–33, 141–42.

37. The exact number of slaves that accompanied the Clarks to Kentucky in 1784 is not known for certain. John Clark's 1799 will identifies twelve slaves as belonging to him at that time, including York, Old York, Rose, Nancy, Tuba, Jane, Cupid, and Harry,

all of whom seem likely prospects for having made the trip from Virginia. See copy of John Clark's Will, October 1, 1799, in William Clark Papers, MHS.

38. Lutie J. Kinkead, "How the Parents of George Rogers Clark Came to Kentucky in 1784–1785," 1–4.

39. Ibid., 2.

40. Ibid., 2–4.

41. Neal O. Hammon, "Early Louisville and the Beargrass Stations," 160, 162; Thomas D. Clark, ed., *A Description of Kentucky in North America . . . by Harry Toulmin,* 91.

42. Ibid., 78.

43. Holmberg, ed., *Dear Brother,* 32–33n1; Alfred Pirtle, "Mulberry Hill: The First Home of George Rogers Clark in Kentucky," 49–54.

44. John Clark to Col. Jonathan Clark, March 29, 1785, Draper Mss., 2L22; John Clark to Jonathan Clark, April 21, 1786, Draper Mss., 2L23.

45. Rowe, *Bulwark of the Republic,* 8; Cayton, *Frontier Indiana,* 95–96.

46. George Rogers Clark to William Clark, September 1, 1797; Invoice of Sundry Merchandize of property of Laurent Bazedone, March 4, 1801; M. Hughes to William Clark, May 16, 1801; Judge Daniel Symmes to Capt. William Clark, June 1, 1801; Symmes to Clark, August 3, 1801, and Heb. Hurst to William Clark, June 25 and August 23, 1803, all in William Clark Papers, MHS.

47. John Clark to Jonathan Clark, April 21, 1786, Draper Mss., 2L23.

48. Clark Family Mathematics Copy Book, MHS.

49. For a brief summary on this subject see Robert B. Betts, "'we commenced wrighting &c.': A Salute to the Ingenious Spelling and Grammar of William Clark," 10–12.

50. Meriwether Lewis to Thomas Jefferson, April 7, 1805, in Jackson, ed., *Letters of the Lewis and Clark Expedition,* vol. 1, 231.

51. William Clark Notebook, 1798–1801, Western Historical Manuscripts Collection, Columbia, Missouri (WHMCC).

52. Clark Family Mathematics Notebook, MHS.

53. Charles Mackenzie's "Narratives" in W. Raymond Wood and Thomas D. Thiessen, eds., *Early Fur Trade on the Northern Plains: Canadian Traders among the Mandan and Hidatsa Indians, 1783–1818,* 238; William Clark to Fanny Clark, July 1, 1795, in Holmberg, ed., *Dear Brother,* 276.

54. William Clark Notebook, 1798–1801, WHMCC.

Two *Kentucky Apprenticeship*

1. George Rogers Clark to Jonathan Clark, April 20, 1788, Draper Mss., State Historical Society of Wisconsin, 2L26.

2. On Kentucky politics during this period see Patricia Watlington, *The Partisan Spirit: Kentucky Politics, 1779–1792.*

3. George Rogers Clark to Jonathan Clark, April 20, 1788, Draper Mss., 2L26.

4. Ibid.

5. Randolph C. Downes, *Council Fires on the Upper Ohio,* 310–12.

6. Ibid.; Journal of Hardin's Campaign, August 5, 1789, to March 18, 1790, William Clark Papers, MHS.

7. Journal of Hardin's Campaign, William Clark Papers, MHS.

8. Ibid. See appended maps and drawings.

9. Ibid.

10. Ibid.

11. Ibid.; Commission of William Clark as Captain in the Militia, Northwest Territory, January 8, 1790, William Clark Papers, MHS.

12. Journal of Hardin's Campaign, William Clark Papers, MHS.

13. William Clark Notebook, 1798–1801, WHMCC.

14. Cayton, *Frontier Indiana*, 154–57.

15. James O'Fallon to Jonathan Clark, May 30, 1791, Draper Mss., 2L28.

16. Journal of General Scott's Proceeding from May 23 to June 16, 1791, William Clark Papers, MHS; Cayton, *Frontier Indiana*, 154–57.

17. Cayton, *Frontier Indiana*, 154–57.

18. Journal of General Scott's Proceeding from May 23 to June 16, 1791, William Clark Papers, MHS; *Kentucky Gazette*, June 25, 1791, as cited in John L. Loos, "A Biography of William Clark, 1770–1813," 18.

19. R. Douglas Hurt, *The Ohio Frontier Crucible of the Old Northwest, 1720–1830*, 110–19.

20. Francis B. Heitman, *Historical Register and Dictionary of the United States Army from September 29, 1789 to March 2, 1903*, vol. 1, 306.

21. Journal and Memorandum Book of William Clark, 1792, William Clark Papers, MHS.

22. Ibid.

23. William Clark to Jonathan Clark, September 2, 1792, in Holmberg, ed., *Dear Brother*, 19.

24. Ibid.

25. Richard H. Kohn, "General Wilkinson's Vendetta with General Wayne: Politics and Command in the American Army, 1791–1796," 362–63; Paul David Nelson, *Anthony Wayne: Soldier of the Early Republic*, 249–57; William Clark to Jonathan Clark, May 25, 1794, Draper Mss., 2L33. See also R. C. McGrane, ed., "William Clark's Journal of General Wayne's Campaign," 418–44.

26. Ibid.

27. Jonathan Clark to William Clark, June 18, 1792, William Clark Papers, MHS.

28. Heitman, *Historical Register*, vol. 1, 306; Journal and Memorandum Book of William Clark, 1792–1794, MHS.

29. Journal and Memorandum Book of William Clark, 1792–1794.

30. Ibid.

31. Ibid.

32. Ibid.; William Clark to Jonathan Clark, May 25, 1794, Draper Mss., 2L33.

33. Ibid.

34. William Clark to Jonathan Clark, May 25, 1794, Draper Mss., 2L33; Thomas D. Clark, ed., *The Voice of the Frontier: John Bradford's Notes on Kentucky*, 224–25.

35. Journal and Memorandum Book of William Clark, 1792–1794, William Clark Papers, MHS.

36. William Clark to Jonathan Clark, May 25, 1794, Draper Mss., 2L33.

37. Ibid.

38. McGrane, ed., "William Clark's Journal of General Wayne's Campaign," 419–30.

39. Ibid., 420–23.

40. Nelson, *Anthony Wayne*, 261–68; Gregory Evans Dowd, *A Spirited Resistance: The North American Indian Struggle for Unity, 1745–1815*, 113.

41. William Clark to Jonathan Clark, August 28, 1794, Draper Mss., 2L34.

42. Nelson, *Anthony Wayne*, 282–83.

43. William Clark to Jonathan Clark, November 25, 1794, Draper Mss., 2L37; William Clark to Edmund Clark, November 25, 1794, Draper Mss., 2L36.

44. William Croghan to Edmund Clark, February 1, 1795, and John Clark to Jonathan Clark, February 4, 1795, both in Draper Mss., 2L38, 2L39; Mary Ellen Rowe, "'A Respectable Independence': The Early Career of John O'Fallon," 395.

45. William Clark to Fanny Clark, May 9, 1795, in Holmberg, ed., *Dear Brother*, 269.

46. William Clark to Fanny Clark, June 1, 1795, and July 1, 1795, in Holmberg, ed., *Dear Brother*, 273–74, 276–77.

47. William Clark to Fanny Clark, June 1, 1795, in Holmberg, ed., *Dear Brother*, 273–74.

48. Unsigned document in William Clark's hand to Major General Wayne, November 4, 1795, William Clark Papers, MHS; "A Scetch of W: Clarks Trip up the Ohio, Sept. Oct. 1795," in Samuel W. Thomas, ed., "William Clark's 1795 and 1797 Journals and their Significance," 278–85.

49. Unsigned document in William Clark's hand to Major General Wayne, November 4, 1795, William Clark Papers, MHS; "A Scetch of W: Clarks Trip up the Ohio, Sept. Oct. 1795," in Samuel W. Thomas, ed., "William Clark's 1795 and 1797 Journals and their Significance," 278–85.

50. Ibid.; William E. Foley, *The Genesis of Missouri: From Wilderness Outpost to State-hood*, 78; Alice Long, "Reclaiming a Lost Connection: A Brief History of Meriwether Lewis and William Clark in West Tennessee," 201; Pen and Ink Sketch Plan of Fort St. Ferdinand and of Gayoso de Lemos's galley, November 1795, William Clark Papers, MHS; Francis Preston to William Preston, December 27, 1795, Preston Family Papers–Joyes Collection, FHS.

51. E. G. Chuinard, "The Court-Martial of Ensign Meriwether Lewis," 12–15.

52. William Clark to Nicholas Biddle, August 15, 1811, in Jackson, ed., *Letters of the Lewis and Clark Expedition*, vol. 1, 572; William Clark to [General Anthony Wayne], November 27, 1795, William Clark Papers, MHS.

53. William Clark to Samuel Gwathmey, July 14, 1823, William Clark Papers, MHS; Heitman, *Historical Register*, vol. 1, 306; William Clark to [General Anthony Wayne] November 27, 1795, William Clark Papers, MHS; George Rogers Clark to Billy [William Clark], June 1796, Carlota Glasgow Collection, MHS; William Clark to Jonathan Clark, August 24, 1796, Draper Mss., 2L42; George Rogers Clark to Billy [William Clark] June 1796, Carlota Glasgow Collection, MHS. He must have delivered on the still because in his 1799 will John Clark bequeathed a still to William.

54. George Rogers Clark to Billy [William Clark] June 1796, Carlota Glasgow Collection, MHS.

55. William Clark to Edmund Clark, February 22, 1797, Draper Mss., 2L44; William Clark to Edmund Clark, August 18, 1797, Draper Mss., 2L45; Bill of Sale to William Clark for land near Vincennes, August 10, 1797, George Rogers Clark Papers, MHS; Draft Notes and Plat Map relating to five-hundred-acre tract in Clarksville, Indiana, conveyed by John Clark to George Rogers Clark, November 16, 1797, in William Clark Papers, MHS.

56. William Clark's Journal, August 20–September 6, 1797, Northwest Territory Collection, Indiana Historical Society. A published version of this journal can be found in Samuel W. Thomas, ed., "William Clark's 1795 and 1797 Journals and their Significance," 287–94.

57. George P. Garrison, ed., "Memorandum of Moses Austin's Journey, 1796–1797," *American Historical Review* 5 (April 1900): 535.

58. William Clark's Journal, September 10–11, 1797, Indiana Historical Society.

59. Ibid.

60. William Clark's Journal, September 12–October 9, 1797, Indiana Historical Society; William Clark to Edmund Clark, December 14, 1797, Draper Mss., 2L46.

61. Concerning the possibility of York's pre-expedition travels with Clark see Holmberg, ed., *Dear Brother,* 274n1.

62. William Clark Notebook, 1798–1801, WHMCC.

63. Ibid.; Holmberg, ed., *Dear Brother,* 29n3.

64. William Clark Notebook, 1798–1801, WHMCC.

65. Ibid.; Holmberg, ed., *Dear Brother,* 29–30n4.

66. John Clark to Edmund Clark, April 25, 1799, Draper Mss., 2L49.

67. William Clark to Jonathan Clark, July 30, 1799, Draper Mss., 2L51.

68. William Clark to Jonathan Clark, June 8, 1799, Draper Mss., 2L50.

69. John Clark's Will and Testament filed at Jefferson County Courthouse, October 1, 1799, copy in William Clark Papers, MHS.

70. Invoice of goods seized by orders of General George Rogers Clark, March 4, 1801, Clark Family Papers, MHS; Abraham Hite to Jonathan Clark, December 13, 1800, Clark Family Papers, FHS; John Thruston to William Clark, May 19, 1799, William Clark Papers, MHS; Abraham Hite to Jonathan Clark, December 13, 1800. Thruston was in all likelihood a severe master. The previous year William Clark had reported that "Thruston has three Negroes back he has lost 6 Negroes this year." William Clark to Jonathan Clark, June 8, 1799, Draper Mss., 2L50.

71. Meriwether Lewis to William Clark, June 27, 1801, William Clark Papers, MHS; William Clark Notebook, 1798–1801, WHMCC.

72. George Rogers Clark to Jonathan Clark, January 8, 1800, 2L53.

73. William Clark to Jonathan Clark, August 13, 1801, in Holmberg, ed., *Dear Brother,* 30, 32.

74. William Clark to Jonathan Clark, February 4, March 2, and April 5, 1802, all in ibid., 40–41, 44–45, 55.

75. William Clark to Samuel Gwathmey, July 4, 1823, with list of payments made by William Clark for George Rogers Clark, William Clark Papers, MHS; Holmberg, ed., *Dear Brother,* 9, 54n29.

Three   *A Most Welcome Invitation*

1. Meriwether Lewis to William Clark, June 19, 1803, William Clark Papers, MHS.

2. Ibid.

3. Ibid.

4. George Rogers Clark to Thomas Jefferson, December 12, 1802, in Jackson, ed., *Letters of the Lewis and Clark Expedition,* vol. 1, 8.

5. Original draft William Clark to Meriwether Lewis, July 17, 1803, William Clark

Papers, MHS, and final letter dated July 18, 1803, in Jackson, ed., *Letters of the Lewis and Clark Expedition,* vol. 1, 110–11; William Clark to Meriwether Lewis, July 24, 1803, and William Clark to Thomas Jefferson, July 24, 1803, both in Jackson, ed., *Letters of the Lewis and Clark Expedition,* vol. 1, 112–13.

6. Journal of Josiah Espy as quoted in Temple Bodley, *George Rogers Clark: His Life and Public Services,* 357–58; William Clark to Meriwether Lewis, July 18, 1803, in Jackson, ed., *Letters of the Lewis and Clark Expedition,* vol. 2, 110.

7. Edward Thornton to Lord Hawkesbury, March 9, 1803, in Jackson, ed., *Letters of the Lewis and Clark Expedition,* vol. 1, 26.

8. Thomas Jefferson to William Dunbar, March 13, 1804, as quoted in Donald Jackson, *Thomas Jefferson and the Stony Mountains: Exploring the West from Monticello,* 86–96.

9. Thomas Jefferson to George Rogers Clark, December 4, 1783, and GR Clark to Jefferson, February 8, 1784, both in Jackson, ed., *Letters of the Lewis and Clark Expedition,* vol. 2, 654–56.

10. Jackson, *Thomas Jefferson and the Stony Mountains,* 74–78.

11. "'So Vast an Enterprise': Thoughts on the Lewis and Clark Expedition," by James P. Ronda in Ronda, ed., *Voyages of Discovery: Essays on the Lewis and Clark Expedition,* 7–9; William Clark to Meriwether Lewis, July 18, 1803, William Clark Papers, MHS.

12. Jefferson's Message to Congress, January 18, 1803, and editorial annotations, in Jackson, ed., *Letters of the Lewis and Clark Expedition,* vol. 1, 10–14.

13. William E. Foley, "Lewis and Clark's American Travels: The View from Britain," 303–7.

14. Thomas Jefferson to Meriwether Lewis, April 27, 1803, in Jackson, ed., *Letters of the Lewis and Clark Expedition,* vol. 1, 44; Meriwether Lewis to William Clark, June 19, 1803, William Clark Papers, MHS.

15. Meriwether Lewis to Thomas Jefferson, July 26, 1803, in Jackson, ed., *Letters of the Lewis and Clark Expedition,* vol. 1, 113–14; Meriwether Lewis to William Clark, August 3, 1803, William Clark Papers, MHS.

16. Thomas Jefferson to Henry Dearborn, August 13, 1803, and Henry Dearborn to Thomas Jefferson, August 28, 1803, as cited in Jackson, ed., *Letters of the Lewis and Clark Expedition,* 117n. In overruling a proposal by Lewis to deploy Clark on a separate winter reconnaissance, Jefferson pointedly stressed the importance of Clark's presence: "By having Mr. Clarke with you we consider the expedition double manned, & therefore the less liable to failure . . ." Thomas Jefferson to Meriwether Lewis, November 16, 1803, in Jackson, ed., *Letters of the Lewis and Clark Expedition,* vol. 1, 137.

17. Thomas Jefferson to Benjamin Rush, February 28, 1803, in Jackson, ed., *Letters of the Lewis and Clark Expedition,* vol. 1, 18–19.

18. See Thomas Jefferson to Benjamin Smith Barton, February 27, 1803, Jefferson to Caspar Wistar, February 28, 1803, Jefferson to Robert Patterson, March 2, 1803, and Andrew Ellicott to Jefferson, March 6, 1803, all in Jackson, ed., *Letters of the Lewis and Clark Expedition,* vol. 1, 16–17, 17–18, 21, 23–25.

19. Meriwether Lewis to William Clark, August 3, 1803, William Clark Papers, MHS.

20. Ibid. Detailed lists of Lewis's purchases can be found in Jackson, ed., *Letters of the Lewis and Clark Expedition,* vol. 1, 69–99.

21. Meriwether Lewis to William Clark, August 3, 1803, William Clark Papers, MHS; William Clark to Meriwether Lewis, July 24, 1803, William Clark Papers, MHS.

22. Affidavit sworn by Humphrey Marshall, November 12, 1803, William Clark Papers, MHS; William Clark to Samuel Gwathmey, August 27, 1823, Gwathmey Family Papers, FHS; Henry Hurst to William Clark, June 25 and August 23, 1803, photostatic copies in Clark Papers, Box 2, folio 1, MHS.

23. Robert Breckinridge to Major William Preston, November 25, 1803, Preston Family Papers–Joyes Collection, FHS.

24. William Clark's notes and observations on hygiene, fruits, vegetables, and drink, ca. 1803, William Clark Papers, MHS.

25. Ibid.

26. William Clark's Scientific Notes, 1803, William Clark Papers, MHS; Donald Jackson, "Some Books Carried by Lewis and Clark," 6–7. Jerome Steffen was one of the first to call attention to Clark's scientific contributions. See *William Clark: Jeffersonian Man on the Frontier.*

27. Meriwether Lewis to Thomas Jefferson, April 20, 1803, Jefferson to Lewis, April 27, 1803, and Lewis to Jefferson, all in Jackson, ed., *Letters of the Lewis and Clark Expedition,* vol. 1, 37–38, 44, 130; Meriwether Lewis to William Clark, August 3, 1803, William Clark to John Conner, August 26, 1803, Clark to Lewis, September 11, 1803, and Lewis to Clark, September 28, 1803, all in William Clark Papers, MHS.

28. Meriwether Lewis to William Clark, June 19, 1803, William Clark to Meriwether Lewis, July 18, 24 and August 21, 1803, William Clark Papers, MHS.

29. Meriwether Lewis to Thomas Jefferson, September 8, 1803, and Lewis to Jefferson, October 3, 1803, in Jackson, ed., *Letters of the Lewis and Clark Expedition,* vol. 1, 121–22, 126–31; Lewis to Clark, September 28, 1803, William Clark Papers, MHS.

30. On the members of the expedition see Appendix A in Gary E. Moulton, ed., *The Journals of the Lewis and Clark Expedition,* vol. 2, 509–29. For the Field connection see Holmberg, ed., *Dear Brother,* 93–96n10.

31. Holmberg, ed., *Dear Brother,* 98–99, 274.

32. Moulton, ed., *Journals,* vol. 2, 85; William Clark to Jonathan Clark, December 16, 1803, in Holmberg, ed., *Dear Brother,* 60.

33. Moulton, ed., *Journals,* vol. 2, 87–94; William Clark to Jonathan Clark, December 16, 1803, in Holmberg, ed., *Dear Brother,* 60.

34. Moulton, ed., *Journals,* vol. 2, 101; William Clark to Jonathan Clark, December 16, 1803, in Holmberg, ed., *Dear Brother,* 60.

35. Moulton, ed., *Journals,* vol. 2, 105–8.

36. Ibid., 112–13.

37. William Clark to Jonathan Clark, December 16, 1803, in Holmberg, ed., *Dear Brother,* 60–61.

38. Ibid.

39. Ibid.; Meriwether Lewis to Thomas Jefferson, December 19 and 28, 1803, in Jackson, ed., *Letters of the Lewis and Clark Expedition,* vol. 1, 145–55.

40. Summary of Distribution of Trade Licenses by Delassus, 1799–1804, in Abraham P. Nasatir, ed., *Before Lewis and Clark: Documents Illustrating the History of Missouri, 1785–1804,* vol. 2, 590–93.

41. William Clark to Jonathan Clark, December 16, 1803, in Holmberg, ed., *Dear Brother,* 60–61; Meriwether Lewis to Thomas Jefferson, December 19 and 28, 1803, in Jackson, ed., *Letters of the Lewis and Clark Expedition,* vol. 1, 145–55.

42. William Clark to Jonathan Clark, December 16, 1803, in Holmberg, ed., *Dear*

Brother, 60–61; Amos Stoddard to Mrs. Samuel Benham, June 16, 1804, Stoddard Papers, MHS.

43. William Clark to Jonathan Clark, June 16, 1804, in Holmberg, ed., *Dear Brother,* 60–61.

44. Meriwether Lewis to Thomas Jefferson, December 19 and 28, 1803, in Jackson, ed., *Letters of the Lewis and Clark Expedition,* vol. 1, 145–55.

45. William Clark to Jonathan Clark, June 16, 1804, in Holmberg, ed., *Dear Brother,* 60–61; Moulton, ed., *Journals,* vol. 2, 129.

46. Meriwether Lewis to Thomas Jefferson, December 28, 1803, in Jackson, ed., *Letters of the Lewis and Clark Expedition,* vol. 1, 155.

47. William Clark to Jonathan Clark, December 16, 1803, in Holmberg, ed., *Dear Brother,* 61–62 and Moulton, ed., *Journals,* vol. 2, 133.

48. Moulton, ed., *Journals,* vol. 2, 131, 134, 139, 140.

49. Ibid., 139.

50. Ibid., 140–42.

51. Ibid., 142, 144.

52. Ibid., 145; William Clark to Major William Croghan, January 15, 1804, William Clark Papers, MHS; Moulton, ed., *Journals,* vol. 2, 147–49, 152.

53. Moulton, ed., *Journals,* vol. 2, 153–55; Thomas Danisi, "James MacKay," in Lawrence O. Christensen et al., *Dictionary of Missouri Biography,* 511.

54. The identity of the draftsman who prepared the Indian Office map has been the subject of considerable scholarly debate. Additional documentation has allowed Thomas Danisi and W. Raymond Wood to authenticate its author and to explain how Lewis and Clark acquired it. See Thomas Danisi and W. Raymond Wood, "The Genesis of James MacKay's Map of the Missouri River: Lewis and Clark's Route Map."

55. Moulton, ed., *Journals,* vol. 2, 66n7, 159–63; Clark to Lewis [April 1804] in Jackson, ed., *Letters of the Lewis and Clark Expedition,* vol. 1, 175.

56. Jackson, ed., *Letters of the Lewis and Clark Expedition,* vol. 1, 168, 173, vol. 2, 174.

57. William E. Foley, "The Lewis and Clark Expedition's Silent Partners: The Chouteau Brothers of St. Louis," 131–46.

58. Ibid.

59. Moulton, ed., *Journals,* vol. 2, 174–76; Meriwether Lewis to William Clark, February 18, 1804, William Clark Papers, MHS.

60. William Clark to Jonathan Clark, February 25, 1804, in Holmberg, ed., *Dear Brother,* 76–77; Foley, *Genesis of Missouri,* 138–40.

61. Foley, *Genesis of Missouri.*

62. Ibid.; Charles Dehault Delassus to Amos Stoddard, February 24, 1804, Stoddard to William C. C. Claiborne and James A. Wilkinson, March 10, 1804, in Stoddard Papers, MHS; Order of Troops of St. Louis, March 8, 1804, in Delassus Papers, MHS; Moulton, ed., *Journals,* vol. 2, 178–79.

63. Stoddard to Claiborne and Wilkinson, March 26, 1804, Stoddard Papers, MHS.

64. Moulton, ed., *Journals,* vol. 2, 178–79.

65. Ibid.

66. Meriwether Lewis to Thomas Jefferson, March 26, 1804, in Jackson, ed., *Letters of the Lewis and Clark Expedition,* vol. 1, 170–71, 172n; Donald Chaput, "The Early Missouri Graduates of West Point: Officers or Merchants?" 262–70.

67. Moulton, ed., *Journals,* vol. 2, 182–83, 187–90; John Ordway to his parents, April 8, 1804, in Jackson, ed., *Letters of the Lewis and Clark Expedition,* vol. 1, 176–77.

68. Moulton, ed., *Journals,* vol. 2, 193; Stoddard to Phoebe Reade Benham, June 16, 1804, Stoddard Papers, MHS.

69. At the time of Stoddard's death in 1813 Clark was still attempting to collect the debt from his estate. William Clark to John O'Fallon, June 18, 1813, O'Fallon Papers, MHS; Moulton, ed., *Journals,* vol. 2, 193; Clark to Lewis, Memorandum of Articles which may be wanting, [April 1804], William Clark Papers, MHS.

70. Meriwether Lewis to William Clark, May 2, 1804, in Jackson, ed., *Letters of the Lewis and Clark Expedition,* vol. 1, 177–78.

71. William Clark to Jonathan Clark, May 3, 1804, in Holmberg, ed., *Dear Brother,* 81–82; William Clark to William Croghan, May 2, 1804, and Meriwether Lewis to William Preston, May 3, 1804, in Jackson, ed., *Letters,* vol. 1, 178–79.

72. Henry Dearborn to Meriwether Lewis, March 26, 1804, in Jackson, ed., *Letters of the Lewis and Clark Expedition,* vol. 1, 172.

73. Meriwether Lewis to William Clark, May 6, 1804, William Clark Papers, MHS.

74. William Clark to Nicholas Biddle, August 15, 1811, and William Clark to Henry Dearborn, October 10, 1806, in Jackson, ed., *Letters of the Lewis and Clark Expedition,* vol. 2, 571–72, vol. 1, 347.

75. Memorandum of Articles in readiness for the voyage, [undated ca. May 14, 1804], in Moulton, ed., *Journals,* vol. 2, 217–18, 213–15.

Four   ·*Westward Ho!*

1. Moulton, ed., *Journals,* vol. 2, 227. James Holmberg has noted that Clark first employed the familiar phrase "we proceeded on" in a December 16, 1803, letter he wrote to his brother Jonathan. See Holmberg, ed., *Dear Brother,* 73n25.

2. Moulton, ed., *Journals,* vol. 2, 227.

3. Ibid., 227–30 and vol. 9, 3.

4. Ibid., vol. 2, 227–31.

5. Georges Henri Victor Collot, *A Journey in North America,* vol. 1, 277; Carl Ekberg and William E. Foley, eds., *An Account of Upper Louisiana by Nicholas de Finiels,* 74; Moulton, ed., *Journals,* vol. 2, 232–33.

6. Ibid., 234.

7. Ibid., 235–37.

8. Ibid., 239.

9. Ibid., 240–44.

10. Ibid., 245.

11. Ibid., 248, 249n8.

12. Ibid., 294–95.

13. Ibid., 248.

14. Ibid., 266.

15. Ibid., 249–51.

16. Ibid., 289.

17. Ibid., 333.

18. Ibid., 317–18.

19. Ibid., 394.

20. Ibid., 329–30.

21. Ibid., 346–47; James P. Ronda's Introduction in Carolyn Gilman, *Lewis and Clark across the Divide,* 29.

22. Moulton, ed., *Journals,* vol. 2, 415–21; Thomas Jefferson's instructions to Meriwether Lewis, June 20, 1803, in Jackson, ed., *Letters of the Lewis and Clark Expedition,* vol. 1, 61, 64.

23. Moulton, ed., *Journals,* vol. 2, 433.

24. Ibid., 436.

25. Jackson, ed., *Letters of the Lewis and Clark Expedition,* vol. 1, 64.

26. Moulton, ed., *Journals,* vol. 2, 438–41. The assessments of Lewis and Clark's dealings with the Indians in this and succeeding chapters draw heavily from James P. Ronda's classic study *Lewis and Clark among the Indians.* Ronda's account of this particular assembly can be found on pp. 17–23.

27. Moulton, ed., *Journals,* vol. 2, 452.

28. Ibid., 488–89; Biddle's Notes in Jackson, ed., *Letters of the Lewis and Clark Expedition,* vol. 2, 474.

29. Moulton, ed., *Journals,* vol. 2, 479, 487–93; Jackson, ed., *Letters of the Lewis and Clark Expedition,* vol. 1, 119n.

30. Moulton, ed., *Journals,* vol. 2, 429, 431n, 492–95.

31. Ibid., 492–95.

32. Ibid., 500–501, vol. 3, 15.

33. Ibid., vol. 3, 7–10.

34. Ibid., 16–19.

35. Ibid., 21–24, vol. 4, 51.

36. Ibid., vol. 3, 23–24, vol. 4, 47–48.

37. Ibid.

38. Ibid., vol. 3, 26–34.

39. Ibid., 27, and Biddle's Notes in Jackson, ed., *Letters of the Lewis and Clark Expedition,* vol. 2, 503.

40. Moulton, ed., *Journals,* vol. 3, 52–53.

41. Ibid., 20–21n, 44–45, 50–51n, 65–66.

42. Ibid., 76–79.

43. Ibid., 90, 93.

44. Ibid., 111–13; Ronda, *Lewis and Clark among the Indians,* 27–41; Gilman, *Lewis and Clark across the Divide,* 81–108.

45. Ibid.

46. Ibid.; *St. Louis Enquirer,* August 12, 1820.

47. Moulton, ed., *Journals,* vol. 3, 111–14, vol. 4, 67–68.

48. Ibid., vol. 3, 115–19.

49. Ibid.

50. Ibid.

51. Ibid., 121–23.

52. Ibid., 123–25; Biddle's Notes in Jackson, ed., *Letters of the Lewis and Clark Expedition,* vol. 2, 518.

53. Moulton, ed., *Journals,* vol. 9, 68; William Clark to William Henry Harrison, April 2, 1805, in Jackson, ed., *Letters of the Lewis and Clark Expedition,* vol. 1, 228; Ronda, *Lewis and Clark among the Indians,* chap. 2.

54. Moulton, ed., *Journals,* vol. 3, 157, 161–63.

55. Ibid., 152.

56. Ibid., 155–66.

57. Ibid., 155–66, 174.

58. Ibid., 169–73.

59. Ibid., 179–80.

60. Ibid., 188.

61. Ibid., 191.

62. Ibid., 195.

63. Ibid., 194–200.

64. Ibid., 203.

65. Ibid., 204.

66. Ibid., 204–10; Ronda, *Lewis and Clark among the Indians,* 84.

67. Moulton, ed., *Journals,* vol. 3, 208–12, 213n3.

68. Ibid., 209–11.

69. Ibid., 215–26.

70. Ibid., 226–28.

71. Moulton, ed., *Journals,* vol. 10, 62, vol. 3, 283; Francois-Antoine Larocque's "Missouri Journal" in Wood and Thiessen, eds., *Early Fur Trade on the Northern Plains,* 143.

72. Moulton, ed., *Journals,* vol. 3, 215–19; Meriwether Lewis's British Passport, February 28, 1803; Lewis and Clark to Charles Chaboillez, October 31, 1804, in Jackson, ed., *Letters of the Lewis and Clark Expedition,* vol. 1, 10–20, 213–14.

73. Larocque's "Missouri Journal," 138–40.

74. Moulton, ed., *Journals,* vol. 3, 243–47.

75. Ibid., 255.

76. Ibid., 257–60; Larocque's "Missouri Journal," 143.

77. Francis Paul Prucha, *The Sword of the Republic: The United States Army on the Frontier, 1783–1846,* 84–85; Ernest S. Osgood, *Field Notes of Captain William Clark, 1803–1805,* 176–77, 188.

78. Larocque's "Missouri Journal," 143; Moulton, ed., *Journals,* vol. 3, 261, vol. 9, 106.

79. Moulton, ed., *Journals,* vol. 3, 261, 265, vol. 9, 106, vol. 10, 67–68.

80. Charles Mackenzie's "Narratives," 233.

81. Moulton, ed., *Journals,* vol. 3, 264, 269, 286–87; Larocque's "Missouri Journal," 151. Also see John Logan Allen, *Passage through the Garden: Lewis and Clark and the Image of the American Northwest,* 212–14.

82. Larocque's "Missouri Journal," 138–40; Moulton, ed., *Journals,* vol. 3, 281, 284.

83. Charles Mackenzie's "Narratives," 238.

84. Ibid.

85. Moulton, ed., *Journals,* vol. 3, 266–67, vol. 9, 107, vol. 10, 68–69.

86. Ibid., vol. 3, 268–69; Jackson, ed., *Letters of the Lewis and Clark Expedition,* vol. 2, 538; *Quarterly Review* 12 (January 1815): 328.

87. Moulton, ed., *Journals,* vol. 3, 403; Ronda, *Lewis and Clark among the Indians,* chap. 5, "Lewis and Clark as Ethnographers," 113–32.

88. Moulton, ed., *Journals,* vol. 3, 285.

89. Ibid., 291.

90. Allen, *Passage through the Garden,* 227–31, 250–51; Gilman, *Lewis and Clark across the Divide,* 150–51.

91. Gilman, *Lewis and Clark across the Divide,* 304–6.

92. Moulton, ed., *Journals,* vol. 3, 297–98, 300–303, 308, 310–11, 317, 321.

93. Ibid., 319–20, 322, 324, 326.

94. Ibid., 327.

95. Ibid., 328–32; William Clark to Thomas Jefferson, April 3, 1805, and Clark to William Henry Harrison, April 2, 1805, in Jackson, ed., *Letters of the Lewis and Clark Expedition,* vol. 1, 227–31.

96. William Clark to William Croghan, April 2, 1805, in Jackson, ed., *Letters of the Lewis and Clark Expedition,* vol. 1, 230; William Clark to Jonathan Clark, April 1805, in Holmberg, ed., *Dear Brother,* 84–86.

Five   *On to the Pacific*

1. Moulton, ed., *Journals,* vol. 4, 9–10; James P. Ronda, "'A Most Perfect Harmony': The Lewis and Clark Expedition as an Exploration Community," 77–88.

2. Moulton, ed., *Journals,* vol. 43, 7–11.

3. Mark Chalkley, "Eagle Feather Goes to Washington," 6–10.

4. William Joseph Clark Diary, May 20, 1805, Filson Historical Society. William Joseph Clark was not related to William Clark. Jackson, *Thomas Jefferson and the Stony Mountains,* 171, 190n47; William Clark to Jonathan Clark, April 1805, in Holmberg, ed., *Dear Brother,* 84–86.

5. Moulton, ed., *Journals,* vol. 4, 14–16.

6. Ibid., 17, 22, 29, 33–34, 41, 48, 51–52, 62–66, 136.

7. Ibid., 70.

8. Ibid., 89, 126–28, 131.

9. Ibid., 152–57.

10. Ibid., 84–85, 161, 185, 201, 204.

11. Ibid., 216.

12. Ibid., 222–25, 228–30.

13. Ibid., 246–56.

14. Ibid., 256–72; John Logan Allen, "Lewis and Clark on the Upper Missouri: Decision at the Marias," 2–17.

15. Moulton, ed., *Journals,* vol. 4, 269–77.

16. Ibid., 271.

17. Ibid., 277–80.

18. Ibid., 287, 294, 297, 301; Gilman, *Lewis and Clark across the Divide,* 170.

19. Moulton, ed., *Journals,* vol. 4, 283–90.

20. Ibid., 307–17.

21. Ibid., 297–303.

22. Ibid., 301, 305, 323–24.

23. Ibid., 318, 324–32.

24. Ibid., 342–46.

25. Ibid., 343–50, 362, 368–71, 374, 379.

26. Ibid., 319, 382–88.

27. Ibid., 401–17, 428–38.

28. Ibid., vol. 5, 7–11, 35–47.

29. Ibid., 59, 62–63.

30. Ibid., 64, 74–76.

31. Ibid., 68–69, 77–84.

32. Ibid., 79–81.

33. Ibid., 81, 88–92.

34. Ibid., 96–97, 104–5.

35. Ibid., 114–15; Biddle's Notes in Jackson, ed., *Letters of the Lewis and Clark Expedition*, vol. 2, 518–19.

36. Moulton, ed., *Journals*, vol. 5, 111–18.

37. Ibid., 130–31, 145–46, 155–56.

38. Ibid., 162–63, 173–75.

39. Ibid., 175, 178–79, 183, 185–88, 207.

40. U.S. Indian Agent Peter Ronan in his *History of the Flathead Indians, Their Wars and Hunts, 1813–1890,* first recorded the Salish tradition concerning Joseph Clark. Ronan records an 1890 account from an elderly Salish woman Ochanee who vividly remembered Lewis and Clark's visit from her girlhood days.

41. Moulton, ed., *Journals*, vol. 5, 206–7, 209.

42. Ibid., 213–14, 219, 222.

43. Ibid., 222–23.

44. Ibid., 226–27, 229–31; Ronda, *Lewis and Clark among the Indians*, 159–60; Gilman, *Lewis and Clark across the Divide,* 220.

45. Moulton, ed., *Journals*, vol. 5, 229–31.

46. Ibid., 232–35.

47. Ibid., 236, 245–46, 248–50, 253.

48. Ibid., 251, 255–56, 266, 271–72.

49. Ibid., 255–56.

50. Ibid., 268, 277–78.

51. Ibid., 285–90, 298, 303–6.

52. Ibid., 315, 318–19.

53. Ibid., 323, 326–27.

54. Ibid., 347, 361.

55. Ibid., 359, 369, 371.

56. Ibid., 373.

57. Ibid., 33.

58. Ibid., 58–62.

59. Ibid., 35–36, 65.

60. Ibid., vol. 10, 171.

61. Ibid., vol. 6, 79.

62. Ibid., 83–85, 108–9, vol. 10, 177.

63. Ibid., vol. 6, 108–9, 114.

64. Ibid., 114–20.

65. Ibid., 121–35.

66. Ibid., 137.

67. Ibid., 138, 145, 156–58.

68. Ibid., 145, 151–53.

69. Ibid., 162–63, 166–67.

70. Ibid., 168–72, 175–78.

71. Ibid., 182–83.

72. Ibid., 180–84.
73. Ibid.
74. Ibid., 245, 201–2, 309–11; Allen, *Passage through the Garden,* 323–26.
75. Moulton, ed., *Journals,* vol. 6, 204–5.
76. Ibid., 219, 230, 239–40, 337, 339; Biddle's Notes in Jackson, ed., *Letters of the Lewis and Clark Expedition,* vol. 2, 503.
77. Moulton, ed., *Journals,* vol. 6, 384–85.
78. Ibid., 330–31.
79. Ibid., 430–31, 441–44.

Six   *Homeward Bound to Blaze New Trails*

1. Moulton, ed., *Journals,* vol. 7, 8.
2. Ibid., vol. 6, 426; Ronda, *Lewis and Clark among the Indians,* 210–12.
3. Moulton, ed., *Journals,* vol. 7, 8, 10.
4. Ibid., 16, 24, 46.
5. Ibid., 52–53.
6. Ibid., 55–60.
7. Ibid.
8. Ibid., 55–60, 62, 64–66, 92–93.
9. Ibid., 92–93, 95.
10. Ibid., 99, 105, 106, 111–12.
11. Ibid., 115–17, 120.
12. Ibid., 124, 128–29, 133.
13. Ibid., 139–40, 143, 148.
14. Ibid., 156, 164, 168, 171.
15. Ibid., 173–81.
16. Ibid., 209–12.
17. Ibid., 212–17.
18. Ibid., 224, 237–40.
19. Ibid., 231–36.
20. Ibid., 237–40, 255.
21. Ibid., 237–51.
22. Ibid., 239–40, 241n5; Biddle's Notes in Jackson, ed., *Letters of the Lewis and Clark Expedition,* vol. 2, 543–44.
23. Moulton, ed., *Journals,* vol. 7, 256–59, 263, 266–67, 275.
24. Ibid., 267–68, 271, 273, 284–85, 288, 294, 299.
25. Ibid., 278, 280, 282, 284, 286, 294, 297, 346.
26. Ibid., 326.
27. Ibid., 326, 328.
28. Ibid., 332, 341.
29. Ibid., 346–49.
30. Ibid., vol. 8, 10, 23, 24.
31. Ibid., 25–26, 32–34.
32. Ibid., 36, 47–48, 51, 53–54, 57.
33. Ibid., 62–64, 74.
34. Ibid., 83, 163, 172–74.

35. Ibid., 179–80, 187, 190.

36. Speech for Yellowstone Indians, William Clark Papers, MHS.

37. William Clark to Hugh Heney, July 20, 1806, and William Clark to Nathaniel Pryor, July 25 [23], 1806, in Jackson, ed., *Letters of the Lewis and Clark Expedition,* vol. 1, 309–14.

38. Moulton, ed., *Journals,* vol. 8, 225–26, 227–28n7, 272, 275–76, 280–81.

39. Ibid., 280–81, 284–85.

40. Ibid., 288–89.

41. Ibid., 290.

42. Ibid., 290, 295.

43. Ibid., 293–95.

44. Ibid., 298–99, 299n1.

45. Ibid., 300–303.

46. Ibid., 304–5. See also William E. Foley and C. David Rice, "The Return of the Mandan Chief," 2–14.

47. Moulton, ed., *Journals,* vol. 8, 305–6; William Clark to Toussaint Charbonneau, August 20, 1806, in Jackson, ed., *Letters of the Lewis and Clark Expedition,* vol. 1, 315–16.

48. William Clark to Toussaint Charbonneau, August 20, 1806, in Jackson, ed., *Letters of the Lewis and Clark Expedition,* vol. 1, 315–16.

49. Moulton, ed., *Journals,* vol. 8, 306–7, 308, 309n2.

50. Ibid., 311–16.

51. Ibid., 317–19, 323–24, 328–29.

52. Ibid., 329.

53. Ibid., 330–31.

54. Ibid., 337–38.

55. Ibid., 346–47.

56. Ibid., 348–49, 352, 357–59; Biddle's Notes in Jackson, ed., *Letters of the Lewis and Clark Expedition,* vol. 2, 541–42.

57. Moulton, ed., *Journals,* vol. 8, 361, 363, 365–66, 366n3, 367.

58. Ibid., 369–70.

59. Ibid., 370.

60. James Ronda, "Wilson Price Hunt Reports on Lewis and Clark," 95–103.

61. Moulton, ed., *Journals,* vol. 8, 370–71.

· 62. Ibid., 371; Meriwether Lewis to Thomas Jefferson, September 23, 1806, in Jackson, ed., *Letters of the Lewis and Clark Expedition,* vol. 1, 319–24; William Clark to Jonathan Clark, September 23, 1806, in Holmberg, ed., *Dear Brother,* 101–6.

63. Meriwether Lewis's Draft of the Clark Letter, September 24, 1806, in Jackson, ed., *Letters of the Lewis and Clark Expedition,* vol. 1, 330–35, 335n; Holmberg, ed., *Dear Brother,* 106–7n; Moulton, ed., *Journals,* vol. 8, 370.

64. William Clark to Jonathan Clark, September 24, 1806, in Holmberg, ed., *Dear Brother,* 115; Jackson, ed., *Letters of the Lewis and Clark Expedition,* vol. 1, 329–30n.

65. Moulton, ed., *Journals,* vol. 8, 371–72; William Clark Account, October 1806, in William Clark Papers, MHS; Frankfort, Kentucky *Western World,* October 11, 1806, in James P. Ronda, "St. Louis Welcomes and Toasts the Lewis and Clark Expedition: A Newly Discovered 1806 Newspaper Account," 19–20.

66. Frankfort *Western World,* October 11, 1806, in Ronda, "St. Louis Welcomes and Toasts the Lewis and Clark Expedition," 19–20; Silas Bent to Jared Mansfield, Septem-

ber 28, 1806, in Clarence E. Carter, ed., *Territorial Papers of the United States,* vol. 13, 12–13.

67. Moulton, ed., *Journals,* vol. 8, 372; Jackson, ed., *Letters of the Lewis and Clark Expedition,* vol. 2, 378, 424.

68. See Holmberg, ed., *Dear Brother,* 116n2, 122n1; Citizens of Fincastle to Lewis and Clark, January 8, 1807, and William Clark to the Citizens of Fincastle, January 1807, William Clark Papers, MHS, also in Jackson, ed., *Letters of the Lewis and Clark Expedition,* vol. 1, 358–60.

69. See Holmberg, ed., *Dear Brother,* 125n8; "William Clark and the Girls on the Pony," in Donald Jackson, *Among Sleeping Giants: Occasional Pieces on Lewis and Clark,* 33–43; Eldon G. Chuinard, "Fincastle-Santillane and William and Judith Clark," 10–15.

70. *National Intelligencer and Washington Advertiser,* January 16, 1807.

71. William Clark to Jonathan Clark, January 22, 1807, in Holmberg, ed., *Dear Brother,* 119, 122.

72. Ibid.; Meriwether Lewis to Thomas Jefferson, September 23, 1806, in Jackson, ed., *Letters of the Lewis and Clark Expedition,* vol. 1, 323–24.

73. Henry Dearborn to Willis Alston, January 14, 1807, Dearborn to Thomas Jefferson, February 24, 1807, and Jefferson to the U.S. Senate, February 28, 1807, in Jackson, ed., *Letters of the Lewis and Clark Expedition,* vol. 1, 363–64, 375, 376, 376n.

74. William Clark to Edmund Clark, March 5, 1807, Draper Mss., State Historical Society of Wisconsin, 2L60; Act Compensating Lewis and Clark, [3 March 1807], Financial Records of the Expedition Account No. 1989 [August 5, 1807] in Jackson, ed., *Letters of the Lewis and Clark Expedition,* vol. 2, 377–78, 427; Henry Dearborn to William Clark, March 9, 1807, and Arlen J. Large, "Captain Clark's Belated Bonus," 12–14.

75. Henry Dearborn to William Clark, March 9, 1807, and William Clark's Commission as Indian Agent, March 7, 1807, in Carter, ed., *Territorial Papers,* vol. 14, 108–9.

76. William Clark to Jonathan Clark, January 22, 1807, in Holmberg, ed., *Dear Brother,* 122; Meriwether Lewis to William Clark, March 11, 1807, in Jackson, ed., *Letters of the Lewis and Clark Expedition,* vol. 2, 385.

77. Meriwether Lewis to William Clark, March 15, 1807; Clark to Lewis [after March 15, 1807] in Jackson, ed., *Letters of the Lewis and Clark Expedition,* vol. 2, 387–88; William Clark's Commission as Brigadier General in the Militia of the Louisiana Territory, March 12, 1807, William Clark Papers, MHS.

Seven   *Soldier, Diplomat, and Businessman*

1. Moulton, ed., *Journals,* vol. 8, 364.

2. Meriwether Lewis to William Clark, March 13, 1807, William Clark Papers, MHS.

3. Meriwether Lewis to William Clark, March 15, 1807, William Clark Papers, MHS.

4. William Clark to Henry Dearborn, May 18, 1807, in Carter, ed., *Territorial Papers,* vol. 14, 122–23; Frederick Bates to Henry Dearborn, May 15, 1807, in Thomas M. Marshall, ed., *The Life and Papers of Frederick Bates,* vol. 1, 119–23.

5. Henry Dearborn to William Clark, March 9, 1807, Clark to Dearborn, May 18, 1807, and Clark to Dearborn, June 1, 1807, in Carter, ed., *Territorial Papers,* vol. 14, 108–9, 122, 126; Foley and Rice, "The Return of the Mandan Chief," 6.

6. William Clark to Henry Dearborn, June 1 and September 12, 1807, in Carter, ed., *Territorial Papers,* vol. 14, 126–28, 146–47.

7. William Clark to Henry Dearborn, May 18 and June 1, 1807, in Carter, ed., *Territorial Papers,* vol. 14, 124–25, 126; William Clark to Col. Thomas Hunt, May 15, 1807, Daniel Bissell Papers, St. Louis Mercantile Library.

8. William Clark to Henry Dearborn, May 18, June 1, 12, 1807, in Carter, ed., *Territorial Papers,* vol. 14, 122–25, 126; Frederick Bates to Meriwether Lewis, May 15, 1807, in Marshall, ed., *Papers of Frederick Bates,* vol. 1, 118.

9. William Clark to Henry Dearborn, May 18, June 1, and September 12, in Carter, ed., *Territorial Papers,* vol. 14, 125, 126, 146; Clark to Jefferson, September 20, 1807, Thomas Jefferson Papers, Library of Congress; Christian Schultz, *Travels on an Inland Voyage,* vol. 2, 88.

10. William Clark [canceled] to Henry Dearborn, June 8, 1807, William Clark Papers, MHS; Frederick Bates to Col. Thomas Hunt, July 22, 1807, Bates to William Clark, July 25, 1807, and Bates to Henry Dearborn, August 2, 1807, in Marshall, ed., *Papers of Frederick Bates,* vol. 1, 163, 166–68, 169.

11. Clark to Dearborn, September 12 and December 3, 1807, in Carter, ed., *Territorial Papers,* vol. 14, 146–47, 153–54; Clark to James Madison, October 6, 1807, Aaron Burr Papers, MHS; William Clark to Jonathan Clark, September 9, 1807, in Holmberg, ed., *Dear Brother,* 126.

12. Clark to Jefferson, September 20 and November 10, 1807, in Jefferson Papers, Library of Congress; Jefferson to Clark, December 19, 1807, William Clark Papers, MHS. These letters along with other pertinent documents can be found in Howard C. Rice, "Jefferson's Gift of Fossils to the Museum of Natural History in Paris," 597–627.

13. Nathaniel Pryor to Clark, October 16, 1807, in Jackson, ed., *Letters of the Lewis and Clark Expedition,* vol. 2, 432–37; Clark to Dearborn, October 24, 30, 1807, in Elliot Coues, ed., "Letters of William Clark and Nathaniel Pryor," 619–20; Clark to Dearborn, December 3, 1807, in Carter, ed., *Territorial Papers,* vol. 14, 153–54.

14. William Clark to Jonathan Clark, January 21, 1809, in Holmberg, ed., *Dear Brother,* 194.

15. Fitzhugh-Rose Account Book, Account of William Clark, April–May 1808, Filson Historical Society.

16. William Clark to Jonathan Clark, June 6, 1808, in Holmberg, ed., *Dear Brother,* 131–32.

17. Ibid., G. R. C. Sullivan to John O'Fallon, June 2, 1808, O'Fallon Papers, MHS; Lewis to Clark, May 29, 1808, William Clark Papers, MHS.

18. Lewis to Clark, May 29, 1808, William Clark Papers, MHS.

19. William Clark to Jonathan Clark, July 2, October 5, and November 9, 1808, in Holmberg, ed., *Dear Brother,* 139, 154, 156, 160; Thomas Riddick to Frederick Bates, July 2, 1808, Bates Family Papers, MHS.

20. William Clark to Jonathan Clark, July 2, 21, 1808, in Holmberg, ed., *Dear Brother,* 139, 144.

21. William Clark to Jonathan Clark, January 21, 1809, in Holmberg, ed., *Dear Brother,* 193.

22. William Clark to Jonathan Clark, November 9, 1808, in Holmberg, ed., *Dear Brother,* 160.

23. William Clark to Jonathan Clark, December 10, 1808, May 28 and August 26, 1809, in Holmberg, ed., *Dear Brother,* 183–84, 201, 210.

24. Aside from Clark's own letters to his brothers in Louisville, by far the best account of the relationship between Clark and York can be found in James Holmberg's "Epilogue: York's Post-Expedition Life and Estrangement from William Clark," in Robert B. Betts, *In Search of York,* 151–70; John O'Fallon to William Clark, April 13, 1811, William Clark Papers, MHS; John Francis McDermott, ed., *The Western Journals of Washington Irving,* 82.

25. William Clark to Jonathan Clark, December 14, 1810, in Holmberg, ed., *Dear Brother,* 251.

26. William Clark to Henry Dearborn, August 18, 1808, in Carter, ed., *Territorial Papers,* vol. 14, 207–10; William Clark to Jonathan Clark, July 21 and December 10, 1808, in Holmberg, ed., *Dear Brother,* 143, 184.

27. William E. Foley, "Different Notions of Justice: The Case of the 1808 St. Louis Murder Trials," 2–13. Clark's subsequent decision to recommend that the president pardon the Sac Indian must have been influenced by Maurice Blondeau's letter stating that while many of the Sacs were favorably disposed to the U.S. government, they remained perplexed by the American system of justice. Maurice Blondeau to William Clark, June 16, 1809, William Clark Papers. Original in French.

28. Lewis to Dearborn, July 1, 1808, in Carter, ed., *Territorial Papers,* vol. 14, 196–98.

29. Jefferson to Lewis, July 21, 1808, Jefferson Papers, Library of Congress; Dearborn to Thomas Hunt, May 17, 1808, in Carter, ed., *Territorial Papers,* vol. 14, 184.

30. Clark to Dearborn, June 25, 1808, and Lewis to Dearborn, July 1, 1808, in Carter, ed., *Territorial Papers,* vol. 14, 194, 196; Kate L. Gregg, ed., *Westward with Dragoons: The Journal of William Clark on His Expedition to Establish Fort Osage, August 25 to September 22, 1808,* 33–51.

31. Gregg, ed., *Westward with Dragoons,* 34–35; William Clark to Jonathan Clark, October 1, 1808, in Holmberg, ed., *Dear Brother,* 151; and Manuscript plan of Fort Osage, showing location of structures, building assignments, and topography, September 1808, William Clark Papers, MHS.

32. Gregg, ed., *Westward with Dragoons,* 35, 38.

33. Ibid., 41; Clark to Dearborn, September 23, 1808, in Carter, ed., *Territorial Papers,* vol. 14, 224–25. On the subject of Jefferson's Indian policies, see Anthony F. C. Wallace, *Jefferson and the Indians: The Tragic Fate of the First Americans.*

34. Gregg, ed., *Westward with Dragoons,* 41–48; William Clark to Jonathan Clark, October 1, 5, 1808, in Holmberg, ed., *Dear Brother,* 151, 154.

35. Clark to Dearborn, September 23, 1808, in Carter, ed., *Territorial Papers,* vol. 14, 224–25; *American State Papers, Indian Affairs,* vol. 2, 763–67.

36. *American State Papers, Indian Affairs,* vol. 2, 763–67; William Clark to Jonathan Clark, October 5, 1808, in Holmberg, ed., *Dear Brother,* 154.

37. J. Frederick Fausz, "Becoming 'A Nation of Quakers': The Removal of the Osage Indians from Missouri," 34–36; and Grant Foreman, ed., *A Traveler in Indian Territory: The Journal of Ethan Allen Hitchcock, Late Major-General in the United States Army,* 56.

38. William Clark to Jonathan Clark, October 5, November 9, 22–24, and December 10, 1808, in Holmberg, ed., *Dear Brother,* 153, 161, 167, 184.

39. William Clark to Jonathan Clark, October 5, November 9, and December 10, 1808, in Holmberg, ed., *Dear Brother,* 156, 160–61, 182–83; Swekosky Data, St. Louis Building Collection, 1808, MHS; John A. Bryan, "A Preliminary Study of William Clark Sites in St. Louis," typescript research report, November 1938, Missouri Historical Society Library.

40. William Clark to Jonathan Clark, November 9, 22–24, 1808, in Holmberg, ed., *Dear Brother,* 160, 167–68, 171–72.

41. William Clark to Jonathan Clark, November 22–24 and December 10, 1808, and William Clark to John Hite Clark, December 15, 1808, in Holmberg, ed., *Dear Brother,* 168, 182–83, 278–79.

42. William Clark to Jonathan Clark, December 10, 1808, and William Clark to John Hite Clark, December 15, 1808, in Holmberg, ed., *Dear Brother,* 182–82, 185n3, 279.

43. William Clark to Jonathan Clark, July 21 and November 22, 24, 1809, and William Clark to Edmund Clark, April 15, 1809, in Holmberg, ed., *Dear Brother,* 143, 144n1, 168–70, 283; William Clark to John O'Fallon, August 25, 1807, and November 22, 1808, O'Fallon Papers, MHS; John O'Fallon to George Rogers Clark, February 19, 1809, Draper Manuscripts, 55J65. Also see Mary Ellen Rowe, "'A Respectable Independence': The Early Career of John O'Fallon," 393–409.

44. William Clark to Jonathan Clark, May 28, 1809, in Holmberg, ed., *Dear Brother,* 201; George R. C. Sullivan to John O'Fallon, April 24, 1809, O'Fallon Papers, Filson Historical Society.

45. William Clark to Jonathan Clark, January 2, 1809, in Holmberg, ed., *Dear Brother,* 189–90.

46. William Clark to Jonathan Clark, January 21, 1809, in ibid., 193.

47. Ibid.; William Clark to Jonathan Clark, May 28, 1809, in ibid., 201.

48. For a full discussion of the Missouri Fur Company and its founding, see Richard E. Oglesby, *Manuel Lisa and the Opening of the Missouri Fur Trade,* 65–75.

49. For a perspective on why Clark felt comfortable in joining a private venture, see Jerome O. Steffen, *William Clark: Jeffersonian Man on the Frontier,* 72–82.

50. John Mason to William Clark, December 31, 1808, in Carter, ed., *Territorial Papers,* vol. 14, 247; William Clark to Jonathan Clark, [ca. March 1, 1809] in Holmberg, ed., *Dear Brother,* 197.

51. Articles of Agreement between Governor Meriwether Lewis and Members of the St. Louis Missouri Fur Company, February 24, 1809, Chouteau Collections, MHS.

52. Foley and Rice, "The Return of the Mandan Chief," 8–9, and *Missouri Gazette,* March 8, 1809.

53. St. Louis Missouri Fur Company Record Book, 1809–1812, MHS; William Clark to Edmund Clark, April 15, 1809, in Holmberg, ed., *Dear Brother,* 283.

54. William Clark to Jonathan Clark, May 28, 1809, in Holmberg, ed., *Dear Brother,* 204; Summons, July 12, 1809, Fur Trade Papers, MHS; Manuel Lisa to William Clark, June 23, 1809, in St. Louis Missouri Fur Company Record Book, 1809–1812; Missouri Fur Company Ledger, 1812–1814, Kansas State Historical Society; and *William Clark (to use of Missouri Fur Company) v. Charles Bourguion; Clark v. Francois St. Michel, Clark v. Nicholas Brazeau, Clark v. Joseph Richard, Clark v. Joseph Manseau,* November 1809, St. Louis Circuit Court Historical Records, St. Louis, Missouri. The St. Louis Circuit Court records contain more than a dozen cases between 1809 and 1823 involving Clark and the interests of the Missouri Fur Company. These cases can all be viewed online at the St. Louis Historical Records Project jointly sponsored by Washington University, St. Louis, and the Missouri State Archives.

55. William Clark to Jonathan Clark, May 28, 1809, in Holmberg, ed., *Dear Brother,* 201–2; William Clark to Henry Dearborn, April 29, 1809, in Carter, ed., *Territorial Papers,* vol. 14, 265–66.

56. William Eustis to Meriwether Lewis, July 15, 1809, in Carter, ed., *Territorial Papers*, vol. 14, 285–86.

57. William Clark to Jonathan Clark, August 26, 1809, in Holmberg, ed., *Dear Brother*, 210; Frederick Bates to Richard Bates, April 15, July 14, and November 9, 1809, in Marshall, ed., *Papers of Frederick Bates*, vol. 2, 64, 68–69, 86–87, 108–11.

58. Frederick Bates to Richard Bates, November 9, 1809, in Marshall, ed., *Papers of Frederick Bates*, vol. 2, 108–11.

59. William Clark to Jonathan Clark, November 22–24, 1808, and August 26, 1809, in Holmberg, ed., *Dear Brother*, 172, 210.

60. William Eustis to William Clark, August 7, 1809, in Carter, ed., *Territorial Papers*, vol. 14, 289–90; Memorandum of books, papers, notes, accounts, and other instruments delivered to Peter Chouteau, Jr., by Genl. William Clark, September 15, 1809, Chouteau Collection, MHS; William Clark to Jonathan Clark, September 16, 1809, in Holmberg, ed., *Dear Brother*, 214–15; William Clark's Certificate of membership in St. Louis Lodge No. 111 of Ancient York Masons, September 18, 1809, William Clark Papers, MHS.

61. William Clark to Jonathan Clark, September 16, 1809, in Holmberg, ed., *Dear Brother*, 215; and William Clark 1809 Memorandum Book, WHMCC.

62. William Clark 1809 Memorandum Book, WHMCC.

63. Ibid., and William Clark to Jonathan Clark, October 28, 1809, in Holmberg, ed., *Dear Brother*, 216, 218.

64. William Clark 1809 Memorandum Book, WHMCC, and William Clark to Jonathan Clark, October 8 [November] 1809, in Holmberg, ed., *Dear Brother*, 225–26.

65. William Clark's 1809 Memorandum Book, WHMCC; and William Clark to Jonathan Clark, November 26, 1809, in Holmberg, ed., *Dear Brother*, 228–29.

66. Ibid.

67. Thomas Jefferson to William Clark, September 10, 1809, William Clark Papers, MHS; William Clark's 1809 Memorandum Book, WHMCC; Thomas Jefferson to C and A Conrad and Co., November 23, 1809, in Jackson, ed., *Letters of the Lewis and Clark Expedition*, vol. 2, 474–75; and Jackson, *Thomas Jefferson and the Stony Mountains*, 272–73.

68. William Clark's 1809 Memorandum Book, WHMCC; William Clark to Jonathan Clark, January 12, 1810, in Holmberg, ed., *Dear Brother*, 233–34.

69. William Clark's 1809 Memorandum Book, WHMCC; William Clark to Jonathan Clark, January 12, 1810, in Holmberg, ed., *Dear Brother*, 233–34.

70. William Clark to Jonathan Clark, January 12, 1810, in Holmberg, ed., *Dear Brother*, 233–34.

71. William Clark to Jonathan Clark, [March] 8, 1810, in ibid., 236–37; Charles Willson Peale to Rembrandt Peale, February 3, 1810, in Jackson, ed., *Letters of the Lewis and Clark Expedition*, vol. 2, 493–94.

72. William Clark to Nicholas Biddle, February 20 and March 25, 1810; Biddle to Clark, March 3 and 17, 1810; Nicholas Biddle Notes [c. April 1810] and Nicholas Biddle Prospectus [c. May 1810] in Jackson, ed., *Letters of the Lewis and Clark Expedition*, vol. 2, 494, 495–97, 545, and 546–48; William Clark to Jonathan Clark, [March] 8, 1810, in Holmberg, ed., *Dear Brother*, 237.

73. William Clark to Jonathan Clark, July 16, 1810, in Holmberg, ed., *Dear Brother*, 248–49; William Clark to William Eustis, July 20, 1810, photocopy only in William

Clark Papers, MHS (original at National Archives); Clark to Eustis, September 12, 1810, in Carter, ed., *Territorial Papers*, vol. 14, 412–13.

74. Clark to Eustis, September 12, 1810, in Carter, ed., *Territorial Papers*, vol. 14, 413; William Clark to Jonathan Clark, July 16 and December 14, 1810, in Holmberg, ed., *Dear Brother*, 248–49, 252.

75. William Clark to Nicholas Biddle, December 7, 1810, in Jackson, ed., *Letters of the Lewis and Clark Expedition*, vol. 2, 562.

76. Allen, *Passage through the Garden*, 375–94.

77. Ibid.; William Clark to Thomas Jefferson, October 10, 1816, in Jackson, ed., *Letters of the Lewis and Clark Expedition*, vol. 2, 624.

78. James P. Ronda, *Finding the West: Explorations with Lewis and Clark*, 54–55.

79. Clark to Eustis, July 20, 1810, photocopy only in William Clark Papers, MHS; William Clark to Jonathan Clark, July 16 and December 14, 1810, in Holmberg, ed., *Dear Brother*, 248, 251–52.

80. Bob Moore, "Pompey's Baptism: A Recently Discovered Document Sheds Light on the Christening of Jean Baptiste Charbonneau," 10–17; John C. Luttig, *Journal of a Fur-Trading Expedition on the Upper Missouri 1812–1813*, 138; Toussaint Charbonneau deed to William Clark, March 26, 1811 [in French]; George Rogers Hancock Clark Papers, MHS.

81. Moore, "Pompey's Baptism," 10–17; Luttig, *Journal of a Fur-Trading Expedition*, 134. According to Stella Drumm, in 1812 Luttig, Clark's sometime clerk, returned to St. Louis from a Missouri Fur Company trading expedition, bringing with him Lizette, a girl about one year old and the child of Toussaint Charbonneau. Drumm speculates that this was perhaps the infant daughter of the recently deceased Sacagawea. Luttig petitioned the St. Louis Orphans' Court on August 11 to be named the guardian of the infant children of Toussaint Charbonneau, a boy about ten years old and Lizette, a girl about one. Someone later crossed out Luttig's name and substituted William Clark. There are no other known references to Lizette, and the outcome of the proceedings in the Orphans' Court is unknown.

82. Dick Steward, *Duels and the Roots of Violence in Missouri*, 30–32; William Clark to Jonathan Clark, January 31, 1810, in Holmberg, ed., *Dear Brother*, 254, 255–56n2; Dr. Bernard G. Farrar to James A. Graham, December 25, 1810, William Clark Papers, MHS.

83. William Clark to Jonathan Clark, January 31, 1810, in Holmberg, ed., *Dear Brother*, 254; *Louisiana Gazette*, January 31, 1811; Steward, *Duels and the Roots of Violence in Missouri*, 45, 49.

84. William Clark to Jonathan Clark, [n.d. ca. March 1, 1811] and August 30, 1811, in Holmberg, ed., *Dear Brother*, 257–58, 262–63; St. Louis Missouri Fur Company Ledger Book, 1809–1812, March 27, 1811, MHS.

85. William Clark to Jonathan Clark, August 30 and September 14, 1811, in Holmberg, ed., *Dear Brother*, 263, 264.

86. William Clark to Jonathan Clark, August 17 and September 14, 1811, in Holmberg, ed., *Dear Brother*, 259, 264.

87. Shawnees to President of the U.S., March 29, 1811, Letters Received by Secretary of War Relating to Indian Affairs, 1800–1816, M271, National Archives; William Clark to James Madison, April 10, 1811, and William Eustis to William Clark, May 31, 1811, in Carter, ed., *Territorial Papers*, vol. 14, 452.

88. *Missouri Gazette*, December 21 and 28, 1811, and February 8 and 29, 1812;

Frederick Bates to William C. Carr, July 31, 1812, in Marshall, ed., *Papers of Frederick Bates,* vol. 2, 232.

89. *Louisiana Gazette,* May 9, 1812; John O'Fallon to Fanny Fitzhugh, August 15, 1812, Fitzhugh Family Papers, MHS.

90. Nicholas Biddle to William Clark, July 4, 1812, Clark to Biddle, August 6 and September 5, 1812, in Jackson, ed., *Letters of the Lewis and Clark Expedition,* vol. 2, 577–79.

91. William Clark to William Eustis, October 24, 1812, in Carter, ed., *Territorial Papers,* vol. 14, 602–3; Christian Wilt to Joseph Hertzog, November 1, 1812, Christian Wilt Letterbook, MHS.

92. Clark to Eustis, December 5, 1812, in Carter, ed., *Territorial Papers,* vol. 14, 609–11; Christian Wilt to Joseph Hertzog, November 22, 1812, Christian Wilt Letterbook, MHS; John Mason to Clark, August 11, 1812, typescript copy only, William Clark Papers, MHS; *Missouri Gazette,* November 28, 1812.

93. Clark to Eustis, December 5, 1812, in Carter, ed., *Territorial Papers,* vol. 14, 609–11; Christian Wilt to Joseph Hertzog, December 13, 1812, Christian Wilt Letterbook, MHS; Clark to Biddle, January 24 [1813]; John Conrad to Biddle, [November 12, 1812], Biddle to Clark, February 23, 1813, Clark Assigns Power of Attorney, [March 29, 1813] in Jackson, ed., *Letters of the Lewis and Clark Expedition,* vol. 2, 580–83.

94. William Clark to John Armstrong [1813], in Carter, ed., *Territorial Papers,* vol. 14, 635–36; *American State Papers, Military Affairs,* vol. 1, 387; John Armstrong to Benjamin Howard, April 10, 1813, Howard to James Monroe, March 30, 1813, Monroe to Howard, April 3, 1813, and Armstrong to Clark, April 8, 1813, in Carter, ed., *Territorial Papers,* vol. 14, 656–57, 645–46, 655.

95. William Clark to John O'Fallon June 18, 1813, O'Fallon Papers, MHS.

Eight   *Mr. Governor*

1. Notice that John B. C. Lucas had administered the oath of office to William Clark, July 6, 1813; typescript of excerpt copied from U.S. State Department Records dated April 8, 1814; Commissions dated June 16 and July 1, 1813, all in William Clark Papers, MHS, and Edward Hempstead to James Madison, March 4, 1813, in Carter, ed., *Territorial Papers,* vol. 14, 637.

2. Clark to Armstrong, July 31, 1813, and Daniel Bissell to John Armstrong, April 12, 1813, in Carter, ed., *Territorial Papers,* vol. 14, 691–92, 662–63; William Clark to John O'Fallon, June 18, 1813, O'Fallon Papers, MHS; *Missouri Gazette,* August 7, 1813.

3. Clark to Armstrong, September 12, 1813, in Carter, ed., *Territorial Papers,* vol. 14, 697–98; *Missouri Gazette,* September 18 and October 2, 1813; Kate L. Gregg, "The War of 1812 on the Missouri Frontier," pt. 2, 198–99.

4. Christian Wilt to Andrew Wilt, October 2, 1813, Christian Wilt Letterbook, MHS; William Clark to Colonel George Hancock, October 27, 1813, in Preston Family Papers–Joyes Collection, FHS; *Missouri Gazette,* November 27 and December 11, 1813; John B. C. Lucas to Mr. Leacock, December 3, 1813, memorandum of a letter, Lucas Collection, MHS, and Gregg, "War of 1812," pt. 2, 202.

5. *Missouri Gazette,* July 31 and December 11, 1813.

6. William Clark to James Monroe, June 19, July 31, and September 18, 1813, in Carter, ed., *Territorial Papers,* vol. 14, 679–80, 692, 699; John G. Heath to Frederick Bates,

January 14, 1816, Bates Family Papers, MHS; John G. Heath to Madison, May 1, 1816, in *Territorial Papers,* vol. 15, 133–34.

7. James Monroe to William Clark, July 30, 1813, and Clark to Monroe, September 18, 1813, in Carter, ed., *Territorial Papers,* vol. 14, 691, 699; John P. Gates to William Clark, March 5, 1814.

8. William Clark to Col. George Hancock, October 27, 1813, Preston Family Papers–Joyes Collection, FHS; Christian Wilt to Joseph Hertzog, March 27, 1815, Christian Wilt Letterbook, MHS.

9. *Missouri Gazette,* November 13, 1813; Julia Hancock to George Hancock, February 27, 1814; Julia Clark's Household Memo Book, n.d., and Recipe for Vinegar Pudding sent to Julia Clark, n.d., in William Clark Papers, MHS.

10. Armstrong to Howard, December 31, 1813, in Carter, ed., *Territorial Papers,* vol. 14, 724; Harrison to Armstrong, December 21, 1813, in Logan Esarey, ed., *Messages and Letters of William Henry Harrison,* vol. 2, 610–11; Hempstead to Armstrong, March 22, 1814, Clark to Armstrong, March 28, 1814, and Howard to Armstrong, March 22, 1814, in *Territorial Papers,* vol. 14, 744, 746–47, 737n; General Orders, February 15, 1814, printed handbill in William Clark Papers, MHS.

11. Clark to Armstrong, January 6, February 2, and March 28, 1814, and endorsement by Armstrong of Clark's letter to him dated May 4, 1814, in Carter, ed., *Territorial Papers,* vol. 14, 727–28, 738–40, 746–47, 763.

12. Clark to Armstrong, May 4 and June 5, 1814, and Joseph Perkins to Benjamin Howard, August 1814, in Carter, ed., *Territorial Papers,* vol. 14, 762–63, 768–69, 784–86; *Missouri Gazette and Illinois Advertiser,* June 25, 1814.

13. *Missouri Gazette and Illinois Advertiser,* June 4 and 11, 1814; Howard to Armstrong, June 20 and August 17, 1814; Joseph Perkins to Benjamin Howard, August 1814, and Clark to Armstrong, July 31 and August 20, 1814, in Carter, ed., *Territorial Papers,* vol. 14, 772–73, 781–82, 784–86, 786–87.

14. Clark to Armstrong, August 20, 1814, in Carter, ed., *Territorial Papers,* vol. 14, 787.

15. Clark to Sibley, March 17, 1814, George Sibley Papers, MHS.

16. Samuel J. Mills and Daniel Smith, *Report on a Missionary Tour Through That Part of the United States which lies West of the Allegany Mountains;* Baptismal Records, 1814–1835, Cathedral of St. Louis the King (Old Cathedral), St. Louis, 1–3; and Clark Family Births, Deaths, Marriages and Baptisms compiled by Meriwether Lewis Clark, Meriwether Lewis Clark Papers, FHS.

17. Clark to Biddle, September 16, 1814, in Jackson, ed., *Letters of the Lewis and Clark Expedition,* vol. 2, 600; William Clark to Edmund Clark, December 25, 1814, Clark Family Papers, FHS.

18. *Missouri Gazette,* August 13, 1814; Clark to Armstrong, August 20, 1814, in Carter, ed., *Territorial Papers,* vol. 14, 786–87.

19. *Missouri Gazette,* October 22 and 29, 1814.

20. Clark to Armstrong, September 18, 1814; and Petition to Congress by U.S. Missouri Rangers, December 17, 1814, in Carter, ed., *Territorial Papers,* vol. 14, 787–88, 805–6; *Missouri Gazette and Illinois Advertiser,* December 10, 1814.

21. Clark to Biddle, September 16, 1814, and June 18, 1815; Biddle to Clark, March 12, 1815, in Jackson, ed., *Letters of the Lewis and Clark Expedition,* vol. 2, 600, 604–5, 605n; American Antiquarian Society Membership Commission, October 24, 1814, William Clark Papers, MHS; Foley, "Lewis and Clark's American Travels," 301–24.

22. *Missouri Gazette,* February 18, 1815.

23. Ibid.; James Monroe to Indian Commissioners, March 11, 1815; Col. William Russell to James Monroe, March 12, 1805, in Carter, ed., *Territorial Papers,* vol. 15, 14–15, 15–16; Christian Wilt to Joseph Hertzog, March 13, 1815, Christian Wilt Letterbook, MHS.

24. *American State Papers, Indian Affairs,* vol. 2, 6; Commission of Alexander McNair as Register of the Land Office, February 28, 1815, in Carter, ed., *Territorial Papers,* vol. 15, 10–11.

25. Clark to Monroe, April 17, 1815, in Carter, ed., *Territorial Papers,* vol. 15, 25–26; Monroe to Indian Commissioners, March 11, 1815; Commissioners Clark, Edwards, and Chouteau to Monroe, October 18, 1815, in *American State Papers, Indian Affairs,* vol. 2, 6, 9–11; Monroe to Clark, March 11, 1815, William Clark Papers, MHS.

26. Clark, Edwards, and Chouteau to Monroe, May 15 and 22, 1815, in *American State Papers, Indian Affairs,* vol. 2, 7; Gregg, "The War of 1812 on the Missouri Frontier," pt. 3, 345.

27. Daniel Bissell to Andrew Jackson, July 2, 1815, photostatic copy only in Daniel Bissell Papers, MHS.

28. William Clark to John O'Fallon, August 28, 1815, O'Fallon Papers, MHS; Clark, Edwards, and Chouteau to William H. Crawford, October 18, 1815, in *American State Papers, Indian Affairs,* vol. 2, 9–11; *Missouri Gazette,* July 8, 1815.

29. James Monroe to John Mason, March 27, 1815, Clark, Edwards, and Chouteau to James Monroe, July 16, and Clark, Edwards, and Chouteau to William H. Crawford, September 18 and October 18, 1815, in *American State Papers, Indian Affairs,* vol. 2, 7, 8–9, 9–12; *Missouri Gazette,* July 15, 1815.

30. *Missouri Gazette,* July 15, 1815; Robert L. Fisher, "The Treaties of Portage des Sioux," 502–3.

31. Clark, Edwards, and Chouteau to Monroe, July 16, 1815, in *American State Papers, Indian Affairs,* vol. 2, 8–9; Fisher, "The Treaties of Portage des Sioux," 503–4; William Clark Kennerly and Elizabeth Russell, *Persimmon Hill: A Narrative of Old St. Louis and the Far West,* 38.

32. Fisher, "The Treaties of Portage des Sioux," 504–5; Clark, Edwards, and Chouteau to Crawford, October 18, 1815, in *American State Papers, Indian Affairs,* vol. 2, 9–12; William Clark to John O'Fallon, August 28, 1815, O'Fallon Papers, MHS.

33. Clark to Crawford, October 1, 1815, in *American State Papers, Indian Affairs,* vol. 2, 77–78.

34. Crawford to Clark, Edwards, and Chouteau, November 24, 1815, in *American State Papers, Indian Affairs,* vol. 2, 12; Osgood, *Field Notes of Captain William Clark,* 176–77, 188.

35. Timothy Flint, *Recollections of the Last Ten Years in the Mississippi Valley,* 104–6, 111–13; Treaties with Sacs of Rock River (May 13, 1816), Sioux (June 1, 1816), Winnebago (June 3, 1816), and Ottawa, Chippewa, and Potawatomi (August 24, 1816), in *American State Papers, Indian Affairs,* vol. 2, 94–96.

36. Jay H. Buckley, "William Clark: Superintendent of Indian Affairs at St. Louis, 1813–1838," 112; Christian Wilt to Joseph Hertzog, March 13, 1815, Christian Wilt Letterbook, MHS; letter signed "Justice" in *Missouri Gazette,* April 12, 1817.

37. Walter A. Schroeder, "Populating Missouri, 1804–1821," 265; William Clark, Report on the names and probable number of the Tribes of Indians in the Missouri

Territory, November 4, 1816, in Letters Received by the Secretary of War Relative to Indian Affairs, 1800–1816, M–271, National Archives; Clark, Edwards, and Chouteau to Crawford, October 18, 1815, *American State Papers, Indian Affairs,* vol. 2, 1; Proclamation by Governor William Clark, December 4, 1815, in Carter, ed., *Territorial Papers,* vol. 15, 191–92; Proclamation of President James Madison, December 12, 1815, in *Missouri Gazette,* January 27, 1816.

38. Resolutions of the Territorial Assembly, January 22, 1816, in Carter, ed., *Territorial Papers,* vol. 15, 105–7, 108–9; John Mack Faragher, "More Motley than Mackinaw: From Ethnic Mixing to Ethnic Cleansing on the Frontier of the Lower Missouri, 1783–1833," 304–26.

39. *Missouri Gazette,* March 2, 1816; Alexander McNair to Josiah Meigs, January 27, 1816, in Carter, ed., *Territorial Papers,* vol. 15, 112; *U.S. Statutes at Large* (1850), 260–61.

40. Resolutions of the Territorial Assembly, January 8, 1815, in Carter, ed., *Territorial Papers,* vol. 15, 37–38; 3 *U.S. Statutes at Large* (1850), 211–12; William Clark's agreement with Theodore Hunt and Charles Lucas, May 19, 1815; William Clark to Charles Lucas, October 10, 1815, and Rufus Easton notes to Thomas Robertson, n.d. [after 1817] in Lucas Collection, MHS.

41. Clark to Monroe, January 26, 1815, in Carter, ed., *Territorial Papers,* vol. 15, 4; Monroe to Clark, March 11, 1816, William Clark Papers, MHS.

42. For a fuller discussion of territorial Missouri's political squabbles, see Foley, *Genesis of Missouri,* 283–93.

43. William Russell to Charles Lucas, December 13, 1815; *Missouri Gazette,* March 29, July 27, and August 3, 1816.

44. Election returns certified by Governor Clark, September 19, 1816, in Carter, ed., *Territorial Papers,* vol. 15, 195; *Missouri Gazette,* September 21 and 28 and October 5 and 12, 1816.

45. E. B. Clemson to Charles Lucas, August 18, 1816; John Scott to Charles Lucas, August 19, 1816; Frederick Bates notes re. Scott-Lucas duel in Lucas Collection, MHS; Steward, *Duels and the Roots of Violence in Missouri,* 45–46.

46. *Report of the Committee of Elections on the memorial of Rufus Easton, contesting the election and returns of John Scott, the Delegate from the Territory of Missouri,* December 31, 1816, and *Report of the Committee of Elections, to which was recommitted their Report of the 31st ult. On the Petition of Rufus Easton, contesting the election of John Scott,* January 10, 1817, in State Historical Society of Missouri Library, Columbia; *Annals of Congress,* 14 Cong., 2nd sess. (January 3, 4, and 13, 1817), 414–19, 472–73.

47. Benjamin O'Fallon to John O'Fallon, June 21, 1816, O'Fallon Collection, MHS; John A. Bryan, Preliminary Study of the William Clark Sites in St. Louis, November 1938, prepared for the National Park Service. Copy in MHS Library.

48. William Clark's Commissions as Governor, June 16, 1816, and January 21, 1817, William Clark Papers, MHS; George Rogers Clark to William Clark, November 5, 1815, George Rogers Hancock Clark Papers, William Clark Estate File, MHS; William Clark to Henry Clay, September 11, 1816, in Jackson, ed., *Letters of the Lewis and Clark Expedition,* 619–21.

49. Jefferson to Clark, September 8, 1816, and Clark to Jefferson, October 10, 1816, in Jackson, ed., *Letters of the Lewis and Clark Expedition,* 619, 623–25.

50. *Missouri Gazette,* February 15, 1817; Timothy Hubbard and Lewis E. Davids, *Banking in Mid-America: A History of Missouri Banks,* 20–21.

51. *Missouri Gazette,* March 8, 1817; Copy of an act of the General Assembly of the Territory of Missouri to incorporate a board of trustees for superintending schools in the Town of St. Louis, approved January 30, 1817, Frank Mosberger Collection, 1813–1857, St. Louis Public School Records Center and Archives.

52. Proceedings of the first Board of Trustees, April 4, 1817; Josiah Meigs to Clark, August 26 and November 3, 1817; Notice of school leasing lands, April 1817, and other miscellaneous documents, Frank Mosberger Collection, St. Louis Public School Records Center and Archives; Minutes of Board of Trustees for St. Louis Schools, April 4, 1817, Schools Papers, MHS.

53. William Russell to Charles Lucas, February 22 and August 17, 1817, Lucas Collection, MHS; William Clark to High Scull, May 29, 1817, William Clark Papers, MHS.

54. *Missouri Gazette,* August 9, 1817.

55. John O'Fallon to Dennis Fitzhugh, August 11, 1817, Fitzhugh Family Papers, MHS; William N. Chambers, "Pistols and Politics: Incidents in the Career of Thomas Hart Benton, 1816–1818," 5–17.

56. William Russell to Charles Lucas, August 17, 1817, Lucas Collection; *Missouri Gazette,* August 9, 1817.

57. *Missouri Fur Company v. Tibeau, Charles,* October 1817, Case No. 62; *Clark, William v. Brazeau, Louis Jr. and Auguste,* October 1817, Case No. 69, Circuit Court Case Files, Office of the Circuit Clerk, City of St. Louis, Missouri.

58. William Clark to George Sibley, January 11, April 4, and November 11, 1817, George Sibley Papers, MHS; William Clark Journal, 1817–1820, and Bernard G. Farrar to Clark, December 29, 1817, in William Clark Papers, MHS.

59. William Clark Journal, 1817–1820, William Clark Papers, MHS; William Clark to John C. Calhoun, February 6, 1818, in *American State Papers, Indian Affairs,* vol. 2, 173; William Clark to Nicholas Biddle, January 27, 1818, in Jackson, ed., *Letters of the Lewis and Clark Expedition,* vol. 2, 634–35; Agreement of the Historical Committee of the American Philosophical Society, April 8, 1818, in William Clark Papers, MHS.

60. William Clark Journal, 1817–1820 in William Clark Papers, MHS.

61. Ibid.; Thomas Hart Benton to Governor Preston, May 20, 1818, photostatic copy in Thomas Hart Benton Papers, MHS.

62. *American State Papers, Indian Affairs,* vol. 2, 171–72; John C. Calhoun to Clark, May 8, 1818; Clark to Calhoun, July 1 and October [n.d.] 1818, in Carter, ed., *Territorial Papers,* vol. 15, 390–91, 406, 454–55.

63. William Clark to Dennis Fitzhugh, September 20, 1818, Fitzhugh Family Papers, MHS; William Clark Journal, 1817–1820, William Clark Papers, MHS; George Hancock to Julia Clark, October 14, 1818, Preston Family Papers–Joyes Collection, FHS.

64. William Clark Journal, 1817–1820, William Clark Papers, MHS; John O'Fallon to General Thomas Smith, June 28, 1819, Thomas A. Smith Collection, WHMCC; William Clark to John O'Fallon, October 18, 1819, O'Fallon Papers, MHS; Kennerly and Russell, *Persimmon Hill,* 52–53.

65. Bernard Farrar to William Clark, January 20, 1820, William Clark Papers, MHS; *St. Louis Enquirer,* March 22, 1820; Beth Rubin, "The Backwoodsman Newly Caught: The Missouri Apprenticeship of Portraitist Chester Harding," 64–73; William Clark Journal, January 2, 1821, William Clark Papers, MHS.

66. *St. Louis Enquirer,* March 29, 1820; *Missouri Gazette and Public Advertiser,* June 28, 1820.

67. William Carr Lane to Mary Lane, April 17, 1819, Letters of William Carr Land, 1819–1831, in *Glimpses of the Past* 7 (July–September), 60; Rough copies of notes addressed to the editor, 1820, William Clark Papers, MHS.

68. O'Fallon to Thomas Smith, June 24, 1820, Thomas A. Smith Collection, WHMCC; William Clark to Thomas Forsyth, June 25, 1820, Draper Mss., 1T54.

69. William Clark Journal, 1817–1820, MHS.

70. Dennis Fitzhugh to John O'Fallon, June 15, 1820, Dennis Fitzhugh Papers, FHS; William Clark to Thomas Forsyth, June 25, 1825, Draper Manuscripts, 1T54.

71. William Clark Memorandum Book, 1820–1825, William Clark Papers, MHS; Gene Crotty, *The Visits of Lewis and Clark to Fincastle, Virginia,* 92.

72. To the People of Missouri, July 2, 1820, political circular in William Clark Papers, MHS; *St. Louis Enquirer,* July 22, 1820; O'Fallon to Smith, June 24, 1820, Thomas A. Smith Collection, WHMCC; *Missouri Gazette and Public Advertiser,* July 5, 1820.

73. *St. Louis Enquirer,* July 22, 1820; Perry McCandless, "Alexander McNair," *Dictionary of Missouri Biography,* 538–40.

74. To the People of Missouri, July 2, 1820, political circular, William Clark Papers, MHS.

75. Ibid.

76. Noah M. Ludlow, *Dramatic Life As I Found It,* 184–85; *Missouri Gazette and Public Advertiser,* August 16 and 23, 1820; Political Notes of John B. C. Lucas on his reasons for favoring McNair, [1820], Lucas Collection, MHS.

77. An Elector in the *Missouri Gazette and Public Advertiser,* August 23, 1820; Alexander McNair's address to Fellow Citizens of the New State of Missouri, Franklin *Missouri Intelligencer,* August 26, 1820.

78. *Missouri Gazette and Public Advertiser,* July 19 and August 16, 1820.

79. A Citizen in the *St. Louis Enquirer,* August 19, 1820.

80. *St. Louis Enquirer,* July 15, 1820.

81. "On the Noble Arts of electioneering," in the *St. Louis Enquirer,* August 2, 9 and 19, 1820; John O'Fallon to Thomas A. Smith, August 27, 1820, Thomas A. Smith Papers, WHMCC.

82. John O'Fallon to Dennis Fitzhugh, August 18, 1820, Fitzhugh Family Papers, MHS; John O'Fallon, "Brief Notices of the Principal Events in the Public Life of Governor Clark, August 9, 1820, copy in MHS Library; *Missouri Gazette and Public Advertiser,* September 6, 1820; Thomas Hart Benton to John Scott, August 30, 1820, photostatic copy in Thomas Hart Benton Papers, MHS.

83. William Clark memorandum and Account Book, 1820–1825, William Clark Papers, MHS.

Nine   *The Graying of the Redheaded Chief*

1. William Clark Memorandum and Account Book, 1820–1825, William Clark Papers, MHS.

2. John C. Calhoun to William Clark, October 21, 1820; John Scott to John Q. Adams, February 27, 1821; Calhoun to Clark, April 2, 1821, in Carter, ed., *Territorial Papers,* vol. 15, 659, 705, 712–15.

3. William Clark's sixty-day note, February 13, 1821, William Clark Papers, MHS; John O'Fallon to Thomas A. Smith, January 22, 1821, Thomas A. Smith Collection,

WHMCC; Notice of election of Board of Directors of Bank of Missouri, January 22, 1821, William Clark Papers, MHS; James Kennerly to George Sibley, August 18, 1821, George Sibley Papers, MHS.

4. Mary Margaret Clark to William Clark, n.d. [marked received July 13, 1821] and September 12, 1821, and William Clark to Col. McClalihan, September 25, 1821, William Clark Papers, MHS.

5. Clark Family Genealogy compiled by Meriwether Lewis Clark, Meriwether Lewis Clark Papers, Family Records 1853, FHS; John O'Fallon to Dennis Fitzhugh, November 2, 1821, Fitzhugh Family Papers, MHS.

6. Marriage certificate dated November 29, 1821, for wedding performed the previous day, William Clark Papers, MHS; Kennerly and Russell, *Persimmon Hill,* 55–56.

7. John O'Fallon to Dennis Fitzhugh, December 22, 1821, Fitzhugh Family Papers, MHS; Margaret Hancock to William Clark, December 19, 1821, William Clark Papers, MHS; John O'Fallon to Dennis Fitzhugh, January 18, 1822, O'Fallon Papers, FHS.

8. Calhoun to Clark, May 28, 1822, Records of the War Department, Letters Sent by the Secretary of War, National Archives; Thomas Hart Benton to Benjamin O'Fallon, April 8, 1824, O'Fallon Family Papers, WHMCC.

9. The authoritative study on Clark's Indian superintendency is Buckley, "William Clark: Superintendent of Indian Affairs at St. Louis, 1813–1838."

10. Clark later summarized his views on the fur trade in William Clark and Lewis Cass to Thomas Hart Benton, December 27, 1828, reprinted in *Message from the President . . . relating to British establishments on the Columbia, and the state of the fur trade.* William Clark to Richard Graham, June 21, 1822, and April 20, 1823, and Osage Treaty, August 31, 1822, Richard Graham Papers, MHS; Clark to Calhoun, August 9, 1822, January 16 and March 12, 1823, in Dale L. Morgan, ed., *The West of William H. Ashley, 1822–1838,* 18, 19–20, 21.

11. Clark to Calhoun, July 4, 1823, and January 14 and March 29, 1824, in Morgan, *West of William H. Ashley,* 45–46, 69–70, 75.

12. William Clark Memorandum and Account Book, 1820–1825, May 18, 1823, William Clark papers, MHS; William B. Faherty, "General William Clark and the Jesuits," WPO 17 (August 1991), 13–17; William Clark to Thomas McKenney, February 28, 1825, Letters Received by the Office of Indian Affairs, 1824–1881, St. Louis Superintendency, M-234, National Archives.

13. Paul Wilhelm, Duke of Wurttemberg, *Travels in North America, 1822–1824,* 190–93.

14. Ibid.

15. *Missouri Republican,* May 2, 1825; John Francis McDermott, "Museums in Early St. Louis," 130–31; Marquis de Lafayette to William Clark, February 1, 1830, William Clark Papers, MHS.

16. Louise Barry, ed., "William Clark's Diary, May 1826–February 1831," pt. 4, 391–93; George Catlin, *Letters and Notes of the Manners, Customs and Condition of the North American Indians,* vol. 2, 30.

17. Maximilian, *Travels in the Interior of North America, 1832–1834,* in Reuben Gold Thwaites, ed., *Early Western Travels, 1748–1846,* vol. 22, 217–36.

18. William Clark to John C. Calhoun, September 5, 1823, and William Clark to Richard Graham, September 5 1823; Graham to Clark, January 15, 1825, all in Richard Graham Papers, MHS; Clark to Calhoun, December 8, 1823, photostatic copy in Forsyth Papers, MHS; Joseph B. Herring, *Kenekuk, the Kickapoo Prophet,* 44–48.

19. William Clark to John O'Fallon, August 8, 1824, O'Fallon Papers, MHS; Treaties with Ioways, Sacs, and Foxes, August 4, 1824, in *American State Papers, Indian Affairs,* vol. 2, 525–26; *Missouri Republican,* November 29, 1824; R. Douglas Hurt, *The Indian Frontier, 1763–1864,* 170.

20. William Clark to John O'Fallon, August 22, 1824, Clark Family Papers, FHS; John O'Fallon to Thomas A. Smith, November 25, 1824, Thomas A. Smith Collection, WHMCC.

21. William Clark to Meriwether Lewis Clark, April 4, 1824, and Appointment for Meriwether Lewis Clark as a cadet at West Point, February 19, 1825, Meriwether Lewis Clark Papers, MHS.

22. William Clark to James Barbour, April 19 and June 1, 1825, Letters Received by the Office of Indian Affairs, 1824–1881, St. Louis Superintendency, M-234, National Archives; Treaties with the Osage and the Kansa, June 2 and 3, 1825, in *American State Papers, Indian Affairs,* vol. 2, 588–89, 589–90; William Clark to the Osages, [1825] U.S. Superintendency of Indian Affairs, St. Louis, Records, 1824–1851, Kansas State Historical Society (KSHS); William Clark to Meriwether Lewis Clark, July 3, 1825, Meriwether Lewis Clark Papers, MHS.

23. William Clark to Meriwether Lewis Clark, July 3, 1825, Meriwether Lewis Clark Papers, MHS.

24. William Clark to James Pierce, September 3, 1825, Clark Family Papers, FHS; William Clark to Meriwether Lewis Clark, Meriwether Lewis Clark Papers, September 24, 1825; Treaties with Sioux, Chippewa, Sac, Fox, Winnebago, Menominees, Ottawa, Potawatomi, and Ioway, August 19, 1825, in *American State Papers, Indian Affairs,* vol. 2, 608–9; William Clark's Journal of Prairie du Chien Conference, July 30–August 31, 1825, U.S. Superintendency of Indian Affairs, St. Louis, Records, 1807–1855, Kansas State Historical Society; Hurt, *The Indian Frontier,* 172.

25. William Clark to Meriwether Lewis Clark, September 24, 1825, Meriwether Lewis Clark Papers, MHS; Official copies of Virginia court ruling in the settlement of George Hancock Estate, July 9, 1825; William Clark to Charles Thruston, January 30, 1823, Clark Family Papers, FHS; William Clark to Samuel Gwathmey, July 4 and August 27, 1823, Gwathmey Family Papers, FHS; Clark to Gwathmey, June 15, 1823, and Conveyance of Land to George Rogers Clark heirs, April 2, 1823, and Jefferson County, Kentucky, Court Award in the estate of Charles Thruston, September 27, 1825, in William Clark Papers, MHS.

26. *Missouri Republican,* November 21, 1825; William Clark to James Barbour, November 22, 1825, and March 28, 1826, William Clark to Thomas McKenney, July 18, 1829, and William Clark to John Eaton, March 19, 1830, Letters Received at Office of Indian Affairs, 1824–1881, St. Louis Superintendency, National Archives, M–234.

27. Larry C. Skogen, *Indian Depredation Claims, 1796–1920,* 57–63; Franklin *Missouri Intelligencer,* April 28, 1826.

28. William Clark to Thomas McKenney, September 25 and November 15, 1825, and January 4, 1826, and William Clark to James Barbour, December 6, 1825, Letters Received by Office of Indian Affairs, 1824–1881, St. Louis Superintendency, NA, M-234.

29. William Clark to James Barbour, March 1, 1826, William Clark Papers, MHS.

30. Ibid.

31. Ibid.

32. *Missouri Intelligencer,* April 14, 1826.

33. Barry, ed., "William Clark's Diary," pt. 1, 3–8; *Missouri Republican,* June 22, 1826.

34. Harriet Clark to Meriwether Lewis Clark, October 3, 1826, April 14, 1828, and William Clark to Meriwether Lewis Clark, January 17 and April 12, 1827, and February 8 and May 18, 1828, Meriwether Lewis Clark Papers, MHS.

35. William Clark to Meriwether Lewis Clark, June 25 and September 10, 1826, Meriwether Lewis Clark Papers, MHS.

36. William Clark to Meriwether Lewis Clark, June 4 and 25 and September 10, 1826; Harriet Clark to Meriwether Lewis Clark, October 3, 1826, in Meriwether Lewis Clark Papers, MHS.

37. Harriet Clark to Meriwether Lewis Clark, July 5, 1826; William Clark to Meriwether Lewis Clark, September 10, 1826, in Meriwether Lewis Clark Papers, MHS; *Missouri Republican,* October 5, 1826; Barry, ed., "William Clark's Diary," pt. 1, 14–15.

38. William Clark to Meriwether Lewis Clark, June 25, 1826; Harriet Clark to Meriwether Lewis Clark, October 3, 1826; William and Harriet Clark to Meriwether Lewis Clark, December 17, 1826, Meriwether Lewis Clark Papers, MHS.

39. William Clark to Meriwether Lewis Clark, February 25, 1827, Meriwether Lewis Clark Papers, MHS; Barry, ed., "William Clark's Diary," pt. 1, 20.

40. William Clark to Meriwether Lewis Clark, September 10, 1826, April 12 and 27, 1827, and Harriet Clark to Meriwether Lewis Clark, October 3, 1826, in Meriwether Lewis Clark Papers, MHS.

41. William Clark to Meriwether Lewis Clark, April 27, 1827, Meriwether Lewis Clark Papers, MHS; Handbill for the sale of town lots in Paducah, 1827, William Clark Papers, MHS; John P. Dyson, "The Naming of Paducah," 149–74.

42. Barry, ed., "William Clark's Diary," pt. 1, 27–34; William Clark to Meriwether Lewis Clark, May 18 and August 3, 1828, Meriwether Lewis Clark Papers, MHS; William Clark to George Rogers Hancock Clark, January 13, February 14, April 28, and November 30, 1828, George Rogers Hancock Clark Papers, MHS.

43. William Clark to Meriwether Lewis Clark, May 18 and October 18, 1828, Meriwether Lewis Clark Papers, MHS; Thomas Hart Benton to Benjamin O'Fallon, January 19, 1830, O'Fallon Family Papers, WHMCC; Barry, ed., "William Clark's Diary," pt. 4, 386; ? to Thomas Forsyth, March 14, 1832, and Thomas Forsyth to William H. Ashley, May 8, 1832, in Draper Manuscript Collection, 2T52 and 6T167–68; Emma Helen Blair, *The Indian Tribes of the Upper Mississippi Valley and Region of the Great Lakes,* vol. 2, 189n67; Jack Gregory and Rennard Strickland, *Sam Houston with the Cherokees, 1829–1833.*

44. William Clark to Meriwether Lewis Clark, October 18, 1828, MLC Papers, MHS; Barry, ed., "William Clark's Diary," pt. 2, 168; James Monroe to William Clark, September 28, 1828, William Clark Papers, MHS.

45. William Clark to John O'Fallon, January 8, 1829, O'Fallon Papers, MHS.

46. Ibid.

47. William Clark and Lewis Cass to Thomas Hart Benton, December 27, 1828, reprinted in *Messages from the President. . . relative to British establishments on the Columbia, and the state of the fur trade,* January 25, 1831; John F. A. Sanford to Benjamin O'Fallon January 30, 1829, O'Fallon Family Papers, WHMCC; Francis Paul Prucha, *The Great Father: The United States Government and the American Indians,* vol. 1, 294–97.

48. William Clark to George Rogers Hancock Clark, February 3, 1829, GRHC Papers, MHS; William Clark to Meriwether Lewis Clark, February 28, 1829, MLC Papers, MHS; George Kennerly to Alzire Kennerly, February 19, 1829, Kennerly Papers, MHS.

49. Thomas L. McKenney to John Eaton, March 21, 1829, and Receipt, December 22, 1829, William Clark Papers, MHS; William Clark to John Eaton, April 8, 1829, Letters Received by Office of Indian Affairs, 1824–1881, St. Louis Superintendency, NA, M-234.

50. William Clark to Meriwether Lewis Clark, April 26 and June 21, 1829, MLC Papers, MHS.

51. William Clark to Meriwether Lewis Clark, April 26, 1829, MLC Papers, MHS; Barry, ed., "William Clark's Diary," pt. 4, 400–401.

52. Dorothy Caldwell, "The Big Neck Affair: Tragedy and Farce on the Missouri Frontier," 391–412.

53. Ibid.

54. Barry, ed., "William Clark's Diary," pt. 4, 396; Treaty with the Sauk, Foxes, Etc., 1830, July 15, 1830, in Charles J. Kappler, ed., *Indian Affairs, Laws and Treaties*, vol. 2, 305–8; Thomas Hart Benton to Benjamin O'Fallon, December 8, [1829?], O'Fallon Family Papers, WHMCC.

55. Barry, ed., "William Clark's Diary," pt. 4, 400, 405; Meriwether Lewis Clark to William Clark, February 16, 1830, William Clark Papers, MHS.

56. William Clark to John Eaton, January 17, 1831, photostatic copy in Forsyth Papers, MHS; William Clark to John O'Fallon, January 21 and February 10 and 27, 1831, John O'Fallon Papers, MHS.

57. Clark to John O'Fallon, January 21 and February 10 and 27, 1831, O'Fallon Papers, MHS; *Missouri Intelligencer*, January 16, 1829, and January 29, 1830; William Clark's Promissory Note to John O'Fallon, April 19, 1831, William Clark Papers, MHS.

58. William Clark to John O'Fallon, February 27, 1831, O'Fallon Papers, MHS; William Preston Clark to William Clark, August 3, [1831], William Clark Papers, MHS.

59. William Clark to Meriwether Lewis Clark, September 5, 1831, MLC Papers, MHS.

60. "Nez Perce Warriors' Journey Memorialized" and "Nez Perce Tribe Finally Will Get Memorial to Two Idaho Warriors," in Boise *Idaho Statesman*, September 2 and December 19, 2002.

61. Ibid.; Catlin, *North American Indians*, vol. 2, 109.

62. William Clark to Secretary of War, September 22, 1830, U.S. Superintendency of Indian Affairs, St. Louis, Records, 1807–1855, Letterbook, Kansas State Historical Society; "Report of William Clark to Lewis Cass, Secretary of War," November 20, 1831, reprinted in Missouri Historical Society, *Glimpses of the Past*, 9 (July–September 1941): 44–54.

63. William Clark to Meriwether Lewis Clark, December 29, 1831, MLC Papers, MHS.

64. Thomas Forsyth to William H. Ashley, May 8 and August 10, 1832, and Report by Thomas Forsyth, October 1, 1832, Draper Mss. 6T167–170 and 9T59.

65. William Clark to General Henry Atkinson, April 16, 1832, William Clark Papers, MHS.

66. William Clark to Lewis Cass, June 8, 1832, in Ellen M. Whitney, ed., *The Black Hawk War 1831–1832*, vol. 2, 549–50.

67. See Anthony F. C. Wallace, "'The Obtaining Lands': Thomas Jefferson and the Native Americans," in James P. Ronda, ed., *Thomas Jefferson and the Changing West*, 38–39.

68. William Clark to Meriwether Lewis Clark, June 19 and 27 and August 2, 1832, Meriwether Lewis Clark Papers, MHS; Roger L. Nichols, *Black Hawk and the Warrior's Path*, 134–41.

69. William Clark to Meriwether Lewis Clark, August 14, 1832, Meriwether Lewis Clark Papers, MHS; William Clark to George Rogers Hancock Clark, August 19, 1832, George Rogers Hancock Clark Papers, MHS.

70. William Clark to George Rogers Hancock Clark, July 30, August 19, and December 2, 1832, and William Preston Clark to George Rogers Hancock Clark, December 3, 1832, GRHC Papers, MHS.

71. McDermott, ed., *The Western Journals of Washington Irving,* 81–82.

72. Ibid.

73. William Clark to George Rogers Hancock Clark, July 30 and November 11, 1832, GRHC Papers, MHS.

74. Joshua Pilcher to T. Hartley Crawford, July 6, 1839, and Thomas Hart Benton to the Commissioner of Indian Affairs, September 16, 1838, as quoted in John E. Sunder, *Joshua Pilcher: Fur Trader and Indian Agent,* 141–42.

75. Donald Jackson, *Voyages of the Steamboat Yellow Stone,* 57–63; William Clark to John Robb, September 25, 1832, Letters Received by Office of Indian Affairs, 1824–1881, St. Louis Superintendency, NA, M-234; William Clark to J. P. Cabanné and P. A. Sarpy, March 9, 1833, and Elbert Herring to William Clark, February 18, 1833, in H. R. Gamble Papers, MHS.

76. Nichols, *Black Hawk and the Warrior's Path,* 141–48; William Clark to Elbert Herring, May 14, 1833, as cited in Donald Jackson, ed., *Black Hawk: An Autobiography,* 7.

77. Pierre Menard to William Clark, January 1, 1833, typescript copy in Indians Collection, MHS.

78. William Clark to Meriwether Lewis Clark, March 13, 1833, and January 30, 1834, MLC Papers, MHS; John O'Fallon to Charles Thruston, March 8, 1834, O'Fallon Papers, FHS; Claims of Wm Clark on the U.S., 1822 to 1 January 1833, William Clark Papers, MHS.

79. John O'Fallon to Charles Thruston, March 8, 1834, O'Fallon Papers, FHS; William Clark to Meriwether Lewis Clark, May 18 and June 22, 1834, MLC Papers, MHS; William Preston Clark to William Clark, April 10, 1834, William Clark Papers, MHS.

80. John O'Fallon to Charles Thruston, March 7, May 24, June 6, 1835, and December 12, 1836, O'Fallon Papers, FHS; Ludlow, *Life as I Found It;* Receipt for share of stock in St. Louis Theatre Company, May 30, 1836, William Clark Papers, MHS; *Missouri Argus,* March 11, 1836.

81. *Missouri Argus,* November 6, 1835.

82. *Missouri Argus,* April 28, 1827; Sunder, *Joshua Pilcher,* 120; Perry McCandless, *A History of Missouri, Volume II, 1820–1860,* 16–17.

83. John O'Fallon to Charles Thruston, January 10 and April 17, 1837, in O'Fallon Papers, FHS.

84. Invitation to dine with corporation of New York, June 28, 1837, William Clark Papers, MHS; William Clark to George Rogers Hancock Clark, July 6 and August 25, 1837, GRHC Papers, MHS; William Clark to Abby Clark, November 14, 1837, MLC Papers, MHS.

85. William Clark to James Herring, January 7, 1838, GRHC Papers, MHS.

86. John O'Fallon to Charles Thruston, January 21 and 27 and May 22, 1838, O'Fallon Papers, FHS; Sarah Mason to Rosalie von Phul, July 17, 1837, Von Phul Collection, MHS; Kennerly and Russell, *Persimmon Hill,* 83. In reporting William's death in 1840

Samuel Churchill reported the following: "Our friend & relative William Clark died suddenly about two o'clock yesterday. A short time before his death he was in his usual state of health, but was carried off in a few minutes by one of those attacks to which he had been subject. Dr. Ruthkawski left him for a short time and whilst setting in the next room heard and slight noise in William's, and entering his chamber found him about to breathe his last. Poor William had a warm generous & noble heart, but as you know he has for a long time been the victim of a disease of which it is melancholy to think." Samuel Churchill to Charles Thruston, May 17, 1840, Churchill Family Papers, Folder 6, FHS.

87. Reginald Horsman, *Frontier Doctor: William Beaumont, America's First Great Medical Scientist,* 227–28; James Kennerly to Jefferson Kearny Clark, January 8 and February 22, 1838, as cited in Kennerly and Russell, *Persimmon Hill,* 84–87; John O'Fallon to Charles Thruston, May 22, 1838, O'Fallon Papers, FHS.

88. Major E. A. Hitchcock to C. A. Harris, September 2, 1838, as printed in Kennerly and Russell, *Persimmon Hill,* 90.

89. Noah Ludlow to Cornelia Ludlow, September 2, 1838, Ludlow Field Maury Collection, MHS.

Epilogue

1. *Missouri Saturday News,* September 8, 1838.

2. "Journal of Henry B. Miller," *Missouri Historical Society Collections* 6, no. 3 (1931): 268–71. William Clark's remains were later reinterred on a grassy knoll in St. Louis's historic Bellefontaine Cemetery, and in 1904, on the occasion of the expedition's centennial, family members erected a stately monument to mark his grave, complete with an impressive granite obelisk and a bust of the renowned explorer under the constant gaze of the heads of two grizzly bears.

3. "Journal of Henry B. Miller," 268–71.

4. William Clark's Last Will and Testament, Missouri State Archives.

5. William Clark to George Rogers Hancock Clark, December 2, 1832, George Rogers Hancock Clark Papers, MHS.

Bibliography

Manuscript Collections

Cathedral of St. Louis the King (Old Cathedral), St. Louis
    Baptismal Records 1814–1835
Filson Historical Society, Louisville, Kentucky
    Churchill Family Papers
    Clark Family Papers
    Jonathan Clark Diary
    Meriwether Lewis Clark Papers
    William Joseph Clark Diary
    Fitzhugh-Rose Account Book
    Gwathmey Family Papers
    O'Fallon Papers
    Preston Family Papers–Joyes Collection
Indiana Historical Society, Indianapolis
    Northwest Territory Collection
Kansas State Historical Society, Topeka
    Missouri Fur Company Ledger, 1812–1814
    U.S. Superintendency of Indian Affairs, St. Louis, Records, 1807–1855
Library of Congress, Washington, D.C.
    Thomas Jefferson Papers
Missouri Historical Society, St. Louis
    Bates Family Papers
    Thomas Hart Benton Papers
    Daniel Bissell Papers
    Aaron Burr Papers

George Rogers Clark Papers
George Rogers Hancock Clark Papers
Meriwether Lewis Clark Papers
William Clark Papers
Delassus Papers
Fitzhugh Family Papers
Forsyth Papers
Hamilton R. Gamble Papers
Carlota Glasgow Collection
Richard Graham Papers
Indians Collection
Ludlow Field Maury Collection
Lucas Collection
O'Fallon Papers
St. Louis Missouri Fur Company Record Book, 1809–1812
St. Louis Building Collection
George Sibley Papers
Amos Stoddard Papers
Von Phul Collection
Christian Wilt Letterbook
Missouri State Archives, Jefferson City
Missouri Supreme Court Records
William Clark's Probate Records
National Archives, Washington, D.C.
Letters Received by the Secretary of War Relating to Indian Affairs,
1800–1816
Letters Received by the Office of Indian Affairs, 1824–1881, St. Louis
Superintendency
St. Louis Circuit Court, Office of Circuit Clark, City of St. Louis
St. Louis Circuit Court Case Files
St. Louis Mercantile Library, University of Missouri–St. Louis
Daniel Bissell Papers
St. Louis Public School Records Center and Archives
Frank Mosberger Collection
State Historical Society of Wisconsin, Madison
Lyman Draper Collection
Western Historical Manuscripts Collection, Columbia, Missouri
William Clark Notebook, 1798–1801
William Clark Memorandum Book, 1807
O'Fallon Family Papers
Thomas A. Smith Collection

Printed Government Documents

American State Papers: Indian Affairs.

American State Papers: Military Affairs.

American State Papers: Public Lands.

Annals of the Congress of the United States, 1789–1824. 42 vols. Washington, D.C.: Gales and Seaton, 1834–1836.

Carter, Clarence E., ed. *Territorial Papers of the United States.* Vols. 13–15. Washington, D.C.: Government Printing Office, 1948–1949, 1951.

Heitman, Francis B. *Historical Register and Dictionary of the United States Army from September 29, 1789 to March 2, 1903.* 2 vols. Washington, D.C.: Government Printing Office, 1903.

Kappler, Charles J., ed. *Indian Affairs, Laws and Treaties.* 2 vols. Washington, D.C.: Government Printing Office, 1904.

Messages from the President . . . relative to British establishments and the state of the fur trade. Washington, D.C., 1831.

Report on the committee of elections on the Memorial of Rufus Easton, contesting the election and returns of John Scott, the Delegate from the Territory of Missouri. N.p, n.n., n.d.

Report on the Committee of Elections, to which was recommitted their Report of the 31st ult. On the Petition of Rufus Easton, Contesting the election of John Scott. N.p., n.n., n.d.

Newspapers and Periodicals

Louisiana Gazette (St. Louis)

Missouri Argus (St. Louis)

Missouri Gazette (St. Louis)

Missouri Gazette and Illinois Advertiser (St. Louis)

Missouri Intelligencer (Franklin and Fayette)

Missouri Republican (St. Louis)

National Intelligencer and Washington Advertiser (Washington, D.C.)

Quarterly Review (London)

St. Louis Enquirer

Books

Allen, John Logan. *Passage through the Garden: Lewis and Clark and the Image of the American Northwest.* Urbana: University of Illinois Press, 1975.

Ambrose, Stephen E. *Undaunted Courage: Meriwether Lewis, Thomas Jefferson and the Opening of the American West.* New York: Simon and Schuster, 1996.

Aron, Stephen. *How the West Was Lost: The Transformation of Kentucky from Daniel Boone to Henry Clay.* Baltimore: Johns Hopkins University Press, 1996.

Betts, Robert. *In Search of York.* Rev. ed. with epilogue by James Holmberg. Boulder: University Press of Colorado and Lewis and Clark Trail Heritage Foundation, 2000.

Blair, Emma Helen. *The Indian Tribes of the Upper Mississippi Valley and Region of the Great Lakes.* Vol. 2. Cleveland: Arthur H. Clark Company, 1912.

Bodley, Temple. *George Rogers Clark: His Life and Public Services.* Boston: Houghton Mifflin Company, 1926.

Catlin, George. *Letters and Notes of the Manners, Customs and Condition of the North American Indians.* 2 vols. Rprt., Minneapolis: Ross and Haines, 1965.

Cayton, Andrew R. L. *Frontier Indiana.* Bloomington: Indiana University Press, 1996.

Christensen, Lawrence O., William E. Foley, Gary R. Kremer, and Kenneth H. Winn, eds. *Dictionary of Missouri Biography.* Columbia: University of Missouri Press, 1999.

Clark, Thomas D., ed. *A Description of Kentucky in North America . . . by Harry Toulmin.* Lexington: University of Kentucky Press, 1945.

———, ed. *The Voice of the Frontier: John Bradford's Notes on Kentucky.* Lexington: University of Kentucky Press, 1993.

Collot, Georges Henri Victor. *A Journey in North America.* 2 vols. Paris: Arthur Bertrand, 1826.

Crotty, Gene. *The Visits of Lewis and Clark to Fincastle, Virginia.* Roanoke: History Museum and Historical Society of Western Virginia, 2003.

Cutright, Paul Russell. *Lewis and Clark: Pioneering Naturalists.* Urbana: University of Illinois Press, 1969.

Dicken-Garcia, Hazel. *To the Western Woods: The Breckinridge Family Moves to Kentucky in 1793.* Cranbury, N.J.: Fairleigh Dickinson University Press, 1991.

Dowd, Gregory Evans. *A Spirited Resistance: The North American Indian Struggle for Unity, 1745–1815.* Baltimore: Johns Hopkins University Press, 1992.

Downes, Randolph. *Council Fires on the Upper Ohio.* Pittsburgh: University of Pittsburgh Press, 1940.

Ekberg, Carl, and William E. Foley, eds. *An Account of Upper Louisiana by Nicholas de Finiels.* Columbia: University of Missouri Press, 1989.

Esarey, Logan, ed. *Messages and Letters of William Henry Harrison.* 2 vols. Indianapolis: Indiana Historical Commission, 1922.

Fisher, David Hackett, and James C. Kelly. *Bound Away: Virginia and the Westward Movement.* Charlottesville: University Press of Virginia, 2000.

Flint, Timothy. *Recollections of the Last Ten Years in the Mississippi Valley.* Boston, 1826. Rprt., George R. Brooks, ed., Carbondale: Southern Illinois University Press, 1968.

Foley, William E. *The Genesis of Missouri: From Wilderness Outpost to Statehood.* Columbia: University of Missouri Press, 1989.

——, and C. David Rice. *The First Chouteaus: River Barons of Early St. Louis.* Urbana: University of Illinois Press, 1983.

Foreman, Grant, ed. *A Traveler in Indian Territory: The Journal of Ethan Allen Hitchcock, Late Major-General of the United States Army.* Cedar Rapids, Iowa: Torch Press, 1930.

Furtwangler, Albert. *Acts of Discovery: Visions of America in the Lewis and Clark Journals.* Urbana: University of Illinois Press, 1993.

Gilman, Carolyn. *Lewis and Clark across the Divide.* Washington, D.C.: Smithsonian Institution Press, 2003.

Gregg, Kate L, ed. *Westward with Dragoons: The Journal of William Clark on His Expedition to Establish Fort Osage, August 25 to September 22, 1808.* Fulton, Mo.: Ovid Bell Press, 1937.

Gregory, Jack, and Rennard Strickland. *Sam Houston with the Cherokees, 1829–1833.* Austin: University of Texas Press, 1967.

Harlan, James D., and James M. Denny. *Atlas of Lewis and Clark in Missouri.* Columbia: University of Missouri Press, 2003.

Herring, Joseph B. *Kenekuk, the Kickapoo Prophet.* Lawrence: University Press of Kansas, 1988.

Holmberg, James, ed. *Dear Brother: Letters of William Clark to Jonathan Clark.* New Haven, Conn.: Yale University Press, 2002.

Horsman, Reginald. *Frontier Doctor: William Beaumont, America's First Great Medical Scientist.* Columbia: University of Missouri Press, 1996.

Hubbard, Timothy, and Lewis E. Davids. *Banking in Mid-America: A History of Missouri Banks.* Washington, D.C.: Public Affairs Press, 1969.

Hurt, R. Douglas. *The Indian Frontier, 1763–1846.* Albuquerque: University of New Mexico Press, 2002.

——. *The Ohio Frontier: Crucible of the Old Northwest, 1720–1830.* Bloomington: Indiana University Press, 1996.

Hutton, Andrew Paul, ed. *Soldiers West: Biographies from the Military Frontier.* Lincoln: University of Nebraska Press, 1987.

Jackson, Donald. *Among Sleeping Giants: Occasional Pieces on Lewis and Clark.* Urbana: University of Illinois Press, 1987.

_____, ed. *Black Hawk: An Autobiography.* Urbana: University of Illinois Press, 1955.

_____. *Letters of the Lewis and Clark Expedition with Related Documents, 1783–1854.* 2 vols. Rev. ed. Urbana: University of Illinois Press, 1978.

_____. *Thomas Jefferson and the Stony Mountains: Exploring the West from Monticello.* Urbana: University of Illinois Press, 1981.

_____. *Voyages of the Steamboat Yellow Stone.* New York: Ticknor and Fields, 1985.

James, James Alton, ed. *George Rogers Clark Papers, 1771–1781.* 2 vols. Springfield: Trustees of the Illinois State Historical Library, 1912–1926.

Kennerly, William Clark, and Elizabeth Russell. *Persimmon Hill: A Narrative of Old St. Louis and the Far West.* Norman: University of Oklahoma Press, 1948.

Ludlow, Noah M. *Dramatic Life as I Found It.* St. Louis: G. I. Jones and Co., 1880.

Luttig, John C. *Journal of a Fur-Trading Expedition on the Upper Missouri, 1812–1813.* Rprt., Stella Drumm, ed., New York: Argosy-Antiquarian Ltd., 1964.

McCandless, Perry. *A History of Missouri, Volume II, 1820–1860.* Columbia: University of Missouri Press, 1972.

McDermott, John Francis, ed. *The Western Journals of Washington Irving.* Norman: University of Oklahoma Press, 1944.

Malone, Dumas. *Jefferson: The Virginian.* Boston: Little Brown, 1948.

Marshall, Thomas Maitland, ed. *The Life and Papers of Frederick Bates.* 2 vols. St. Louis: Missouri Historical Society, 1926.

Maximilian, Prince of Wied. *Travels in the Interior of North America, 1832–1834.* Reprinted in Reuben Gold Thwaites, ed., *Early Western Travels, 1748–1846,* vol. 22. Cleveland: Arthur H. Clark, 1906.

Mills, Samuel J., and Daniel Smith. *Report on a Missionary Tour through that Part of the United States which Lies West of the Allegany Mountains.* Andover, Mass.: Flagg and Gould, 1815.

Morgan, Dale, ed. *The West of William H. Ashley, 1822–1838.* Denver: Old West Publishing Company, 1964.

Moulton, Gary, ed. *The Journals of the Lewis and Clark Expedition.* 13 vols. Lincoln: University of Nebraska Press, 1983–2001.

Nasatir, Abraham P., ed. *Before Lewis and Clark: Documents Illustrating the History of Missouri, 1785–1804.* 2 vols. St. Louis: St. Louis Historical Documents Foundation, 1952.

Nelson, Paul David. *Anthony Wayne: Soldier of the Early Republic.* Bloomington: Indiana University Press, 1985.

Nichols, Roger L. *Black Hawk and the Warrior's Path.* Arlington Heights, Ill.: Harlan Davidson, Inc., 1992.

Oglesby, Richard E. *Manuel Lisa and the Opening of the Missouri Fur Trade.* Norman: University of Oklahoma Press, 1963.

Osgood, Ernest S. *Field Notes of Captain William Clark, 1803–1805.* New Haven, Conn.: Yale University Press, 1964.

Prucha, Francis Paul. *The Great Father: The United States Government and the American Indians.* 2 vols. Lincoln: University of Nebraska Press, 1984.

_____. *The Sword of the Republic: The United States Army on the Frontier, 1783–1846.* New York: Macmillan, 1969.

Rankin, Hugh F. *George Rogers Clark and the Winning of the West.* Richmond: Virginia Independence Bicentennial Commission, 1976.

Rogers, Ann. *Lewis and Clark in Missouri.* 3rd ed. Columbia: University of Missouri Press, 2002.

Rollings, Willard H. *The Osage: An Ethnohistorical Study of Hegemony on the Prairie-Plains.* Columbia: University of Missouri Press, 1992.

Ronan, Peter. *History of the Flathead Indians, Their Wars and Hunts, 1813–1890.* Rprt., Minneapolis: Ross and Haines, 1965.

Ronda, James P. *Finding the West: Explorations with Lewis and Clark.* Albuquerque: University of New Mexico Press, 2001.

_____. *Jefferson's West: A Journey with Lewis and Clark.* Monticello, Va.: Thomas Jefferson Foundation, 2000.

_____. *Lewis and Clark among the Indians.* Lincoln: University of Nebraska Press, 1984.

_____, ed. *Thomas Jefferson and the Changing West: From Conquest to Conservation.* Albuquerque: University of New Mexico Press, 1997.

_____, ed. *Voyages of Discovery: Essays on the Lewis and Clark Expedition.* Helena: Montana Historical Society Press, 1998.

Rowe, Mary Ellen. *Bulwark of the Republic: The American Militia in the Antebellum West.* Westport, Conn.: Praeger, 2003.

Schultz, Christian. *Travels on an Inland Voyage.* New York: Isaac Riley, 1810.

Skogen, Larry C. *Indian Depredation Claims, 1796–1920.* Norman: University of Oklahoma Press, 1996.

Slaughter, Thomas P. *Exploring Lewis and Clark: Reflections on Men and Wilderness.* New York: Alfred A. Knopf, 2003.

Steffen, Jerome. *William Clark: Jeffersonian Man on the Frontier.* Norman: University of Oklahoma Press, 1977.

Steward, Dick. *Duels and the Roots of Violence in Missouri.* Columbia: University of Missouri Press, 2000.

Sunder, John E. *Joshua Pilcher: Fur Trader and Indian Agent.* Norman: University of Oklahoma Press, 1968.

Wallace, Anthony F. C. *Jefferson and the Indians: The Tragic Fate of the First Americans.* Cambridge, Mass.: Harvard University Press, 1999.

Watlington, Patricia. *The Partisan Spirit: Kentucky Politics, 1779–1792.* New York: Atheneum, 1972.

Whitney, Ellen M., ed. *The Black Hawk War 1831–1832*. Vol. 2 in *Collections of the Illinois Historical Library*. Vol. 36. Springfield: Illinois State Historical Library, 1973.

Wilhelm Paul, Duke of Wurttemberg. *Travels in North America, 1822–1824*. Translated by W. Robert Nitske, edited by Savoie Lottinville. Norman: University of Oklahoma Press, 1973.

Wood, W. Raymond, and Thomas D. Thiessen, eds. *Early Fur Trade on the Northern Plains: Canadian Traders among the Mandan and Hidatsa Indians, 1783–1818*. Norman: University of Oklahoma Press, 1985.

Articles

Allen, John Logan. "Lewis and Clark on the Upper Missouri: Decision at the Marias." *Montana, the Magazine of Western History* 21 (Summer 1971): 2–17.

Barry, Louise, ed. "William Clark's Diary, May 1826–February 1831." Four-part series. *Kansas Historical Quarterly* 16 (February 1948): 1–39; (May 1948): 136–74; (August 1948): 274–305; (November 1948): 384–410.

Betts, Robert B. "'we commenced wrighting &c': A Salute to the Ingenious Spelling and Grammar of William Clark." *We Proceeded On* 6 (November 1980): 10–12.

Caldwell, Dorothy. "The Big Neck Affair: Tragedy and Farce on the Missouri Frontier." *Missouri Historical Review* 64 (July 1970): 391–412.

Chalkley, Mark. "Eagle Feather Goes to Washington." *We Proceeded On* 29 (May 2003): 6–10.

Chambers, William N. "Pistols and Politics: Incidents in the Career of Thomas Hart Benton, 1816–1818." *Bulletin of the Missouri Historical Society* 5 (October 1948): 5–17.

Chaput, Donald. "The Early Missouri Graduates of West Point: Officers or Merchants?" *Missouri Historical Review* 72 (April 1978): 262–70.

Chuinard, Eldon G. "The Court-Martial of Ensign Meriwether Lewis." *We Proceeded On* 8 (November 1982): 12–15.

_____. "Fincastle-Santillane and William and Judith Clark." *We Proceeded On* 14 (February 1988): 10–15.

_____. "Lewis and Clark—Master Masons." *We Proceeded On* 15 (February 1989): 12–14.

Coues, Elliott, ed. "Letters of William Clark and Nathaniel Pryor." *Annals of Iowa* 1 (1895): 613–20.

Danisi, Thomas, and W. Raymond Wood. "The Genesis of James MacKay's Map of the Missouri River: Lewis and Clark's Route Map." *Western Historical Quarterly* (Spring 2004).

Dyson, John P. "The Naming of Paducah." *Register of the Kentucky Historical Society* 92 (Spring 1994): 149–74.

Faragher, John Mack. "More Motley than Mackinaw: From Ethnic Mixing to Ethnic Cleaning on the Frontier of the Lower Missouri, 1783–1833." In Andrew R. L. Cayton and Frederika J. Teute, eds., *Contact Points: American Frontiers from the Mohawk Valley to the Mississippi, 1750–1830* (Chapel Hill: University of North Carolina Press), 304–26.

Fausz, J. Frederick. "Becoming `A Nation of Quakers': The Removal of the Osage Indians from Missouri." *Gateway Heritage* 21 (Summer 2000): 28–39.

Fisher, Robert L. "The Treaties of Portage des Sioux." *Mississippi Valley Historical Review* 19 (March 1933): 495–508.

Foley, William E. "Different Notions of Justice: The Case of the 1808 St. Louis Murder Trials." *Gateway Heritage* 9 (Winter 1988–1989): 2–13.

_____. "Lewis and Clark's American Travels: The View from Britain." *Western Historical Quarterly* 34 (Autumn 2003): 301–24.

_____. "The Lewis and Clark Expedition's Silent Partners: The Chouteau Brothers of St. Louis." *Missouri Historical Review* 77 (January 1983): 131–46.

_____, and C. David Rice. "The Return of the Mandan Chief." *Montana the Magazine of Western History* 29 (Summer 1979): 2–14.

Gatten, Robert E., Jr. "Clark Land in Virginia and the Birthplace of William Clark." *We Proceeded On* 25 (May 1999): 6–11.

Gregg, Kate L. "The History of Fort Osage." *Missouri Historical Review* 34 (July 1940): 439–88.

_____. "The War of 1812 on the Missouri Frontier." Three-part series. *Missouri Historical Review* 33 (October 1938): 3–22; (January 1939): 184–202; (April 1939): 326–48.

Hammon, Neal O. "Early Louisville and the Beargrass Stations." *Filson Club Historical Quarterly* 52 (April 1978): 147–65.

Holmberg, James J., ed. "`This Report Has Vexed Me a Little': William Clark Reports of an Affair of Honor." *We Proceeded On* 24 (November 1988): 28–31.

Jackson, Donald. "Some Books Carried by Lewis and Clark." *Bulletin of the Missouri Historical Society* 16 (October 1959): 3–13.

Kinkead, Lutie J. "How the Parents of George Rogers Clark Came to Kentucky in 1784–85." *Filson Club Historical Quarterly* 3 (October 1928): 1–4.

Kohn, Richard H. "General Wilkinson's Vendetta with General Wayne: Politics and Command in the American Army, 1791–1796." *Filson Club Historical Quarterly* 45 (October 1971): 361–72.

Large, Arlen J. "Captain Clark's Belated Bonus." *We Proceeded On* 23 (November 1997): 12–14.

————. "Lewis & Clark Meet the 'American Incognitum.'" *We Proceeded On* 2 (August 1995): 12–18.

"Letters of William Carr Lane, 1819–1831." *Glimpses of the Past* 7 (July–September 1940), 47–56.

Long, Alice. "Reclaiming a Lost Connection: A Brief History of Meriwether Lewis and William Clark in West Tennessee." *West Tennessee Historical Papers* 50 (1996): 200–206.

McDermott, John Francis. "Museums in Early St. Louis." *Bulletin of the Missouri Historical Society* 4 (April 1948): 129–38.

McGrane, R. C., ed. "William Clark's Journal of General Wayne's Campaign." *Mississippi Valley Historical Review* 1 (December 1914): 418–44.

Moore, Robert. "Lewis and Clark and Dinosaurs." *We Proceeded On* 24 (May 1998): 26–29.

————. "Pompey's Baptism: A Recently Discovered Document Sheds Light on the Christening of Jean Baptiste Charbonneau." *We Proceeded On* 26 (February 2000): 10–17.

Pirtle, Alfred. "Mulberry Hill: The First Home of George Rogers Clark in Kentucky." *Register of the Kentucky Historical Society* 15 (September 1917): 49–54.

Rice, Howard C. "Jefferson's Gift of Fossils to the Museum of Natural History in Paris." *Proceedings of the American Philosophical Society* 95 (December 1951): 597–627.

Ronda, James P. "'A Most Perfect Harmony': The Lewis and Clark Expedition as an Exploration Community." In Ronda, ed., *Voyages of Discovery: Essays on the Lewis and Clark Expedition* (Helena: Montana Historical Society Press, 1988), 77–88.

————. "St. Louis Welcomes and Toasts the Lewis and Clark Expedition: A Newly Discovered 1806 Newspaper Account." *We Proceeded On* 13 (February 1987): 19–20.

————. "'So Vast an Enterprise': Thoughts on the Lewis and Clark Expedition." In Ronda, ed., *Voyages of Discovery*, 1–25.

————. "Why Lewis and Clark Matter." *Smithsonian* 34 (August 2003): 98–101.

————. "Wilson Price Hunt Reports on Lewis and Clark." *Filson Club Historical Quarterly* 62 (April 1988): 95–103.

Rowe, Mary Ellen. "'A Respectable Independence': The Early Career of John O'Fallon." *Missouri Historical Review* 90 (July 1996): 393–409.

Rubin, Beth. "The Backwoodsman Newly Caught: The Missouri Apprenticeship of Portraitist Chester Harding." *Gateway Heritage* 12 (Summer 1991): 64–73.

Schroeder, Walter A. "Populating Missouri, 1804–1821." *Missouri Historical Review* 97 (July 2003): 263–94.

Steffen, Jerome O. "William Clark." In Paul Andrew Hutton, ed., *Soldier's West: Biographies from the Military Frontier* (Lincoln: University of Nebraska Press, 1987), 11–24.

————. "William Clark: A New Perspective on Missouri Territorial Politics, 1813–1820." *Missouri Historical Review* 67 (January 1973): 171–97.

Thomas, Samuel W., ed. "William Clark's 1795 and 1797 Journals and their Significance." *Bulletin of the Missouri Historical Society* 25 (July 1969): 278–85.

Thruston, C. Ballard. "Some Recent Findings Regarding the Ancestry of George Rogers Clark." *Filson Club Historical Quarterly* 9 (January 1935): 1–27.

Wallace, Anthony F. C. "'The Obtaining Lands': Thomas Jefferson and the Native Americans." In James P. Ronda, ed., *Thomas Jefferson and the Changing West* (Albuquerque: University of New Mexico Press, 1977), 25–41.

Theses, Dissertations, and Unpublished Papers

Bryan, John A. "A Preliminary Study of William Clark Sites in St. Louis." Typescript research report for the National Park Service, November 1938. Copy in Missouri Historical Society Library.

Buckley, Jay. "William Clark: Superintendent of Indian Affairs at St. Louis, 1813–1838." Ph.D. diss., University of Nebraska–Lincoln, 2001.

Loos, John L. "A Biography of William Clark, 1770–1813." Ph.D. diss., Washington University, St. Louis, 1953.

Index

About the Author

Photo by Tom Mitchell

WILLIAM E. FOLEY is Professor Emeritus of History at Central Missouri State University. He is the General Editor of the Missouri Biography Series and author or editor of numerous books, including *The Genesis of Missouri: From Wilderness Outpost to Statehood, Dictionary of Missouri Biography,* and *A History of Missouri, Volume I: 1673–1820,* all available from the University of Missouri Press.